Residential Leases

Residential Leases

Stuart Bridge, MA

Barrister, of the Middle Temple and the North-Eastern Circuit;
University Lecturer in Law, University of Cambridge;
Fellow, Queens' College, Cambridge

BLACKSTONE
PRESS LIMITED

First published in Great Britain 1994 by Blackstone Press Limited, 9-15 Aldine Street, London W12 8AW. Telephone: 081-740 1173

ISBN: 1 85431 356 8

British Library Cataloguing in Publication Data
A CIP catalogue record for this book is available from the British Library.

Typeset by Montage Studios Ltd, Tonbridge, Kent
Printed by Livesey Ltd, Shrewsbury

Contents

Preface

This book had its beginnings in *Blackstone's Guide to the Housing Act 1988*, published in 1989 shortly after that hugely significant piece of legislation was brought into force. Certain passages in this book bear very close resemblance to what was then written. But, as the title of this book suggests, this is a much broader treatment of the law of residential leases than the earlier work. It is in no sense a 'Second Edition' of the Housing Act Guide. But neither is it a comprehensive statement of all the legal principles applying to residential leases. The objective of this book is to set out in intelligible and readable form the current law governing the security afforded to residential tenants, and the statutory rights of acquisition and enfranchisement they presently enjoy. Both private and public sectors of housing are covered. Whilst other obligations arising out of the landlord/tenant relationship may be referred to in the text, treatment will be incidental only. Both practitioner and student must be ready to supplement this book by resort to the huge body of statute, case law, and statutory regulation which makes up the law of residential leases.

I must express my considerable gratitude to Louise Tee, Fellow of Lucy Cavendish College, and Tim Meakin, Barrister of Fenners Chambers, Cambridge, for reading earlier drafts and making useful comments and practical suggestions for improvements, many of which have been acted upon in the final text. My wife, Jane, despite her own writing commitments (see the Fourth Edition of Black, Bridge and Bond's *Practical Approach to Family Law* for the results), gave much by way of practical assistance, support and encouragement. The redoubtable staff of the Cambridge Law Faculty Office cheerily gave efficient secretarial help when it was most needed and Ellen Zwingli at Cornell greatly expedited the galley stage with enthusiasm and good humour. Blackstones, much to their credit, let me get on with it, loyally expecting a manuscript by the agreed date. The responsibility for the final product must however remain mine. I have striven to state the law of England and Wales as at 1 August 1994.

Stuart Bridge
Cornell Law School
Ithaca
New York

Table of Cases

Table of Statutes

ONE

INTRODUCTION

1 RESIDENTIAL LEASES AND STATUTORY INTERVENTION

Few tenants will realise, when they sign their tenancy agreement for the letting of their house or flat, the extent to which that document misrepresents the true legal relationship between them and their landlord. Few areas of the law have been subjected to so much statutory intervention over the course of the last century, intervention which has been heavily party-political, and which has, as a result, been riddled with inconsistencies. The complexity of the present law, to which the length of this book, for all its relatively modest objectives, bears witness, can best be approached by a basic understanding of the changing social background, and the changing political initiatives, which have so stunted its development.

2 THE PRIVATE SECTOR: 1915–1979

At the time of the enactment of the first Rent Act in 1915, the private sector formed by far the largest part (of the order of 90%) of the housing stock in England and Wales. There was a shortage of urban housing, and the Act was passed, as a war-time 'emergency' measure, in order to avert rent strikes threatened by munitions workers and others who responded angrily to their landlords' attempts to exploit the situation by increasing rents. The Rent and Mortgage Interest Restrictions Act 1915 froze rents, and in an attempt to prevent consequential mass evictions, conferred protection on occupying tenants. The measure was perceived as being a temporary answer to an immediate and pressing social need. Ironically, over 70 years later, rent control is still a significant feature of a large proportion of residential housing in this country.

The housing shortage did not end with the War, and measures passed immediately afterwards further improved the security of the residential tenant. The 1920 Rent Act, for instance, introduced protection for widows of deceased tenants, and increased the number of dwellings to which the Acts applied. The years between the Wars saw the many-talented Court of Appeal, led by the likes of Atkin, Scrutton and Bankes LJJ, working out and applying a formidable Rent Act jurisprudence, whilst Parliament gradually whittled away at tenant protection. From 1923, landlords were given an incentive to repossess, as new lets were taken outside rent control. The Acts of 1933 and 1938 were similarly regressive. But at no stage did wholesale repeal, and thereby complete deregulation, take place.

The commencement of hostilities in 1939 required Parliament to step in again to assist the residential tenant, and the majority of houses were brought under control. In 1946, a statutory code for furnished tenancies, previously excluded from protection, was introduced, conferring some rent control and security of tenure. The first concerted post-war attack on the Rent Acts came in 1957, the Conservative administration providing for immediate deregulation of higher value houses, and for phased deregulation of the rest. However, the legislation did not survive the Wilson Labour Government, which largely returned the Acts to the status quo, adding further layers of complexity by introducing a distinction (which is fortunately no longer relevant) between 'controlled' and 'regulated' tenancies, and responding to the much publicised forced evictions (for which phased deregulation was held partly to blame) by creating criminal offences of unlawful eviction and harassment.

The next major statute was the Rent Act 1974, bringing furnished tenancies into the Rent Acts proper, and creating at the same time an exclusion in favour of 'resident landlords', a concept which was to spawn much litigation. The final measures of a Labour administration were the Rent Act 1977, and the Protection from Eviction Act 1977, consolidating all that had gone before. Indeed, at the time of the 1979 election, the law of residential leases was in a reasonably coherent and comprehensible state, but it was not to last for long.

3 THE PUBLIC SECTOR: UP TO 1979

As we have seen, in 1914 the domination of the private sector was almost total, and very few residential properties were in public ownership. Only after 1945 did the councils and similar bodies, burdened with wider public duties to house, begin to accumulate a substantial body of housing, as the contemporaneous mass house building programmes resulted in the construction of a vast number of publicly owned dwellings. By 1966, the public rented sector had grown to 27% of the nation's housing stock, and now exceeded the private rented sector (at 24%). It was, however, many years before any government identified a need for statutory protection of these tenants against their council landlords, and Parliament consistently maintained a policy of non-intervention. The retention of residential property by the councils came to be identified with the retention of political power, and it was only under the Thatcher administration that public sector tenants were given significant legally enforceable rights of security.

4 THE HOUSING ACT 1980

The two most important measures of the Thatcher administration in the context of housing law were the Housing Acts of 1980 and 1988. The Act of 1980 (subsequently consolidated in the Housing Act 1985) contained the public sector tenant's charter, most notably the politically popular 'right to buy', whereby tenants were entitled to compel their local authority landlords to sell the freehold reversion in their dwellings to them, at a discount calculated with reference to the length of time they had been public sector tenants. In addition, tenants of local authorities and other public sector bodies were given statutory security (as 'secure tenants') for the first time. The introduction of the right to buy had an inevitable, and intended, impact on the quantity of housing stock held by local authorities, but more was to come, as by further legislation (the Housing and Planning Act 1986; the Housing Act 1988, Part IV) local authorities were first given the power, and then placed under a duty, to sell their interests in housing to private sector purchasers. The effect has been substantial. Between 1981 and 1993, the number of dwellings rented from English local authorities (and new town corporations) fell from 5,118,000 to 3,742,000. As a percentage of the housing stock, the public rented sector declined from over 28% to below 18%.

5 THE HOUSING ACT 1988

The Thatcher Government sought at the same time to encourage private sector, and housing association, lettings. The 1980 Act made small but significant amendments to the Rent Act 1977, introducing the protected shorthold tenancy as a means for landlords to let dwellings without conferring security of tenure. Much more radical was the approach of Part I of the Housing Act of 1988, which sought to phase out Rent Act tenancies, with their restrictive rent controls, and introduce as the major form of private sector tenure the assured tenancy. It is this piece of legislation, together with its heavily influential and practically important counterpart, the Rent Act 1977, which is central to an understanding of how the current law of residential leases works.

The 1988 Act does not repeal the 1977 Act. The two systems will continue to operate in tandem for many years to come. But the first question a practitioner will require to ask when faced with a problem concerning a private sector residential lease will be 'When was the lease granted?' If before 15 January 1989 (the day Part I of the Housing Act 1988 came into force, and a date to remember), the lease will almost certainly be governed by the Rent Act 1977, and the reader should turn to chapter 3 of this book. If on or after 15 January 1989, the lease will in all likelihood be an assured tenancy, and reference should be made to chapter 2.

The 1988 Act also created a new form of tenure for landlords seeking to avoid the conferment of security on the tenant: the much used assured shorthold tenancy. This device is very attractive to landlords, as it enables them to recover possession without difficulty at the end of the term they grant. They must be prepared to part with possession for a minimum of six months, and to risk the tenant applying to a rent assessment committee to have the rent reduced to the appropriate market level. Early indications are that, as was expected, assured shortholds are proving popular for landlords, but, as was not, they are also obtaining higher rents than the 'standard' assured tenancy. The overall effect of the enactment of the 1988 Act appears to have been inflationary: between 1988 and 1990, the mean weekly rent for privately rented accommodation rose by 43%, from £30 to £43 (see generally Rauta & Pickering, *Private Renting in England 1990*, HMSO, p. 24 et seq.).

A further incentive to private sector lettings was announced in the 1988 Budget, which extended the Business Expansion Scheme (BES) to investments in companies which specialise in letting residential property on assured tenancy. This enables such companies to attract investors by the incentive of income tax relief on their investment (for further details see Income and Corporation Taxes Act 1988, Part VIII, Chapter III, and Finance Act 1988, s. 50, sch. 4). The provisions are complex, and there are important exclusions. In particular, companies seeking to utilise BES must not let on assured shorthold tenancy.

6 HOUSING ASSOCIATIONS

There has been a voluntary sector of housing in this country for centuries, but it has never been more important, or substantial, than today. The expansion can be dated from the Housing Act 1974, which introduced a new system of funding for housing associations, and the encouragement for this sector from the subsequent Conservative administration, which has seen it as a more acceptable alternative to local authorities as a large-scale housing provider. The Housing Corporation (and in Wales, Housing for Wales) is a statutory body which maintains a register of housing associations and has an overall supervisory juridiction. It issues management guidance to housing associations, and is responsible for determining whether a particular association (or other person or body) should be approved to enable it to purchase local authority housing stock.

The Housing Act 1988 made highly significant changes to the funding of housing associations, as a result of which they have come to be viewed by government as belonging to the private rather than the public sector. Nevertheless, housing associations, many of which are charitable bodies, do work closely with local authorities. In some cases, local authorities have alienated their entire stock to housing associations or similar bodies by the process known as 'LSVT' (large scale voluntary transfer). In others, arrangements are in place whereby housing associations will assist the local authority in discharging its functions, for example its statutory duty to house the homeless.

Prior to 1989, housing associations, depending on their precise legal definition, would let either on secure tenancy or on 'housing association tenancy', pursuant to provisions contained in Part VI of the Rent Act 1977. Indeed, many lettings by housing associations would fall within both definitions. The secure tenancy would confer on the occupier a security of tenure, as well as in some cases the right to buy (but see exceptions applying to certain housing associations: chapter 7). Part VI of the Rent Act 1977 afforded the housing association tenant the benefits of rent control, where the tenant would be protected under the 1977 Act but for ss. 15 and 16 (see chapter 3, para. 10). Part I of the Housing Act 1988 carried forward the government policy of distancing the housing association movement from the public sector by providing that new tenancies granted by housing associations would in general not be 'secure', nor would Part VI of the Rent Act 1977 apply to them. Most lettings by housing associations are now on assured tenancy.

It should be noted, however, that there are certain constraints imposed on registered housing associations by the Housing Corporation, which requires them to observe the 'Tenants' Guarantee' (i.e., *Guidance on the Management of Accommodation let on Assured Tenancies by Registered Housing Associations,* Housing Corporation Circular 29/91, in force since 1 October 1991 and published in Sweet & Maxwell's *Encyclopaedia of Housing Law,* 2-5931). Although this document does not state legal obligations enforceable by individual tenants against their housing association landlords, compliance by associations is enforced by the Housing Corporation, which has effective sanctions such as the withdrawal of grant where associations do not manage their tenancies properly. Separate guidance has been issued for fully mutual housing associations, almshouse charities, and associations providing special needs housing in shared accommodation and hostels or letting on long leases.

7 LONG LEASEHOLDERS

The long leaseholder is in many ways closer to a person who owns the freehold rather than a tenant. The leasehold will be relatively freely assignable, the leaseholder will have paid a substantial premium in much the same way that a freehold purchaser pays for his property. Yet the law has recognised the need to accord him greater protection in the form of statutory security and rights to expand or extend his interest. Treatment of the long leaseholder by Parliament has been uneven, and inconsistent. The position has now been reached where most long leaseholders have a form of statutory security (generally under Part I of the Landlord and Tenant Act 1954), and some method of compelling the freeholder either to sell the freehold to them, or to grant a new or extended lease. The statutes do not provide a code which is either rational or readily comprehensible. The latest Parliamentary offering, the Leasehold Reform, Housing and Urban Development Act 1993, is the least user friendly of them all. In chapters 4 and 5 an attempt is made to digest the provisions affecting long leaseholders (and in the case of certain rights to compel the sale of the landlord's reversion, some others) into some sensible form.

8 AGRICULTURAL TIED COTTAGES

A separate regime for agricultural workers occupying tied accommodation modelled on the Rent Acts was contained in the Rent (Agriculture) Act 1976. This scheme is now being phased out, and such occupiers are now accorded a security which is provided to 'assured agricultural occupancies' by the Housing Act 1988, ss. 24 to 26. Such occupancies are closely equated to assured tenancies. No further reference to them will be made in this book.

9 THE CURRENT STATE OF THE HOUSING STOCK

The Government publication *Housing and Construction Statistics* indicates that the housing stock of England is in a state of some flux. In 1981 (April), in the early days of the Conservative administration, the stock comprised some 17,912,000 dwellings. 57.7% of these were owner-occupied (and therefore outside the scope of this book), 11.4% were rented privately (or with a job or business), 2.3% were rented from housing associations and 28.6% were rented from local authorities or housing associations. By 1993 (December), the stock had grown to 20,068,000 dwellings. Owner-occupation now accounts for 67.3%, the private rented sector for 10.2%, housing associations for 3.8%, and the public sector for 18.6%. The most dramatic changes have been the fall in public sector housing, and the increase in owner-occupation, both clear legacies of government policy.

However, the expansion of housing association lettings is also highly significant.

An assessment of the impact of the new tenures introduced by the Housing Act 1988 is no doubt premature, but such indications as there are demonstrate a small increase in the availability of housing in the private sector. In December 1988, shortly before the Act came into force, 1,848,000 dwellings were let privately, representing some 9.6% of the English housing stock. The first year did not see any improvement (by December 1990, the sector had fallen as a percentage to 9.5%, an all-time low), but it has since rallied. By December 1993, some 2,045,000 homes were let in the private sector, which now accounted for 10.2% of the total.

The balance between private sector (now including housing associations) and public sector is becoming rather fine: as at December 1993, 14% as against 18.6%. Owner-occupation remains, and no doubt will continue to be, the most popular method of land-holding in this country. But the rented sector, comprising as it does almost one third of all houses and flats in this country, is hugely significant, and it is likely to remain so for the foreseeable future.

TWO

ASSURED TENANCIES

Housing Act 1988, Part I

1 INTRODUCTION

If a private sector landlord offers accommodation today, it will, more likely than not, be on assured tenancy. This chapter will explain what an assured tenancy is, and what rights it gives to the landlord and tenant respectively. Many assured tenancies are 'assured shortholds' (it will be very clear from the lease if this is the case), and special rules apply to them.

1.1 Assured tenancies under the 1980 Act

The term 'assured tenancy' first entered the lawyer's vocabulary in 1980, when the Housing Act of that year created a special status of 'assured tenancy' for lettings of newly erected dwellings where the landlords were specifically approved by Order of Parliament (Housing Act 1980, ss. 56–58, repealed with savings by the Housing Act 1988, s. 140(2), sch. 18). This status enabled approved landlords to charge their tenants a market rent outside the constraints of the Rent Act, the tenants in return obtaining security of tenure modelled on the statutory code which applies to business tenants. These '1980 Act assured tenancies' have been phased out by HA 1988, ss. 1(3) and 37, so that no tenancy entered into on or after 15 January 1989 can be a 1980 Act assured tenancy, and, with one exception, 1980 Act assured tenancies are converted into assured tenancies under the Housing Act 1988. The exception is transitional. Where a 1980 Act assured tenant applied to the court prior to 15 January 1989 for a new tenancy, then he would remain subject to the 1980 Act whilst the application was pending. Once the court made an order for the grant of a new tenancy in favour of the tenant, however, that new tenancy would be an assured tenancy under the Housing Act 1988. Where the 1988 Act effects such a conversion, it will do so even though the tenancy would normally be excluded from being a 1988 Act assured tenancy by sch. 1 to that Act, unless that exclusion relates to the interest of the landlord (see further, HA 1988, ss. 1(4), 1(5), 37(5)).

The effect of these provisions must be that there are very few, if any, 1980 Act assured tenancies still in existence. The assured tenancy of the Housing Act 1988 is wholly different to that of the 1980 Act. References in this book to 'assured tenancies' and 'assured tenants' will be to those subject to the Housing Act 1988.

1.2 Status of 1988 Act assured tenant

As we have seen, the Housing Act 1988 was enacted in an attempt by the government to revitalise the private sector of residential housing, most notably by permitting landlords to let at a commercial rent. Thus, although Part I of the 1988 Act confers on the assured tenant a security of tenure, whereby the landlord will not normally be able to recover possession without obtaining a possession order from the court on proof of certain prescribed grounds, the statute imposes few restraints beyond this. Subject only to a minor exception in the case of assured shorthold tenancies, there is no rent control of assured tenancies.

The legal relationship between the landlord and the assured tenant will depend to a very large extent on the lease which they have negotiated, and the tenant has in all likelihood signed. Unlike under the Rent Acts, where statute imposes its own type of tenancy when the original contractual tenancy terminates (see chapter 3, para. 1), the Housing Act 1988 allows the parties to negotiate freely and to enforce the terms which they have agreed with very few exceptions. The philosophy of the free market underpins the assured tenancy. Although there is no 'contracting out' of the status of assured tenancy, the terms of the contract still largely dictate the respective rights and obligations of landlord and tenant.

2 DEFINITION

The principal definition of 'assured tenancy' is to be found in HA 1988, s. 1(1). This definition is qualified by various exceptions, contained in HA 1988, s. 1(6) and sch. 2. By s. 1(1):

> A tenancy under which a dwelling-house is let as a separate dwelling is for the purposes of this Act an assured tenancy if and so long as—
>
> (a) the tenant or, as the case may be, each of the joint tenants is an individual; and

(b) the tenant or, as the case may be, at least one of the joint tenants occupies the dwelling-house as his only or principal home; and

(c) the tenancy is not one which, by virtue of subsection (2) or subsection (6) below, cannot be an assured tenancy.

Each of these elements will be taken in turn.

2.1 'Tenancy'

An assured tenancy must be a tenancy (or 'lease'). A mere licence to occupy the dwelling-house will not suffice, but any form of tenancy will do. Since *Street* v *Mountford* [1985] AC 809 most agreements for the occupation of residential property will be tenancies, but it remains important to define a tenancy or lease clearly, and to make the distinction between tenancy or lease and licence. The case law which is now described has a much broader utility, and application, than the definition of assured tenancy, as most significant statutory rights are conferred exclusively on tenants.

In *Street* v *Mountford*, a landlord conferred exclusive possession of two furnished rooms on an occupier pursuant to a written agreement whereby the occupier agreed to pay a 'licence fee' of £37 per week. The agreement was expressed to be terminable at 14 days' notice, and the occupier expressly accepted 'that a licence in the above form does not and is not intended to give me a tenancy protected under the Rent Acts. ' The House of Lords decided nevertheless that the agreement did create a tenancy. The three vital *indicia* were present, namely (i) exclusive possession; (ii) for a term; (iii) at a rent. The clear evidence from the written agreement that the parties did not intend to create a tenancy was irrelevant, in so far as they did intend exclusive possession to be granted. However, Lord Templeman, giving the only reasoned speech in the House of Lords conceded that there were certain restricted circumstances where the presence of the three *indicia* would not be decisive:

(a) *'Sometimes it may appear from the surrounding circumstances that there was no intention to create legal relationships'*. This must be distinguished from situations (of which *Street* v *Mountford* is of course one) where the parties do not intend to create a lease. Lord Templeman envisages informal family arrangements where the motive has been affection, kindness or generosity, and where no legal relationship giving rise to enforceable rights and obligations is intended. Examples are *Booker* v *Palmer* [1942] 2 All ER 674 (cottage owner agreed to allow a friend to install an evacuee in the cottage rent free for the duration of the war); *Marcroft Wagons Ltd* v *Smith* [1951] 2 KB 496 (landlord allowed daughter of deceased tenant to occupy a property temporarily, albeit paying for the privilege, while they considered her position); *Heslop* v *Burns* [1974] 1 WLR 1241 (family occupying cottage rent free); and see also *Monmouth Borough Council* v *Marlog* [1994] Times Law Reports 238. The scope of this exception is limited.

(b) *'Sometimes it may appear from the surrounding circumstances that the right to exclusive possession is referable to a legal relationship other than a tenancy. Legal relationships to which the grant of exclusive possession might be referable and which would or might negative the grant of an estate or interest in the land include . . . occupancy under a contract for the sale of the land'*. In *Isaac* v *Hotel de Paris Ltd* [1960] 1 WLR 239, an employee agreed 'subject to contract' to purchase shares in his employer's company, and was allowed to run their nightclub (and pay the rent under the employer's lease) in the expectation that the share purchase would be completed. The Privy Council held that he was not a tenant but was occupying pursuant to the informal, and unenforceable, agreement with his employer. In *Bretherton* v *Paton* (1986) 18 HLR 257, although there had been negotiations with a view to a purchase of the freehold by the occupier, the parties never agreed a price. The occupier, who enjoyed exclusive possession and made a periodic payment of £1.20 per week in respect of her occupation was held by the Court of Appeal to be a tenant.

(c) *'Occupancy pursuant to a contract of employment or occupancy referable to the holding of an office'*. Where an employee is accommodated by his employer, he will be a licensee (a 'service occupier') if the employer requires him to occupy the premises in order the better to perform his contractual duties (*Smith* v *Seghill Overseers* (1875) LR 10 QB 422). There must be something more than mere convenience to the employee. In *Norris* v *Checksfield* [1991] 1 WLR 1241, an employer allowed his employee, a semi-skilled mechanic, into possession of a bungalow on condition he would, in the future, drive coaches for the employer's business. The employee's occupation of the bungalow was not necessary, but was desirable: the employer required him to occupy the premises for the better performance of his duties, as he would then be available at short notice to drive coaches. Although, being disqualified from driving, a fact unknown to the employers when engaging him, the employee could not lawfully perform this duty, it was enough that the employer contemplated the employee fulfilling this role. The Court of Appeal held that the employee was a licensee rather than a tenant. See further case law on the analogous exception applicable to secure tenancies (see chapter 6, para. 3.2).

2.1.1 Proof of intention

A major practical problem is working out exactly what the 'landlord' and 'tenant' did 'intend'. The occupier may have gone into occupation having been told by word of mouth what rent he must pay, when he must pay it, and nothing else: there may be no written agreement at all. On the other hand, there may be a lengthy document which purports to inform the occupier in detail what his rights (if any) are, and what his (somewhat more extensive) obligations. Or the situation may be one where some of the terms of the agreement are oral, and some are in writing. Ultimately, the question is the same: does the agreement as a whole grant exclusive possession of the premises to the occupier, that exclusive possession being for a term at a rent? Matters are complicated by the tendency of many private landlords to attempt to obviate the effect of what they rightly perceive to be legislation which protects the tenant. Whilst they operated under the shadow of rent control, landlords would commonly seek by their written agreements to confer a licence or some other interest falling short of a tenancy on their occupier: indeed, that was the very tactic of the landlord (himself a solicitor) in *Street* v *Mountford*. Written agreements are therefore carefully examined by the courts: 'an express statement of intention is not decisive and . . . the court must pay attention to the facts and surrounding circumstances and to what people do as well as to what people say' (per Lord Templeman in *AG Securities* v *Vaughan* [1990] 1 AC 417).

There is less incentive now for landlords to beat the system. The absence of rent control means that the assured tenancy is not the item of value which the Rent Act protected tenancy was (and continues to be). The assured shorthold frankly offers little more by way of 'assurance' than a mere licence to occupy does. But the words of Lord Templeman in *Street* v *Mountford* remain of relevance (replacing 'Rent Acts' with 'Housing Act' where appropriate):

> Although the Rent Acts must not be allowed to alter or influence the construction of an agreement, the court should, in my opinion, be astute to detect and frustrate sham devices and artificial transactions whose only object is to disguise the grant of a tenancy and to evade the Rent Acts.

2.1.2 Sham transactions

A 'sham' in its strictest sense connotes 'acts done or documents executed by the parties to the "sham" which are intended by them to give to third parties or to the court the appearance of creating between the parties legal rights and obligations different from the actual legal rights and obligations (if any) which the parties intend to create' (per Diplock LJ in *Snook* v *London & West Riding Investments Ltd* [1967] 2 QB 786, 802). As the parties to a purported licence will have a common intention to create a licence rather than a tenancy, this test will rarely be satisfied. It does not follow that if a court finds that a written agreement is not a sham it must go on to apply the terms of the agreement as committed to writing. The court must apply the same rules of construction as it would apply to any other legal document, bearing in mind that the situation may be as envisaged by Mustill LJ in *Hadjiloucas* v *Crean* [1988] 1 WLR 1006, 1019, that is:

> . . . one in which the document does precisely reflect the true agreement between the parties, but where the language of the document (and in particular its title or description) superficially indicates that it falls into one legal category whereas when properly analysed in the light of the surrounding circumstances it can be seen to fall into another.

The consolidated appeals before the House of Lords in *AG Securities* v *Vaughan*; *Antoniades* v *Villiers* [1990] 1 AC 417 saw Lord Templeman moderating his choice of words. His Lordship considered that 'fewer misunderstandings would have been caused' if in *Street* v *Mountford* he had used the word 'pretence' to describe a written agreement or clause which was intended to act as a smokescreen obscuring the parties' real intentions. Moreover, in determining whether an agreement or clause is a 'pretence', the court may look at the conduct of the parties subsequent to the agreement in question as evidence of whether they genuinely intended to act upon it. Thus, in the *Antoniades* v *Villiers* appeal, a clause whereby an occupier could be required to share the premises with the landlord or any nominee of his was struck down partly because the landlord, who might be expected to make the maximum profit out of the property, never sought to exercise this right.

2.1.3 Exclusive possession

Exclusive possession was not itself in issue in *Street* v *Mountford*. It has caused difficulties before and since. It is generally recognised that the tenant has exclusive possession if he can lawfully exclude all others, including the landlord, from the property. The landlord (or others) may reserve rights of entry, for example in order to inspect the state of repair, but such rights should be restricted and well defined. Landlords should be aware that attempts to exclude exclusive possession may be subjected to rigorous scrutiny by the courts as they examine whether they are nothing more than 'shams' which the landlord does not intend to invoke.

A bald statement that the agreement does not confer exclusive possession on the occupier will be carefully scrutinised. In *Skipton Building Society* v *Clayton* (1993) 25 HLR 596, a written agreement purported to confer on a married couple a licence to occupy a dwelling-house for their joint lives and the life of the survivor. A clause vesting 'possession management and control' of the property in the defendant landlords was rejected as a sham, as it did not accord with the parties' true intentions (as evidenced by their subsequent conduct).

In *Crancour Ltd* v *Da Silvaesa* (1986) 18 HLR 265, a written agreement purported to require the occupier to vacate the property for one and a half hours each day. If this were a genuine term, it would no doubt rebut exclusive possession. It was, however, held to be a sham, as was the case in

Aslan v *Murphy (No 1); Duke* v *Wynne* [1990] 1 WLR 766, where the Court of Appeal described the term as 'wholly unrealistic and clearly a pretence'. In *Aslan* v *Murphy*, the Court evaluated the significance of the landlord's retention of a key to the premises. It did not have any magic in itself, and would only be significant if the purpose of keeping the key was to enable the landlord to provide services such as 'frequent cleaning, daily bed-making, the provision of clean linen at regular intervals and the like'.

2.1.4 Tenant or lodger

If extensive services are provided by the landlord, the occupier may not then have exclusive possession. In *Marchant* v *Charters* [1977] 1 WLR 1181, a case which must be treated with some caution in view of subsequent criticisms of Lord Denning's dicta in *Street* v *Mountford*, the landlord's daily cleaning of the 'bachelor service apartments' and weekly provision of clean linen was enough to deny the occupier exclusive possession. In colloquial terms, the occupier was a 'lodger'. A 'lodger' is a licensee rather than a tenant. He is not a tenant because he does not have exclusive possession, the owner retaining control and unrestricted access for the purpose of providing attendance and services (see Lord Templeman in *Street* v *Mountford* at 818).

The extent of services required to render the occupier a licensee is a matter of degree, and no hard and fast rules can be given. Access needs to be 'unrestricted' in so far as the landlord requires 'to go into and out of the lodger's rooms at the convenience of the landlord and without the lodger being there to let the landlord in' (per Ralph Gibson LJ in *Crancour* v *da Silvaesa* at 273). But not all licensees are lodgers. In *Brooker Settled Estates Ltd* v *Ayers* (1987) 19 HLR 246, the County Court judge, having held that the occupier was not a lodger, concluded that she must be a tenant. The Court of Appeal allowed the appeal, and ordered a re-hearing. The lodger is but one kind of licensee.

2.1.5 Exclusive possession and multiple occupiers

The landlord who attempts to deny the occupier exclusive possession by insisting that he share with another individual runs the very substantial risk that the two occupiers will together be deemed to be joint tenants. The high water mark of so-called 'non exclusive occupation agreements' was the Court of Appeal decision in *Somma* v *Hazelhurst* [1978] 1 WLR 1014. A young unmarried couple shared a double bed sitting room, each signing identical documents whereby they agreed to share the room with the landlord (termed 'the licensor') 'and with such other licensees or invitees whom the licensor shall from time to time permit to use the room.' They were held to be licensees as neither occupier had the individual right to exclusive possession. This decision was overruled in *Street* v *Mountford*, as (in Lord Templeman's words, at 825) 'the agreements signed by H and S [the occupiers] constituted the grant to H and S jointly of exclusive possession at a rent for a term for the purposes for which the room was taken and the agreement therefore created a tenancy.'

Street v *Mountford* was not itself concerned with multiple occupiers of one dwelling. However, in *Antoniades* v *Villiers* the House of Lords had to consider whether agreements which were very similar to those in *Somma* v *Hazelhurst* created a joint tenancy or two licences to occupy in respect of a single room furnished with a double bed. A clause permitting the landlord to occupy the rooms himself at any time and to permit other persons to use them together with the licensee was a pretence, and should be disregarded. The two agreements were interdependent. Reading them together, in the light of the surrounding circumstances (the physical layout and size of the flat, and the fact that the occupiers, though not married, were living together as husband and wife), it was clear that the landlord did not genuinely intend the agreements to be a true statement of the nature of the possession to be enjoyed by the occupiers. Evidence of their sham nature was provided by the physical arrangement of the premises (unsuited for the sharing the agreements contemplated), the lack of any discussion between the parties as to how the clause might operate, not to mention that the landlord never attempted to obtain increased income from the flat by introducing further occupiers (as by the agreements he was allegedly entitled to do). The true effect of the agreement between the parties was to confer on the occupiers a joint right to exclusive possession of the flat, and they were accordingly joint tenants.

In *Mikeover Ltd* v *Brady* [1989] 3 All ER 618, the Court of Appeal distinguished *Antoniades* v *Villiers*. A clause imposing an obligation on the occupier to share with those 'who have been granted' a like right did not permit the landlord to introduce further occupiers in the future, and so, as a matter of construction, did not itself derogate from a grant of exclusive possession. However, the agreements, in providing for the occupiers to make separate payments of rent, imposed several rather than joint liability for the rent. The occupiers could not be joint tenants as they lacked the requisite unity of interest, and the Court of Appeal decided that they were accordingly licensees only. Particularly striking on the facts was the landlord's refusal to accept the proferred payment of the whole rent by the occupier who remained following the departure of her fellow occupier.

Mikeover Ltd v *Brady* is an authority which should be treated with care. In a similar case, a court may well find the purported imposition of several rather than joint liability on two or more occupiers a pretence or a sham, as it was not seriously intended to be so enforced. This was so in several other cases (most notably *Antoniades* v *Villiers*, where the agreements *prima facie* indicated several liability for a half share of the rent). Alternatively, a court may infer a periodic tenancy has been created by the acceptance of rent proferred by the remaining occupier to the landlord.

The effect of these decisions can be summarised as follows. If the agreement, or agreements, read together in the light of the surrounding circumstances, confer exclusive possession on the occupiers, then as long as the other *indicia* of tenancy are present and the liability of the occupiers for the rent is joint, they will be joint tenants. Otherwise they will hold under separate licences.

In the *AG Securities* v *Vaughan* appeal, agreements were held to confer separate licences on the occupiers rather than a joint tenancy. The landlord company entered into four separate written agreements with four separate individuals between 1982 and 1985 for the occupation of a large flat in a mansion block which consisted of four bedrooms, a sitting room, a lounge, a kitchen, and a bathroom. The agreements were independent, each individual having entered his own following separate negotiations with the landlord. Although each agreement was in standard form, the rent payable by each occupier was different, as they had arrived at the flat at different times. When one occupier left the flat, the three remaining would decide whether they wished to change their bedrooms, and the replacement occupier would be offered the room the others did not want.

The House of Lords held that the occupiers were not joint tenants of the flat. The written agreements accurately reflected the flexible relationship between the landlord and the occupiers, and they were not shams. Construing the written agreements, their Lordships held that there was no grant of exclusive possession to the occupiers jointly as, in the event of one of the occupiers leaving, the three remaining could not exclude a fourth person nominated by the landlord. It is significant that the occupiers did not contend that they each had exclusive possession of their bedroom. Had they been granted an identifiable part of the flat, the tenancy having been granted on or after 15 January 1989, they would be able to argue that their tenancy was assured by virtue of the Housing Act 1988, s. 3 (see para. 2.3.7 below, and also Lord Oliver in *AG Securities* at 471).

2.1.6 For a term

A tenancy must be sufficiently certain. This will rarely be a difficulty with residential lettings. The landlord may let on a fixed term or on periodic tenancy. In *Prudential Assurance plc* v *London Residuary Body* [1992] 2 AC 386, the London County Council had in 1930 purported to lease a strip of land to predecessors in title of the plaintiff 'until the said land is required by the Council for the purposes of the widening' of the adjacent road. The House of Lords held that these words were not sufficiently certain to comprise a 'term', and whether a lease is for a fixed term or is a periodic tenancy, the requirement of certainty must be satisfied. The duration of a fixed term must be known at the outset. Thus, a provision that the tenancy is for six months, or three years, or will terminate on a given date, will be sufficient. A periodic tenancy (weekly, monthly and so on) is rendered sufficiently certain by the power of landlord and tenant to terminate by giving notice of the appropriate length. Restrictions on the right to terminate (e.g., that one party cannot give notice until a certain length of time has elapsed from the beginning of the lease) are unobjectionable as long as they are clearly prescribed (*Breams Property Investment Co. Ltd* v *Stroulger* [1948] 2 KB 1). In *Centaploy Ltd* v *Matlodge Ltd* [1974] Ch 1, parties purported to create a lease which was determinable by the tenant only. Whitford J held that a term preventing the landlord from terminating a periodic tenancy was repugnant to the nature of such a tenancy. The lease was validated by striking down the offending term.

2.1.7 At a rent

In *Street* v *Mountford*, Lord Templeman appeared to indicate that the existence of rent, in one form or another, was an essential ingredient of a tenancy. This is not consistent with the definition of 'term of years absolute' in the Law of Property Act 1925, s. 205 ('whether or not at a rent'), and in *Ashburn Anstalt* v *Arnold* [1989] Ch 1, the Court of Appeal denied that the reservation of a rent was a requirement. That said, in the protective codes it is usual to exempt rent-free tenancies, and a tenancy for which no rent is payable cannot be an assured tenancy (HA 1988, sch. 1, para. 3).

2.1.8 Informal tenancies

It remains the case that tenancies which are created very informally may nevertheless be assured tenancies for the purposes of the 1988 Act. Although a rent is required (as the statute so demands), it has been held that a tenancy 'at will', and even a tenancy 'by sufferance' can be regulated under the Rent Acts, and the same would no doubt apply in relation to assured tenancies (see, for example, *Artizans, Labourers and General Dwellings Co. Ltd* v *Whitaker* [1919] 2 KB 301; *Chamberlain* v *Farr* (1942) 112 LJKB 206).

2.2 'Dwelling-house'

A dwelling-house may be a house or a part of a house, such as a flat (HA 1988, s. 45(1)), and an assured tenant has the same degree of protection whether his property is a house or a flat (which may be a single bedsitting room). Little is likely to turn on whether a particular house or flat is a dwelling, that is a house which is capable of being inhabited, as the tenant will only be assured where he occupies the house as his only or principal home, and if he does so occupy it, it is surely inevitable that it is a dwelling so called. The proper interpretation of 'house' is more problematical. In *R* v *Nottinghamshire Rent Officer, ex parte Allen* (1985) 17 HLR 481, the Divisional Court held that a caravan was capable of being a dwelling-house.

The question was one of fact and degree, the dominant factor being the extent to which the caravan could be moved. If, unlike the facts in *ex parte Allen*, the caravan was completely immobile, it was more likely to come within the term 'dwelling-house'. Although never judicially considered, it seems, in the light of this authority, that tenancies of house-boats, or, more particularly, their moorings, could not be assured.

2.3 Let as a separate dwelling

The dwelling-house must be let as a dwelling, not, by inference, a shop or an office. Mixed lettings, such as shops with flats over, will be business tenancies, and excluded from assured tenancy status by para. 4 of sch. 1 to the 1988 Act. That schedule excludes no less than four types of potentially mixed letting (see para. 3 below).

2.3.1 Use of the property

The requirement that the dwelling-house be a *separate* dwelling means that it must be a coherent unit of occupation where the 'essential operations of living' (*per* Jenkins LJ in *Wimbush* v *Cibulia* [1949] 2 KB 564) go on. 'The right to retain possession is dependent on the tenant establishing that the premises are used by him as a home' (*per* Sir John Arnold P in *Kavanagh* v *Lyroudias* [1985] 1 All ER 560). It is the use of the property which is contemplated at the time of the letting which is material. As Eveleigh LJ stated in *St Catherine's College, Oxford* v *Dorling* [1980] 1 WLR 66, 68:

> ... one has to consider the terms of the lease and the surrounding circumstances at the time that the lease was granted. It may be that in some cases assistance can be obtained from the subsequent user of the premises. In my opinion generally speaking such assistance will be found to be a matter of last resort.

If all the tenant does in the property is sleep, it is not let as a separate dwelling, as he will presumably cook, eat, wash and so forth elsewhere (*Curl* v *Angelo* [1948] 2 All ER 189). Likewise if the tenant does everything there *except* sleep (*Wimbush* v *Cibulia*). Sleeping appears to be essential but not sufficient. In *Kavanagh* v *Lyroudias*, the tenant was granted at different times tenancies of adjoining houses. The house of which possession was sought was used by the tenant for sleeping in, and occasionally doing work which he brought home. The house had no hot water, and the tenant never cooked or ate there; he would do those things in the adjoining house. The Court of Appeal held that the house was not let as a separate dwelling, clearly evidenced by the fact that the tenant did not occupy it as a complete home.

2.3.2 Two units as one dwelling

A landlord may let two physically separate living units to the tenant, the intention being that the tenant will occupy them as a single dwelling. Despite the reference in the statutory provisions to 'a' dwelling, the courts have held that a dwelling-house need not be in one location only. In *Langford Property Co. Ltd* v *Goldrich* [1949] 1 KB 511, two flats on the same floor, although not structurally connected or even adjacent, were let 'as a separate dwelling' to the tenant and his family: see also *Whitty* v *Scott-Russell* [1950] 2 KB 32. In *Hampstead Way Investments Ltd* v *Lewis-Weare* [1985] 1 WLR 164, the House of Lords criticised the failure of the Court of Appeal in *Kavanagh* v *Lyroudias* [1985] 1 All ER 560 to consider

> whether the defendant tenant occupied [the two houses] as a combined or composite home of the kind contemplated in *Wimbush* v *Cibulia*, bearing in mind that the leases of both houses had originally been granted to the tenant by a person who was the owner of both, and that it was only subsequently that the reversions of the two houses passed into different hands.

It was not apparently conclusive that the landlord's interests in the two adjoining houses no longer belonged to the same person.

2.3.3 Tenancy comprising units separately occupied

In *Horford Investments Ltd* v *Lambert* [1976] Ch 39, the tenant converted two houses let to him by the same landlord into a number of 'accommodation units'. The Court of Appeal held that neither house could in consequence be said to be let as a separate dwelling. A similar conclusion was reached in *St Catherine's College, Oxford* v *Dorling* [1980] 1 WLR 66, where the landlord let a house to a college on the understanding (supported by a covenant by the college to like effect) that the house was to be occupied by undergraduates of the college, each student having the use of a room as a study bedroom, and sharing with the others the kitchen and the bathroom. The Court of Appeal held that the college did not have a protected tenancy of the house, as it was not let as a separate dwelling to the college, but as a building for multiple occupation in various units.

2.3.4 Business tenancy construction

In *Groveside Properties Ltd* v *Westminster Medical School* (1983) 47 P & CR 507, the Court of Appeal, on similar facts to *St Catherine's College, Oxford* v *Dorling*, construed an agreement between a landlord and a medical school as giving rise not to a protected tenancy but to a business tenancy within Part II of the Landlord and Tenant Act 1954. The medical school occupied the premises for the purposes of an 'activity' it carried on, namely the provision of residential accommodation for its student body (see Landlord and Tenant Act 1954 (LTA 1954), s. 23). The possibility of such a finding makes schemes of this kind rather less attractive to the landlord, although it does depend on the tenant exercising sufficient control over the property in the way it provides for its students or other residents as to comprise 'occupation' within the 1954 Act (see, by way of contrast, *Bagettes Ltd* v *G.P. Estates Ltd* [1956] Ch 290).

2.3.5 Tenants sharing accommodation

The invocation that the property must be let as a separate dwelling implies that those tenants who share some part of their living accommodation with others cannot be assured: 'the occupier must have the exclusive use of the essential living rooms of a separate dwelling-house', *per* Mackinnon LJ in *Cole* v *Harris* [1945] KB 474, 479. Thus, in *Cole* v *Harris*, a tenant who had exclusive use of a living room, bedroom and kitchen, but joint use with the landlord of a bathroom, w.c., and the garden, was a protected tenant under the Rent Acts as the property was let as a separate dwelling. However, in *Neale* v *del Soto* [1945] KB 144, sharing the kitchen with the landlord took the letting outside the protection of the Acts. In *Goodrich* v *Paisner* [1957] AC 65, where the House of Lords approved the distinction between the above two decisions of the Court of Appeal, Lord Morton of Henryton (at 83) considered that a kitchen, a dining room, a bedroom, and a sitting room were all living accommodation, the sharing of which would negative a protected tenancy, whereas a bathroom and w.c. were not. However, the Housing Act 1988 (as the Rent Act 1977 did) provides some protection for those who share their accommodation with other occupiers, but not with the landlord.

2.3.6 Sharing with the landlord

An occupier who shares living accommodation with his landlord (whether alone, or in conjunction with other occupiers) is unlikely to be an assured tenant on one of three grounds:

(a) the landlord's use of the accommodation is such as to deny the occupier exclusive possession (see, for example, *Marchant* v *Charters* at para. 2.1.4 above), and so he is not a tenant; or

(b) the property of which the occupier is tenant is not 'let as a separate dwelling'; or

(c) the resident landlord exception (para. 3.10 below) applies.

Whereas many occupiers who were not protected tenants by reason of the sharing with their landlord would nevertheless have the residual protection of a restricted contract (Rent Act 1977, s. 21: chapter 3, para. 9), this is not the case where they are not assured tenants, as restricted contracts can no longer be created (see chapter 3, para. 9.3).

2.3.7 Sharing with other occupiers

Where the tenant shares with other occupiers (whether tenants or licensees), not including his landlord, ss. 3 and 10 of the Housing Act 1988 must be carefully examined. A common sharing arrangement is one where individual tenants are given a room of their own, where they sleep, but they share common facilities such as the kitchen, living room, bathroom and so on with other tenants. A tenant could not without more claim that the room let to him under such an arrangement was 'let as a separate dwelling'. Nor could it be argued successfully that the tenants had together a joint tenancy of the whole house: they do not have a joint right of exclusive possession to the bedrooms. However, s. 3 deems certain units to be let on assured tenancy. The tenancy of the 'separate accommodation' (i.e., the bedroom in the above example) will be deemed to be an assured tenancy if the following conditions are satisfied:

(a) The tenant has exclusive occupation of the separate accommodation (cf. the arrangement in *AG Securities* v *Vaughan*, para. 2.1.5 above, where no occupier had exclusive rights to their bedroom).

(b) The terms on which he holds that room include the use of the other accommodation (i.e., the kitchen, living room, etc.) in common with others, not the landlord.

(c) The letting of the bedroom must not be excluded from assured tenancy status by any provision other than s. 1 itself.

The tenant does not obtain an assured tenancy of the shared accommodation. However, the court is prohibited from making an order for possession of that shared accommodation while the tenant remains in possession of the separate accommodation. Only when the court makes, or has made, a possession order relating to the separate accommodation will it have the necessary jurisdiction to order that possession of the shared accommodation be given up. As the separate accommodation is held on assured tenancy, the landlord who seeks possession will have to prove grounds.

Any term of the tenancy terminating or modifying the tenant's right to use the shared accommodation, or allowing the landlord so to terminate or modify, is of no effect whilst the tenant remains in possession of the separate accommodation (HA 1988, s. 3(3)). The landlord who seeks to prevent the tenant from using common rooms without authority in the tenancy agreement would be acting in breach of contract, and a tenant could apply for an injunction restraining the landlord's conduct.

Certain actions are however open to the landlord:

(a) He may invoke a term in the lease allowing him to terminate or modify the tenant's right to use shared accommodation in so far as that accommodation is not 'living accommodation' (HA 1988, s. 3(3)). 'Living accommodation' is 'accommodation of such a nature that the fact that it constitutes or is included in the shared accommodation is sufficient, apart from this section, to prevent the tenancy from constituting an assured tenancy of the dwelling-house' (HA 1988, s. 3(5)). In other words, it is the exclusion of this accommodation from the lease itself which prevents the dwelling-house being 'let as a separate dwelling', as required by HA 1988, s. 1(1).

(b) If, under the lease, the landlord is entitled to increase the number of persons with whom the tenant has to share, he will be free to invoke such a term, despite the fact that by increasing the number of sharers the landlord will be to some extent modifying the use of the shared accommodation by the existing tenants (HA 1988, s. 3(4)).

The landlord is entitled to apply to the court to enforce the above contractual rights, and on such application the court may make such order as it thinks just (HA 1988, s. 10(3)).

2.3.8 Sharing with sub-tenant(s)

Where a tenant sub-lets part, but not the whole, of the dwelling-house let, then no part of the dwelling-house is to be treated as excluded from being a dwelling-house let on assured tenancy by reason only that the terms on which the sub-tenant holds include the use of accommodation in common with other persons (HA 1988, s. 4). Thus the tenant may still be an assured tenant although the accommodation is being shared in part with a sub-tenant. The landlord cannot contend that the dwelling-house is not, as a result, let as a separate dwelling. Where a tenant sub-lets the whole of the dwelling-house let, he will thereupon cease to be an assured tenant as he will not satisfy the residence condition (see para. 2.5 below).

2.4 'Individual'

A tenancy is only assured if and so long as the tenant, or in the case of joint tenancy, each of the joint tenants, is an individual. This provision is intended to prevent companies or other institutions from holding on joint tenancy, although it is arguably unnecessary as it has been held in the context of the Rent Acts that a company or other artificial person cannot occupy a dwelling-house as its residence (*Hillier* v *United Dairies Ltd* [1934] 1 KB 57).

2.4.1 Company lets

Landlords have on occasion let residential property to companies rather than individuals, in the certain knowledge that the company would allow an individual into occupation. This 'company let' arrangement has the benefit of avoiding the protective legislation, at least in so far as it is not struck down as a sham or artificial device. The letting to the individual would be outside the assured tenancy provisions either because it was a licence (difficult since *Street* v *Mountford*), or because the individual paid no rent. Most schemes involved a company which had a pre-existing connection with the individual concerned (*Firstcross Ltd* v *East West (Export/Import) Ltd* (1981) 41 P & CR 145), and in such a case, Stocker LJ stated:

> I would not wish to express any view . . . as to what the situation might be under the Rent Acts where there is a letting in which the company does not perform genuinely the obligations under the lease and in which a company had been put in as tenant solely as a cloak to avoid the operation of the Rent Acts which would otherwise apply. (*Estavest Investments Ltd* v *Commercial Express Travel Ltd* (1987) 21 HLR 106).

Despite this comment, company let schemes have since been upheld where the landlord has required the intending occupier to purchase a company 'off the shelf', that company then becoming the tenant. In *Hilton* v *Plustitle Ltd* [1989] 1 WLR 149, the Court of Appeal considered that as a company let was the intention of both parties, and they had full knowledge of what this involved, the written agreement was effective and not a sham. In *Kaye* v *Massbetter Ltd* (1990) 24 HLR 28, the individual was guarantor of the rent payable by the company purchased 'off the shelf'. The Court of Appeal placed the onus of proving that the written documents were sham firmly on the occupier, who, according to Nicholls LJ, 'has to establish that, contrary to the terms of the document, the common intention of himself and [the landlord] was that the company . . . was not to be subject to an obligation in law to pay rent or to perform the obligations imposed by the agreement on the tenant.'

The company let scheme has proved surprisingly successful at avoiding protective legislation. The assured tenancy provisions, with their insistence that the tenant be an 'individual', allow for its continued use. That said, one must doubt whether it will be as popular as before. A landlord will obtain most practical advantages he can hope for with the assured shorthold tenancy, a mode of letting with express Parliamentary approval and without the risk inherent in using a mere device.

2.5 Occupation as only or principal home

A tenancy will only be assured if and so long as the tenant, or one of joint tenants, occupies the dwelling-house as *his only or principal home*. This terminology is identical to that used for secure tenancies (see chapter 6, para. 2.6), but differs from the residence condition for Rent Act statutory tenants, who have to occupy the dwelling in question '*as a residence*'. There is no significant distinction between 'home' and 'residence' (see *Hampstead Way Investments Ltd* v *Lewis-Weare* [1985] 1 WLR 164, 169). In imposing the requirement for an assured tenancy that the dwelling be the tenant's only or principal home, Parliament has set out to prevent privileged tenants who have two or more residences, claiming security of tenure in a property which is not in fact their main home. Thus, in construing the residence condition for assured tenancies, considerable care must be taken in using Rent Act authorities (discussed fully in chapter 3, para. 4.1), as the question being asked is subtly different. There are many decisions under the Rent Acts where the tenant had two homes, of which the one he was claiming to hold as statutory tenant was clearly not, at the time, the principal one (see, for example, *Gofor Investments Ltd* v *Roberts; Brickfield Properties Ltd* v *Hughes; Duke* v *Porter*). There are other decisions where the tenant absents himself, sometimes involuntarily, and cannot truly be said to have occupied another dwelling as his 'home' (see, for example, *Brown* v *Brash; Tickner* v *Hearn*). It would be unlikely, and ungenerous, to term a prison or a mental hospital a tenant's 'principal home', and it could be argued that such a tenant would remain assured in so far as he intended to return to the property, and sufficient evidence of his intentions was left there (i.e., the necessary *animus* and *corpus* were present). It will be necessary in each such case to consider where the tenant has been living during his period of absence, and on what basis he has been living there.

2.5.1 Occupation a question of fact

There can be little doubt that the courts will adopt the same stance they have taken in relation to occupation under the Rent Act 1977, and state that whether a tenant occupies the dwelling as his only or principal home is a question of fact for the first instance judge (see, for example, *Gofor Investments Ltd* v *Roberts* (1975) 29 P & CR 366, chapter 3, para. 4.1). Although there are no examples of applying the only or principal home test in the context of the 1988 Act, reference can be made to decisions under the Leasehold Reform Act 1967 (see chapter 5, para. 3.4) and the Housing Act 1985 (see chapter 6, para. 2.6).

2.5.2 Husband and wife

The Matrimonial Homes Act 1983 makes important qualifications to the requirement of occupation where a husband and wife are concerned, and where the tenanted property is, or has at some time since the contract of tenancy been, the matrimonial home. Where one spouse only is assured tenant of the property, the other will have statutory rights of occupation

(Matrimonial Homes Act 1983 (MHA 1983), s. 1(1)). These rights are treated, for the purposes of Part I of the Housing Act 1988, as occupation by the tenant spouse (MHA 1983, s. 1(6), as amended by the Housing Act 1988, sch. 17, para. 33). Thus, if the tenant spouse (for ease of exposition, let us say the husband, although the provisions are gender neutral) leaves the wife, not intending to return, her occupation will be enough for his assured tenancy to persist. She will be entitled to make payments of rent and rates herself, and would be well advised to do so in the event of her husband defaulting, as the landlord may otherwise have grounds for possession (MHA 1983, s. 1(5)).

However, the operation of the Matrimonial Homes Act 1983 depends on the parties being married, and the tenanted property being their matrimonial home. If the parties have never been married at all, the 1983 Act cannot apply, and the deserted 'common law spouse' of an assured tenant has no right to remain as against the landlord under the Housing Act 1988. If the parties have been married, but are no longer, the same applies: see, applying the provisions in relation to a Rent Act regulated tenancy, *Metropolitan Properties Ltd* v *Cronan* (1982) 44 P & CR 1, at chapter 3, para. 4.1.9. On divorce, the wife should protect herself by applying in the ancillary relief proceedings for the assured tenancy to be transferred to her (MHA 1983, sch. 1, as amended by HA 1988, sch. 17, para. 34(1)). If the property has never been the matrimonial home of the married couple, rights under the 1983 Act cannot be asserted (see, for example, *Hall* v *King* (1987) 19 HLR 440). Where the spouses were joint tenants of the matrimonial home, problems of this nature should not arise, as in such a case, the tenancy will remain assured as long as one of them occupies the dwelling as his or her only or principal home: HA 1988, s. 1(1)(b).

2.5.3 Loss of assured status

If an assured tenant ceases to occupy, he thereby ceases to be an assured tenant. He does not, however, lose his tenancy. The contractual relationship between landlord and tenant will continue, and the landlord will only be able to recover possession once it has terminated, paying due heed to the provisions of the Protection from Eviction Act 1977 (see chapter 8). This is significantly different from the position of the Rent Act statutory tenant, who is holding only by virtue of the statute. When he ceases to occupy, the only right by virtue of which he remains on the property is extinguished, and the landlord will be entitled to repossess (although, similarly, restrictions on the way in which possession is recovered are imposed by the Protection from Eviction Act: see chapter 8).

3 EXCLUSIONS

Subject to the rules regarding '1980 Act' assured tenancies (see chapter 2, para. 1.1), a tenancy cannot be an assured tenancy 'if and so long as' it falls within any paragraph of sch. 1 to the 1988 Act. These will now be dealt with in turn. Many of the excluded categories are very similar, and sometimes identical, to exclusions from protected tenancy status under the Rent Acts.

3.1 Tenancies pre-dating the Housing Act 1988: para. 1

As a general rule, tenancies (whether or not Rent Act regulated) entered into before 15 January 1989, or pursuant to a contract made before that date, cannot be assured tenancies. However, there are important exceptions.

3.1.1 Savings for Rent Act protected tenancies

The Housing Act 1988, sch. 1, para. 1, implements the policy of retaining Rent Act status for those protected or statutory tenancies existing at the time the Act came into force. In three further situations, set out in s. 34 and outlined in chapter 3, para. 3.1 below, a tenancy will be protected although it was entered into on or after 15 January 1989. As a protected tenancy cannot also be an assured tenancy (see para. 3.13 below), these situations comprise exceptions to the conferment of assured status on tenancies post-dating the Housing Act which otherwise satisfy the stipulated criteria.

3.1.2 Transfers to the private sector

A further important exception to the general rule is found in HA 1988, s. 38. By this provision, a tenant of a 'public body' (e.g., a local authority, a new town corporation, an urban development corporation, a housing action trust: see s. 38(5) for full definition) whose tenancy was entered into before 15 January 1989 or pursuant to a contract made before that date, and whose landlord subsequently alienates its interest to a non-public body, will become an assured tenant of that new landlord, if in all other respects the conditions necessary for an assured tenancy are fulfilled. The broad effect can be summarised by stating that tenants who move from the public to the private sector after the commencement of the 1988 Act will become assured tenants on transfer irrespective of the dates their tenancies were entered into.

> *Example:* In 1988, district council L lets a house on secure tenancy to T. In 1990, L sells the house to P, which is not a 'public body' within s. 38(5). On the date of completion, T will cease to be a secure tenant, as the 'landlord condition' of Housing Act 1985, s. 80 (see chapter 6, para. 2.5) is no longer satisfied. T's tenancy will become assured, as long as it fulfils the usual conditions, although it was entered into before the commencement of the 1988 Act.

There are special provisions concerning new town corporations (see HA 1988, s. 38(4), as amended by the Local Government and Housing Act 1989, s. 194(1), sch. 11), and, of wider relevance, housing associations (see chapter 3, para. 10).

3.2 High value properties: para. 2

The abolition of the domestic rating system has led to considerable complexity in ascertaining whether a property is within the scope of the Housing Act 1988. Amendments have been made to the Act by the References to Rating (Housing) Regulations 1990, SI 1990, No 434.

3.2.1 Tenancy entered into prior to 1 April 1990

If the tenancy was entered into before, or pursuant to a contract made before, 1 April 1990, then the test is rateable value of the dwelling-house on 31 March 1990. If in Greater London this exceeded £1,500, or elsewhere £750, the tenancy cannot be assured. For the definition of 'rent', see para. 3.3.3 below.

3.2.2 Tenancy entered into on or after 1 April 1990

If the tenancy was entered into on or after 1 April 1990, or the dwelling-house had no rateable value on 31 March 1990, then the test is the rent payable. If this exceeds £25,000 a year 'for the time being', the tenancy cannot be assured. For the definition of 'rent', see para. 3.3.3 below.

3.3 Tenancies at a low rent (or no rent): para. 3

There is no prohibition as such on 'long tenancies' (where the tenant obtains a lease exceeding 21 years, probably for a substantial premium) being assured tenancies. However, many will be caught by this provision. As with para. 2 above, complexities have arisen from the abolition of domestic rates: see again for relevant amendments SI 1990, No 434.

3.3.1 Tenancy entered into prior to 1 April 1990

If the tenancy is entered into before 1 April 1990, or in pursuance of a contract made before that date, then it cannot be assured if the rent for the time being payable is less than two thirds of the rateable value of the dwelling-house on 31 March 1990.

3.3.2 Tenancy entered into on or after 1 April 1990

If the tenancy was entered into on or after 1 April 1990, or the dwelling-house did not have a rateable value on that date, the tenancy cannot be assured if the rent for the time being is payable at a rate of £1,000 or less per year in Greater London, £250 or less per year elsewhere.

3.3.3 Definition of rent

For the purposes of paras. 2 and 3, 'rent' does not include sums payable by the tenant which are expressed to be payable in respect of rates, services, management, repairs, maintenance or insurance, unless they could not have been regarded by the parties as sums so payable. 'Rent' has been held not to include the value of services rendered by the tenant for the benefit of the landlord (*Barnes* v *Barratt* [1970] 2 QB 657). Where a tenant was employed by his landlord, and occupied rent-free accommodation, receiving a smaller wage as a result, it was held proper to quantify the rent by reference to the reduction in wages (*Montagu* v *Browning* [1954] 1 WLR 1039).

A landlord may seek to avoid the creation of an assured tenancy by charging a rent below these limits, but combining it with a high premium at the commencement of the lease. Under the Rent Act 1977, the courts were known to strike down premiums which were essentially a capitalised pre-payment of rent (*Samrose Properties Ltd* v *Gibbard* [1958] 1 WLR 235), premiums being in any case restricted in relation to protected or statutory tenancies. However, it is perfectly lawful to charge a premium as consideration for an assured tenancy, and it may be more difficult for the courts to rationalise intervention where assured tenancies are concerned.

3.4 Business tenancies: para. 4

A tenancy to which Part II of the Landlord and Tenant Act 1954 applies (i.e., a 'business tenancy') cannot be an assured tenancy. The definition of business tenancy is:

> any tenancy where the property comprised in the tenancy is or includes premises which are occupied by the tenant and are so occupied for the purposes of a business carried on by him or for those or other purposes.
> (LTA 1954, s. 23(1).)

'Business' is in turn widely defined, so as to include a trade, profession or employment, and it 'includes any activity carried on by a body of persons, whether corporate or unincorporate.' (LTA 1954, s. 23(2).)

3.4.1 Mixed user

The definition in section 23(1) is wide, including as it does property which 'includes premises' which are occupied for business 'and other purposes'. A small but significant amount of business user of a dwelling-house will be enough to make the tenancy a business tenancy, and therefore not an assured tenancy. Thus, a doctor who uses a room in his rented house as a consulting room will occupy the premises for the purposes of his business (i.e., 'profession'). A shopkeeper who holds under his lease a shop with a flat above will be a business tenant. However, the business user must be a significant purpose of the occupation, and not merely incidental to occupation as a residence, for the tenancy to fall within the 1954 Act. In *Royal Life Saving Society* v *Page* [1978] 1 WLR 1329, a doctor rented a maisonette as his home. With the landlords' consent, he saw the occasional patient at his home in an emergency, and he used the telephone in the flat for professional purposes. The business user was not significant enough for the tenancy to be a business tenancy. Geoffrey Lane LJ said (at 1339):

> The businessman . . . who takes work home in the evening which he does in a study set aside for the purpose may very well be using the premises partly for carrying on thereat a business, but he could scarcely be said to be occupying the premises for the purposes of a business, any more than the person who watches the television regularly every evening can be said to be occupying his house for the purpose of watching television. It is only if the activity is part of the reason for, part of his aim and object in occupying the house that the section will apply.

The test contained in the final sentence was approved by the Court of Appeal in *Gurton* v *Parrot* (1990) 23 HLR 418, holding that a tenant who carried on a business grooming, breeding, and kennelling dogs 'as a hobby which provided her with some money to help with living expenses and upkeep of the property' was not occupying the premises for that purpose.

3.4.2 Change of user: from residence to business

In *Cheryl Investments Ltd* v *Saldanha* [1978] 1 WLR 1329 (consolidated with *Royal Life Saving Society* v *Page* in the Court of Appeal), a protected tenant equipped his flat with a telephone, a work table, and printed notepaper, and commenced to carry on a seafood importing business from the flat. He had no other place of work. Lord Denning MR held that the tenancy was a business tenancy under the 1954 Act rather than a Rent Act protected tenancy. The change of use effected a change in the status of the tenancy once it could be said that the premises were being occupied for the purposes of a business. It was immaterial that the landlord did not know about the business use being carried on.

3.4.3 Change of user: from business to residence

In *Pulleng* v *Curran* (1980) 44 P & CR 58, a tenant attempted to argue that his tenancy, which he acknowledged had started life as a business tenancy, had become protected under the Rent Act 1977 by virtue of his cessation of trading. The premises comprised a grocer's and dairyman's shop, with rooms at the rear and living accommodation above. The tenant contended that he had ceased to trade in 1965, and thereupon the tenancy became protected under the Rent Acts. The Court of Appeal, whilst refusing to subvert the judge's finding of fact that significant business use had continued up to the date of the relevant proceedings, denied the basic premise of the tenant's argument that a cessation of business use would automatically lead to premises which were being lived in becoming protected under the Rent Acts, following *Wolfe* v *Hogan* [1949] 2 KB 194.

The Housing Act 1988 (and the Rent Act 1977) in setting the criteria for an assured (or, as the case may be, protected) tenancy requires the court to examine the agreement between the parties ('let as a dwelling': HA 1988, s. 1(1)). Part II of the Landlord and Tenant Act 1954 requires the court to look at the purpose of the occupation at the given time ('occupied for the purposes of a business'). The combined effect is that while a tenancy may change from being a residential tenancy to being a business tenancy without the knowledge, actual or assumed, of the landlord, the converse is not the case. The issue received its closest analysis in *Russell* v *Booker* (1982) 5 HLR 10, where the Court of Appeal was asked to decide whether on termination of agricultural use a property, originally let as an agricultural holding, which included a dwelling-house, became a protected tenancy. Slade LJ stated:

> If a tenant changes the user of the premises and the fact of change is fully known to, and accepted by, the landlord, it may be possible for the court to infer a subsequent contract to let them 'a separate dwelling-house', although this would be a contract different in essentials from the original tenancy agreement ... However, unless a contract of the last-mentioned nature can be spelt out, a mere unilateral change of user will not enable a tenant to claim the protection of the Rent Acts in a case where the terms of the tenancy agreement itself provide for and contemplate the use of the premises for some particular purpose which does not attract the protection of the Acts — for example as a shop or agricultural holding ... Where the tenancy agreement does not provide or contemplate the use of the premises for any particular purpose, actual subsequent user has to be looked at in determining whether a house is 'let as a separate dwelling-house', so as to attract the protection of the Rent Acts.

3.4.4 Tenant tactics

Whilst the above case law proceeds on the rational assumption that a tenant is better off as a Rent Act regulated tenant (enjoying as he does the benefit of rent control) rather than a business tenant (whose tenancy will not have a controlled rent), it may not always be in the tenant's interests to argue that he is an assured tenant rather than a business tenant. The procedure for obtaining possession of property let on a business tenancy is highly technical and fraught with pitfalls, and the tenant may on advice see himself in a stronger bargaining position as a business tenant. This will nowhere more clearly be the case than where the landlord has initiated proceedings on the basis that the defendant is an assured tenant, as the landlord will clearly be unable to succeed in such an action if the tenant can establish that his tenancy is protected by Part II of the Landlord and Tenant Act 1954.

3.5 Licensed premises: para. 5

A tenancy under which the dwelling-house consists of or comprises premises licensed for the sale of intoxicating liquors for consumption on the premises cannot be an assured tenancy. This exclusion largely affects public houses. Since 11 July 1992, such tenancies have been brought within the business tenancy code contained in Part II of the Landlord and Tenant Act 1954 (see Landlord and Tenant (Licensed Premises) Act 1990), and so most of these tenancies will now be denied assured status anyway by para. 4 above. Tenancies of 'off-licences' will be business tenancies under the 1954 Act.

3.6 Tenancies of agricultural land: para. 6

A tenancy under which 'agricultural land' (as defined in the General Rate Act 1967, s. 26(3)(a)), exceeding two acres, is let together with the dwelling-house cannot be an assured tenancy. If not more than two acres of agricultural land is let with the dwelling (or any amount of non-agricultural land), that other land is to be treated as part of the dwelling-house as long as the 'main purpose' of the letting is the provision of a home for the tenant or one of two or more joint tenants (HA 1988, s. 2).

3.7 Tenancies of agricultural holdings: para. 7

A tenancy under which the dwelling-house is comprised in an agricultural holding, and is occupied by the person responsible for the control (whether as tenant or as servant or agent of the tenant) of the farming of the holding cannot be an assured tenancy. 'Agricultural holding' is defined in the Agricultural Holdings Act 1986, s. 1(1), as the aggregate of land (whether agricultural or not) comprised in a contract of tenancy which is a contract for an agricultural tenancy. There is a contract for an agricultural tenancy if having regard to the terms of the tenancy, the actual and contemplated use of the land, and all other relevant circumstances, the whole of the land is let for use as agricultural land, here defined as land used for agriculture which is so used for the purposes of a trade or business. Finally, 'agriculture' is widely defined so as to include horticulture, fruit growing, seed growing, market gardening, and so forth (see Agricultural Holdings Act 1986, ss. 1, 96(1)). Certain 'contracts of tenancy' are further excluded from protection by virtue of the agricultural holdings legislation. The purpose of such exclusion is to prevent duplication of protection. Lettings which fall within para. 7 will be protected by the Agricultural Holdings Act 1986.

A property which is initially let as a dwelling-house, with no, or purely subsidiary, use for agriculture, may be converted from being an assured tenancy to a tenancy within the Agricultural Holdings Act 1986 by a change of use. However, although a dwelling-house which is initially let as part of an agricultural holding will, on a cesser of agricultural use, no longer be within the 1986 Act, it does not follow that it will thereupon convert into an assured tenancy as a matter of course. To qualify as an assured tenancy, the property must be 'let as a dwelling' (HA 1988, s. 1(1)), and the tenant must therefore prove that a new contract has been made, either on the parties' express agreement or by inference from the landlord's tacit acceptance of the position (*Russell* v *Booker*: see para. 3.4.3 above).

3.8 Lettings to students: para. 8

Despite this heading in sch. 1, by no means all lettings to students are excluded from protection as assured tenancies. The identity of the landlord is the determining factor. Paragraph 8 excludes tenancies which are granted to students by a 'specified educational institution or body of persons'. The institution must have been specified by the Secretary of State by statutory instrument. The current instrument is the Assured and Protected Tenancies (Lettings to Students) Regulations 1988, SI 1988 No 2236, as substantially amended by SI 1992 No 515, which lists universities, university colleges, other publicly funded further or higher education institutions, registered housing associations, and various named bodies. The student need not be full time: he must be merely pursuing, or intending to pursue, a course of study at a specified educational institution. If an educational institution is specified by regulation, any tenancy it grants to a student cannot be assured, even if it is desired by the institution. Whilst many such institutions have recently established business expansion (BES) schemes, under which lettings to their students must be on assured tenancy, the landlord is the BES company, which is not itself a specified institution, and so there is no difficulty with para. 8.

Vacation lettings of student accommodation to other persons are not covered by para. 8. However, the landlord has the opportunity of availing himself of a mandatory ground for possession on termination of such a fixed term tenancy (HA 1988, sch. 2, Ground 4).

3.9 Holiday lettings: para. 9

Tenancies the purpose of which is to confer on the tenant the right to occupy the dwelling-house for a holiday are excluded from assured tenancy status.

'Holiday' has been defined judicially as 'a period of cessation of work or a period of recreation' (*Buchmann* v *May* [1978] 2 All ER 993). In *Buchmann* v *May*, a dancer from New Zealand had been the tenant of a dwelling-house for two years when she signed a new agreement which stated that 'the letting hereby made is solely for the purpose of the tenant's holiday'. The Court of Appeal, holding that the onus was on the tenant to displace this *prima facie* evidence of the parties' true purpose, decided that she had failed to do this, and the tenancy was accordingly unprotected. In the light of *Street* v *Mountford*, where Lord Templeman adverted to the need to detect shams and other artificial devices intended to avoid the application of protective statutes, *Buchmann* v *May* should be treated with caution. In *R* v *Camden Rent Officer, ex parte Plant* (1980) 7 HLR 15, Glidewell J, sitting in the Divisional Court, took a more sanguine view of a purported 'holiday let'. The landlord let to four student nurses, the written agreement stating that the letting was for the purposes of a holiday. As there was clear evidence that the landlord knew that his tenants were nurses working in the area, Glidewell J held that the tenancy was not excluded from protection.

3.10 Resident landlords: para. 10

The resident landlord exception, based upon the 'social embarrassment' which would arise from involuntary 'close proximity' of landlord and tenant (*Bardrick* v *Haycock* (1976) 31 P & CR 420, 424), is long established in relation to Rent Act protected tenancies (see further, chapter 3, para. 3.11). However, whereas tenants of resident landlords would normally hold restricted contracts under the Rent Acts, this is not the case with lettings entered into on or after 15 January 1989 (see chapter 3, para. 9.3). If a resident landlord shares 'accommodation' with such a tenant, the tenant will not even enjoy the most basic protection of a statutory minimum period of notice (Protection from Eviction Act 1977, ss. 3, 3A(2), 5, as amended by HA 1988, ss. 30, 31: see further, chapter 8, para. 4.1).

3.10.1 Purpose-built block of flats

Three conditions (which we will refer to as the 'Rules') must be fulfilled before the resident landlord exception is established. The way in which the Rules operate depend on whether or not the dwelling let to the tenant forms part of a 'purpose-built block of flats', as defined by HA 1988, sch. 1, para. 22. The building must *as constructed* contain two or more 'flats'. (A 'flat' is a dwelling-house which forms part only of a building which is separated horizontally from another dwelling-house forming part of the same building.) As 'purpose-built' implies, it cannot include buildings which are converted from their former use, perhaps as a single dwelling-house, into self-contained flats. In *Barnes* v *Gorsuch* (1981) 43 P & CR 294, an attempt was made to argue that a Victorian house which was in 1959 divided into three flats, and then subsequently sub-divided so as to make six flats in all was nevertheless a 'purpose-built block of flats'. O'Connor LJ rejected this argument, holding that the ordinary meaning of the statutory words ('as constructed') referred to 'the building as it was originally designed and built'. The only circumstances in which later works could have a bearing would be where the works were so extensive that the building changed its character and became a different building altogether.

3.10.2 The Rules

3.10.2.1 Where the building is a purpose-built block of flats

Rule A: The dwelling-house let to the tenant must form part of one of the flats.

Rule B: The person who granted the tenancy (the first landlord) must have been an individual (i.e., not a company), and he must have occupied another dwelling-house in the same flat as his only or principal home.

Rule C: Subject to the various qualifications below, at all times each of the later landlords, if any, must have been an individual and have occupied another dwelling-house in the flat as his only or principal home.

3.10.2.2 Where the building is not a purpose-built block of flats

Rule A: The dwelling-house let to the tenant must form part only of the building.

Rule B: The first landlord must have been an individual and he must have occupied another dwelling-house in the same building as his only or principal home.

Rule C: Subject to the various qualifications below, at all times each of the later landlords, if any, must have been an individual and have occupied another dwelling-house in the same building as his only or principal home.

3.10.3 Part of the building (or flat)

Whether the dwelling let to the tenant forms part of the same building or flat as the dwelling occupied by the landlord is a question of fact and degree. In *Bardrick* v *Haycock*, a substantial house was converted into six flats, which were then let to and occupied by tenants. The landlord lived in a two-storey extension which, although physically attached to the house, did not have any internal means of communication to it. The Court of Appeal upheld the decision of the county court judge that the landlord did not occupy a dwelling-house forming part of the same building as that of which the tenants' dwellings formed part, and the resident landlord exception did not apply. Scarman LJ stated:

> The English word 'building' covers an immense range of all sorts of structures. It is an ordinary English word, and its meaning must therefore be a question of fact, always assuming that the court directs itself correctly as to the intention and meaning of the statute which uses it. As a matter of law, to give a defined or precise meaning to the word 'building' is an impossibility. It is beyond the capacity of even the most consummate master of the English language to do so. This itself is, in my judgment, an indication that Parliament is leaving the question of fact to the judge.

The cases which follow *Bardrick* v *Haycock* are illustrative only, and should not be considered 'authorities' save for the recurring proposition that the question whether the dwellings respectively occupied by landlord and tenant are parts of the same building is one of fact for the judge: see *Griffiths* v *English* (1981) 2 HLR 127, *Wolff* v *Waddington* (1989) 22 HLR 72, *Lewis-Graham* v *Conacher* (1991) 24 HLR 132.

3.10.4 Occupation by the landlord

The landlord must occupy a dwelling-house in the same building or flat as the tenant's dwelling, and must do so *as his only or principal home*. This test is the same which must be satisfied for a tenant to be assured (HA 1988, s. 1(1)(b): see chapter 2, para. 2.5). It is essentially a question of fact, but the mere retention of a sparsely furnished room in the building, which the landlord sleeps in only occasionally, will not be sufficient. As landlords may frequently have more than one home, it is important to check what other residences, if any, the landlord has, and, if he has, whether this is his principal home. It is not enough for the landlord to prove merely that he is occupying this property as a residence, and care must be taken in using case law on the Rent Act resident landlord exception. In *Wolff* v *Waddington*, above, it was observed that a resident landlord for the purposes of the Rent Act could have two homes much as a statutory tenant. This could not be the case in relation to the 1988 Act.

3.10.4.1 Joint landlords

Where the landlord's interest is held by more than one person, the occupation of one will suffice to fuel the resident-landlord exception. As long as at least one of those holding the landlord's interest is an individual, and that individual or one of them is occupying at the relevant times, it is immaterial that a company, or institution, is a joint owner of that interest (HA 1988, sch. 1, para. 10(2)).

3.10.4.2 Occupation throughout the tenancy

It can be seen from the above statement of the basic Rules, in particular Rule C, that where the tenant has had different landlords, the evaluation of whether that tenancy is excluded from assured tenancy status by reason of the resident-landlord exception may involve a close analysis of the way in which the landlord's interest has been passed on, and the residence of each and every subsequent landlord. One must not lose sight also that the first landlord must have been in occupation at the time of the tenancy agreement (i.e., Rule B), although there appears to be a certain amount of latitude for landlords where they move property together with their tenants (see *O'Sullivan* v *Barnett* (1994) Times Law Reports 295). The analysis is made more complex still by the various qualifications which must now be explained.

3.10.4.3 Rule C 'deemed to be fulfilled'

The effect of Rule C being deemed to be fulfilled in one of the instances set out below is that, if Rules A and B are also satisfied, the tenancy will not be assured. Nor will the tenancy be a restricted contract, having been entered into on or after 15 January 1989, and the landlord will be able to obtain possession by any common law method of terminating the tenancy (forfeiture, notice, expiry of fixed term, etc.), subject only to compliance with the Protection from Eviction Act 1977 (chapter 8, para. 2).

Rule C *will be deemed to be fulfilled* in three instances:

(1) Where the landlord's interest is vested in trustees on trust for a beneficiary or beneficiaries, at least one of whom occupies the dwelling-house as his only or principal home (HA 1988, sch. 1, para. 18).

(2) Where the landlord's interest has been so vested in trustees, and the tenancy has come to an end, during the full duration of any new tenancy of the same (or substantially the same) dwelling-house which the trustees grant to the sitting tenant (para. 19).

(3) For a period, not exceeding two years, throughout which the landlord's interest is vested in personal representatives (i.e., the persons who, following the death of the resident landlord, have his estate vested in them by his will or on his intestacy) (para. 20).

Example: Occupation by beneficiary under trust

A house is settled on trust by settlor S, the beneficiaries being A, B and C. C occupies a room in the house (which is not a purpose built block of flats) as his principal home, and has done so ever since the other rooms in the house were let in 1990. The tenants of those rooms will not be assured tenants as long as C continues to reside, and the trustees will be able to obtain possession of any of the rooms by giving the tenants the notice to which they are entitled under the terms of their tenancy agreements. (Note: the tenants would be entitled to a minimum of four weeks' notice in writing, unless the tenancy is an 'excluded tenancy': Protection from Eviction Act 1977, s. 5(1)).

3.10.4.4 Periods of disregard

A 'period of disregard' is a period of grace where for a specific reason the landlord may find it difficult to satisfy the condition of residence. The period of disregard will end on the residence condition being once more fulfilled, whether by the individual owning the landlord's interest commencing to occupy the dwelling as his only or principal home, or by activation of the deeming provisions above. During a period of disregard, no order for possession of the dwelling-house shall be made other than an order which might be made were the tenancy an assured tenancy (HA 1988, sch. 1, para. 21). However, although possession cannot be ordered during a period of disregard, the tenancy may be terminated by any of the common law methods of termination which may be available (e.g., by giving notice in relation to a periodic tenancy). If the tenancy is so terminated, possession can be obtained when the period of disregard ends. The tenancy does not temporarily become an assured tenancy during the period of disregard (if it did, it could not be terminated by the landlord: HA 1988, s. 5(1)).

The fact that the landlord's occupation condition is not for the time being fulfilled *will be disregarded* in four instances:

(a) For a period of 28 days following the vesting of the landlord's interest in an individual who does not occupy the dwelling-house as his only or principal home (e.g., the landlord sells his interest to a purchaser) (HA 1988, sch. 1, para. 17(1)(a)).

(b) For a further period of six months following the vesting of the landlord's interest in such an individual, *provided that* the individual has notified the tenant in writing of his intention to occupy the dwelling-house as his only or principal home during the initial 28-day period above. The six months runs from the date the landlord's interest was vested in the individual concerned (*not* the date of the written notice) (para. 17(1)(b)).

(c) A period of two years following the vesting of the landlord's interest in trustees or the Probate judge (i.e., on death intestate) (para. 17(1)(c)).

(d) A period of two years following the death of a beneficiary behind a trust whose occupation of the dwelling-house has until then caused Rule C to be deemed to be fulfilled (para. 18(2)).

The leading decision on the effect of a period of disregard is that of the House of Lords in *Landau* v *Sloane* [1982] AC 490. Lord Fraser of Tullybelton there stated (at 502):

> where a tenancy ... comes to an end during the period of disregard, the tenant, or more properly now the ex-tenant, is left with no relevant rights under the Act except the right not to have an order for possession made against him during the disregard period. It seems inappropriate to describe a person in that position as a trespasser, but I see no alternative.

Landau v *Sloane* concerned the period of disregard which then applied (for the purposes of the Rent Act 1977) where the landlord's interest was vested in personal representatives of a deceased person. Under both the Housing Act 1988 and the Rent Act 1977 (as amended by the Housing Act 1980, s. 65, which was enacted in consequence of the Court of Appeal decision in *Landau* v *Sloane*), the landlord's occupation condition is in such circumstances now 'deemed to be fulfilled' for a period of two years. Despite this, the decision of the House of Lords remains the leading authority on the effect of a period of disregard (i.e., the meaning of Housing Act 1988, sch. 1, para. 21, and Rent Act 1977, sch. 2, para. 3). The clear position is that during the period of disregard, the tenant's contractual tenancy can be terminated if the agreement so permits, and then on expiry of that period, a possession order sought from the court.

> *Example: Purchasing the resident landlord's interest*
> L, the landlord, lives in a basement flat of a house of which he owns the freehold and which has been converted into several one-bedroom flats. T lives in the ground-floor flat which was let to him under a weekly tenancy on 1 January 1990. L has satisfied the condition of residence throughout the period of T's tenancy. On 1 January 1993, L sells the freehold in the house to P, who thereupon becomes T's landlord. On 21 January 1993, P serves written notice on T stating that he intends to occupy the basement flat within the six-month period which commenced on 1 January 1993. Until he goes into occupation, P cannot obtain possession of T's flat unless he can show that were T an assured tenant an order for possession would be made. However, following *Landau* v *Sloane*, P can terminate the weekly tenancy by giving notice of the appropriate length (four weeks': Protection from Eviction Act 1977, s. 5(1), unless the agreement falls within s. 3A thereof). If, however, P does not terminate the tenancy, and does not go into occupation until after 30 June 1993, he will fail to satisfy Rule C, the resident landlord exception will cease to apply, and T will become a fully fledged assured tenant. The result will be the same if P neither goes into occupation nor serves written notice stating his intention to do so before 29 January 1993.

3.10.5 Re-grants

A landlord may be tempted to sidestep the horribly complicated residence conditions by the simple expedient of granting his tenants new tenancies. Thus, he could argue, at the time of grant, and at all times thereafter, Rules B and C have been satisfied. It would be an effective method of wiping the slate clean. However, this tactic is countered by para. 10(3) of sch. 1 to the Housing Act 1988. The resident landlord exception will not apply if the tenancy is granted to a person (alone, or jointly) who, immediately before it was granted, was a tenant under an assured tenancy of the same dwelling-house or of another dwelling-house which forms part of the building in question, and the landlord under the old and the new tenancy is the same person or, if either of the tenancies was granted by two or more persons jointly, the same person is the landlord or one of the landlords under each tenancy.

While this provision will be effective in most simple cases, it is not by any means watertight. As the new tenancy must be granted to someone who immediately before the grant was an assured tenant of the landlord, the landlord may seek to engineer a brief lapse of time between the ending of the old tenancy and the commencement of the new. Nor does the provision appear to take account of the landlord who sells his interest, and contemporaneously with that sale, obtains a surrender of the old assured tenancies, the incoming resident landlord then offering the new tenancies.

3.11 Crown tenancies: para. 11

A tenancy under which the landlord's interest belongs to Her Majesty in right of the Crown (save where it is under the management of the Crown Estate Commissioners) or a government department or is held in trust for Her Majesty for the purposes of a government department cannot be an assured tenancy. If the landlord's interest is assigned to or from one of these bodies during the existence of the tenancy, the tenancy will cease to be, or become, an assured tenancy, as the case may be.

3.12 Local authority tenancies etc.: para. 12

A tenancy under which the landlord's interest belongs to a local authority (as defined in para. 12(2)), the Commission for New Towns, the Development Board for Rural Wales, an urban development corporation, a development corporation, a waste disposal authority, a residuary body, a fully mutual housing association (the only kind of housing association to be so excluded), or a housing action trust, cannot be an assured tenancy. Many of these 'public' bodies will let on secure tenancy (see chapter 6).

3.13 'Transitional cases': para. 13

A tenancy which is a protected tenancy (see chapter 3), a housing association tenancy (see chapter 3, para. 9), a secure tenancy (see chapter 6) or a tenancy by virtue of which a protected occupier under the Rent (Agriculture) Act 1976 occupies a dwelling-house, cannot be an assured tenancy. These are not, as the title to the paragraph indicates, purely 'transitional' cases. Secure tenancies are not being phased out as a result of the Housing Act 1988, and there will be protected tenancies and Rent (Agriculture) Act protected occupancies for many years to come.

3.14 Accommodation for homeless persons: s. 1(6)

Where accommodation is provided in pursuance of statutory duties to house the homeless, a local authority may use its own housing stock, or (as is becoming more frequent as the public housing stock declines) use accommodation provided by others, particularly housing associations, which, if registered with the Housing Corporation, are under a duty to co-operate with local authorities in the discharge of their homelessness functions (HA 1985, s. 72). If a person applies to a local authority for housing, he will not become a secure tenant of that authority until the expiry of one year from the date he receives his notification of the housing authority's decision on the question whether he is homeless or threatened with homelessness, or of the name of the authority which has the duty to house him (HA 1985, sch. 1, para. 4: see chapter 6, para. 3.4). If the letting is by a landlord which does not satisfy the 'landlord condition' in the Housing Act 1985, s. 80, (e.g., by a housing association), and which does not fall within para. 12 of sch. 1 to the 1988 Act, the tenancy could be an assured tenancy.

The Housing Act 1988, s. 1(6) accordingly makes equivalent provision for lettings to the homeless by the landlord who assists the local authority as is provided for the authority itself. Where the tenancy is granted in pursuance of arrangements between the authority and some other person to provide accommodation for the homeless, there will be a one-year period during which the tenancy cannot be assured. The period runs from the date the tenant receives notification under Part III of the 1985 Act (HA 1988, s. 1(7)). If the period expires before the landlord terminates the tenancy, the tenancy may then become assured, and the landlord is unlikely to succeed in an argument that, the accommodation being essentially of a temporary nature, the occupier is a licensee rather than a tenant (see *Eastleigh Borough Council* v *Walsh* [1985] 1 WLR 525). If the tenant is notified by the landlord during the one-year period that the tenancy is to be regarded as an assured tenancy, then it will no longer be excluded from assured status by the Housing Act 1988, s. 1(6).

It should, however, be noted that certain agreements between local authorities and homeless persons may not evince an intention to grant exclusive possession on the part of the landlord, when that intention is construed against the appropriate background of statutory duties and obligations (see, for example, *Ogwr Borough Council* v *Dykes* [1989] 1 WLR 295; *Westminster City Council* v *Clarke* [1992] 2 AC 288 (see further chapter 6, para. 2.1), overruling *Family Housing Association* v *Jones* [1990] 1 WLR 779). In such circumstances, the agreement is unlikely to give rise to a tenancy.

4 THE TERMS OF THE ASSURED TENANCY

4.1 The property

The assured tenancy is not restricted to the physical structure of the dwelling-house the subject of the lease. If, under the terms of the lease, the dwelling-house is let together with other land (e.g., a garden, outhouses, or even a small paddock) that land will also be let on assured tenancy, if and so long as the main purpose of the letting is the provision of a home for the tenant (or one of joint tenants) (HA 1988, s. 2(1)). The question of 'main purpose' will involve balancing the various purposes of the letting concerned. In *Feyereisel* v *Turnidge* [1952] 2 QB 29, a camp site was let to the tenant, as well as a bungalow for his personal occupation. It was held that the main purpose of the letting was the use of the site for the tenant's business of camp-site proprietor. In such circumstances, not only the land but also the house is excluded from assured tenancy status. Where the other land consists of agricultural land exceeding two acres, the tenancy cannot be an assured tenancy (HA 1988, sch. 1, para. 6: see para. 3.6 above).

4.2 Types of tenancy

The assured tenancy can take one of three forms: fixed term, 'contractual' periodic or statutory periodic. Of these, the first two are created by the agreement of the parties, whereas the third is created by operation of law.

4.2.1 Fixed term tenancy

A fixed term tenancy arises where the landlord and tenant agree that the tenancy will terminate on a fixed date. Thus a tenancy 'until 31 December 1994' or 'for three years' is a fixed term tenancy. It is essential to satisfy the condition of certainty that it is possible to state the maximum duration of the lease at its commencement. It is perfectly possible, and indeed usual, for the lease to provide for earlier termination, either as a result of the tenant's breach of covenant (forfeiture) or by the giving of a notice of the length prescribed by the parties (a break clause). However, it should not be thought that such terms in a fixed term assured tenancy will operate so as to entitle the landlord to recovery of possession.

4.2.2 Periodic tenancy

A periodic tenancy derives conceptual certainty from the ability of either party to terminate the lease by giving notice to quit. It is not possible to state from the beginning of the tenancy how long the tenant will be in possession, other than to say that he is entitled to be there for the duration of the first 'period'. But unless landlord or tenant serve notice on the other to expire at that time, the tenancy will continue. A periodic tenancy may be created by express agreement of the parties, the lease stating that the tenancy is 'weekly', 'monthly', or 'yearly' as the case may be. It may also be created by implication from the parties' conduct, the tenant being let into possession and paying rent to the landlord on a periodic basis. In these circumstances, the period of the tenancy will be ascertained according to the period with reference to which rent is calculated. A periodic tenancy is under the general law (outside the Housing Act 1988) terminable by notice given by either party, but unless and until notice is given the tenancy will continue from period to period. Termination of an assured periodic tenancy by a landlord's notice to quit is not, however, possible.

4.2.3 Statutory periodic tenancy

A statutory periodic tenancy is part of the machinery of security provided by the Housing Act 1988. When a fixed term assured tenancy comes to an end by effluxion of time, and the tenant under the fixed term tenancy is not expressly granted another tenancy of the same, or substantially the same, dwelling-house, he will nevertheless hold over as statutory periodic tenant (HA 1988, s. 5(2), (4)). However, a statutory periodic tenancy will not arise if the fixed term tenancy comes to an end by the tenant's own action, such as surrendering the lease, or by an order of the court (HA 1988, s. 5(2)). The statutory periodic tenancy need not be an assured tenancy itself (although it usually will be).

4.3 Terms of the assured tenancy

As a general rule, the terms contained in the assured tenancy are those agreed by landlord and tenant. The assured tenancy is based on the contract between them, and the courts will enforce the terms which they have agreed. Although the statutory periodic tenancy is not as such agreed by the parties, its terms will largely derive from the fixed term tenancy which preceded it. Certain terms concerning repairs, assignment and sub-letting are imposed by law, and there is only a limited freedom for the parties to agree otherwise. Where the landlord is a registered housing association, the 'Tenants' Guarantee' places some constraints on the terms of an assured tenancy.

4.3.1 Statutory periodic tenancy

By HA 1988, s. 5(3), the statutory periodic tenancy:

(a) takes effect in possession immediately the fixed term tenancy comes to an end;

(b) has as its landlord and tenant those persons who were landlord and tenant under that fixed term;

(c) is of the same dwelling-house as was let under the fixed term;

(d) has as its periods those by which rent was last payable under the fixed term (e.g., if under the fixed term the rent was £2,000 per year payable monthly, the statutory periodic tenancy will be a monthly tenancy);

(e) has as its other terms those of the fixed term tenancy, with one exception. Any provision in the fixed term for determination by landlord or tenant shall not have effect while the statutory periodic tenancy remains an assured tenancy. This exception is highly significant, placing the matter of termination of the tenancy, and recovery of possession, firmly in the province of the court, which, as will be seen, can only order possession on statutorily prescribed grounds.

4.4 Variation of terms

The landlord and tenant to any assured tenancy may agree to vary the terms of the tenancy at any time, with the one qualification that terms providing for determination by either of them will have no effect whilst a statutory periodic tenancy remains assured. The parties cannot unilaterally vary the terms of a statutory periodic tenancy, but a procedure is provided by HA 1988, s. 6, whereby a proposal by either party to vary can be made, and a binding determination made by a rent assessment committee in the event of opposition by the other party.

The s. 6 procedure cannot be used:

(a) where the tenancy is not an assured tenancy by virtue of paras. 11 or 12 of sch. 1 to the 1988 Act (i.e., the landlord is the Crown or a listed public body: s. 6(1));

(b) to vary the rent as such. A separate procedure is provided whereby rent increases can be effected (see para. 4.6 below). The rent assessment committee may however make adjustments to the rent to take account of the terms they have determined in the course of a s. 6 reference (HA 1988, s. 6(5)).

The s. 6 procedure takes the following course:

(a) The fixed term ends, and a statutory periodic tenancy takes effect.

(b) Not later than the first anniversary of the ending of the fixed term, the landlord (or tenant) serves a notice in prescribed form (SI 1988 No 2203, Form 1) proposing varied terms.

(c) Within three months of notice being served, the tenant (or landlord) refers the notice to the rent assessment committee, again using a form prescribed for the purpose (SI 1988 No 2203, Form 2, as amended by SI 1990 No 1532). If the tenant (or landlord) fails so to refer the notice within the three-month period, the variation, and any adjustment of rent, will take effect.

(d) The committee considers the proposed terms and makes a determination.

(e) The committee specify an adjustment to the rent to take account of their determination.

(f) The committee direct the date (no earlier than the date specified in the notice proposing variation) from which the terms they have determined shall become terms of the statutory periodic tenancy, and the adjustment in rent, if any, takes effect.

4.4.1 The criteria for variation

The rent assessment committee must determine whether the terms proposed in the notice are such as might reasonably be expected to be found in an assured periodic tenancy of the dwelling-house concerned. This hypothetical tenancy is to be viewed as one beginning on the date of termination of the fixed term tenancy, granted by a willing landlord, and having the same terms as the statutory periodic tenancy before them except for those terms which 'relate to the subject matter of the proposed terms'. In other words, the rent assessment committee should take the lease as it currently stands with the exception of the terms being proposed, and terms which would be closely affected by the variation in question.

4.4.2 Powers of the committee

The rent assessment committee may accept the terms as proposed. They may reject them outright, and refuse any variation. They may, if they wish, devise terms of their own in place of the currently implied terms and the proposed terms, as long as the terms they devise deal with the same subject-matter as the proposal before them. The committee shall, if they consider it appropriate, specify a rent adjustment, even though the initial notice of variation did not propose one. In making their determination and specifying a rent adjustment, the committee must disregard any effect on the terms or rent attributable to the tenancy being granted to a sitting tenant.

The rent assessment committee may require the parties to provide such information as they may reasonably require for the performance of their functions, and failure to comply with such a requirement may result in the imposition of a fine in the magistrates' court (HA 1988, s. 41). If there are concurrent applications before a rent assessment committee for variation of the terms of a lease and increase of the rent payable (under HA 1988, s. 13), the rent assessment committee may 'consolidate' the applications, and should then hear the s. 6 reference first (HA 1988, s. 14(6)). This is common sense. The committee will only be able to fix the market rent when the terms of the tenancy have been properly established.

4.4.3 Appeals

The 1988 Act provides no right of appeal from a determination of a rent assessment committee under s. 6, but it appears that appeal under the Tribunals and Inquiries Act 1971, s. 13, will be available. Where the committee have misdirected themselves in law, there will be a remedy by way of judicial review.

4.5 Statutorily imposed terms

4.5.1 Access for repairs

Section 16 of the Housing Act 1988 implies a term into *every assured tenancy* that the tenant shall afford the landlord access to the dwelling-house, and all reasonable facilities for executing therein any repairs which the landlord is entitled to execute. The most important statutory repairing obligation imposed on landlords is to be found in the Landlord and Tenant Act 1985, s. 11 (as amended by HA 1988, s. 116), whereby landlords letting dwelling-houses on leases for less than seven years are obliged to keep in repair the structure and exterior, and keep in repair and proper working order installations for the supply of water, gas and electricity and for sanitation, and for space heating and for heating water. By the Landlord and Tenant Act 1985, s. 11(6), a covenant by the tenant is implied into leases to which that section applies that the landlord, or persons authorised by him in writing, may at reasonable times of the day and on giving 24 hours' notice, enter the premises for the purpose of viewing their condition and state of repair. Assured tenants are under an additional obligation by HA 1988, s. 16, to allow access and facilities to execute the repairs themselves.

4.5.2 Assignment and sub-letting

See para. 7 below.

4.6 Rents

Parties to an assured tenancy are free to agree the amount of rent, and to provide for rent reviews if they consider it appropriate. The degree of statutory intervention is strictly limited. Save where assured shorthold tenancies are concerned (on which see para. 9.3 below), the only circumstances where statutory procedures are to be invoked relate to assured periodic tenancies. Where the landlord is a registered housing association, the association should in setting its assured tenancy rents comply with the 'Tenants' Guarantee' (see para. 4.7 below).

4.6.1 Fixed term tenancies

While a fixed term tenancy is continuing, the parties will be bound by the terms of the lease. If the tenant has agreed to pay £*x* per week or month for *y* years, that is the sum which can be enforced. The landlord cannot claim any more, nor can he increase the rent unilaterally: if he purports to do so, the tenant can simply refuse to pay. The landlord cannot go before a rent assessment committee and ask for an increase in the rent. Nor can the tenant seek a reduction. Both are bound by the lease. There may be a rent review clause in that lease. The timing and frames of reference of the rent review will be as stipulated in the lease: there is nothing in the Housing Act 1988 which has any bearing upon it.

4.6.2 Statutory periodic tenancies

A statutory periodic tenancy arises when an assured fixed term tenancy comes to an end, generally by expiry of the term (HA 1988, s. 5(2)). Under the tenancy which is imposed by statute, the rent payable will continue at the same level as before (HA 1988, s. 5(3)). However, the landlord now has the right to propose a rent increase. This is justified on the basis that the tenant is holding over by force of statute, and the parties' agreement as such has ended. Without a statutory procedure, the landlord would be powerless to increase the rent in view of the tenant's security of tenure, as there would be little effective sanction available to the landlord when faced with a tenant who refused to agree any increase in the rent. Accordingly, the landlord may propose a rent increase at the earliest opportunity following the expiry of the tenant's fixed term, and he has the same right where a tenant has succeeded as assured periodic tenant to a tenancy which was previously Rent Act regulated. The provisions presuppose a rising market, the tenant being given no corresponding right to propose rent reduction. The rent increase provisions apply to all statutory periodic tenancies, even where they are no longer assured tenancies (as long as the landlord's interest does not belong to the Crown or one of the public bodies listed in HA 1988, sch. 1, paras. 11 and 12).

4.6.3 'Contractual' periodic tenancies

Where a periodic tenancy has been created by agreement, express or implied (from payment and acceptance of rent), the landlord would normally seek to obtain a rent increase by threatening notice to quit in the event of the tenant refusing to come to terms. The availability of this course of action is curtailed by the security afforded to assured periodic tenants by the 1988 Act, and thus it is necessary to enable landlords to seek rent increases by some other means. If there is provision in the lease for the rent to be greater (or to be made greater) for a particular, later, period of the tenancy, then s. 13 cannot be used for as long as such provision is binding on the tenant. Freedom of contract will there prevail.

4.6.4 Rent increase procedure

The landlord serves on the tenant a notice in prescribed form (SI 1988 No 2203, Form No 5). The notice proposes a new rent and the date it is to take effect. The notice must inform the tenant of his rights in relation to the procedure. If the tenant wishes to contest the rent proposed, he must refer the notice to a rent assessment committee (SI 1988 No 2203, Form No 6) before the date on which the proposed rent is to take effect. If he fails to do so, the rent as proposed will take effect on the date shown in the notice.

The procedure for the increase of rent, which may be initiated only by the landlord, is quite distinct from the procedure whereby the terms of a statutory periodic tenancy may be varied (at the behest of either landlord or tenant). The latter procedure (outlined at para. 4.4 above) may only increase rent in the sense of 'adjusting' it to take account of the terms which have been determined. The rent increase procedure does not entitle the rent assessment committee to vary any terms other than rent. As the rent assessment committee are the tribunal in both cases, it is possible that the committee will have two references pending which relate to the same tenancy. The committee are not obliged to hear the two references together, but it would seem to be common sense to do so. If they do, the variation of terms reference should be heard first. Once the terms of the tenancy have been determined, the committee can go on to consider what the appropriate rent should be for an assured tenancy having those terms (HA 1988, s. 14(6)).

The date on which the new rent is proposed to take effect must comply with s. 13(2) and (3), provisions which are at first sight complex, but not difficult in application. Two examples follow, relating to the different kinds of tenancy in relation to which a rent increase may be sought.

Example A Landlord lets house on a fixed term tenancy of 12 months, which expired by effluxion of time on 22 April 1994. A statutory periodic tenancy then takes effect, the rent being the same as under the old fixed term, and the periods of the tenancy being those for which the rent was payable (HA 1988, s. 5(2)). As the rent was payable monthly, the new tenancy is a monthly tenancy. The landlord may propose a new rent to take effect on 22 May 1994 (HA 1988, s. 13(3)(c)). It is unclear from the statute whether the landlord may serve notice of increase before the fixed term has expired, to take effect when it has. The cautious landlord will wait until the fixed term has ended, and then serve his notice.

Example B Landlord lets house on a weekly tenancy (i.e., a contractual periodic tenancy) commencing on 1 July 1993. The earliest date for a rent increase will be 1 July 1994 (the first anniversary of the tenancy: HA 1988, s. 13(2)(b)). If the landlord wishes to propose an increased rent from that date, he must serve his notice no later than one month before (i.e., 1 June 1994), as the period of the tenancy is less than a month (HA 1988, s. 13(3)(b)). If the rent is increased from that date, the landlord will next be able to propose an increase of rent to be effective from 1 July 1995 (HA 1988, s. 13(2)(c)), notice to be served no later than 1 June 1995.

4.6.5 Market rent

The rent assessment committee must determine the rent at which they consider the dwelling-house concerned might reasonably be expected to be let in the open market by a willing landlord under an assured tenancy having the same terms as the tenancy in question (HA 1988, s. 14(1)). In making the determination, the committee must disregard any effect on the rent attributable to the grant of a tenancy to a sitting tenant, any increase in value of the dwelling-house attributable to certain tenants' improvements (defined in s. 14(3)), and any reduction in value of the house attributable to a breach of covenant by the tenant (s. 14(2): not including a predecessor of the tenant: *N & D (London) Ltd* v *Gadsdon* (1991) 24 HLR 64). 'Rent' is defined for these purposes by s. 14(4). The committee is to assume that rates in respect of the dwelling-house are not borne by the landlord or superior landlord, even if they are (HA 1988, s. 14(5)).

The formula to be applied by rent assessment committees in determining assured tenancy rents is very different from that applicable to the 'fair rents' procedure under the Rent Acts, although, as will be seen, rents under the two regimes are gradually being drawn closer together (chapter 3, para. 11.3). The committee determining rents for assured tenancies are expected to consider the local 'market', the number of potential tenants for this particular property, and then assess the sum at which a 'willing landlord', i.e., someone who wants to let, given a reasonable return on his property, being appraised of the market conditions, would reasonably expect the property to be rented for. The committee are not being asked to determine what is a reasonable rent for this tenant to pay, or, indeed, what a reasonable rent for the property would be. Their task is to determine what a landlord's reasonable expectation for the rent for this property should be, if it is let on an assured tenancy with the same terms on which the tenant presently holds.

The committee may, in determining the rent, wish to refer to comparable assured tenancy rents in the vicinity, and the president of each rent assessment panel is placed under a duty to keep and make publicly available certain information with respect to rents under assured tenancies (including assured shortholds). By this means there is a ready source of comparables for those appearing before rent assessment committees (HA 1988, s. 42; SI 1988 No 2199).

4.6.6 Effect of determination

When the rent assessment committee have made their determination of the rent, the rent thus determined will be the rent under the tenancy with effect from the date specified in the landlord's initial notice proposing the increase. Only if the committee form the view that this would cause undue hardship to the tenant may they specify a later date, and that date may not in any circumstances be later than the date of the committee's determination (HA 1988, s. 14(7)). If there is a substantial delay between the landlord's notice and the decision of the rent assessment committee, and the rent is then increased, the tenant may find himself with a substantial amount of back rent to pay off. At all stages of the proceedings (including after the determination by the rent assessment committee), the parties may come to an agreement about the rent to be charged, and withdraw the reference to the committee or vary the decision which the committee has reached (HA 1988, s. 14(7), (8)).

For the regulations governing the procedure before rent assessment committees, see SI 1971 No 1065, as amended by SI 1988 No 2200. Appeals from rent assessment committees are governed by the Tribunals and Inquiries Act 1971, s. 13(1): appeal is on a point of law, and is to the High Court. Unlike the Rent Act 'two-tier' system of rent officer and rent assessment committee, neither party may appeal on a question of fact, such as the quantum of the market rent. Only if the committee have misdirected themselves in law will an appeal be tenable. For a full treatment of review of the decisions of rent assessment committees, see Megarry, *The Rent Acts*, 11th ed., chapters 24 and 33.

4.7 Assured tenancies of housing associations

Where the landlord is a registered housing association, the terms of the assured tenancy should normally comply with the 'Tenants' Guarantee' (see chapter 1, para. 6). The tenancy should provide 'long-term security of tenure wherever possible' . . . 'it is expected that most association tenancies will be periodic assured tenancies'. The use of assured shortholds is greatly discouraged (see para. 9.1 below). The tenancy agreement should be in writing, and should fully inform the tenant of his security of tenure under the 1988 Act, including the specified grounds on which the courts would be able to end the tenancy, and rights to succeed to the tenancy. Associations are expected to give their assured tenants additional contractual rights, which should include the right to exchange tenancies with tenants of other associations, New Towns or local authorities (subject to the landlords' agreement, which should not be unreasonably withheld); the right to take in lodgers and sub-let (provided no security is thereby granted, and subject to the landlord's agreement, which should not be unreasonably withheld); the right to carry out improvements (with the landlord's permission, not to be unreasonably withheld); the right to carry out repairs and refund the cost where the landlord is in breach of its repairing obligations; the right to be consulted about housing management changes, and to be informed about association management policies.

5 SECURITY OF TENURE

The landlord will only be able to recover possession of a dwelling-house let on assured tenancy by obtaining a possession order from the court. However, should the assured tenant lose his status, the Housing Act will no longer stand in the landlord's way. Moreover, an assured tenant is not immune from the exercise of powers by public bodies such that the possession of their property is gained. Before considering the means whereby the landlord can regain possession by seeking an order of the court, we should elaborate briefly upon these other options.

5.1 Loss of assured status

Nothing in the Housing Act 1988 prevents the tenant from exercising his right to terminate the lease subject to its terms. Thus, he can give notice to quit of whatever length the lease demands of him (subject to the statutory minimum of four weeks: Protection from Eviction Act 1977, s. 5(1)). He can surrender the lease by agreement with the landlord, and he can terminate it by invoking a break clause. In each of these cases, the action of the tenant, if effective to terminate the tenancy (in itself dependant on its terms), will result in the occupier ceasing to be an assured tenant. If, following termination of the tenancy, he remains in occupation, the landlord will be entitled to repossess. Indeed, it is doubtful whether in these circumstances the landlord needs to obtain a possession order from the court, as the statutory prohibition on eviction without due process of law does not apply where a 'statutorily protected tenancy' (which includes an assured tenancy) has come to an end (Protection from Eviction Act 1977, s. 3(1)). A possession order is however desirable, as it would protect the landlord from possible civil or criminal liability (see generally, chapter 8).

The power of the assured tenant (if contained in the lease) to terminate the tenancy, and thereby enable the landlord to enforce the right to possession which arises, makes the position of the assured tenant somewhat different to that of the Rent Act protected tenant. It gives the landlord a route to possession which does not involve the proof of a ground for possession. But if the assured tenant has not terminated the tenancy, and the landlord seeks possession pursuant to Part I of the 1988 Act, the court has jurisdiction to make an order only on proof of a ground. If the parties come to terms at that stage, and agree to a consent order, it is important that an admission of the existence of a ground is made by the tenant (see further, chapter 3, para. 5.5).

Another possibility is that the occupier remains a tenant, but ceases for some reason to be an assured tenant. For example, he may cease to occupy the dwelling-house as his only or principal home, having recently bought another property closer to his workplace, but wishing to spend the occasional weekend at the dwelling-house. The landlord will not in these circumstances be entitled to immediate possession. He must terminate the tenancy first, complying with its terms and the provisions of the Protection from Eviction Act 1977 (in particular ss. 3 and 5). The tenancy no longer being assured, however, he will not be required to prove grounds for possession under the Housing Act 1988. It should be noted that courts are reluctant to find that a tenant has ceased to occupy, and landlords who act precipitously may run into serious difficulties (see, e.g., *Love & Lugg* v *Herrity* (1990) 23 HLR 217).

An agreement at or before the time of the lease that the assured tenant will give up possession on a particular future date will be unenforceable. By Housing Act 1988, s. 5(5), where *on or before the date the tenancy is entered into*, a tenant enters into an obligation to do any act which will cause the tenancy to come to an end at a time when it is an assured tenancy, or executes, signs or gives any surrender, notice to quit or other document which has the effect of bringing an assured tenancy to an end, the obligation, surrender, notice to quit or other document will be of no effect. A landlord seeking to enforce such an agreement would therefore fail.

5.2 Exercise of statutory powers

The Housing Act 1985 contains many of the statutory duties owed by local authorities with regard to housing, and it is provided by s. 612 of that Act that where in the exercise of their powers 'under any enactment in relation to housing' possession is required, nothing in Part I of the 1988 Act will prevent possession being obtained. Further specific provisions are contained in the Housing Act 1985 exempting the assured tenant's security in the event of:

(a) enforcement of an undertaking that premises will not be used for human habitation (s. 264(5));
(b) a demolition order (s. 270(3));
(c) a closing order (s. 276);
(d) an obstructive building order (s. 286(3));
(e) power to secure that part of a house is not used for human habitation to provide means of escape from fire (s. 368).

5.3 Landlord initiated recovery of possession

5.3.1 Outline

The Housing Act 1988 seriously restricts the availability to the landlord of the normal methods of termination of tenancies (such as forfeiture for breach of covenant, and notice) where the property is let on assured tenancy. The provisions are complex, and have caused much confusion. It may be useful to set out clearly their effect before considering them in any detail. It is important to establish first whether the dwelling of which possession is sought is held on fixed term or periodic tenancy (see para. 4.2 above).

(a) Where the tenant holds under *a fixed term tenancy which has not expired*, the landlord may:

(i) terminate the fixed term by giving the tenant notice pursuant to a right to do so reserved by the lease (e.g., a break clause). This will almost certainly result in the tenant holding over as a statutory periodic tenant. Termination of the fixed term will not entitle the landlord to recover possession.

(ii) seek a possession order from the court on any of Grounds 2, 8, or 10 to 15 inclusive, as contained in sch. 2 to the Act. He can only do this if the lease expressly provides for termination on the particular ground relied upon.

The landlord cannot forfeit the fixed term pursuant to a right reserved in the lease. If he wishes to recover possession to prevent future breaches of covenant, he must seek a possession order as under (ii) above.

(b) Where the tenant holds pursuant to *a periodic tenancy* (whether statutory or 'contractual'), the landlord may seek a possession order from the court on any of the grounds set out in sch. 2 to the Act. No other method of termination is open to him. In particular, service of a notice to quit will be of no effect.

5.3.2 Explanation

The security of tenure of assured tenants is firmly based upon a statutory prohibition on termination of the tenancy by the landlord, contained in s. 5(1), and a statutory requirement of recovery of possession by court order, contained in s. 7(1). Section 5(1) reads:

> An assured tenancy cannot be brought to an end by the landlord except by obtaining an order of the court in accordance with the following provisions of this Chapter or Chapter II [assured shorthold tenancies] below or, in the case of a fixed term tenancy which contains power for the landlord to determine the tenancy in certain circumstances, by the exercise of that power and, accordingly, the service by the landlord of a notice to quit shall be of no effect in relation to a periodic assured tenancy.

Where the tenancy is *fixed term*, the landlord can terminate by exercising a 'power to determine' the lease which has been expressly reserved. Despite appearances to the contrary, the landlord may not terminate the fixed term tenancy by exercising a power of re-entry or forfeiture for breach of a term or condition of the tenancy. Section 45(4) declares 'for the avoidance of doubt' that any reference in Part I of the Act to 'a power for a landlord to determine a tenancy does not include a reference to a power of re-entry or forfeiture for breach of any term or condition of the tenancy'. Thus s. 5(1) can only be referring to a power to give notice, possibly at certain defined times during the term, by invoking a 'break clause' (see HA 1988, s. 45(4)). But termination of an assured fixed term by invoking a break clause does not entitle the landlord to repossess, as on termination, a statutory periodic tenancy will arise by operation of law (HA 1988, s. 5(2)). An order of the court will still be necessary to recover possession from him.

Where the assured tenancy is *periodic*, whether contractual periodic or statutory periodic, the position appears to be (and is) straightforward. Section 5(1) permits of no exceptions. The landlord cannot unilaterally bring such tenancy to an end, and the final clause confirms the already apparent: service of a notice to quit is of no effect. The landlord must take the tenant to court.

5.3.3 Orders for possession

It is then necessary to turn to s. 7 of the Act, titled 'Orders for possession'. Section 7(1) reads:

> The court shall not make an order for possession of a dwelling-house let on an assured tenancy except on one or more of the grounds set out in sch. 2 to this Act; but nothing in this Part of this Act relates to proceedings for possession of such a dwelling-house which are brought by a mortgagee, within the meaning of the Law of Property Act 1925, who has lent money on the security of the assured tenancy.

As we have seen, where an assured tenancy is a *fixed term* tenancy, the landlord can only terminate by giving notice pursuant to an expressly reserved right to do so. He cannot forfeit. What course of action is appropriate where the tenant is in flagrant breach of covenant (or is in substantial rent arrears)? He cannot be powerless to act. As long as the tenancy contains express provision for it to be brought to an end on the particular ground on which possession is being sought, the landlord can seek a possession order from the court. Most confusingly, this 'express provision' *may* 'take the form of a provision for re-entry, for forfeiture, or for determination by notice or otherwise' (HA 1988, s. 7(6)). Thus, although a landlord cannot terminate an assured fixed term by forfeiture etc., the presence of a forfeiture clause in the lease is essential, as without it he has no effective remedy in terms of regaining possession where the tenant is in default. The grounds on which the landlord can obtain an order for possession where the assured tenancy is a fixed term are limited to Grounds 2, 8, and 10 to 15 inclusive in sch. 2 to the 1988 Act (HA 1988, s. 7(6)).

Where the assured tenancy is a *periodic* tenancy, whether contractual or statutory, the landlord may seek possession on any of the grounds in sch. 2. There is no need for the landlord to terminate the tenancy prior to commencing proceedings (as is necessary where a tenancy is Rent Act protected). Indeed, the landlord cannot terminate. He should however ensure that he follows the appropriate procedure before action.

5.4 Possession procedure

5.4.1 Notice before action

Before the landlord commences proceedings, he should serve on the tenant a notice seeking possession (HA 1988, s. 8). This notice must be in prescribed form (SI 1988 No 2203, Form 3), and must inform the tenant:

(a) that the landlord intends to begin proceedings for possession of the dwelling-house on one or more grounds specified in the notice;
(b) that those proceedings will not begin earlier than a date specified in the notice; and
(c) that proceedings will begin not later than 12 months from the date the notice was served.

5.4.2 Prescribed form

Although the s. 8 notice must be in the prescribed form, strict adherence to Form 3 annexed to SI 1988 No 2203 is not necessary. By reg. 2 of the instrument, service of a completed form 'substantially to the same effect' as Form 3 will suffice. In *Mountain* v *Hastings* (1993) 25 HLR 427, the Court of Appeal had to consider whether a notice served on an assured tenant satisfied the statutory requirements. The landlord responded to the invocation in Form 3 to 'give the full text of each ground which is being relied on' by stating 'At least three months rent is unpaid.' The Court of Appeal held that this was not an adequate notice on which the landlord could proceed under Ground 8, as it made no reference to the requirements that the rent be 'lawfully due' and that it be in arrear both at the date of the notice and at the date of the hearing. Ralph Gibson LJ conceded (at 433):

> . . . the ground in sch. 2 may validly be 'specified in the notice' as required by Parliament, in words different from those in which the ground is set out in the Schedule, provided that the words used set out fully the substance

> of the ground so that the notice is adequate to achieve the legislative purpose of the provision. That purpose, in my judgment, is to give to the tenant the information which the provision requires to be given in the notice to enable the tenant to consider what she should do and, with or without advice, to do that which is in her power and which will best protect her against the loss of her home.

The safest policy for the landlord to adopt is to repeat the ground on which reliance is placed verbatim from the Housing Act 1988.

5.4.3 Alteration or addition to grounds in notice

By s. 8(2) of the 1988 Act, the grounds specified in a s. 8 notice may be altered or added to with the leave of the court. If, however, the notice is initially defective, the notice may be invalid, and not susceptible to amendment by the court. This occurred in *Mountain* v *Hastings*, where the Court of Appeal denied that the court had jurisdiction to add Ground 8 subsequently once it had been improperly and invalidly specified.

5.4.4 Commencing proceedings

Having served notice under s. 8, the landlord then commences his possession action in the county court, which is given statutory jurisidiction by HA 1988, s. 40. The action is commenced in compliance with County Court Rules 1981, ord. 3, pursuant to r. 3(1A) of which (added by SI 1993 No 2175) the plaintiff must prepare the summons. Where the basis of the claim is non-payment of rent, the particulars of claim must be in prescribed form (SI 1993 No 2174, N.119), and give certain specific details (see County Court Rules 1981, ord. 3, r. 3(3), added by SI 1993 No 2175). There is an accelerated possession procedure applicable to assured tenancies which are subject to recovery of possession on Grounds 1, 3, 4 and 5, and to assured shorthold tenancies (see paras. 6.1.8 and 9.5 below).

6 GROUNDS FOR POSSESSION

The grounds for possession are either mandatory (on proof of which the court *must* order possession) or discretionary (on proof of which the court *may* order possession if it considers it reasonable to do so). The mandatory grounds are Grounds 1 to 8 in sch. 2 to the 1988 Act; the discretionary grounds are Grounds 9 to 16.

6.1 Mandatory grounds

Where the landlord satisfies the court that one or other of the mandatory grounds is established, the court *must* order possession. Moreover, the order must take effect within 14 days, unless it appears to the county court that exceptional hardship would be caused by the imposition of such a requirement. In a case of exceptional hardship, the delivery up of possession can be postponed for a maximum of six weeks (see generally HA 1980, s. 89). The extended power to adjourn proceedings, etc. (contained in HA 1988, s. 9) does not apply where the court is satisfied that the landlord is entitled to possession by virtue of a mandatory ground (s. 9(6)). However, until the court is satisfied of this, its general power to adjourn 'to control and direct the conduct of the trial' may be exercised (*Mountain* v *Hastings* (1993) 25 HLR 427, 438).

6.1.1 Grounds 1 to 5: notice in writing

Grounds 1 to 5 all require the giving of a written notice to the tenant not later than the beginning of the tenancy. No forms are prescribed for these notices: the landlord is simply required to give a notice in writing that possession might be recovered on this ground. If such notice is given, the landlord has a 'cast iron' ground for possession, and the tenant's security is from the outset highly precarious. Indeed, where Grounds 1, 3, 4 or 5 (but not 2) are invoked by a landlord, he may be able to make use of an accelerated possession procedure. The lesser security afforded by assured tenancies granted subject to these Grounds is acknowledged by the refusal to accept that accommodation on such terms can be suitable alternative accommodation, where possession is sought on that basis (see HA 1988, sch. 2, Part III, para. 2).

6.1.2 Dispensing with the requirement of notice

Grounds 1 and 2 expressly provide for the court dispensing with this requirement where it is satisfied that 'it is just and equitable' to dispense with it. Grounds 3 to 5 do not. It appears, therefore, that a failure to give notice at the relevant time will be fatal where these latter grounds are concerned.

With Grounds 1 and 2, it is necessary to consider when the court will use its dispensation power. The court may be invited to use its discretion to dispense with notice in all kinds of circumstances. The landlord, ignorant of the finer points of the 1988 Act, and rushing off abroad on business for a few months, may tell the tenant that the property he is about to rent is his home, but not put the information in writing. The landlord may send the tenant written notice, but it is delayed in the post and arrives after he has gone into possession. Or the landlord may not think about recovering the house at all at the time of the initial letting, but two years later when he wants to reclaim possession so that he can live there he reads Ground 1 and regales the court with tales of the hardship he is now under.

On a literal reading of Grounds 1 and 2, the discretion appears to be unfettered. When the Court of Appeal had to consider a dispensation power which was couched in identical terms (Case 11 of the Rent Act 1977), it held that the judge must look at all the circumstances of the case:

> Those would embrace the circumstances affecting the landlord, or his successors in title, the circumstances of the tenant and, of course, the circumstances in which the failure to give written notice arose. It is only if, having considered all those circumstances, the court considers that it would be just and equitable to give possession that it should do so, because it must be borne in mind that, by failing to give the written notice, the tenant may well have been led into a wholly false position (*per* Griffiths LJ in *Bradshaw* v *Baldwin-Wiseman* (1985) 49 P & CR 382).

To return to our hypotheses, the landlord who gives the tenant oral notice and the landlord whose notice is delayed in the post may argue strongly, and possibly with some success, that the dispensation power should be exercised in their favour: see *Fernandes* v *Parvardin* (1982) 5 HLR 33 and *Minay* v *Sentongo* (1983) 6 HLR 79. Where the landlord did not at the outset envisage that recovery of possession could be attained by the use of these grounds, however, the courts should take a strong line and refuse to dispense with the notice requirement. In *Bradshaw* v *Baldwin-Wiseman*, Griffiths LJ stated that it could not be 'just and equitable' to dispense where there was no initial intention [to create a 'Case 11 tenancy'], and the same can be said in relation to Grounds 1 and 2 of the 1988 Act. See further *White* v *Jones* (1993) 26 HLR 477.

6.1.3 Ground 1: past or future occupation by landlord

Not later than the beginning of the tenancy, and subject to the power of the court, considered above, to dispense with the requirement where it is just and equitable to do so, the landlord must have given written notice to the tenant that possession might be recovered on this ground. Then, the landlord will obtain possession as of right if he can prove one of two alternatives:

> (a) at some time before the beginning of the tenancy, the landlord seeking possession or, in the case of joint landlords seeking possession, at least one of them occupied the dwelling-house as his only or principal home; or
>
> (b) the landlord who is seeking possession or, in the case of joint landlords seeking possession, at least one of them requires the dwelling-house as his or his spouse's only or principal home and neither the landlord (or, in the case of joint landlords, any one of them) nor any other person who, as landlord, derived title under the landlord who gave the notice mentioned above acquired the reversion on the tenancy for money or money's worth.

(For occupation as one's only or principal home, see para. 2.5.) Although these are combined in the one ground they are wholly distinct alternatives, (a) relying on past occupation by the landlord, and (b) relying on the landlord's future intentions. It should also be noted:

(a) that (a) above does not require the landlord to have occupied the dwelling at any particular time save that it be before the commencement of the tenancy. In particular, it is not necessary that he occupied it immediately before the tenancy commenced. Nor does the landlord relying on (a) need to show any intention to reoccupy it in the future. It is perfectly legitimate for the landlord to recover possession simply in order to facilitate the sale of his interest in the property.

(b) that (b) above does not require the landlord to have occupied the dwelling-house previously at all. He must simply, subject to what is said below, have been sufficiently perspicacious to have given the tenant notice under this ground prior to granting the tenancy. He may wish to obtain possession to house himself, or, possibly, his spouse (making this ground a useful device in the event of the landlord's divorce or separation). Whilst he may rely on a written notice served by an earlier landlord, neither he nor any predecessor of his must have acquired the interest he now has 'by purchase': thus the Act seeks to prevent its abuse by persons buying up reversions simply in order to repossess by virtue of a relatively short-term intention to occupy. There is no need for the requirement to occupy to be reasonable, although it must, obviously, be genuine.

6.1.4 Ground 2: mortgagee seeking possession

The dwelling-house is subject to a mortgage granted before the beginning of the tenancy, and three further conditions are satisfied, namely:

(a) the mortgagee is entitled to exercise a power of sale conferred on him by the mortgage or by section 101 of the Law of Property Act 1925; and

(b) the mortgagee requires possession of the dwelling-house for the purpose of disposing of it with vacant possession in exercise of that power; and

(c) *either* notice was given as mentioned in Ground 1 above *or* the court is satisfied that it is just and equitable to dispense with the requirement of notice.

This ground is in a sense ancillary to Ground 1. It contemplates the situation where the landlord lets his house, over which there is a pre-existing mortgage, to an assured tenant, serving prior to the tenancy a notice reserving his rights under Ground 1, perhaps because he intends to occupy at a future date ((b) rather than (a)). The landlord then defaults on the mortgage. The mortgagee wishes to realise its security. The landlord cannot viably argue in these circumstances that he intends to occupy the property as his only or principal home, as once possession is recovered the mortgagee will insist on sale. However, he will be able to utilise Ground 2.

Mortgagees are well advised to insert a clause into their mortgage deeds which contemplate lettings requiring service of a Ground 1 notice on assured tenants. However, the mortgagee's rights outside the Housing Act 1988 are quite effective. In *Dudley & District Benefit Building Society* v *Emerson* [1949] Ch 707, a mortgagor let a dwelling-house in breach of a term in the mortgage deed. The Court of Appeal held that the mortgagee's right of possession prevailed over the rights of a Rent Act protected tenant.

Where a mortgage is secured on the interest of the tenant, Part I of the 1988 Act does not restrict the rights of the mortgagee to recover possession pursuant to the mortgage agreement (see proviso to HA 1988, s. 7(1)).

6.1.5 Ground 3: off-season holiday lets

By sch. 1, para. 9, to the 1988 Act, holiday lets are excluded from assured tenancy status. If at some time within the period of 12 months prior to the commencement of the tenancy, the dwelling-house has been occupied under a right to occupy it for a holiday, then a tenancy for a fixed term not exceeding eight months will, although an assured tenancy, carry with it a mandatory ground for possession. However, the landlord must have given notice in writing to the tenant no later than the beginning of the tenancy that Ground 3 was applicable. The landlord will not be able to obtain possession under Ground 3 until the fixed term has expired, but once it has, on proper application the court must order possession. Although it is convenient to think of these as off season lettings of holiday accommodation, the provisions are not so limited in their terms.

6.1.6 Ground 4: vacation lets of student accommodation

As with off season lettings of holiday accommodation, so with vacation lettings of student accommodation. Within the 12 months prior to the tenancy, the dwelling must have been let on a tenancy falling within sch. 1, para. 8, to the 1988 Act. The present tenancy must be a fixed term tenancy not exceeding 12 months, and the landlord must have given notice in writing to the tenant no later than the beginning of the tenancy that Ground 4 was applicable. It is not necessary that the tenancy is granted by a specified educational institution, but that will normally be the case. The landlord will not be able to recover possession pursuant to Ground 4 until the fixed term has expired.

6.1.7 Ground 5: residence of minister of religion

The dwelling-house must be held for the purpose of being made available for occupation by a minister of religion as a residence from which to perform the duties of his office, and the court must be satisfied that the dwelling-house is now required for occupation by a minister of religion as such a residence. Notice in writing must have been given to the tenant by the landlord at the beginning of the tenancy that Ground 5 was applicable. The ground enables lettings of ministers' residences without significant statutory security both to the ministers themselves, and to outsiders.

6.1.8 Grounds 1, 3, 4 and 5: accelerated possession procedure

The attraction of these Grounds has been enhanced by the introduction for landlords of a 'fast track' to repossession by amendment to the County Court Rules which took effect on 1 November 1993 (County Court (Amendment No 3) Rules, SI 1993 No 2175). It is not available merely by satisfying the usual conditions for the application of the Ground in question. The following conditions must all be satisfied:

(a) The tenancy and any agreement for the tenancy was entered into on or after 15 January 1989;

(b) The proceedings are brought on one of Grounds 1, 3, 4, or 5;

(c) The only purpose of the proceedings is to recover possession, and no other claim (e.g., for rent arrears) is being made;

(d) The assured tenancy is the subject of a written agreement, or is a statutory periodic tenancy on the same terms (save as to rent) as such a tenancy, or relates to the same or substantially the same premises which were let to the same tenant, and is on the same terms (save as to rent and/or duration) as such a tenancy;

(e) The proceedings are brought against the tenant to whom written notice was given (i.e., there has been no assignment);

(f) The tenant was given written notice, not later than the beginning of the tenancy (thus the procedure is not available where the landlord wishes to invoke the court's dispensation power);

(g) The tenant was given notice of the proceedings in accordance with s. 8.

These conditions being satisfied, the landlord may bring proceedings for possession under the rule (what is now County Court Rules, ord. 49, r. 6). Application must be in prescribed form (County Court (Forms) (Amendment No 2) Rules 1993, SI 1993 No 2174, Form N.5A), and must contain information and attach copies of documents as listed in detail in the rules (ord. 49, r. 6(6) as amended). Statements must be verified on oath. Should the application be opposed, the defendant must within 14 days of its service on him deliver a reply (also in prescribed form: SI 1993 No 2174, Form N.11A). The application and any reply are then referred to the judge, who may either make an order for possession 'without delay' and 'without requiring the attendance of the parties' (ord. 49, r. 6(15), or, (*only* where he is not satisfied that the prior notice was served before the tenancy, or that a notice was served in accordance with s. 8, or that service of the application was duly effected, or that the plaintiff has established he is entitled to recover possession under the Ground relied upon against the defendant) fix a hearing date and give directions. In the event of an order for possession being made under this expedited procedure, the court has discretion to set aside, vary, or confirm it on application being made on notice within 14 days of the order, or of its own motion (ord. 49, r. 6(17)). For the form of order of possession where possession is granted pursuant to the accelerated procedure, see SI 1993 No 2174, N.26A.

There are many potential pitfalls where a landlord seeks to invoke the accelerated possession procedure, but it has clear advantages in terms of speed (and therefore cost) to those who take care to satisfy its requirements.

6.1.9 Ground 6: intention to demolish etc.

Ground 6 is complex. The landlord who is seeking possession must intend to demolish or reconstruct the whole or a substantial part of the dwelling-house, or carry out substantial works on the dwelling-house or any part thereof, or any building of which it forms part, three conditions being fulfilled:

(a) the work cannot be carried out without the tenant giving up possession, for one of four stated reasons (the tenant is not willing to agree to variation of the terms of the lease; the nature of the work is such that no such variation is practicable; the tenant is not willing to accept an assured tenancy of part of the dwelling-house; the nature of the work is such that such a tenancy is not practicable);

(b) since the grant of the tenancy, no person holding the landlord's interest has acquired it for money or money's worth;

(c) the assured tenancy did not arise by succession to a Rent Act protected or statutory tenancy (or, if an assured agricultural occupancy, did not arise by succession to a Rent (Agriculture) Act 1976 tenancy).

Although Ground 6 was an innovation in private sector housing law, there has been a similar ground in relation to secure tenancies since 1980 (see chapter 6, para. 6.2.2), and the analogous provision in the business tenancy code has given rise to much litigation. One particular difficulty which the courts have had to face in relation to the latter has been the proof of intention. In relation to Ground 6, it is the intention of the landlord which is material save where the landlord is a registered housing association or charitable housing trust, in which case the intention of a superior landlord may suffice. In *Cunliffe* v *Goodman* [1950] 2 KB 237, Asquith LJ stated:

> An 'intention' . . . connotes a state of affairs which the party 'intending' . . . does more than merely contemplate: it connotes a state of affairs which, on the contrary, he decides, so far as in him lies, to bring about, by his own act of volition.

Denning LJ in *Fisher* v *Taylors Furnishing Stores Ltd* [1956] 2 QB 78, 84 stated that:

> . . . the court must be satisfied that the intention to reconstruct is genuine and not colourable; that it is a firm and settled intention, not likely to be changed, that the reconstruction is of a substantial part of the premises, indeed so substantial that it cannot be thought to be a device to get possession; that the work is so extensive that it is necessary to get possession of the holding in order to do it; and that it is intended to do the work at once and not after a time.

In seeking to prove intention, the landlord should come to court armed with the planning permission, if necessary, proof of ability to finance the operation and sufficient details of the intended works to convince the court that the plan is not merely colourable. If the landlord is a company, its intention is best shown by a resolution of the directors as recorded in the minutes or, if the matter is beyond their powers, by a resolution of the company in general meeting. The landlord may undertake to the court that it will take the requisite steps, and this has been considered an effective course of action in relation to business tenancies (*Espresso Coffee Machine Co. Ltd* v *Guardian Assurance Co. Ltd* [1959] 1 WLR 250).

Landlords 'by purchase' are excluded from Ground 6 by condition (b) referred to above. This is designed to prevent property developers from buying up the reversions of dwelling-houses let on assured tenancy, and then using Ground 6 as a means of obtaining vacant possession.

It would be particularly easy for such landlords to offer attractive new tenancies to the sitting tenants, and then argue Ground 6 on the basis that they have not acquired the interest as landlord since the date of the tenancy. This abuse is, however, obviated by the second paragraph of Ground 6. If, immediately before the grant of the tenancy, the tenant (or any one of joint tenants) was the tenant under an earlier assured tenancy, then the landlord must not have acquired his interest for money or money's worth since the grant of that earlier tenancy.

Where the court makes an order for possession by virtue of Ground 6, the landlord must pay the tenant his reasonable removal expenses (HA 1988,

s. 11). The landlord who obtains a possession order by misrepresenting or concealing material facts may be ordered by the court to pay compensation to his former tenant (HA 1988, s. 12). While this latter provision has general application to assured tenancies, it may have particular use in relation to Ground 6, where landlords may be tempted to disguise their true intentions in the interests of obtaining a possession order.

6.1.10 Ground 7: death of periodic tenant

> The tenancy is a periodic tenancy (including a statutory periodic tenancy) which has devolved under the will or intestacy of the former tenant and the proceedings for the recovery of possession are begun not later than 12 months after the death of the former tenant . . .

Assured periodic tenancies cannot be terminated by notice to quit (HA 1988, s. 5(1)). On the death of the assured periodic tenant, his interest will vest in his spouse, subject to the various exceptions and qualifications of HA 1988, s. 17, irrespective of whether his will states otherwise, or the rules of intestacy would otherwise indicate (see para. 8 below). If, however, the tenant does not leave a surviving spouse, or for some other reason s. 17 does not operate, the periodic tenancy will devolve in accordance with the tenant's will or the intestacy rules. The effect could well be that the landlord is left with a tenant whom he does not want.

Ground 7 gives the landlord a 12-month period of grace following the death of a periodic tenant to assess the character and financial viability of the person who has inherited the tenancy under the general law. If the landlord does not wish him to remain tenant, he need not justify his decision to seek possession, since if proceedings are commenced within the 12-month period the court must make the order sought. The court has a discretion to calculate the 12 months from the date the landlord became aware of the tenant's death, in circumstances where he did not become immediately aware of it. However, the landlord would be safer in proceeding, if he can, in the period beginning with the tenant's death, as he is not then reliant on the exercise of discretion in his favour.

If the court were to imply that a *new* periodic tenancy had been created during the 12-month period from the tender and acceptance of rent, the policy of Ground 7 would be frustrated. The tenancy would not any longer be the periodic tenancy which had devolved under the will or intestacy of the former tenant, and Ground 7 would not apply. A rider therefore provides that the court must not make such an implication, unless the landlord agrees in writing to a change 'in the amount of rent, the period of the tenancy, the premises which are let, or any other term of the tenancy.' However, a tenant could argue in an appropriate case that a new periodic tenancy had been expressly orally agreed with the landlord, and was not merely inferred from tender and acceptance of rent. Such a contention, if established on the evidence, would prevent the landlord from claiming possession by virtue of Ground 7.

6.1.11 Ground 8: non-payment of rent

> Both at the date of the service of the notice under section 8 of this Act relating to the proceedings for possession and at the date of the hearing—
>
> (a) if rent is payable weekly or fortnightly, at least thirteen weeks' rent is unpaid;
>
> (b) if rent is payable monthly, at least three months' rent is unpaid;
>
> (c) if rent is payable quarterly, at least one quarter's rent is more than three months in arrears; and
>
> (d) if rent is payable yearly, at least three months' rent is more than three months in arrears;
>
> and for the purpose of this ground 'rent' means rent lawfully due from the tenant.

Ground 8 is particularly attractive to landlords seeking possession. It is a mandatory ground, and so if the landlord can establish the requisite amount of rent outstanding (broadly based in each case on three months' arrears), then the court must grant him possession, and cannot, for example, allow the tenant time to pay. It can be used even though the assured tenant is holding under a fixed term tenancy.

Where the landlord is proceeding on Ground 8, he must serve a s. 8 notice. The court has no power to dispense with service (HA 1988, s. 8(5)). At the date of service of that notice, there must be the appropriate amount of rent due. The tenant then has the opportunity to pay off a sufficient amount to ward off the threat of repossession. As the landlord has to prove that at the date of the hearing there is still the requisite amount of rent due, the tenant who pays enough rent to take the level below that for possession to be granted under Ground 8 will probably frustrate the landlord's proceedings. A prudent landlord will have particularised Grounds 10 and 11 as alternatives in his s. 8 notice, but they are discretionary, and if the tenant has shown a recent ability and willingness to pay the rent, the court is unlikely to make an immediate order for possession against him. It is particularly important that the landlord proceeding under Ground 8 gets his s. 8 notice right. The court has no power to dispense with service of a valid notice. Reference should be made to *Mountain* v *Hastings*, above.

The tenant may defend proceedings under Ground 8 on the basis that the rent is not due, or that he would have a defence to an action by the landlord for the rent itself. He may argue, for instance, that the landlord is in breach of his repairing covenant (perhaps under Landlord and Tenant Act 1985, s. 11) and he the tenant either has a counterclaim for damages which he can set off against the entirety of the landlord's claim (*British Anzani (Felixstowe) v International Marine Management (UK) Ltd* [1980] QB 637; *Televantos* v *McCulloch* (1990) 23 HLR 412) or has had to pay for repairs which the landlord had failed to perform out of the rent moneys (*Lee Parker* v *Izzet* [1971] 1 WLR 1688). It is not a defence to a rent action that the tenant has not been able to obtain, or has had difficulties obtaining, housing benefit.

6.2 Discretionary grounds

6.2.1 Reasonableness

Where a discretionary ground is proved, the court may order possession to be given up if it considers it reasonable to make the order. The burden of proof is on the plaintiff seeking possession to show that it is reasonable to make the order. According to Lord Greene MR in *Cumming* v *Danson* [1942] 2 All ER 653, 655:

> The duty of the judge is to take into account all relevant circumstances as they exist at the date of the hearing. That he must do in what I venture to call a broad commonsense way giving weight as he thinks right to the various factors in the situation. Some factors may have little or no weight: others may be decisive.

By virtue of s. 9 of the 1988 Act, the court has an extended discretion to adjourn proceedings 'for such period or periods as it thinks fit', and on making an order for possession or at any time before execution it may stay or suspend execution of the order, or postpone the date of possession, for such period as it thinks just. On exercise of these powers, the court must impose conditions with regard to the payment of rent arrears (if any) or other payments in respect of occupation after the termination of the tenancy, unless it considers that to do so would cause exceptional hardship to the tenant or would otherwise be unreasonable. It may impose such other conditions as it thinks fit. The flexibility of these provisions is in part to enable the court to use its powers to make the tenant pay the rent, or comply with the other obligations of the tenancy, and to allow the tenant to remain in possession if that is possible.

6.2.2 Ground 9: suitable alternative accommodation

> Suitable alternative accommodation is available for the tenant or will be available for him when the order for possession takes effect.

'Suitable alternative accommodation' is defined in Part III of sch. 2 to the 1988 Act. The landlord has two main options open to him in establishing this ground. He may produce a certificate of the local housing authority stating that the authority will provide suitable alternative accommodation, and such a certificate will be conclusive evidence that such accommodation will be provided by the date there specified. However, local authority certificates are hard to come by, as local authorities have diminishing (and sometimes no) housing stock, and the needs of a person who already holds an assured tenancy are not pressing.

Alternatively, the landlord may suggest that some accommodation which he, or some other landlord, can provide is suitable. It will be deemed to be suitable if it satisfies two requirements, one concerning the security of tenure of the premises, the other concerning the suitability of the accommodation itself. The premises must be let on assured tenancy, or alternatively on terms affording 'reasonably equivalent' security to that offered by an assured tenancy. A public sector letting to the tenant might suffice, if the tenancy was secure and therefore within Part IV of the Housing Act 1985. However, the letting must not be an assured shorthold tenancy, nor must it be on assured tenancy where the landlord has given notices pursuant to Grounds 1 to 5. The accommodation offered must in any case be reasonably suitable to the needs of the tenant and his family as regards proximity to place of work, and must either satisfy the comparison with local authority accommodation in the area which is provided for persons with similar needs to the tenant and his family as regards extent or be otherwise reasonably suitable to their needs as regards extent and character. The 'character' of the accommodation is only significant if the accommodation is not being compared with the local authority accommodation. 'Character' may include the physical environs of the property concerned (*Redspring* v *Francis* [1973] 1 WLR 134), but not the provision of on-site recreations (e.g., a pony: *Hill* v *Rochard* [1983] 1 WLR 478). The accommodation must be furnished if that under the assured tenancy was furnished, and the furniture provided must be either similar to that in the present house or reasonably suitable to the needs of the tenant and his family. There is no reason why part of the dwelling-house presently let to the tenant should not constitute suitable alternative accommodation in an appropriate case (see, for example, *Mykolyshin* v *Noah* [1970] 1 WLR 1271).

The court must determine the question whether it is reasonable to order possession independently of the question whether the accommodation offered is suitable (*Battlespring Ltd* v *Gates* (1983) 11 HLR 6). Where the landlord obtains an order for possession under Ground 9, the tenant is entitled to his reasonable removal expenses from the landlord, and can sue the landlord if he fails to pay them (HA 1988, s. 11).

6.2.3 Ground 10: non payment of rent

Some rent lawfully due from the tenant—

(a) is unpaid on the date on which the proceedings for possession are begun; and

(b) except where subsection (1)(b) of section 8 of this Act applies, was in arrears at the date of service of the notice under that section relating to those proceedings.

It is not necessary for proof of this ground that any rent remain unpaid at the date of the hearing. However, there must have been some rent due at the date of the commencement of proceedings, and at the date of service of the s. 8 notice. The court may dispense with service of the s. 8 notice in relation to this ground (unlike Ground 8), and in such circumstances, rent due at the commencement of proceedings will suffice for proof of the ground. On proof of Ground 10, the court is much more likely to make a suspended order for possession, imposing conditions for the payment of rent arrears by the tenant (HA 1988, s. 9).

6.2.4 Ground 11: persistent delay in paying the rent

Whether or not any rent is in arrears on the date on which proceedings for possession are begun, the tenant has persistently delayed paying rent which has become lawfully due.

The landlord need not show that rent is or has been in arrears at any particular time. He will, however, have to show 'persistent delay', and the court is not likely to be satisfied with an unparticularised statement to this effect. A detailed record of the tenant's rent payments may be required. Even if the landlord establishes Ground 11, the court may be reluctant to order possession in the exercise of its discretion when the landlord has been paid all the rent which is then due to him.

6.2.5 Ground 12: breach of obligation

Any obligation of the tenancy (other than one related to the payment of rent) has been broken or not performed.

Any breach will do for proof of the ground. However, the landlord is only likely to obtain possession if the breach is serious and/or continuing despite requests to remedy.

6.2.6 Ground 13: deterioration of dwelling-house

The condition of the dwelling-house or any of the common parts [as defined in Ground 13] has deteriorated owing to acts of waste by, or the

> neglect or default of, the tenant or any other person residing in the dwelling-house . . .

This does not require proof of a breach of a covenant or obligation of the tenancy by the tenant. An act of 'waste' is any act which alters the nature of the land let to the tenant (see Megarry & Wade, *Law of Real Property,* 5th ed., p. 96); the expression here is intended to cover the tenant whose action, as opposed to inaction ('neglect') causes the condition of the dwelling-house to deteriorate. In *Holloway* v *Povey* (1984) 15 HLR 104, a failure to attend to the garden (which is part of the premises let on the assured tenancy: HA 1988, s. 2(1)) fell within the similar ground in the Rent Act 1977. Where the act of waste, or neglect or default, is that of a person lodging with the tenant or of a sub-tenant of his, the landlord must also prove that the tenant has not taken such steps as he ought reasonably to have taken for the removal of the lodger or sub-tenant in question.

6.2.7 Ground 14: tenant misconduct or conviction

> The tenant or any other person residing in the dwelling-house has been guilty of conduct which is a nuisance or annoyance to adjoining occupiers, or has been convicted of using the dwelling-house or allowing the dwelling-house to be used for immoral or illegal purposes.

The landlord must prove either misconduct or a criminal conviction. If he alleges misconduct, it must have comprised a nuisance or annoyance to adjoining occupiers. In *Cobstone Investments Ltd* v *Maxim* [1985] QB 140, the Court of Appeal broadly defined 'adjoining occupiers' so as to include occupiers of premises which were near enough to be affected by the conduct in question. It was not necessary that they physically touched the dwelling-house occupied by the tenant or other person. 'Nuisance' is given its ordinary, everyday meaning; 'annoyance' has been held to be something which 'reasonably troubles the mind and pleasure, not of a fanciful person . . . but of the ordinary sensible [English] inhabitant of a house' (*Tod-Heatley* v *Benham* (1888) 40 Ch D 80, 98).

If the landlord bases his claim on a conviction, it is necessary for him to show that the conviction relates to use of the dwelling-house for immoral or illegal purposes. The meaning of this requirement was fully discussed by the Court of Appeal in *Schneiders & Sons Ltd* v *Abrahams* [1925] 1 KB 301. Whilst the criminal indictment or charge need not specify the premises (and thus the ground is not limited to offences of which user of premises is an essential element), the landlord must be able to establish that the tenant has taken advantage of the opportunity the premises afford of committing the offence. The mere fact of a crime being committed on the premises (for example an assault on a visitor to the dwelling-house) is not enough. Using the premises as a storage place for stolen goods (as in *Schneiders* itself), or for dangerous drugs (see *Abrahams* v *Wilson* [1971] 2 QB 88, 94) are good examples of the kind of conduct which will fall within the ground. There is no need for the use to be continuous, frequent or repeated (*Schneiders & Sons Ltd* v *Abrahams* [1925] 1 KB 301, 307).

The premises will have been used for immoral purposes where the conviction relates to an offence involving unlawful sexual intercourse such as living on the earnings of prostitution or keeping a brothel (Sexual Offences Act 1956, ss. 30 and 33). Using the premises for immoral purposes may in itself cause nuisance or annoyance to adjoining occupiers, and in those circumstances, a conviction will not be necessary. However, the occupation of a dwelling by two unmarried adults will no longer be considered 'immoral': *Heglibiston Establishment* v *Heyman* (1977) 36 P & CR 351.

6.2.8 Ground 15: deterioration of furniture

Ground 15 is similar to Ground 13, save that the deterioration is in the condition of furniture rather than the dwelling-house itself.

6.2.9 Ground 16: termination of tenant's employment

> The dwelling-house was let to the tenant in consequence of his employment by the landlord seeking possession or a previous landlord under the tenancy and the tenant has ceased to be in that employment.

It is not necessary for proof of Ground 16 for the landlord to show that he has a need for possession of the dwelling (perhaps because the tenant's replacement as employee wishes to occupy the dwelling-house). However, such evidence would be useful to the landlord as he attempts to convince the court that it is reasonable to order possession against the tenant. Ground 16 is not available as a ground for possession of dwelling-houses let on assured agricultural occupancies.

7 ASSIGNMENT AND SUB-LETTING

7.1 Implied terms

Section 15(1) of HA 1988 implies a term into all statutory periodic tenancies (which are assured tenancies) that the tenant shall not assign the tenancy, in whole or in part, or sub-let or part with possession of the whole or part of the dwelling-house without the landlord's consent. A similar term is implied into all contractual periodic tenancies unless the parties have themselves expressly prohibited or permitted assignment or sub-letting or parting with possession in the lease (absolutely or conditionally) or a premium is payable on grant or renewal of the lease (HA 1988, s. 15(3)). No such term is, however, implied into fixed term assured tenancies. In such cases, the landlord is expected to make appropriate provision in the lease itself.

If a qualified covenant against assignment or sub-letting, etc. is implied into a residential lease as a result of HA 1988, s. 15, the tenant will not be able to complain that the landlord's refusal to consent to a proposed assignment etc. is unreasonable, as the relevant provision of the Landlord and Tenant Act 1927 (s. 19) is excluded by HA 1988, s. 15(2). Moreover, as the statutory covenant against alienation is not qualified by a provision that the landlord's consent is not to be unreasonably withheld, the landlord will not be under a statutory duty to make his decision whether or not to consent to alienation within a reasonable time of the tenant's application to him (Landlord and Tenant Act 1988, s. 1).

The effect of these provisions is that an assignment or sub-letting by an assured periodic tenant without the landlord's consent will usually be in breach of covenant, and the landlord will be able to institute proceedings for possession based upon Ground 12 (breach of obligation).

7.2 Sub-tenancies

It can be seen that the term implied by s. 15 into assured periodic tenancies outlaws sub-letting of the whole or part of the premises without the landlord's consent. Further provision concerning subtenancies is made by s. 18, whereby on the termination of the landlord's interest in the property occupied by the assured tenant, the tenant (i.e., the sub-tenant) will hold directly from the former landlord's landlord, provided that the assured tenancy is lawful and that the new landlord can hold on assured tenancy (i.e., the tenancy is not now excluded from the Housing Act 1988 by sch. 1 to the 1988 Act).

> *Example:* An assured tenant (S) holds under a periodic tenancy from his landlord (T). T's 10-year fixed term tenancy, held of L, expires. S will now hold as assured periodic tenant from L, provided that his tenancy from T was lawful (i.e., was not in breach of covenant) and that L is not, for example, the Crown or some other landlord which cannot grant assured tenancies.

7.3 Lawfully let

The sub-letting will not be lawful if it is in breach of a covenant against sub-letting in the head lease (*Maley* v *Fearn* [1946] 2 All ER 583). If the immediate landlord is himself an assured tenant, then the sub-letting is very likely to be in breach of such a covenant, in view of HA 1988, s. 15 above. However, a sub-letting which is at the outset unlawful may become lawful if the landlord waives the breach (see further, chapter 3, para. 7.3.6).

7.4 Reversionary leases and assured tenancies

If a landlord grants a fixed term assured tenancy, and then subsequently grants a lease of his reversion, the assured tenant will take priority over the reversionary lessee, and can assert possession against him. On expiry of the fixed term, the assured tenant holding over as statutory periodic tenant, that tenancy will continue to bind the leaseholder (see s. 18(3), (4)).

8 STATUTORY SUCCESSION

On the death of an assured tenant, the devolution of the tenancy will depend on whether, at the time of death, it is for a fixed term or is periodic (see chapter 2, para. 4.2). If it is a fixed term tenancy, it will pass according to the will of the tenant, or, in the event of no testamentary provision being made which covers the tenancy, in accordance with the rules of intestacy (see Administration of Estates Act 1925, ss. 46–49; Intestate Estates Act 1952, s. 5, sch. 2, as variously amended). If the tenancy is periodic, whether 'contractual' periodic or statutory periodic, the tenancy may still devolve according to the will, or the intestacy rules, but only if s. 17 of the Housing Act 1988 does not apply. By s. 17(1):

> In any case where—
>
> (a) the sole tenant under an assured periodic tenancy dies, and
> (b) immediately before the death, the tenant's spouse was occupying the dwelling-house as his or her only or principal home, and
> (c) the tenant was not himself a successor, as defined in subsection (2) or subsection (3) below,
>
> then, on the death, the tenancy vests by virtue of this section in the spouse (and, accordingly, does not devolve under the tenant's will or intestacy).

8.1 Joint tenants

If at the date of death, there are two (or more) persons holding the tenancy, s. 17 will not apply. Instead, the tenancy will pass by virtue of the right of survivorship to the surviving joint tenant(s). This will then preclude the tenancy passing, on the subsequent death of the survivor, by s. 17 (see s. 17(2)(b)).

8.2 Spouse

The only person who is capable of succeeding the assured tenant under s. 17 is his or her spouse. The ordinary meaning of spouse (of a person lawfully married to the tenant) is extended to include a person who was living with the tenant as his or her wife or husband (s. 17(4)). This terminology appears to exclude the possibility of the survivor of a homosexual relationship qualifying as a 'spouse' (see, on the similar succession provisions for secure tenancies, *Harrogate Borough Council* v *Simpson* (1984) 17 HLR 205, chapter 6, para. 7.1.1). In the unlikely event of there being more than one person who qualifies as a spouse, the successor will be decided by agreement between them, failing which the county court will decide (s. 17(5)).

8.3 Occupying the dwelling-house as his or her only or principal home

This is the same test to be applied as in determining whether a tenant is assured (HA 1988, s. 1; para. 2.5 above). The tenant whom the claimant is seeking to succeed must also have been occupying the dwelling-house as his only or principal home up to the time of death in order to remain assured tenant. There is no express requirement that the tenant was 'living with' the claimant unless they were not lawfully married (see then s. 17(4)). If, therefore, a husband and wife, who were lawfully married, the husband being the assured tenant of their dwelling-house, were living in separate households under the same roof, the wife would succeed on the death of her husband.

8.4 Tenant not himself a successor

This is the most important limitation on statutory succession under the Housing Act. The basic principle which is being promoted is that there should be no more than one succession to a periodic tenancy. Succession is widely defined in s. 17(2) and (3). A tenant will be a successor if he has himself become tenant by virtue of s. 17, or by virtue of survivorship, or by succession to a Rent Act regulated tenancy (chapter 3, para. 8). The grant of a new tenancy to a person who was at the time of grant a successor will not 'wipe the slate clean', as that person will still be deemed a successor if the new tenancy is of the same or substantially the same dwelling-house. Where a successor to an assured tenancy transfers the tenancy to his spouse or former spouse on or after a decree of divorce, the transferee will be deemed to be a successor also, and on her death, no further statutory succession will be possible (Matrimonial Homes Act 1983, sch. 1, para. 2(3), as amended by HA 1988, sch. 17, para. 34(2)).

8.5 Devolution under the will or on intestacy

If s. 17 does not apply, for whatever reason, it does not follow that the death of the assured periodic tenant will terminate the tenancy. It will form part of the tenant's estate, and fall to be disposed of under the terms of his will or in accordance with the intestacy rules. However, the landlord has the right to recover possession in the period of 12 months from the date of the death (or, if the court directs, the date the landlord became aware of the tenant's death) by invoking Ground 7, a mandatory ground of possession. This provision will only be required where the person entitled to the tenancy goes into occupation: if he does not, the tenancy will cease to be assured, and the landlord will then be free to terminate it by giving notice of the appropriate length.

9 ASSURED SHORTHOLD TENANCIES

9.1 Introduction

The assured shorthold tenancy has proved a highly popular form of letting. It is attractive to landlords in that it confers no security of tenure ('assured' is legally accurate but factually misleading), yet has few of the traps for the unwary on the route to repossession which so bedevilled its predecessor, the protected shorthold. Somewhat surprisingly, despite the availability of a procedure whereby the assured shorthold tenant can apply for a rent reduction, such evidence as there is suggests that rents agreed for assured shorthold tenancies have been significantly higher than for 'standard' assured tenancies (see *Private Renting in England 1990*, HMSO, p. 24).

A landlord which is hoping to seek to attract investment by means of a business expansion scheme should not use assured shortholds, as they are not effective for such purposes (see Finance Act 1988, s. 50(3)). Nor should registered housing associations normally let on assured shorthold. The 'Tenants' Guarantee' (see chapter 1, para. 6) reads:

> Assured shorthold tenancies should be used only in exceptional circumstances, which an association may be expected to justify to the Housing Corporation, where shorthold is the only practicable way of meeting the association's housing objectives. This might include lettings in property available to the association for a limited period (e.g., before redevelopment or sale) or lettings to students. It is expected that other cases will be very rare.

9.2 Definition

By s. 20(1), HA 1988:

Subject to subsection (3) below, an assured shorthold tenancy is an assured tenancy—

(a) which is a fixed term tenancy granted for a term certain of not less than six months; and

(b) in respect of which there is no power for the landlord to determine the tenancy at any time earlier than six months from the beginning of the tenancy; and

(c) in respect of which a notice is served as mentioned in subsection (2) below.

If a landlord wishes to grant an assured shorthold tenancy to a person who does not already have an assured shorthold, all three of these conditions must be met. It should also be stressed that the tenancy must be an assured tenancy, thus satisfying the necessary criteria outlined at para. 2 above, and not being a tenancy which by sch. 1 to the 1988 Act or otherwise cannot be an assured tenancy.

9.2.1 Fixed term of not less than six months

There is no maximum duration for assured shorthold tenancies. Thus, despite the terminology, the term is not necessarily 'short'.

9.2.2 No power for landlord to determine earlier than six months from commencement

This provision is deceptive. It is perfectly in order, and indeed it is highly advisable, for the landlord to reserve a right of re-entry for breach of covenant and so forth which is exercisable during the first six months. By s. 45(4) of the 1988 Act, 'any reference in [Part I] of this Act (however expressed) to a power for a landlord to determine a tenancy does not include a reference to a power of re-entry or forfeiture for breach of any term or condition of the tenancy.' We will see in due course, when we consider methods of recovery of possession from assured shortholders, why reservation of such a right is essential. What the landlord cannot do, if the tenancy is to be a valid assured shorthold, is provide for termination earlier than six months from the commencement of the tenancy by the giving of notice. Not only will such a clause be ineffective, its presence will prevent the tenancy from being an assured shorthold. It will take effect instead as an assured tenancy. The landlord may insert a break clause which is effective during the fixed term, as long as it is only effective once the first six months have elapsed (e.g., an assured shorthold is granted for three years, whereby the landlord can give notice to the tenant terminating the fixed term at any time following the expiry of six months).

9.2.3 Notice prior to tenancy

The notice must be in prescribed form, served before the assured tenancy is entered into by the person who is to be landlord on the person who is to be tenant, and must state that the assured tenancy to which it relates is to be a shorthold tenancy (HA 1988, s. 20(2)). The form is contained in SI 1988 No 2203, as amended by SI 1990 No 1532 (Form 7). There is no power in the court to dispense with the requirement for such a notice, and if none is served, or it is served late, the tenancy will take effect as a standard assured tenancy. A notice 'substantially to the same effect' as that in the prescribed form will satisfy the rules (SI 1988 No 2203, reg. 2).

In *R* v *London Borough of Newham, ex parte Ugbo* (1993) 26 HLR 263, a notice gave the wrong address for the premises. Sir Louis Blom-Cooper, QC, sitting as a Deputy High Court Judge, at 266, held that this did not invalidate the notice:

> So long as the s. 20 notice could reasonably be understood as having obviously mistakenly recorded the address of the premises under the assured shorthold tenancy, and no-one . . . was misled, the court would overlook the defect, and for that proposition, I cite *Carradine Properties Ltd* v *Aslam* [1976] 1 WLR 442.

Where, however, the notice contains a material perplexity as opposed to an evident error, failure to comply with the rules will be fatal. In *Panayi* v *Roberts* (1993) 25 HLR 421, the tenant was granted a term certain of one year from 7 November 1990. Despite this, the landlord served prior notice on the tenant indicating that the tenancy terminated on 6 May 1991. This notice could not be 'substantially to the same effect' as a notice which gave the correct date, and the Court of Appeal held that in consequence the tenancy was not an assured shorthold. Where the date of termination was obviously wrong (Mann LJ cited as an example '1793' for '1993'), the notice may nevertheless be effective (*Panayi* v *Roberts* at 425).

9.2.4 No assured shorthold if tenant previously assured

If the landlord serves notice on an existing standard assured tenant that his new tenancy is to be a shorthold, this will be of no effect. By s. 20(3), the grant of a new tenancy to a person who immediately before its grant was a standard assured tenant (or to persons, one of whom was a standard assured tenant) by the landlord who was landlord under that assured tenancy cannot take effect as an assured shorthold. Thus, landlords cannot by the simple expedient of granting new fixed term tenancies of the appropriate length, with the appropriate notice, convert their existing tenants into assured shortholders.

9.2.5 Other methods of creation

In the majority of cases, the assured shorthold is created by the landlord serving notice on the tenant prior to the commencement of the tenancy, and the tenant will from reading that form understand roughly his rights and obligations. However, there are several other ways in which an assured shorthold may come into being:

(a) An assured shorthold tenancy (or a shorthold tenancy which was, but no longer is, assured) comes to an end. If a new tenancy of the same, or substantially the same premises, 'comes into being', under which the landlord and tenant are the same as under the shorthold, then it will be an assured shorthold tenancy if and so long as it remains assured. This will be so irrespective of the length of the fixed term (if it is a fixed term), and the reservation by the landlord of rights to terminate, and there is no need for notice to be served. The tenancy will not be assured shorthold in the unlikely eventuality that the landlord serves notice on the tenant that the tenancy is *not* to be an assured shorthold. (HA 1988, s. 20(4), (5)). These provisions are drafted so as to cover not only the situation where the landlord expressly grants a new tenancy to his assured shorthold tenant, but also the situation where the tenant holds over following expiry of the fixed term. He will hold over as statutory periodic tenant by virtue of HA 1988, s. 5(2), and that statutory periodic tenancy will itself be an assured shorthold.

(b) A *protected* shorthold tenant (see chapter 3, para. 6.2.9) who obtains a new tenancy from his landlord on or after 15 January 1989, will become an assured shorthold tenant unless the landlord serves notice to the contrary, even though the usual conditions in HA 1988, s. 20(1) are not satisfied. This is the apparent effect of the highly convoluted transitional provisions contained in HA 1988, s. 34. Normally, the grant of a new tenancy to an existing Rent Act protected or statutory tenant subsequent to the coming into force of the 1988 Act will not be effective to grant an assured tenancy, still less an assured shorthold, and the tenancy will remain subject to the Rent Act 1977. But protected shorthold tenancies were not deemed worthy of preservation, and the 1988 Act therefore facilitates their conversion into assured shortholds. Accordingly, the landlord who grants a new tenancy on or after 15 January 1989 to a protected shorthold tenant will without more grant an assured shorthold tenancy (HA 1988, s. 34(3)). This provision affects tenants holding under protected shorthold tenancies, and protected or statutory tenants of dwelling-houses which were let under protected shortholds which ended prior to 15 January 1989, and in respect of which at that date there had either been no grant of a further tenancy or any grant of a further tenancy had been to the person who, immediately before the grant, was in possession of the dwelling-house as a protected or statutory tenant. 'Protected shorthold tenancy' includes a tenancy which is treated as a protected shorthold tenancy for the purposes of possession proceedings under Case 19 (HA 1988, s. 34(2).)

(c) Where a Rent Act protected or statutory tenant dies on or after 15 January 1989, he may be succeeded on certain conditions being fulfilled by a member of his family (i.e., not his spouse or common law spouse). Such person will take as assured tenant by succession. If the Rent Act tenant whom he is succeeding held a protected shorthold tenancy, or was otherwise vulnerable to a claim for possession based on Case 19 of sch. 15 to the Rent Act 1977, the successor will take as assured shorthold tenant, whether or not s. 20(1) of the 1988 Act is otherwise fulfilled. See further on succession, chapter 3, para. 8.

9.3 Terms of assured shortholds

In most respects, the terms of an assured shorthold tenancy are as determined by the agreement of the parties, subject only to the foregoing provisions, and to the terms which are implied into all assured tenancies by the 1988 Act, ss. 15 and 16 (see paras. 4.5 and 7.1, above). Termination of the tenancy by the tenant will depend on the lease. Assured shorthold tenants have no statutory entitlement to give notice (cf. protected shorthold tenants, chapter 3, para. 6.2.9.1). However, the rent payable under an assured shorthold may be challenged by the tenant on the basis that it is above the appropriate market rent for the dwelling-house, and the rent be reduced in consequence. This jurisdiction we should now consider.

9.3.1 Rents: reduction by the tenant

Section 22(1) of the 1988 Act enables an assured shorthold tenant to apply to a rent assessment committee for a determination of the rent which, in the committee's opinion, the landlord might reasonably be expected to obtain under an assured shorthold. Where the committee make such a determination, the rent which exceeds the rent so determined will thereafter be irrecoverable from the tenant (HA 1988, s. 22(4)). However, the determination does not bind the property (it does not act *in rem*), and thus on the recovery of possession by the landlord he can let the property to a new tenant at whatever rent that tenant will agree.

Application can only be made to the rent assessment committee during the initial fixed term of the assured shorthold. It is to be made by notice in prescribed form (SI 1988 No 2203, Form No 8). If the tenant is successful in his application, he cannot apply at any later date (HA 1988, s. 22(2)(a)). Even if the landlord and tenant enter into a new fixed term assured shorthold on expiry of the old one, the tenant cannot apply for a rent reduction (HA 1988, s. 22(2)(b)). The rationale for this restriction is that once the initial fixed term has ended, the landlord who has elected not to exercise his right to repossession should not be penalised by having his commercial return diminished.

The committee must determine the rent the landlord might reasonably be expected to obtain under the assured shorthold tenancy. Although no express provision is made to this effect, the inference is that the landlord who lets on assured shorthold tenancy should not reasonably expect to obtain as much as a landlord who lets on an assured tenancy which is not shorthold. The price to the landlord of conferring no security of tenure is a potential return on the property somewhat lower than that otherwise obtainable. The committee is expected to consider comparables (lists should be available: see HA 1988, s. 42), and should not make a determination at all unless they consider there is a sufficient number of similar dwelling-houses in the locality let on assured tenancies (shorthold or not) (HA 1988, s. 22(3)(a)). The committee should not tamper with the agreed rent: unless they consider the rent he pays is 'significantly higher' than the rent the landlord might reasonably be expected to obtain (having regard to the comparables), they should not make a determination at all (HA 1988, s. 22(3)(b)).

The Secretary of State has powers (which have not to date been exercised) to order that the rent reduction procedure will not apply in certain areas or in certain circumstances (HA 1988, s. 23). Appeals from rent assessment committees are tenable pursuant to the Tribunal and Inquiries Act 1971, s. 13.

The shortcomings of the procedure of rent reduction should be noted. Although at the time of the application to the rent assessment committee, the tenant has the protection of a fixed term tenancy, the tenant's continued occupation of the property after its expiry will be wholly dependant on the goodwill of his landlord, who has up his sleeve an unassailable right to recover possession. If the tenant wishes to stay beyond the term, it may be in his interests not to apply for rent reduction. Moreover, the landlord is not in any real sense 'bound' by the determination, as the landlord and tenant may agree a new rent before, during, or after proceedings before the committee. The tenant's negotiating position is at all times undermined by the power of the landlord to recover possession on two months' notice following expiry of the fixed term.

9.3.2 Rents: increase by landlord

As with any other assured tenancy, the landlord has no right to increase the rent during the fixed term unless the lease so provides. Generally, the lease will not do so, and the landlord will be bound by the agreement. When the fixed term has expired, and the tenant holds over as a statutory periodic tenant, the landlord may then invoke the rent increase procedure applicable to all assured periodic tenancies (HA 1988, s. 13, on which see para. 4.6 above). If, however, a determination has been made reducing the rent on application by the tenant, the landlord cannot seek to increase the rent until 12 months have elapsed from the date the determination takes effect (HA 1988, s. 22(4)(c)). Where the rent increase procedure is invoked, the rent assessment committee must determine the rent at which the dwelling-house might reasonably be expected to be let in the open market by a willing landlord under an assured shorthold tenancy (HA 1988, ss. 14, 20(7)). The committee would have regard to the inferior security thus afforded.

9.4 Recovery of possession

9.4.1 During the first six months

During the first six months of the assured shorthold tenant's fixed term, the landlord can only recover possession by obtaining a possession order from the court based upon one of Grounds 2, 8, or 10 to 15 inclusive. Furthermore, the tenancy must make provision for it to be brought to an end on the ground in question (HA 1988, s. 7(6)). Thus, reservation of a right of entry which is exercisable during the first six months is necessary to provide an effective sanction for default by the assured shortholder.

9.4.2 During the remainder of the fixed term

The landlord has the same rights during the remainder of the fixed term as he has during the first six months, with one possible addition. He may have incorporated a break clause into the lease which is exercisable by giving notice to the tenant subsequent to the expiry of the first six months. Such a break clause is perfectly legitimate: in particular, it does not offend HA 1988, s. 20(1). If, therefore, the landlord chooses, he may exercise the break clause, and thereby terminate the fixed term. The tenant will then hold as statutory periodic tenant by virtue of HA 1988, s. 5(2), that statutory periodic tenancy being an assured shorthold (HA 1988, s. 20(4)).

9.4.3 Serving notice whilst fixed term subsists, to take effect on expiry or shortly thereafter

Section 21(1) to (3) of the 1988 Act deal with the situation where the landlord wishes to exercise his rights to repossess without proving a ground for possession, doing so whilst the fixed term is still current. He should realise that although he can initiate the proceedings before the fixed term expires, possession will not be recovered until expiry has occurred. The landlord must in these circumstances give the tenant two months' notice (for which no form is prescribed), stating that he requires possession of the dwelling-house. That done, the landlord is entitled to a possession order if the court is satisfied 'that the assured shorthold tenancy has come to an end and no further assured tenancy (whether shorthold or not) is for the time being in existence, other than an assured shorthold periodic tenancy (whether statutory or not)'. These rather wordy provisions (which were amended by the Local Government and Housing Act 1989) mean that the landlord is entitled to possession as of right unless he grants a new fixed term tenancy to the assured shorthold tenant. As we have seen, on expiry of the fixed term, the tenant will hold over as statutory periodic tenant. Alternatively, the landlord may agree to a new periodic tenancy with the tenant on new terms. In either of these circumstances, the landlord can during the fixed term give two months' notice and go on to claim possession as of right.

9.4.4 Serving notice following expiry of fixed term

The landlord's rights are not greatly different from those where notice is served towards the end of the fixed term. The court must be satisfied, by HA 1988, s. 20(4):

> (a) that the landlord, or in the case of joint landlords, at least one of them has given to the tenant a notice stating that, after a date specified in the notice, being the last day of a period of the tenancy and not earlier than two months after the date notice was given, possession of the dwelling-house is required by virtue of this section; and
> (b) that the date specified in the notice under paragraph (a) above is not earlier than the earliest day on which, apart from section 5(1) above, the tenancy could be brought to an end by a notice to quit given by the landlord on the same date as the notice under paragraph (a) above.

Example A L lets to T on an assured shorthold tenancy for a fixed term of two years. For the first six months, L can recover possession only if he can satisfy HA 1988, s. 7(6), i.e., by proof of Grounds 2, 8, 10 to 15. For the final 18 months of the term, L may terminate the fixed term by using a break clause if he has reserved one in the lease. If he does this, a statutory periodic tenancy will then arise.

Example B T's fixed term is due to expire on 1 April 1995. L can give T written notice at any time before 1 February 1995 seeking recovery of possession on 1 April. Here s. 20(1) of the 1988 Act will apply, and the court must make an order for possession. The same provision would apply to any notice of not less than two months given before or on the day on which the fixed term comes to an end.

Example C T's fixed term has expired, and he is either holding over as statutory periodic tenant, or occupying pursuant to a new contractual periodic tenancy agreed with the landlord. The periodic tenancy is a monthly tenancy. L must give T two months' notice stating possession is required after a certain date, which must be the last day of a period of the tenancy. Only if the periodic tenancy is quarterly or yearly would L have to give longer notice, i.e., that stipulated in the contract (HA 1988, s. 20(4)).

9.5 Accelerated possession procedure

As a result of the recommendations made by the Civil Justice Review (Cm. 394), the County Court (Amendment No 3) Rules, SI 1993 No 2175, introduced an accelerated possession procedure for assured shorthold tenancies by way of amendment of the existing County Court Rules. The new procedure came into force on 1 November 1993. Similar provisions were also enacted in relation to assured tenancies under Grounds 1, 3, 4 and 5 (see para. 6.1.8 above).

The 'fast track' procedure has the undoubted advantage to landlords of obtaining a possession order expeditiously in cases which are either uncontested or the tenant has no apparent defence to the proceedings. The order can be made by a district judge without the need for attendance of either party, in little more than 14 days from the date of the service of the application on the tenant. However, it should not be assumed that all assured shorthold tenancies will be susceptible to an accelerated claim, or that the procedure is anything but complex. It will be necessary to check very carefully that all the requirements of the rules are satisfied. There are numerous pitfalls lying in wait for the unwary.

9.5.1 Conditions to be satisfied

The procedure is only available where both of the following conditions are satisfied:

(a) The tenancy and any agreement for the tenancy were entered into or or after 15 January 1989. Thus, it cannot be used where an assured shorthold tenancy has come into being as a result of the operation of the 'transitional' provisions.

(b) The only purpose of the proceedings is to recover possession of the dwelling-house. Thus, the landlord cannot make any other claim in the proceedings (e.g., for rent).

Additional conditions must be satisfied. These differ according to whether the fixed term has, or has not, expired.

Where the fixed term of an assured shorthold tenancy has not yet expired, the additional conditions are:

(c) The assured shorthold tenancy did not immediately follow a full assured tenancy; ss. 20(1)(a) to (c) of the 1988 Act must be satisfied; and the tenancy must be the subject of a written agreement.

(d) A notice in writing under s. 20(2) was served on the tenant, and that tenant is the defendant to these proceedings.

(e) A notice in accordance with s. 21(1)(b) of the 1988 Act has been given to the tenant in writing.

Of these, only (d) may cause difficulty. The fast-track procedure is not available where the present assured shorthold tenant is an assignee from the original tenant.

Where the initial fixed term of the assured shorthold tenancy has expired, the additional conditions are:

(f) The assured shorthold tenancy must not have followed a full assured tenancy, and must either be the subject of a written agreement, or be a statutory periodic tenancy on the same terms (save as to rent) as a tenancy which was the subject of a written agreement, or relate to the same or substantially the same premises which were let to the same tenant and be on the same terms (save as to rent or duration) as a tenancy which was the subject of a written agreement.

(g) Notice in writing under s. 20(2) was served in relation to the first assured shorthold tenancy of the premises, and proceedings are brought against the tenant on whom notice was served.

(h) Notice in writing under s. 21(4) must have been given to the tenant.

9.5.2 Mode of application

Where the conditions are satisfied as above, the landlord may bring possession proceedings under the accelerated procedure instead of making a claim under County Court Rules 1981, Ord. 6, r. 3. The application must be in the prescribed form, and a copy (with a copy for each defendant) must be filed at the court. The contents of the application are set out in detail in the rules, but adherence to the prescribed form will see the landlord safely through. The landlord must verify any documents (e.g., the written tenancy agreement, which must be attached to the application) on oath.

9.5.3 Role of the court

On receipt of the landlord's application for possession, the court should send it, with attached documents, to the defendant tenant by way of service. The defendant then has 14 days in which to deliver a reply (the form for which must be attached to the plaintiff's application). If no reply is received within that time scale, the plaintiff may file a written request for a possession order. If a reply is received, it is referred with the plaintiff's application to the judge. The judge then ('without delay' if no reply, or a late reply, is received) considers the application and the reply, if any, and must do one of two things. He must either order possession or fix a hearing date (giving directions). He may only do the latter if he is not satisfied that the appropriate written notices were served or given, that service of the application was duly effected, or that the plaintiff has established that he is entitled to possession under s. 21 of the 1988 Act against the defendant. The presumption, once the conditions for the use of the procedure are satisfied, is in favour of repossession.

9.5.4 Setting aside

Quite apart from its general jurisdiction (County Court Rules, Ord. 37), the court has jurisdiction to set aside, vary, or confirm, an order made pursuant to the accelerated possession procedure, of its own motion or on application made within 14 days of service of the order.

THREE

REGULATED TENANCIES

Rent Act 1977

1 INTRODUCTION

For nearly 75 years, from 1915 until 1989, the Rent Acts dominated the private sector of rented housing by imposing a system of rent control, and providing security of tenure for tenants within that system. The 'regulated tenancy' is a generic term for the two stages of Rent Act status, the 'protected tenancy' and the 'statutory tenancy'. In essence, whilst the tenant holds under the contract of tenancy, he is, in the event of the Rent Act applying to him, a 'protected tenant'. On termination of his contractual tenancy, he will become a 'statutory tenant' provided that the conditions laid down in the 1977 Act are satisfied, most particularly the condition that he occupies the dwelling-house in question as his residence. Regulated tenants, whether protected or statutory, enjoy rent control, together with security of tenure.

The Rent Act 1977 (RA 1977) was not amended substantially by the Housing Act 1988 (HA 1988). However, the intention of the latter Act being to phase out the former, immediate attention must be drawn to s. 34 of the 1988 Act, which prevents almost all tenancies entered into on or after 15 January 1989 from being protected tenancies. It may at first seem surprising that there is no similar prohibition regarding statutory tenancies. The point is that such tenancies are entirely derivative from protected tenancies: they take effect 'by operation of law' on the termination of a protected tenancy. The general policy of the Housing Act 1988 is to keep existing regulated tenancies within the Rent Act. In that sense, the 1988 Act does not 'deregulate'. Thus on termination of a protected tenancy on or after 15 January 1989, which tenancy must (subject to certain exceptions) by definition have been entered into before the 1988 Act came into force, the tenant will hold over as statutory tenant under the 1977 Act. If and so long as the tenant continues to occupy the dwelling-house as his residence, the statutory tenancy will remain in being. Should the statutory tenant die, the 1977 Act will dictate whether any succession to that tenancy will occur. In certain circumstances, a successor will take as assured tenant rather than as statutory tenant, and then the 1988 Act will come into operation (see further on succession on death, para. 8 below).

2 PROTECTED TENANCY: DEFINITION

By s. 1, RA 1977,

> Subject to this Part of this Act, a tenancy under which a dwelling-house (which may be a house or part of a house) is let as a separate dwelling is a protected tenancy for the purposes of this Act. Any reference in this Act to a protected tenant shall be construed accordingly.

Each of these elements will be taken in turn.

2.1 'Tenancy'

A protected tenancy must be a tenancy (or 'lease'). A mere licence to occupy the dwelling-house will not suffice, but any form of tenancy (including a tenancy at will or by sufferance) will do. See further, chapter 2, para. 2.1, where the relevant case law is extensively discussed. A sub-tenancy can be a protected tenancy (RA 1977, s. 152(1)). The Rent Act protects certain sub-tenants against actions of the head landlords: see further, para. 7 below.

2.2 'Dwelling-house'

Section 1 of the 1977 Act indicates that the dwelling-house may be a house or part of a house, and so tenants of flats can clearly be protected tenants: see further, chapter 2, para. 2.2.

2.3 'Let as a separate dwelling'

There is a large body of case law on the meaning of this phrase: see further, chapter 2, para. 2.3. Where a tenant shares accommodation with his landlord, the tenancy is unlikely to be protected (for the reasons set out at chapter 2, para. 2.3.6). However, the tenant may in such circumstances have a restricted contract (see para. 9 below). Where a tenant shares accommodation with other occupiers, s. 22 of the Rent Act 1977 may come to his aid in much the same way as ss. 3 and 10 of HA 1988 do in relation to agreements entered into on or after 15 January 1989 (see further, chapter 2, para. 2.3.7).

Gray v *Brown* (1992) 25 HLR 144 is a recent example of the application of this provision. In 1978 the occupier was granted exclusive possession of a bed-sitting room, with a right to share a kitchen and bathroom with others. The Court of Appeal, construing the written agreements to determine whether the landlord had the right to share this accommodation, held that he did not, and accordingly s. 22 of the 1977 Act applied so as to confer a protected tenancy on the occupier.

2.4 Corporate tenants

The protected tenant need not be an individual, and need not satisfy a residence qualification (cf. the assured tenant, chapter 2, para 2.4). This means that corporate tenants who fall within s. 1 of the 1977 Act can claim the benefit of rent control (*Carter* v *SU Carburetter Co.* [1942] 2 KB 288; *Feather Supplies Ltd* v *Ingham* [1971] 2 QB 348.) However, the statutory tenant must occupy the dwelling-house as his residence. This requirement of residential occupation cannot be satisfied by an artificial person, and so a company or other institution cannot be a statutory tenant (*Hillier* v *United Dairies Ltd* [1934] 1 KB 57). Thus once the protected tenancy is terminated, the landlord will be able to recover possession in accordance with the general law: the corporate tenant has no security of tenure outside the contract.

3 PROTECTED TENANCY: EXCEPTIONS

There are numerous exceptions to the conferment of a protected tenancy within the 1977 Act itself, in ss. 4 to 16A, and they must now be considered. Many of these are very similar to the exceptions relevant to assured tenancies contained in the 1988 Act, and cross-reference to chapter 2 will be made where appropriate. The first exception to be dealt with, however, is contained in the 1988 Act, and it is in many respects the most important.

3.1 Tenancies post-dating the 1988 Act

Section 34(1), HA 1988 begins:

> A tenancy which is entered into on or after the commencement of this Act [15 January 1989] cannot be a protected tenancy, unless—

There then follows a list of qualifications to the general rule, detailing those tenancies which may be protected tenancies despite being entered into after the Housing Act came into force (it should be noted that protected shorthold tenancies are given special treatment in the transitional provisions: see further, para. 6.2.9 below):

(a) Tenancies 'entered into in pursuance of a contract made before the commencement of this Act' (HA 1988, s. 34(1)(a)). This provision was primarily intended to prevent landlords agreeing to let before the 1988 Act came into force, but delaying the execution of the lease until afterwards. It is of course essential that an enforceable contract be proved. However, the contract need not satisfy s. 2 of the Law of Property (Miscellaneous Provisions) Act 1989 (which does not apply anyway in relation to certain short leases: see s. 2(5)), as that provision has no application to contracts made before 28 September 1989. Reference should be made instead to s. 40 of the Law of Property Act 1925.

(b) A tenancy 'granted to a person (alone or jointly with others) who, immediately before the tenancy was granted was a protected or statutory tenant, and is so granted by the person who at that time was the landlord (or one of the joint landlords) under the protected or statutory tenancy' (HA 1988, s. 34(1)(b)). This provision is a similar, essential, anti-avoidance device. A landlord cannot by the simple expedient of offering a new tenancy to his existing Rent Act regulated tenant after the 1988 Act is in force claim that the new tenancy is no longer Rent Act regulated. An example of the operation of this provision is provided by the county court decision of *Kotecha* v *Rimington*, Legal Action, March 1991, p. 15. The tenant was granted a protected tenancy in 1984. The premises were sold, and, after the coming into force of the 1988 Act, the new landlord purported to grant an assured shorthold tenancy. Judge Appleby QC held, applying s. 34(1)(b), that the new tenancy was a Rent Act protected tenancy. The intention of Parliament in passing the 1988 Act 'was not to release [onto the market] property which was already protected, but to encourage landlords to release property not already let.'

If there is a period of time between the ending of the regulated tenancy and the commencement of the new tenancy, this provision will not apply, as the tenant must have been protected or statutory tenant 'immediately before' the grant of the new tenancy. But such a situation would be very difficult for the landlord to engineer: it would require the tenant to go out of occupation altogether, as otherwise on termination of the protected tenancy by whatever means the tenant will hold over as statutory tenant. Where the new tenancy is offered by a different landlord, the tenancy cannot be protected. It is not clear what the position would be if the old landlord assumed a new identity, for example where an individual landlord began trading as a company.

It is not clear from s. 34(1)(b) what the position is, where, subsequent to the 1988 Act coming into force, the landlord grants the protected or statutory tenant a tenancy of different accommodation. A county court decision, *Goringe* v *Twinsectra Ltd*, Legal Action, June 1994, p. 11, supports the view that the tenant will remain subject to the Rent Acts. This view has the advantage of depriving landlords of the incentive to move tenants around their properties to take them outside the protection of the Rent Acts.

(c) The tenancy 'is granted to a person (alone or jointly with others) in the following circumstances:

(i) prior to the grant of the tenancy, an order for possession of a dwelling-house was made against him (alone or jointly with others) on the court being satisfied as mentioned in s. 98(1)(a) of, or Case 1 in sch. 16 to, RA 1977 or Case 1 in sch. 4 to the Rent (Agriculture) Act 1976 (suitable alternative accommodation available); and

(ii) the tenancy is of the premises which constitute the suitable alternative accommodation as to which the court was so satisfied; and

(iii) in the proceedings for possession the court considered that, in the circumstances, the grant of an assured tenancy would not afford the required security and, accordingly, directed that the tenancy would be a protected tenancy' (HA 1988, s. 34(1)(c)).

This provision contemplates the court, after the coming into force of the 1988 Act, making an order for possession against a protected or statutory tenant on the basis that suitable alternative accommodation is available for the tenant (and that it considers it reasonable to make such an order) (RA 1977, s. 98(1)(a)). The tenancy of the alternative accommodation, being entered into on or after 15 January 1989, would normally be an assured tenancy. If, however, the court takes the view that an assured tenancy does not afford 'security reasonably equivalent to the security afforded' by the 1977 Act to protected tenants (other than protected tenants who have been served with written notices pursuant to Cases 11 to 20 of sch. 15 to the 1977 Act), then it has jurisdiction to order that the tenancy of the alternative accommodation is to be protected under the 1977 Act. If the court could not do this, it would not be able to make an order, as it is strongly arguable that assured tenancies do not as a matter of course confer 'equivalent security' to that enjoyed by such protected tenants.

(d) By s. 38 of the 1988 Act, on transfer of a tenancy from the public to the private sector on or after 15 January 1989, the tenancy may become an assured tenancy even though it was entered into before that date (see chapter 2, para. 3.1.1). It cannot in those circumstances become a protected tenancy. There is a saving in relation to transfers of reversions by new town corporations: see further HA 1988, s. 34(1)(d).

3.2 High value properties: s. 4

The provision excluding higher value dwellings from Rent Act protection has always been complex. A further layer of difficulty has been added by the abolition of the domestic rating system and the associated notion of 'rateable value' which necessitated the amendment of s. 4 of the 1977 Act by the References to Rating (Housing) Regulations 1990, SI 1990 No 434.

3.2.1 Tenancy entered into before 1 April 1990

If the tenancy was entered into before 1 April 1990 or (where the dwelling-house had a rateable value on 31 March 1990) pursuant to a contract made before 1 April 1990, the test is the rateable value on 'the appropriate day', i.e., the date when the rateable value of the hereditament which comprised the dwelling-house was first shown in the valuation list, unless that date was before 23 March 1965, in which case the appropriate day is 23 March 1965. The rateable value on the appropriate day must not exceed:

(a) (Class A) where the appropriate day is on or after 1 April 1973, £1,500 (if in Greater London) or £750 (if elsewhere);

(b) (Class B) where the appropriate day is on or after 22 March 1973 but before 1 April 1973, both £600 (if in Greater London) or £300 (elsewhere) on the appropriate day and £1,500 or £750 (respectively) on 1 April 1973.

(c) (Class C) where the appropriate day is before 22 March 1973, £400 or £200 on the appropriate day, and £600 or £300 on 22 March 1973, and £1,500 or £750 on 1 April 1973.

The burden of proof that a dwelling-house is excluded from the Rent Act by virtue of being contained in one of the above classes is on he who alleges it, in most cases the landlord.

3.2.2 Tenancy entered into on or after 1 April 1990

If the tenancy was entered into on or after 1 April 1990 (otherwise than, where the dwelling-house had a rateable value on 31 March 1990, in pursuance of a contract made before 1 April 1990), then the test is rent payable. If it is payable at a rate which exceeds £25,000 a year, then it cannot be a protected tenancy. For these purposes (but not for s. 5 below save in the case of a long tenancy) 'rent' does not include any sum payable by the tenant which is expressed to be payable in respect of rates, services, repairs, maintenance or insurance, unless it could not have been regarded by the parties as a sum so payable (RA 1977, s. 4(5)). Of course, the vast majority of tenancies entered into on or after 1 April 1990 will not be protected tenancies anyway owing to the Housing Act 1988, s. 34.

3.3 Tenancies at a low rent (or no rent): s. 5

There is no specific exclusion of long tenancies (i.e., tenancies exceeding 21 years) as such from the 1977 Act, but as most such tenancies of residential property are granted for a premium at a low ground rent, they are excluded by virtue of this exception. As with s. 4, the abolition of the domestic rating system has caused difficulties: see for amendments SI 1990 No 434. 'Rent' is not defined in the Act, but it has been held to include rent payable in kind if it has been quantified in money terms (*Barnes* v *Barratt* [1970] 2 QB 657; cf. *Bostock* v *Bryant* (1990) 22 HLR 449).

3.3.1 Tenancy entered into before 1 April 1990

If the tenancy is entered into before 1April 1990 or subsequently (where the dwelling-house had a rateable value on 31 March 1990) pursuant to a contract made before that date, the tenancy will not be protected if there is no rent payable, or the rent payable is less than two-thirds of the rateable value on 'the appropriate day' (for which see RA 1977, s. 25). If the appropriate day is before 22 March 1973, and the dwelling-house had on the appropriate day a rateable value exceeding £400 (in Greater London) or £200 (elsewhere) the tenancy will not be protected if on 22 March 1973 the rent payable was less than two-thirds of the rateable value.

3.3.2 Tenancy entered into on or after 1 April 1990

If the tenancy is entered into on or after 1 April 1990 other than, where the dwelling-house had a rateable value on 31 March 1990, in pursuance of a contract made before 1 April 1990 the tenancy will not be protected if under the tenancy no rent is payable or the rent is payable at a rate of £1,000 or less a year (if in Greater London) or £250 or less a year (if elsewhere).

The above tests are to be applied at the date the question falls to be determined. Thus, tenancies can move in and out of the Acts as rent levels rise and fall, as they could in previous years where rateable values were reassessed (see *J. & F. Stone Lighting and Radio Co. Ltd* v *Levitt* [1947] AC 209). Where the tenancy is a long tenancy (i.e., granted for a term certain exceeding 21 years which term is not terminable by notice to the tenant), sums expressed to be payable by the tenant in respect of rates, services, repairs, maintenance or insurance are to be disregarded in determining whether the tenancy is at a low rent and thereby excluded from protected status (RA 1977, s. 5(4), (5)).

3.4 Shared ownership leases: s. 5A

A lease which is a 'qualifying shared ownership lease' cannot be a protected tenancy. These include leases granted under Part V of the Housing Act 1985 ancillary to the tenant's right to buy (see further, chapter 7), and certain leases granted by housing associations at a prescribed premium for a term of at least 99 years (not terminable save in pursuance of a right of re-entry), whereby *inter alia* the tenant can obtain additional shares and/or acquire the landlord's interest on terms specified in the lease. This exception was introduced by the Housing and Planning Act 1986, s. 18 and sch. 4: see further, SI 1987 No 1939, SI 1987 No 1940. Shared ownership leases can no longer be granted under Part V of the Housing Act 1985 (with effect from 11 October 1993) (Leasehold Reform, Housing and Urban Development Act 1993, s. 107; SI 1993 No 2134).

3.5 Dwelling-houses let with other land: s. 6

A tenancy cannot be protected if the dwelling-house is let together with land other than the site of the dwelling-house. However, by s. 26 any land or premises let together with the dwelling-house shall, unless it consists of agricultural land exceeding 2 acres in extent, be treated as part of the dwelling-house. The question is whether the prime purpose of the letting is the land or the house. In *Feyereisel* v *Turnidge* [1952] 2 QB 29, a camp-site was held to be the main purpose of the letting, and the dwelling (a cottage) ancillary to the land: what is now s. 6 applied to exclude the tenancy from the Rent Acts.

3.6 Payments for board or attendance: s. 7

The Rent Acts have excluded tenancies with board or attendance for most of their existence: until 1974, furnished tenancies were similarly excluded. The relevant provision is s. 7 of the 1977 Act, whereby:

> (1) A tenancy is not a protected tenancy if under the tenancy the dwelling-house is bona fide let at a rent which includes payments in respect of board or attendance.

3.6.1 *Bona fide* let

It has been said (by Viscount Simon in *Palser* v *Grinling, Property Holding Co. Ltd* v *Mischeff* [1948] AC 291, 310) that *bona fide*:

> governs the whole of the words which follow. The words amount to a stipulation that the rent to be paid genuinely includes payments in respect of board [or] attendance . . .: the Act is not to be evaded . . . by a merely colourable use of words which do not correspond with what is really provided.

It is clear from *Palser* v *Grinling* that the court will examine closely what is provided by the landlord, and it is not enough that part of the rent is expressly apportioned to services which are not in fact rendered. Subject to this qualification, the court will look at the position at the commencement of the tenancy ('is let'), as it would be undesirable if subsequent minor fluctuations in the quantum of services provided resulted in a tenancy moving in and out of Rent Act protection. However, a fundamental change might affect the character of the letting and bring the premises within the Acts (see generally *Stagg* v *Brickett* [1951] 1 KB 648). Motive is not as such relevant. As long as the rent includes payments in respect of board or attendance, which service(s) are in fact provided, it is immaterial that the sole motive for their provision is to prevent the application of the Rent Acts to the premises.

3.6.2 Board

The ordinary meaning of 'board' is the provision of a meal. The leading authority is the decision of the House of Lords in *Otter* v *Norman* [1989] AC 129, where a landlord let a room to a tenant at a rent which included payment for the daily provision by the landlord of a continental breakfast served in a communal dining room. This was sufficient to take the tenancy out of protection, as there was no requirement in the Act (unlike where attendance is concerned: see below) that board be substantial. Subject to the *de minimis* rule (to use Lord Bridge's example at 146, the provision of an early morning cup of tea) any amount of board would suffice. The House of Lords endorsed the *obiter dicta* to this effect of the majority of the Court of Appeal in *Wilkes* v *Goodwin* [1923] 2 KB 86.

3.6.3 Attendance

'Attendance' is qualified by s. 7(2) of the 1977 Act:

> ... a dwelling-house shall not be taken to be *bona fide* let at a rent which includes payments in respect of attendance unless the amount of rent which is fairly attributable to attendance, having regard to the value of the attendance to the tenant, forms a substantial part of the whole rent.

The House of Lords subjected the meaning of 'attendance' to the closest scrutiny in *Palser* v *Grinling, Property Holding Co. Ltd* v *Mischeff*. Viscount Simon (at 310) gave a somewhat limited definition of 'attendance' as follows:

> It means service personal to the tenant performed by an attendant provided by the landlord in accordance with his covenant for the benefit or convenience of the individual tenant in his use or enjoyment of the

> demised premises. 'Service' is a wider word than attendance. Attendance, being personal in its nature, may be dispensed with by an individual tenant at his pleasure, though it is not on that account excluded from what the tenant pays for when the landlord has covenanted to supply it. But services common to others (e.g., the heating of a communal water supply, or the cleaning of passages, halls, etc., outside the demised premises) will not constitute attendance.

The first question to determine is whether the rent includes payments in respect of attendance. The court must then consider how substantial the attendance covenanted by the landlord is. In assessing (as required by s. 7(2)) the amount of the rent which is 'fairly attributable' to attendance, the value of that attendance to the actual tenant whose lease is under examination must be taken into account. This calls for 'the exercise of a broad judgment', any arithmetical conclusion being qualified by what is deemed to be fair and reasonable: see *per* Viscount Simon at 315. Finally, a comparison must be made with 'the whole rent' (i.e., the entire contractual rent payable by the tenant to his landlord): if the amount attributable to attendance forms a substantial part of the whole rent, the tenancy will not be protected:

> 'Substantial' in this connexion is not the same as 'not insubstantial', i.e., just enough to avoid the *de minimis* principle. One of the primary meanings of the word is equivalent to considerable, solid or big.
> (*per* Lord Simon in *Palser* v *Grinling* at 317).

Both of the consolidated appeals in *Palser* v *Grinling*, *Property Holding Co. Ltd* v *Mischeff* were decided in favour of the tenant. In the former, the only attendance provided within Viscount Simon's definition was the service of a porter in carrying coals up to the tenant's flat, and removing refuse therefrom, and the amount of the tenant's rent which could be fairly attributable to this attendance did not form a substantial part of the whole rent. In the latter appeal (which also concerned the provision of furniture), none of the services provided by the landlord came within the definition of attendance: they were either services rendered voluntarily by the porter, or else services under the landlord's covenant which did not involve personal attendance.

In *Nelson Developments Ltd* v *Taboada* (1992) 24 HLR 462, a landlord was more successful in arguing for the application of s. 7 in a case of attendance. The landlord covenanted to provide services in the form of daily room cleaning, full weekly laundry, refuse removal, and the provision of clean bed linen and towels. The tenant argued that washing the bed linen and towels could not constitute attendance, as it took place out of the house, and therefore lacked the 'personal' quality emphasised by Viscount Simon in *Palser* v *Grinling*. Nolan LJ, with whom the other judges in the Court of Appeal agreed, rejected this submission:

> ... the personal service, the personal attendance covenanted and performed by the landlords, was the taking away of dirty linen and the supply of clean linen. The washing operation in between was an essential part of the service.

The tenant also appealed on the basis that such attendance as was provided was not substantial enough to take the tenancy out of protection. The Court of Appeal examined the figures with care, reminded itself that arithmetic was not the determining factor, and upheld the decision below that the tenancy was not protected.

3.6.4 Provision of services may indicate licence

If the services provided by the landlord are so extensive that they require him or his agents to have unrestricted access to the occupied property, they may negate the grant of exclusive possession, in which case the occupier will not be a tenant at all, but a mere licensee (see, for example, *Marchant* v *Charters* [1977] 1 WLR 1181, at chapter 2, para. 2.1.4). Such a licence, if made before the coming into force of the Housing Act 1988 (15 January 1990), may however enjoy protection as a restricted contract (see further, para. 9 below).

3.7 Lettings to students: s. 8

This exclusion is identical in all respects to the assured tenancy exclusion contained in HA 1988, sch. 1, para. 8. Educational institutions which can benefit are listed in SI 1988 No 2236, as substantially amended by SI 1992 No 515. See the text at chapter 2, para. 3.8. Where a dwelling-house has at some time within the past 12 months been subject to a 'section 8 tenancy', the landlord may, if he lets for a term of years certain not exceeding 12 months and serves notice on the tenant that possession might be recovered under Case 14, claim possession as of right (see para. 6.2.5 below).

3.8 Holiday lettings: s. 9

This exclusion is identical to the assured tenancy exclusion in sch. 1, para. 9, to the 1988 Act, the text for which appears at chapter 2, para. 3.9. Where a dwelling-house has been occupied under a right to occupy it as a holiday at some time within the period of 12 months ending with the beginning of a tenancy for a term of years certain not exceeding eight months, that tenancy will carry a mandatory ground for possession for the landlord in so far as the landlord gave written notice to the tenant before then that possession might be recovered under Case 13 (see further, para. 6.2.4 below).

3.9 Certain agricultural tenancies

A tenancy is not a protected tenancy if the dwelling-house is comprised in an agricultural holding and is occupied by the person responsible for the control of the farming of the holding. This is identical to the assured tenancy exclusion in HA 1988, sch. 1, para. 7, on which see chapter 2, para. 3.7.

3.10 Licensed premises: s. 11

A tenancy is not a protected tenancy if the dwelling-house consists of or comprises premises licensed for the sale of intoxicating liquors for consumption on the premises. Neither can such a dwelling-house be the subject of a statutory tenancy. The likelihood is that as a result of the Landlord and Tenant (Licensed Premises) Act 1990 such a tenancy will be a business tenancy within Part II of the Landlord and Tenant Act 1954. See the similar assured tenancy exclusion contained in Housing Act 1988, sch. 1, para. 5 (chapter 2, para. 3.5).

3.11 Resident landlords: s. 12

A tenancy which falls within the 'resident landlord' exception contained in s. 12, RA 1977 is not a protected tenancy. This provision is very similar to, although not identical with, the resident landlord exception for assured tenancies contained in sch. 1, para. 10, HA 1988. Cross reference will be made to the relevant text in order to avoid unnecessary repetition.

In every case, the tenancy must have been granted on or after 14 August 1974 (on which date the Rent Act 1974, which created this exception, came into force). Three further conditions must be satisfied, and how they will be characterised will depend on whether the dwelling let to the tenant forms part of a 'purpose-built block of flats': see RA 1977, s. 12(1); sch. 2, para. 4, and chapter 2, para. 3.10.1.

3.11.1 Where the building is a purpose-built block of flats

(a) The dwelling-house let to the tenant forms part of one of the flats.

(b) The person who granted the tenancy must at the time of grant have occupied as his residence another dwelling-house which forms part of the same flat.

(c) Subject to various qualifications below, at all times each of the later landlords must have occupied as his residence another dwelling-house which formed part of the same flat.

3.11.2 Where the building is not a purpose-built block of flats

(a) The dwelling-house let to the tenant must form part only of the building.

(b) The person who granted the tenancy must at the time of grant have occupied another dwelling-house in the same building as his residence.

(c) Subject to various qualifications below, at all times each of the later landlords must have occupied as his residence another dwelling-house which formed part of the same building.

3.11.3 Part of the building (or flat)

See chapter 2, para. 3.10.3.

3.11.4 Joint landlords

Where the landlord's interest is held by more than one person at a particular time, the occupation of one landlord will be sufficient. The Court of Appeal resolved this issue, on which the 1977 Act is silent, in *Cooper* v *Tait* (1984) 15 HLR 113.

3.11.5 Occupation by the landlord

The landlord must occupy a dwelling-house in the same building or flat as the tenant's dwelling, and must do so *as his residence*. This test is the same as that to be satisfied where a tenant claims a statutory tenancy, and statute dictates that the same case law is to be applied (RA 1977, sch. 2, para. 5). The landlord does not have to show that the dwelling-house in question is his only or principal home, and thus it is possible for the landlord to occupy another property or properties elsewhere. In *Wolff* v *Waddington* (1989) 22 HLR 72, the landlord lived in the same building as the tenant throughout the relevant period (some 13 months) save for two short visits to the United States. She admitted in evidence that she regarded America as her home and intended to return there. The Court of Appeal held that she nevertheless continued to occupy the tenanted building as her residence. The question was one of fact and degree, and it was perfectly possible for her to be a resident landlord although her main home was in the States.

In *Jackson* v *Pekic* (1989) 22 HLR 9, the landlord's predecessor in title (her mother) had for a period of four years whilst the tenancy subsisted left some furniture in the first floor flat which she at other times lived in, but then let it, furnished, to another tenant. In those circumstances, the Court of Appeal could not accept that she had during that period both *animus possidendi* and *corpus possessionis*. Although furniture has been held to be capable of comprising the required corpus (or 'visible sign' of continued occupation (see, for example, *Gofor Investments Ltd* v *Roberts* (1975) 29 P & CR 366)), here there was nothing to show that it was other than such furniture as was required for a room to be let at a furnished rent. Moreover, the letting of the house or flat which the landlord is claiming to occupy will almost always prove fatal to the claim (see further *Lyons* v *Caffery* (1982) 5 HLR 63). In *Palmer* v *McNamara* (1990) 23 HLR 168, the landlord did not sleep in the room which he claimed to occupy as his residence so as to satisfy the resident landlord exception. On the unusual facts of the case (the landlord needed assistance in dressing and undressing, and accordingly slept at the house of a friend who could give that assistance, a mile or so away, but spent the rest of his time in the building occupied by his tenant), the Court of Appeal accepted that he did nevertheless satisfy the residence qualification.

3.11.6 Occupation throughout the tenancy: qualifications

Schedule 2, RA 1977 contains provisions qualifying the requirement that 'at all times' since the grant of the tenancy the person then owning the landlord's interest has occupied as his residence a dwelling which is part of the same building or flat which contains the tenant's dwelling. This requirement is in certain circumstances 'deemed to be fulfilled', and certain periods are disregarded. These provisions are very similar to those for assured tenancies contained in sch. 1 to the 1988 Act, and reference should be made to the text of the 1977 Act and to chapter 2, para. 3.10.4.2.

3.11.7 Re-grants

A landlord is not able to sidestep the residence qualifications by granting a new tenancy to his existing tenant. By s. 12(2), RA 1977, the resident landlord exception does not apply to a tenancy granted to a person who, immediately before it was granted, was a protected or statutory tenant of the dwelling-house, or of any other dwelling-house in the same building. Reference should be made to the commentary on the analogous provision in the 1988 Act chapter 2, para. 3.10.5.

3.11.8 Restricted contracts

By s. 20, RA 1977, if and so long as a tenancy is precluded from being a protected tenancy by virtue only of s. 12 of the 1977 Act, it shall be treated as a restricted contract notwithstanding that the rent may not include payment for the use of furniture or for services. Although s. 20 was 'repealed with savings' by the 1988 Act (sch. 18), the 'savings' are substantial. See further, para. 9 below.

3.12 Landlord's interest belonging to Crown: s. 13

A tenancy shall be neither protected nor statutory at any time when the interest of the landlord belongs to Her Majesty in right of the Crown, or a government department, or is held in trust for Her Majesty for the purposes of a government department, unless the interest in question is under the management of the Crown Estate Commissioners.

3.13 Landlord's interest belonging to local authority etc: s. 14

A tenancy shall be neither protected nor statutory at any time when the interest of the landlord belongs to any one of a number of public bodies: a county council, a district council, the Council of the Isles of Scilly, the Broads Authority, a London borough council, the Common Council of the City of London, a joint authority (within Part IV of the Local Government Act 1985), the Commission of the New Towns, a development corporation (under the New Towns Act 1981), the Development Board for Rural Wales, an urban development corporation (under Part XVI of the Local Government, Planning and Land Act 1980), or a housing action trust.

3.14 Landlord's interest belonging to housing association, etc.: s. 15

A tenancy shall be neither protected nor statutory at any time when the interest of the landlord belongs to a registered or co-operative housing association, the Housing Corporation, Housing for Wales, or a housing trust (defined in s. 15(5)) which is a charity.

3.15 Landlord's interest belonging to housing co-operative: s. 16

A tenancy will not be protected at any time when the landlord's interest belongs to a housing co-operative, and the dwelling-house is comprised in a housing co-operative agreement (see further, HA 1985, s. 27B, as amended by the Housing and Planning Act 1986, sch. 5, para. 15).

3.16 Assured tenancies: s. 16A

This provision, which excluded assured tenancies within the Housing Act 1980 (see chapter 2, para. 1.1) from Rent Act protection was repealed by the Housing Act 1988, as it became obsolete with the demise of the 1980 Act assured tenancy. The one small saving related to 1980 Act assured tenancies which were continued transitionally by s. 37(2) of the 1988 Act.

3.17 Business tenancies: s. 24

A tenancy cannot be a regulated tenancy if it is a tenancy to which Part II of the Landlord and Tenant Act 1954 applies (in other words it is a 'business tenancy'). This exclusion is identical to that contained in the Housing Act 1988, sch. 1, para.4. Reference should be made to chapter 2, para. 3.4, where the relevant case law is discussed.

4 STATUTORY TENANCY

4.1 Conditions to be fulfilled

By s. 2(1), RA 1977,

> Subject to this Part of this Act—
>
> (a) after the termination of a protected tenancy of a dwelling-house the person who, immediately before that termination, was the protected tenant of the dwelling-house shall, if and so long as he occupies the dwelling-house as his residence, be the statutory tenant of it. . .

It may be useful at this point to summarise briefly the relationship between the protected and the statutory tenancy. The statutory tenancy comes into being on termination of the protected tenancy. The two cannot co-exist; the one follows the other. The route to recovery of possession for the landlord of a Rent Act property is long and arduous. First, he must terminate the protected (contractual) tenancy (by notice to quit; by forfeiture; or on expiry of the fixed term). That done, the statutory tenancy will normally arise (provided the tenant satisfies the condition of occupation). The landlord must then go to court for an order for possession, which the court may only grant if he can prove a relevant ground for possession (see for detail, para. 6 below). The statutory tenancy will continue in existence until the tenant ceases to occupy, or the court executes an order for possession obtained by the landlord. A statutory tenancy cannot be terminated by means of the orthodox methods of tenancy termination.

The two stage process can be expedited. For example, if the protected tenant holds a fixed term which has not expired, the usual means of seeking possession where the tenant is in breach of covenant is to seek forfeiture of the protected tenancy, and use the same breach as the ground for possession (pursuant to Case 1, RA 1977; see para. 6.1.1 below). The protected tenancy may be forfeited by a statement to that effect in the particulars of claim, which pleading will go on to claim possession against the statutory tenant pursuant to the relevant Case.

4.1.1 Company lets

A company or other artificial person cannot become a statutory tenant, as it cannot occupy a dwelling as a residence (*Hillier* v *United Dairies Ltd* [1934] 1 KB 57). Some landlords have sought to use corporate tenants in order to prevent the operation of the Rent Acts, with considerable recent success: see further, chapter 2, para. 2.4.1, where company lets are discussed in connection with assured tenancies.

4.1.2 Occupation of the dwelling-house as his residence

By s. 2(3) of the 1977 Act, 'the phrase "if and so long as he occupies the dwelling-house as his residence" shall be construed as it was immediately before the commencement of this Act (that is to say, in accordance with s. 3(2) of the Rent Act 1968).' This formula has been accepted to impose the somewhat artificial judicial interpretation of this terminology which evolved following the decision of the Court of Appeal in *Skinner* v *Geary* [1931] 2 KB 546. At the time of *Skinner* v *Geary*, the relevant Act did not impose an express requirement of personal residence by the tenant, but the Court, applying considerable judicial imagination and ingenuity, imposed one itself.

4.1.3 Occupation a question of fact

There is a plethora of case law on the subject of the personal occupation required to perpetuate a statutory tenancy. Despite (or perhaps because of) this, the courts have time and again asserted that whether a particular tenant is in occupation is a question of fact and degree. The cases, many of which are outlined below, should not therefore be treated as more than useful examples of how courts have in the past defined occupation. The question being one of fact, the Court of Appeal will not reverse the decision of a first instance judge who has asked himself the right question unless his findings on the evidence are 'so unreasonable as to be perverse' (per Lawton LJ in *Gofor Investments Ltd* v *Roberts* (1975) 29 P & CR 366, 375.) It should not be thought that simply because a Court of Appeal has upheld the decision of a county court judge that a tenant is or is not in occupation the judges in the Court of Appeal would necessarily have come to the same conclusion themselves, or that a subsequent county court judge will do so.

4.1.4 Meaning of occupation as his residence

The leading authority is *Brown* v *Brash & Ambrose* [1948] 2 KB 247, the leading judgment that of Asquith LJ. He made the obvious point that no tenant can be expected to remain inside his house 24 hours a day, 365 days a year, in order to 'occupy' it. A tenant will inevitably leave the property, sometimes overnight, sometimes for weeks on end, on business, holiday, and so forth, and absences of this kind should not lead to a cessation of his occupation. However, where the absence is so prolonged or uninterrupted as to compel the *prima facie* inference that the tenant has ceased to occupy, he will then, in the event of a claim for possession being made, have the burden of proving that he had not ceased to occupy. To do this, he will have to show:

(a) that this property remains his residence; and
(b) that he intends to return to the property after his absence, having left some physical manifestation of that intention behind him. To use the everyday Latin, he must prove an *animus possidendi* and a *corpus possessionis*.

4.1.5 Intention to return

The intention to return need not be immediate, and it may even be conditional. In *Gofor Investments Ltd* v *Roberts*, the Court of Appeal upheld a decision of a judge who found *animus possidendi* where the tenant did not intend to return for eight to 10 years from the date of her departure (although two years from the date of the hearing). In *Tickner* v *Hearn* [1960] 1 WLR 1406, a tenant had been a patient in a mental home for over six years, and was very unlikely to leave hospital. The Court of Appeal considered that sufficient intention to return was proved, emphasising that there had to be 'a real hope [of return] coupled with the practical possibility of its fulfilment within a reasonable time.' In *Brickfield Properties Ltd* v *Hughes* (1987) 20 HLR 108, a tenant, now aged 74, was absent from a London flat from 1978 until 1987, excepting two brief visits. His children lived in the flat, whilst he lived in a cottage in Lancashire with his wife. The Court of Appeal upheld the decision of the judge that the tenant still occupied the London flat: he intended to return to London if his wife predeceased him, or if they found living alone too difficult, and this was enough.

On the other side of the line are the following decisions of the Court of Appeal. In *Duke* v *Porter* (1986) 19 HLR 1, the tenant left the cottage in 1975 to live with his children in a flat above his work place following the death of his wife. Although he visited the cottage frequently, and claimed that he intended to return to live there (and did in fact go back following the commencement of proceedings), he no longer occupied it as his residence. In *D. J. Crocker Securities (Portsmouth) Ltd* v *Johal* [1989] 2 EGLR 102, the tenant left the flat in 1977, returning to his native Malaysia where he established a thriving practice as a lawyer. On proceedings being commenced in 1985, the tenant claimed an intention to return to live in the London flat, but this was summarily rejected by the Court of Appeal: it was an 'abuse of language' to describe him as occupying the flat as his home. In *Robert Thackray's Estates* v *Kaye* (1988) 21 HLR 160, the tenant left her flat at the request of the landlord as he wished to carry out repairs. When she refused to return to the flat unless the landlord did further works, she was held to have thereby lost her statutory tenancy: her *animus revertendi* had been relinquished.

It is important that the tenant intends to live in the dwelling. It is not enough that he merely wishes to use it intermittently for storage purposes, or otherwise for his personal convenience (see, for example, *Regalian Securities Ltd* v *Scheuer* (1982) 47 P & CR 362, following *Beck* v *Scholz* [1953] 1 QB 570).

4.1.6 Visible sign of continued occupation

In *Brown* v *Brash*, the Court of Appeal stressed the importance of the tenant leaving some physical manifestation of his intention to return on the property, a *corpus possessionis*. The tenant was sentenced to two years' imprisonment for stealing tea. He intended at all times to return to the property when he was free to do so. For the first six months of his incarceration, his common law wife and children carried on living there. They comprised the necessary *corpus*, being 'some visible state of affairs in which the *animus possidendi* finds expression.' The mistress was in a sense a 'caretaker' (using the word in its widest sense), charged with the function of preserving the premises for the tenant's homecoming. When the family left the property, however, the tenant ceased in law to occupy, as there was no longer a 'symbol of continued occupation'. Later cases have been more generous to the tenant, holding that even the presence of furniture on the property may be enough to satisfy this element (*Gofor Investments Ltd* v *Roberts*; *Hoggett* v *Hoggett* (1980) 39 P & CR 121). Thus, the tacit departure of the caretaker, or even the removal of furniture by a third party (but presumably not the landlord), can deprive the tenant of his statutory status even though he does not know that this has occurred, and still intends to return to the property. The presence of furniture in the premises will not of itself be sufficient if the tenant is unable to show that it was indicative of his intention to return. Mere use of the premises for storage is not enough (see, for example, resident landlord case of *Jackson* v *Pekic* at 3.11.5 above).

4.1.7 When condition to be satisfied

In *Gofor Investments Ltd* v *Roberts* (1975) 29 P & CR 366, the Court of Appeal differed as to the date at which the residential qualification has to be assessed. Mackenna J, at 375, stated that the tenant's intention and other similar matters must be considered at the date when his right to continue as a statutory tenant is challenged. Cairns LJ (at 372) believed that if at any time between the ending of the contractual tenancy and the hearing the tenant ceased to occupy the dwelling as her residence, then she could not be a statutory tenant. The latter view accords more closely with the wording of the statute, which preserves a statutory tenancy *if and so long as* the tenant occupies the dwelling as his residence. It certainly cannot be the case that a tenant who is physically absent from the dwelling (and has in law ceased to occupy) can on receipt of the summons return to the property and claim that at the date of the hearing he is in occupation.

4.1.8 'Two-homes' tenants

It is quite possible for a statutory tenant to occupy more than one dwelling at once. He may own a property elsewhere, and still retain a statutory tenancy in the property which he rents. He may even have two (or more) contemporaneous statutory tenancies in two different dwellings. In the words of Lord Brandon in *Hampstead Way Investments Ltd* v *Lewis-Weare* [1985] 1 WLR 164, 168, 'there is no principle of law to prevent a person occupying two dwelling-houses as his residences at the same time, and being the statutory tenant of either or both.' Thus, in *Langford Property Co. Ltd* v *Tureman* [1949] 1 KB 29, it was acknowledged that a person could be statutory tenant of a London flat and a country house to which he resorted at weekends. In *Hampstead Way Investments Ltd* v *Lewis-Weare*, the tenant was a night club employee who used a flat of which he was tenant to sleep in after work. He was also the owner of a three bedroom house which he occupied with his wife and children. The House of Lords emphasised that it was simply a question of fact and degree whether the tenant occupied the flat as his residence: the limited use made of the flat by the tenant was not sufficient to make it his second home.

The Rent Act 1977 appears to be alone in offering protection to the 'two-homes' tenant in this way. The Housing Acts 1985 and 1988, governing secure and assured tenants respectively, adopt the formula of the Leasehold Reform Act 1967, requiring the property in question to be the *principal* home of the tenant. The policy of the more recent statutes has been to deny double statutory security to those with the privilege of two homes, and this certainly appears consistent with the overall objectives of such legislation.

4.1.9 Husband and wife

As has been explained in relation to assured tenancies above (chapter 2, para. 2.5.2), the Matrimonial Homes Act 1983 (MHA 1983) makes important qualifications to the requirement of occupation where a husband and wife are concerned. Similar principles apply with regard to statutory tenancies under the Rent Act 1977. Where the tenanted property is, or has at some time since the contract of tenancy been, the matrimonial home, and one spouse only is the protected or statutory tenant of the property, the other will have statutory rights of occupation (MHA 1983, s. 1(1)). These rights are treated, for the purposes of the Rent Act 1977, as occupation by the tenant spouse (MHA 1983, s. 1(6)), and a husband who leaves his wife occupying the property remains liable for the rent under the tenancy: he cannot effectively terminate his liability whilst she continues in occupation (*Griffiths* v *Renfree* (1989) 21 HLR 338).

If the parties have never been married at all, the 1983 Act cannot apply, and the deserted 'common law spouse' of a statutory tenant has no right to remain as against the landlord under the Rent Act 1977 (see *Colin Smith Music Ltd* v *Ridge* [1975] 1 WLR 463). If the parties have been married, but are no longer, the same applies. In *Metropolitan Properties Ltd* v *Cronan* (1982) 4 HLR 47, decree absolute was pronounced whilst the wife was occupying the dwelling. Her rights of occupation thereupon terminated, and the landlord could recover possession on the basis that the statutory tenant (her former husband) had ceased to occupy the property as a residence. The appropriate course of action for the wife in such circumstances is to apply in the ancillary relief proceedings for the tenancy to be transferred to her (MHA 1983, sch. 1)).

In *Hall* v *King* (1987) 19 HLR 440, a husband provided his estranged wife with a cottage rented from a landlord for her and their child to live in. At the termination of the contractual tenancy, the wife argued that a statutory tenancy under the Rent Acts arose in favour of her husband, her occupation being deemed to be his. The Court of Appeal rejected her contention. The cottage had never been the 'matrimonial home' of the parties, and accordingly the 1983 Act did not apply to it (MHA 1983, s. 1(10)).

The above principles do not apply where the spouses were joint tenants of the matrimonial home. In such a case, the tenancy will remain statutory as long as one of them occupies the dwelling as his or her residence: *Lloyd* v *Sadler* [1978] QB 774.

4.1.10 Bankruptcy

The Housing Act 1988, s. 117, made important amendments to the legal effect of the bankruptcy of a protected tenant. Whereas previously the tenancy would vest automatically in the tenant's trustee in bankruptcy (and would thereby deprive the now former tenant of the security of becoming statutory tenant on termination of the tenancy: *Smalley* v *Quarrier* [1975] 1 WLR 938; *Eyre* v *Hall* (1986) 18 HLR 509), this is no longer the case. The protected tenancy does not become part of the bankrupt's estate unless a notice to that effect is served on the bankrupt tenant by the trustee in bankruptcy (Insolvency Act 1986, s. 308A, added by HA 1988, s. 117). In the absence of such notice being served, the bankrupt will remain protected tenant, and, on termination of the tenancy, hold over as statutory tenant provided the usual conditions are satisfied.

As a statutory tenancy is not a proprietary interest, it cannot vest in the trustee in bankruptcy as part of the bankrupt's estate. A statutory tenancy will therefore continue unless and until the landlord can satisfy s. 98 of the Rent Act 1977 (see para. 5.4 below; *Sutton* v *Dorf* [1932] 2 KB 304).

4.2 Terms of the statutory tenancy

The statutory tenancy is, as its name suggests, the creature of statute. Its terms are those of the protected tenancy which precedes it, so far as they are consistent with the provisions of the RA 1977, s. 3(1). Thus, a term requiring the tenant to give up possession at the end of the contractual term, or on ceasing to be in the employment of the landlord, is clearly inconsistent with the security of tenure provisions and would be excluded from the statutory tenancy (see *Artizans Labourers & General Dwellings Co. Ltd* v *Whitaker* [1919] 2 KB 301; *R.M.R. Housing Society Ltd* v *Coombs* [1951] 1 KB 486). Terms inconsistent with the landlord's right to recover rent up to the permitted limit under the statute are likewise to be excluded (*Regional Properties Ltd* v *Oxley* [1945] AC 347). However, it has been held that an option to extend the term is not inconsistent with the provisions of the Act, and will therefore be carried forward into the statutory tenancy (*William McIlroy Ltd* v *Clements* (1923) 155 LTJo 362). Repairing obligations in the protected tenancy (e.g., those imposed on the landlord pursuant to Landlord and Tenant Act 1985, s. 11) will be carried forward into the statutory tenancy, as will the covenant to pay the rent, the landlord's covenant for quiet enjoyment, and any covenants restricting the use of the property.

The Rent Act implies two terms into statutory tenancies:

(1) That the statutory tenant shall afford to the landlord access to the dwelling-house and all reasonable facilities for executing therein any repairs which the landlord is entitled to execute (RA 1977, s. 3(2)).

(2) That the statutory tenant must give notice to quit as required under the original contract of tenancy, or, if no notice would have been so required, notice to quit of not less than three months (RA 1977, s. 3(3)). The notice must be in writing and comply with Protection from Eviction Act 1977, s. 5 (see chapter 8, para. 2.2).

The statutory tenancy confers a 'status of irremovability' (*Keeves* v *Dean* [1924] 1 KB 685, 686, *per* Lush LJ), but is not proprietary in effect. The statutory tenant has no interest in the property which he may assign *inter vivos* (*Keeves* v *Dean*) or by will (*Lovibond & Sons Ltd* v *Vincent* [1929] 1 KB 687). There is however limited assignment by virtue of the statute (RA 1977, sch. 1, paras. 13, 14), as well as statutory succession on death (see further, para. 8 below). A statutory tenant has no 'title' as such, and is vulnerable to an action by a mortgagee of the landlord seeking possession in order to realise his security (*Britannia Building Society* v *Earl* [1990] 1 WLR 422). However, a statutory tenant may apply for a vesting order following disclaimer of his landlord's leasehold interest by a liquidator, as 'interest' in Insolvency Act 1986, s. 181, is not confined to proprietary interests but includes any financial interest in the continuation of the landlord's lease (*Re Vedmay Ltd* (1993) 26 HLR 70).

As the statutory tenancy is dependant for its continued existence upon the tenant's occupation of the dwelling-house as his residence, a sub-letting of the whole will terminate it (*Roe* v *Russell* [1928] 2 KB 117). A sub-letting of part only will not, provided the statutory tenant continues to occupy the part retained as his residence (although it may give rise to a ground for possession if the sub-letting is in breach of covenant) (*Berkeley* v *Papadoyannis* [1954] 2 QB 149: see further on assignment and sub-letting, para. 7 below).

5 SECURITY OF TENURE

A landlord will only be able to recover possession of a dwelling-house let on a Rent Act regulated tenancy by obtaining a possession order from the court. However, if the occupier ceases to be a regulated tenant, the Rent Act will no longer apply, and recovery of possession will be much facilitated. As with assured tenants, regulated tenants are also vulnerable to the exercise of powers by public bodies.

5.1 Loss of status of occupier

One possible line of attack for the landlord who cannot prove Rent Act grounds is that by reason of a change in circumstances, the occupier is no longer within the protection of the Rent Act, as it only safeguards the position of those who are protected or statutory tenants at the time of the hearing. Thus, in *Foster* v *Robinson* [1951] 1 KB 149, the landlord let a cottage on periodic tenancy to a farm labourer. The tenancy was protected until 1946, when on the labourer's retirement the landlord allowed him to continue living there rent free for the rest of his life. When he died in 1950, the Court of Appeal held that his daughter could not succeed to a statutory tenancy. The arrangement in 1946 had effected a surrender by operation of law of the protected tenancy, and the occupier had thereupon become a licensee. A similar result occurred in *Scrimgeour* v *Waller* (1981) 257 EG 61, where on the plaintiff's purchase of the landlord's interest the protected tenancy was transformed into a rent-free service occupancy.

The more common means whereby a statutory tenancy ceases to exist is on the tenant ceasing to occupy the dwelling-house as his residence. The landlord may still have to obtain a possession order, in the event of some person (presumably not the former tenant) continuing to occupy (see Protection from Eviction Act 1977, s. 3; chapter 8, para. 3). Where a dwelling-house is destroyed, or so seriously damaged that it ceases to exist, any statutory tenancy will thereby terminate, as the tenant can no longer satisfy the condition of residential occupation (*Ellis & Sons Amalgamated Properties Ltd* v *Sisman* [1948] 1 KB 653; cf. *Morleys (Birmingham) Ltd* v *Slater* [1950] 1 KB 506). A protected tenancy does not terminate by reason of the tenant going out of occupation, as it is not a requisite condition of protected status.

In *Killick* v *Roberts* [1991] 1 WLR 1146, the plaintiff landlord granted a tenancy to the defendant in 1988, having been induced to do so by his fraudulent representation that he was having a house built which would be ready in three to four months. The Court of Appeal held that the landlord was entitled to have the protected tenancy rescinded. Although that tenancy had expired, and the tenant was therefore holding over as a statutory tenant by the time of the hearing, the statutory tenancy could not survive the rescission of the protected tenancy on which it was based, and the landlord was accordingly entitled to recover possession although no grounds for possession had been proved.

5.2 Recovery of possession by mortgagee

The Rent Act does not prevent a court granting possession to a mortgagee exercising its rights to possession as against the landlord. In *Dudley & District Building Society* v *Emerton* [1949] Ch 707, a mortgagee in exercise of its statutory power of sale sought to repossess the dwelling occupied by a protected tenant of the mortgagor, the tenancy having been granted without the mortgagee's knowledge, and in breach of an express provision in the mortgage deed. The Court of Appeal held that the predecessor of s. 98 (RA 1977; see para. 5.4 below) did not prevent the mortgagee obtaining an order for possession, as what it 'must be taken to contemplate is a proceeding for possession against the tenant by someone who may be fairly described . . . as a landlord.' An attempt to restrict this decision to proceedings against protected tenants failed in *Britannia Building Society* v *Earl* [1990] 1 WLR 422, where the Court of Appeal held that a mortgagee could recover possession against a statutory tenant without satisfying the requirements of s. 98.

Furthermore, as the statutory tenant did not derive title from the mortgagor (having no title but merely a statutory right to occupation), he could not invoke the jurisdiction of the court contained in the Administration of Justice Act 1970, s. 36, to adjourn proceedings for possession to enable sums due under the mortgage to be paid off.

5.3 Exercise of statutory powers

As outlined at chapter 2, para. 5.2, there are many powers conferred on local authorities to obtain possession of dwelling-houses in compliance with their statutory duties. In these cases, the Housing Act 1985 provides that the Rent Act will not prevent possession being obtained.

5.4 Landlord initiated recovery of possession

The Rent Act 1977 confers security of tenure on regulated tenants by restricting the circumstances in which an order for possession can be made. Section 98, RA 1977 is the centrepiece of the regulated tenant's security of tenure:

> (1) Subject to this Part of this Act, a court shall not make an order for possession of a dwelling-house which is for the time being let on a protected tenancy or subject to a statutory tenancy unless the court considers it reasonable to make such an order and either —
>
> (a) the court is satisfied that suitable alternative accommodation is available for the tenant or will be available for him when the order in question takes effect, or
>
> (b) the circumstances are as specified in any of the Cases in Part II of sch. 15 to this Act.
>
> (2) If, apart from subsection (1) above, the landlord would be entitled to recover possession of a dwelling-house which is for the time being let on or subject to a regulated tenancy, the court shall make an order for possession if the circumstances of the case are specified in any of the Cases in Part II of sch. 15.

From the earliest days of the Rent Acts, this provision, and its predecessors, have been given a strictly literal interpretation. If a tenant is regulated, the court has no jurisdiction to order possession against him unless section 98 is satisfied. In *Barton* v *Fincham* [1921] 2 KB 291, the plaintiff purchased the freehold of premises occupied by the defendant pursuant to a monthly protected tenancy. The defendant agreed in writing to give up possession for the sum of £20 at a future date. The plaintiff having paid this sum, and the date having passed, he sued the defendant for possession. The Court of Appeal refused to order possession, as the plaintiff had not proved a ground of possession or otherwise come within the statute. In the words of Lord Greene MR in *Brown* v *Draper* [1944] 1 KB 309, 313:

> A tenant remaining in possession cannot lawfully contract not to avail himself of the protection which the Acts give him, if and when the landlord takes proceedings against him to recover possession. If he wishes to place himself outside the protection of the Acts without putting the

> landlord to the necessity of taking proceedings, his proper course is to deliver up possession. Unless and until he does so, he is under the shelter of the Act, whether or not he so desires. No contract, and *a fortiori*, no mere statement of his wishes or intentions, can deprive him of the statutory protection.

In *Appleton* v *Aspin* [1988] 1 WLR 410, a protected tenant agreed in writing with a purchaser of the freehold (which was being sold by her daughter) that she would give vacant possession on completion, and then reneged upon the agreement. The Court of Appeal held that the plaintiff could only recover possession from her under s. 98 of the 1977 Act, and, as in *Barton* v *Fincham*, no Rent Act ground for possession had been proved.

5.5 Consent orders

As an agreement to give up possession is unenforceable, care must be taken when drawing up the terms of a court order on which the parties have agreed (see also, on secure tenancies, chapter 6, para. 5.2.4). The fact that the agreement to leave is embodied in an order of the court will not make it any more enforceable against a tenant who changes his mind. In *R* v *Bloomsbury & Marylebone County Court, ex parte Blackburne* (1985) EGLR 157, the landlords brought proceedings against a statutory tenant, arguing in the alternative that he had ceased to occupy the dwelling-house as his residence or that possession should be granted under Case 1, substantial rent arrears being outstanding. The action was settled at the doors of the court, the tenant agreeing to give up possession on payment by the landlords of £11,000 on or before a certain date. When the tenant reneged, and sought judicial review, Glidewell J quashed the order of the county court judge, on the basis that he lacked the necessary jurisdiction to make it. The fact of consent could not confer upon the court a jurisdiction it did not otherwise have.

A consent order can be rendered enforceable if the practice endorsed by Atkin LJ in *Barton* v *Fincham* at 299 is followed:

> If the parties before the court admit that one of the events have happened which give the court jurisdiction, and there is no reason to doubt the *bona fides* of the admission, the court is under no obligation to make further inquiry as to the question of fact.

More recently, McNeill J indicated in *R* v *Newcastle-upon-Tyne County Court, ex parte Thompson* (1988) 20 HLR 430:

> If it is desired to reach terms of agreement to be embodied in an order whereby possession of premises covered by section 98 of the Rent Act

1977 is to be given up, for the court to have jurisdiction to make an order there must be plain admissions of the qualifying conditions which must be fulfilled before such an order can be made. That is to say, a concession that it is reasonable for the order to be made, that whichever the case may be, suitable alternative accommodation is or will be available to the tenant, or that the relevant circumstances specified in the appropriate case exist, and where relevant, that it is accepted by the tenant that greater hardship would not be caused by granting the order than by refusing to grant it.

5.6 Termination of the tenancy

It is essential to establish whether the occupier is a protected or statutory tenant: in other words, whether he is holding under the contract with the landlord, or pursuant to his statutory rights. As we have seen, if the occupier is a protected ('contractual') tenant, the landlord must first terminate the contract, by whatever means are open to him (notice, forfeiture) before he brings possession proceedings, or, at the latest, in the course of those proceedings. There are no restrictions contained in the Rent Act 1977 on termination of the protected tenancy. It is important, though, that the landlord comply with any terms contained in the lease, and with the provisions of the Protection from Eviction Act 1977 (see further, chapter 8).

Once the occupier is a statutory tenant, there is no need for the landlord to give notice to quit prior to commencing proceedings for possession, or subsequent to an order for possession being granted (RA 1977, s. 3(4)). Nor is it necessary to serve any other notice on the tenant as a prelude to the commencement of proceedings. The statutory tenant is holding by force of the statute. His occupation is subject to the jurisdiction of the court.

The court has jurisdiction to order possession under s. 98, RA 1977:

(a) where the landlord establishes a 'discretionary ground' (Cases 1 to 10 in sch. 15) or 'suitable alternative accommodation', in either situation where the court considers it reasonable to make such an order;

(b) where the landlord establishes a 'mandatory ground' (Cases 11 to 20 in sch. 15), in which situation the court has no choice: it must order possession.

6 GROUNDS OF POSSESSION

6.1 Discretionary grounds (Cases 1 to 10)

Where a discretionary ground is proved, the court may order possession only if it considers it reasonable to make an order (see the words of Lord Greene

MR in *Cumming* v *Danson* quoted at chapter 2, para. 6.2.1). The burden of proof of the ground and of reasonableness is on the landlord. By s. 100 of the 1977 Act, the court is given discretion to adjourn proceedings, stay or suspend execution of any order which is made, or postpone the date of giving up possession, provided that it imposes conditions on the tenant (unless to do so would cause exceptional hardship or be otherwise unreasonable). As with the like powers relating to assured tenancies (contained in s. 9 of the 1988 Act: see chapter 2, para. 6.2.1), the court is encouraged to be flexible: to enforce the covenants, but also to allow the tenant to remain in possession if that is at all possible.

6.1.1 Case 1: rent unpaid or breach of obligation

Case 1 applies where any rent lawfully due from the tenant has not been paid, or any other obligation under the tenancy has been broken or not performed. If the claim is based on rent, the landlord must prove that some rent was in arrear at the date proceedings were initiated. The rent must be due from the tenant in possession, not a predecessor of his (*Tickner* v *Clifton* [1929] 1 KB 207). If the landlord has failed to notify the tenant of his address for service, or to state his name and address in a rent demand, rent is not due (Landlord and Tenant Act 1987, ss. 47, 48; *Hussain* v *Singh* [1993] 2 EGLR 70).

The tenant has the defence of tender. In *Bird* v *Hildage* [1948] 1 KB 91, the landlord commenced proceedings despite the tenant having tendered the amount due. Although the rent was late, the landlord could not establish Case 1. In any event, proof of small arrears, or trivial breaches of obligation, will be of little moment, as the court would be unlikely in such circumstances to order possession if there is a prospect of the arrears being satisfied in the reasonably foreseeable future. The court has a wide discretion, which it will readily exercise in relation to this Case, to make suspended orders conditional on payments being made (RA 1977, s. 100). Eager landlords may seek some solace from *Dellenty* v *Pellow* [1951] 2 KB 858, where, despite full satisfaction of the rent arrears by the time of trial, the Court of Appeal upheld the judge's order for possession on Case 1, as there had been a long history of default on the part of the tenant (see also *Lee-Steere* v *Jennings* (1986) 20 HLR 1).

In *Televantos* v *McCulloch* (1990) 23 HLR 412, the tenant failed to pay the rent as she was exercising her right of equitable set off which arose out of the landlord's breach of repairing covenant. Leaving the question open as to whether in such circumstances rent 'lawfully due' from the tenant had not been paid (and therefore Case 1 had been proved), the Court of Appeal held that in any event it was not reasonable to make an order for possession in such circumstances. It can certainly be argued by a tenant whose landlord is in breach of a covenant to repair that relatively insubstantial rent arrears (albeit exceeding the tenant's counter-claim or set-off) should not justify the court in holding that it is reasonable to make an order for possession.

Where the landlord proceeds on the basis of breach of obligation other than that to pay rent, it is not necessary for him to show that the tenant remained in default at the date proceedings were instigated. It is enough that there has at some time previously been a breach of an obligation under the tenancy (*Brown* v *Davies* [1958] 1 QB 117), although the presence of a continuing breach of covenant at the date of the hearing may make it easier for the landlord to leap the hurdle of judicial discretion. Case 1 only applies in relation to obligations of the tenancy which are consistent with Part VII of the 1977 Act: thus, rather obviously, breach of an express obligation in the tenancy to give up possession at the end of term cannot activate this Case (*Artizans Labourers and General Dwellings Co. Ltd* v *Whitaker* [1919] 2 KB 301).

6.1.2 Case 2: tenant misconduct or conviction

This Case is for most practical purposes identical to Ground 14 in the assured tenants' code of security, which is derived from it. See chapter 2, para. 6.2.7.

6.1.3 Case 3: deterioration of dwelling-house

This Case is very similar to Ground 13 in the assured tenants' code of security. See chapter 2, para. 6.2.6. The one small exception concerns deterioration of common parts, which is not covered by Case 3, but is by Ground 13.

6.1.4 Case 4: deterioration of furniture

This Case is virtually identical to Ground 15 in the assured tenants' code of security. See chapter 2, para. 6.2.8.

6.1.5 Case 5: tenant's notice to quit

> Where the tenant has given notice to quit and, in consequence of that notice, the landlord has contracted to sell or let the dwelling-house or has taken other steps as the result of which he would, in the opinion of the court, be seriously prejudiced if he could not obtain possession.

The mere giving of a notice to quit by the tenant will clearly not activate Case 5 (see, for example, the facts of *Appleton* v *Aspin* at para. 5.4 above). If, however, the landlord can establish that he has contracted to sell his reversion, or suffered some other serious prejudice, an order for possession may be made effective in an appropriate case against both the tenant and any sub-tenants (*Lord Hylton* v *Heal* [1921] 2 KB 438.)

6.1.6 Case 6: assignment or sub-letting of dwelling-house

The tenant has (at any time after certain dates) assigned or sub-let the whole of the dwelling-house or sub-let part of the dwelling-house the remainder being already sub-let. This Case is fully discussed below (see para. 7).

6.1.7 Case 7: repealed in 1980

6.1.8 Case 8: dwelling reasonably required as residence for landlord's employee

> Where the dwelling-house is reasonably required by the landlord for occupation as a residence for some person engaged in his whole-time employment, or in the whole-time employment of some tenant from him or with whom, conditional on housing being provided, a contract for such employment has been entered into, and the tenant was in the employment of the landlord or a former landlord, and the dwelling-house was let to him in consequence of that employment and he has ceased to be in that employment.

Case 8 is significantly different from Ground 16 in the 1988 Act, which it superficially resembles. It requires the landlord to prove not only the termination of the employment of the tenant, but also that he has a reasonable need for accommodation for his new or current employee. There are two hurdles of reasonableness to overcome: the reasonableness of the landlord's requirement, and the reasonableness of granting the order for possession against the tenant.

The first element to be proved is that the dwelling-house was let to the tenant *in consequence* of his employment by the landlord. It is assumed that the agreement is not a service occupancy (in which case it would not be a tenancy at all) (see chapter 2, para. 2.1). In *Read* v *Gordon* [1941] 1 KB 495, the Court of Appeal found that a new agreement had been entered into with an existing tenant following his employer's death, at which time the business had ceased to function. As at the date of the landlord's notice to quit, the relevant time for these purposes, the dwelling was not let to the tenant in consequence of his employment, and Case 8 was therefore inapplicable. However, the mere fact of termination of the tenant's employment, together with his continued occupation, will not lead to the implication of a new agreement as a matter of course (see Morton LJ in *Benninga (Mitcham) Ltd* v *Bjistra* [1946] 1 KB 58, 65.) Nor is it necessary for the landlord to show that the tenant knew that the dwelling was let to him in consequence of his employment. The court should look at the intention of the landlord only, and in *Braithwaite & Co. Ltd* v *Elliot* [1947] 1 KB 177, the Court of Appeal overturned the decision of the county court that a tenant who did not know his landlord's motive could not be the subject of a possession claim under Case 8.

The second element to be proved is that the dwelling is reasonably required for the occupation as a residence for another employee. This is to be judged at the date of the hearing (*Benninga (Mitcham) Ltd* v *Bijstra.*) By that date, the person who is to occupy must either be 'engaged in' the whole-time employment of the landlord (or tenant), or be a party to a contract of employment which is conditional on the housing being provided.

6.1.9 Case 9: reasonably required for occupation by landlord etc.

Case 9 is one of the most complex Rent Act grounds, and it has as a result generated a substantial body of case law. It reads:

> Where the dwelling-house is reasonably required by the landlord for occupation as a residence for —
>
> (a) himself, or
> (b) any son or daughter of his over 18 years of age, or
> (c) his father or mother, or
> (d) . . . the father or mother of his wife or husband,
>
> and the landlord did not become landlord by purchasing the dwelling-house or any interest therein after — [certain dates: in almost all cases now, 23 March 1965 will be the relevant one].

By Part III, para. 1, of sch. 15 to the 1977 Act, the court is further required to adjudicate on 'greater hardship', as follows:

> A court shall not make an order for possession of a dwelling-house by reason only that the circumstances of the case fall within Case 9 in Part I of this sch. if the court is satisfied that, having regard to all the circumstances of the case, including the question whether other accommodation is available for the landlord or the tenant, greater hardship would be caused by granting the order than by refusing to grant it.

6.1.9.1 Reasonably required for occupation by the landlord

In *Smith* v *Penny* [1947] 1 KB 230, the landlord required the house currently occupied by the tenant as a home for his minor children, who would live there with two friends of his who would act as housekeepers and child carers. The landlord would not personally occupy, as he was a publican who was required under his agreement with the brewery to reside on the licensed premises. The Court of Appeal held that he could nevertheless base a claim for possession on Case 9. Referring to what is now para. (b) above (see para. 6.1.9), Scott LJ said:

> It is quite impossible that the legislature could have put in that downward age of limitation, unless they had recognised the word 'himself' — the father, and husband — necessarily included the children and the mother and wife . . .

Smith v *Penny* was however distinguished in *Richter* v *Wilson* [1963] 2 QB 426, where an elderly landlord wished to place in the tenant's flat (which was in the same building as the landlord's residence) persons who could look after him. As they would be living in a separate household to the landlord, it could not be said that the landlord was intending to use the flat occupied by them as a residence for himself.

In *Patel* v *Patel* [1981] 1 WLR 1342, the plaintiffs let the dwelling-house as administrators of the estates of a deceased husband and wife. They were held to be 'landlords' within Case 9, and able to invoke the Case when they wished to occupy the house with the orphaned children of the deceased (whom they had legally adopted). It was not material that the plaintiffs had no beneficial interest in the property, as here, somewhat unusually, the circumstances allowed the personal representatives to occupy the trust property without breach of trust.

The court must evaluate the landlord's requirement at the date of the hearing (*Alexander* v *Mohamadzadeh* (1985) 18 HLR 90), although proof of a need for the accommodation in the 'ascertainable and not distant future' may suffice (*Kidder* v *Birch* (1982) 5 HLR 28).

6.1.9.2 Joint landlords

Serious difficulties have been encountered in relation to Case 9 where joint landlords are concerned. It was held in *Baker* v *Lewis* [1947] KB 186 that the Case was applicable where more than one person held the interest of the landlord, but the Court of Appeal did not have to decide the difficult issue (on which Case 9 is itself silent) as to whether it is necessary to activate the Case for both (or all) landlords to require to occupy, or whether it is enough for one to do so. In *McIntyre* v *Hardcastle* [1948] 2 KB 82, the Court of Appeal appeared to resolve this issue in favour of the former alternative, rejecting a claim for possession under Case 9 where one only of two joint landlords required to occupy the dwelling as his residence.

It would be unwise, even in the twilight of the Rent Acts, to regard the issue as definitively settled by *McIntyre* v *Hardcastle*. In 1979, in *Tilling* v *Whiteman* [1980] AC 1, the House of Lords had to consider the same issue in relation to what is now Case 11, and, whilst noting that the language and object of the two Cases were 'strikingly dissimilar' (*per* Lord Salmon at 22), their Lordships took the view that it was enough for one of two joint landlords to satisfy the necessary condition to activate that Case. An analogy can also be drawn with the principle that the continued occupation by one former protected tenant on termination of that contractual tenancy will suffice for a statutory tenancy to be upheld (*Lloyd* v *Sadler* [1978] QB 774).

In *Potsos & Potsos* v *Theodotou* (1991) 23 HLR 356, joint landlords, a married couple, claimed possession pursuant to Case 9, on the basis that the dwelling was reasonably required for the occupation as a residence of '(b) any son or daughter of his [sic] over 18 years of age.' The son in question was 22. Although he had lived with Mr Potsos since he was 18 months old, he was the child of Mrs Potsos' previous marriage, and was neither the adopted nor natural son of Mr Potsos. So, the tenant argued, applying *McIntyre* v *Hardcastle* to this part of Case 9, the landlords should fail in their claim, as any son for whom the dwelling was required had to be the son of both the joint landlords. The Court of Appeal rejected this argument, restricting the application of *McIntyre* v *Hardcastle* to part (a) of Case 9. Indeed, as Parker LJ forcefully stated, to read the plural into parts (c) and (d) would make no sense whatsoever of the situation. On the basis of *Potsos* v *Theodotou*, it is enough that the son or daughter who is to occupy the dwelling is the son or daughter of one of the joint landlords, and, applying the same reasoning to parts (c) and (d) (see para. 6.1.9, above), which one would hope will now follow, intended occupation by a parent, or parent-in-law, of one of the joint landlords should also suffice.

6.1.9.3 Landlords by purchase

Denning LJ summarised the mischief which these provisions were aimed at in *Littlechild* v *Holt* [1950] 1 KB 1 as follows:

> The intention of the legislature was that people should not be able to buy houses over the heads of the tenants and then turn them out without giving them alternative accommodation.

To a certain extent, the courts have taken something of a purposive approach in construing these provisions, and they have admitted that 'by purchase' is to be given its ordinary, rather than technical, 'conveyancing', meaning. Clearly, the purchase of property untenanted (or subject to a wholly different tenancy) prior to the letting in question is not caught by the provisions, even if that purchase was subsequent to the relevant date as listed in Case 9, for in such a situation the landlord did not become landlord *by purchase*, but by grant (*Epps* v *Rothnie* [1945] 1 KB 562). Almost as obviously, the disposition of the landlord's interest by will does not fall within these provisions (*Baker* v *Lewis* [1947] 1 KB 186), nor does an *inter vivos* transfer by way of gift. A conveyance of the landlord's interest in a flat to a child 'in consideration of mutual love and affection' was treated as equivalent to a gift in *Mansukhani* v *Sharkey* (1992) 24 HLR 600.

The tendency of the courts to look favourably on transfers of the reversion within a family context is exemplified by *Thomas* v *Fryer* [1970] 1 WLR 845. The tenanted house was bequeathed by a mother to her four children together with other items of property in equal shares. The children agreed between themselves that one of them should be allowed the house (and certain securities) on payment to her siblings of one third of its probate value. The Court of Appeal held that she was not a landlord by purchase, as the transaction would not be termed a purchase by 'an ordinary and reasonable person': it was a domestic arrangement between members of a family for the division of their mother's estate. However, the facts must be carefully analysed in each case. In *Amaddio* v *Dalton* (1991) 23 HLR 332, a testatrix expressed the wish in her will that her son should offer to sell the tenanted property to her gardener at market value. In the event of such an offer being made (it was), the purchase money was to be provided for the gardener out of the estate. Staughton LJ, distinguishing *Thomas* v *Fryer*, held that this transaction would be viewed by an ordinary and reasonable person as a purchase and sale, and the gardener was accordingly a landlord by purchase.

It would be particularly easy for a landlord, trapped by these provisions, to alienate the interest to a tame donee, that person (not apparently themselves a landlord by purchase) then seeking possession under Case 9. It appears that any such device would fail, however. In *Littlechild* v *Holt* [1950] 1 KB 1, a house was purchased in 1944 subject to a statutory tenancy. The owner died in 1948, and an action to recover possession was carried on by his widow, as administratrix of the estate and in her own right as universal legatee and devisee. The Court held that the widow could be in no better position than her husband: 'It certainly would be a very remarkable hiatus in the Act if she were' (*per* Lord Goddard CJ at 5). The rationale could be found in what is now s. 152 of the 1977 Act, where 'landlord' is defined as including 'any person deriving title under the original landlord'.

Another possible escape for landlords was discussed in *Wright* v *Walford* [1955] 1 QB 363. In 1952, the plaintiff who was now seeking possession purchased the freehold reversion of a house of which the defendant was tenant. He then negotiated a surrender of the defendant's lease, on the basis that a new tenancy would be granted of that part of the house which the defendant had previously been occupying. In 1954, the plaintiff brought proceedings pursuant to Case 9, in which the defendant contended that the plaintiff was a landlord by purchase. The Court of Appeal held that although the precise character and incidents of the landlord/tenant relationship had varied, nevertheless the landlord had become landlord of the rooms which the tenant now occupied by purchase of the reversion, and had so remained landlord ever since. Sir Raymond Evershed MR stated:

> It seems to me that if a person was in occupation of a dwelling-house when the reversion on his tenancy was acquired by another, and if he has never ceased to occupy that dwelling-house as the tenant of that other, then it would offend against the sense and intention of ... [Case 9] and of the plain words used, to say that because the precise relationship which governs the relationship of landlord and tenant has undergone a change, and a change made by agreement, therefore the tenant can no longer allege against the landlord that he is a landlord who has become landlord by purchasing the dwelling-house.

6.1.9.4 Greater hardship

The landlord has to prove that the requirement of the dwelling for his (or some other listed person's) residential occupation is reasonable. However, in the event of the other elements of the Case being satisfied, it is for the tenant to establish that greater hardship will be caused by granting the order for possession than by refusing it (*Piper* v *Hartley* [1958] 1 QB 439; *Manaton* v *Edwards* (1985) 18 HLR 116). The nature of the court's duty was outlined by Scott LJ in *Chandler* v *Strevett* [1947] 1 All ER 164, 165:

> ... it is to the balance of hardship that the judge is directed to turn his mind, and that means that he has to add up the items of hardship proved in evidence on each side of the statutory profit and loss account or balance sheet (for either metaphor will serve) and then see on which party the greater hardship falls. The second [aspect] is that the judge is called upon to operate the process by putting a hardship value on the various items on each side.

The court may take account of, *inter alia*, the financial resources of the parties (e.g., *Kelley* v *Goodwin* [1947] 1 All ER 810), the alternative accommodation available to each (e.g., *Chandler* v *Strevett*), and their physical, and mental, health (e.g., *Thomas* v *Fryer*). It should be noted, however, that the court must still consider that it is reasonable to make an order for possession, Case 9 being a discretionary ground only, and so although the tenant may fail to establish the greater hardship defence the making of an order for possession is not inevitable.

6.1.10 Case 10: excessive rent for sub-lettings

The court may order possession where the tenant is charging or has charged a sub-tenant of any part of the dwelling a rent which (if let as a protected or statutory tenancy) is in excess of the maximum rent for the time being recoverable for that part, or which (if the sub-tenant holds a restricted contract) is in excess of the maximum then lawful for the lessor to require or receive (see generally para. 11 below). This Case is not much utilised, and as most sub-tenancies which are entered into on or after 15 January 1989 will not be protected or statutory tenancies, or restricted contracts, the tenant will be free, in those circumstances, to impose whatever rent his sub-tenant will agree to pay. He will need to be cautious of giving the landlord the opportunity of claiming possession pursuant to Case 6 (or Case 1, if the sub-letting is in breach of covenant.)

6.2 The mandatory grounds: Cases 11 to 20

When the landlord satisfies the court that the circumstances are as specified in one of Cases 11 to 20, the court must order possession (RA 1977, s. 98(3)). It has a very limited power to postpone the date on which possession is to be given up: for 14 days, unless exceptional hardship would thereby be caused, in which case possession may be postponed for up to six weeks (Housing Act 1980, s. 89(1)). The wide power to adjourn which applies where the plaintiff is proceeding on a discretionary ground is not applicable where the circumstances are as specified in Cases 11 to 20 (RA 1977, s. 100(5)).

6.2.1 Notice in writing: the relevant date

Cases 11 to 20 have one other common feature: all require the landlord to have given a notice in writing to the tenant that possession might be recovered under the Case in question. This notice must have been given *not later than the relevant date*. In almost all cases, this date is the date of the commencement of the tenancy, but where the tenancy pre-dates 8 December 1965, or became regulated by reason of the Counter-Inflation Act 1973, or was previously a regulated furnished tenancy, a later date may apply (see further Rent Act 1977, sch. 15, Part III, para. 2). A failure to give the notice in time will be fatal in relation to most Cases, but Parliament has reserved to the court the power to dispense with service of notice where Cases 11, 12, 19 or 20 are concerned. The scope of this dispensation power has been examined by the courts in several decisions which are dealt with in chapter 2, para. 6.1.2.

There is no form prescribed for the written notice under any of these Cases. In *Fowler* v *Minchin* (1987) 19 HLR 224, Stephen Brown LJ said that any notice 'must state quite specifically that possession might be recovered under the provisions of the Act: that is to say, to make it clear that a situation would obtain which would be a compulsory situation as far as the tenant was concerned.' Thus, a term in the written tenancy agreement that the tenant would vacate on 28 days' notice if the landlord required it for another farm worker could not satisfy Case 16, as no reference whatsoever was made to the Case. In *Springfield Investments Ltd* v *Bell* (1990) 22 HLR 440, on the other hand, the service of a certificate of fair rent on the tenant by the landlord before the tenancy commenced, which certificate indicated that the letting was to be subject to the provisions of Case 16, was sufficient to satisfy the Case. It did not matter that the tenant did not read the certificate, or that the landlord did not draw her attention to this particular part of it. However, certain dicta of Staughton LJ (at 118) may assist a tenant in defending an action for possession. Accepting that the form of the notice must be reasonably sufficient to bring its function to the landlord's attention, His Lordship stated:

> A notice would be bad if it were in such small print as to be legible only by those with the sharpest eyes or the strongest spectacles. It would be bad if it were buried in the middle of some document on a quite different topic, or written in a foreign language which the tenant did not understand, or enclosed in an envelope which had the appearance of containing junk mail.

6.2.2 Case 11: owner-occupier

The person who let the dwelling-house ('the owner-occupier') must have occupied it as his residence at any time before (i.e., not necessarily immediately before) the letting, and three further elements must be satisfied. Two of these will relate back, probably to the time of the letting; the third must be satisfied at the date of the hearing.

6.2.2.1 Pre-conditions

First, no later than the relevant date, the landlord must have given notice in writing to the tenant that possession might be recovered under Case 11 (see above). Secondly, the dwelling-house must not have been let by the owner-occupier on a protected tenancy (since 8 December 1965, or other later dates) without having served a Case 11 notice. The court has power to dispense with either or both of these pre-conditions if it is just and equitable to make an order for possession of the dwelling-house.

The court must be satisfied that one of the following conditions is satisfied at the date of the hearing. They are printed as set out in Part V of sch. 15 to the 1977 Act:

> (a) the dwelling-house is required as a residence for the owner or any member of his family who resided with the owner when he last occupied the dwelling-house as a residence; . . .
>
> (c) the owner has died and the dwelling-house is required as a residence for a member of his family who was residing with him at the time of his death;
>
> (d) the owner has died and the dwelling-house is required by a successor in title as his residence or for the purpose of disposing of it with vacant possession;

(e) the dwelling-house is subject to a mortgage, made by deed and granted before the tenancy, and the mortgagee:

(i) is entitled to exercise a power of sale conferred on him by section 101 of the Law of Property Act 1925; and

(ii) requires the dwelling-house for the purpose of disposing of it with vacant possession in exercise of that power;

(f) the dwelling-house is not reasonably suitable to the needs of the owner, having regard to his place of work, and he requires it for the purpose of disposing of it with vacant possession and of using the proceeds of that disposal in acquiring, as his residence, a dwelling-house which is more suitable to those needs.

6.2.2.2 Occupation as residence prior to the letting

The test of occupation as a residence is the same as that which is applied to statutory tenants (para. 4.1 above), and to resident landlords (para. 3.11 above). A practical difficulty for the court may be in the evaluation of evidence concerning a possibly distant time in the past. There will certainly be little evidence available to the tenant in most cases. *Ibie* v *Trubshaw* (1990) 22 HLR 191 is an example of a case where the landlord failed at the first hurdle. He was a Nigerian businessman whose presence in the UK was intermittent, and who installed a female occupier ('a girl friend') in the property concerned. The county court judge held that the landlord had failed to prove that he had occupied the property himself as a residence, and the Court of Appeal upheld this decision as one of fact and degree.

6.2.2.3 Condition (a): dwelling-house required as a residence

Unlike Case 9, the landlord's requirement to occupy (etc.) need not be reasonable. Megaw LJ emphasised this in *Kennealy* v *Dunne* [1977] QB 837, 851:

> It is to my mind clear that the legislature has deliberately omitted the word 'reasonably' in Case [11], and has deliberately inserted it in Case [9]. It may well be that there are good reasons of policy within the general policy of the Rent Act . . . why that distinction should have been drawn. Whether that be so or not, the result of it, I have no doubt, is that in order to comply with . . . Case [11] what has to be proved by the person who had previously occupied the dwelling-house as his residence and now desires to occupy it again is that he desires to occupy it and that he intends so to do. I need scarcely say that the desire must be a genuine desire; the intention must be a genuine intention; but no more than that.

In *Naish* v *Curzon* (1984) 17 HLR 220, the landlord was a chartered surveyor who practised in South Africa. He wished to use the dwelling as his base in London, and intended to visit the UK once or twice each year, for periods of between two and six weeks. The Court of Appeal upheld the order for possession granted pursuant to Case 11: there was no requirement that the landlord's intended occupation need be permanent, or lacking intermittency, and the question was essentially one of fact and degree for the judge. *Davies* v *Peterson* (1988) 21 HLR 63 is a similar case, the landlord being a lawyer practising in Sierra Leone, who intended to visit the UK every year for between three weeks and three months. Not surprisingly, the Court of Appeal again upheld the judge's application of Case 11 to the circumstances. See also *Mistry* v *Isidore* (1990) 22 HLR 281.

6.2.2.4 Joint landlords

In *Tilling* v *Whiteman* [1980] AC 1, the House of Lords had to decide whether condition (a) was satisfied above where one of the two joint owner-occupiers who had served notice under Case 11 required the dwelling-house as a residence. Distinguishing *McIntyre* v *Hardcastle* (para. 6.1.9.2 above) on the basis that it concerned the differently framed Case 9, the House of Lords held that the condition was satisfied, and a possession order must be made.

6.2.3 Case 12: retiring landlord

Case 12 has close affinity to Case 11. The landlord ('the owner') must intend to occupy the dwelling as his residence at such time as he might retire from regular employment, and he must have let it on regulated tenancy before his retirement. The advantage of Case 12 over Case 11 to landlords who fell within its provisions was that there was no need for the owner to have occupied the dwelling at any time previously. The three further elements which must be satisfied (two 'pre-conditions' and one at the date of the hearing) echo those of Case 11.

6.2.3.1 Pre-conditions

No later than the relevant date (para. 6.2.1 above), the landlord must have given notice to the tenant that possession might be recovered under Case 12 (see above). The dwelling must not have been let by the owner on a protected tenancy since 14 August 1973 without having served a Case 12 notice. The court has power to dispense with either or both of these pre-conditions if it is just and equitable to make an order for possession of the dwelling-house.

The court must be satisfied at the date of the hearing that 'the owner has retired from regular employment and requires the dwelling-house as a residence', or that one of the conditions (c) to (f), as set out at para. 6.2.2.1 above, is satisfied, in either case at the date of the hearing.

6.2.4 Case 13: off season holiday accommodation

Case 13 applies where within the period of 12 months ending on the relevant date the dwelling-house was occupied under a right to occupy it for a holiday (itself presumably outside the Rent Act: see para. 3.8 above), and the landlord then let for a term of years certain not exceeding eight months having given written notice to the tenant that Case 13 was to apply. In both this Case and Case 14, a tenancy will be for a term of years certain although the landlord has reserved the right to determine by re-entry or on the happening of any event other than the giving of notice by the landlord to determine the term.

6.2.5 Case 14: vacation lets of student accommodation

Case 14 applies where within the period of 12 months ending on the relevant date, the dwelling-house was subject to a tenancy referred to in s. 8(1) of the 1977 Act (i.e., a letting to a student by a specified educational institution: see para. 3.7 above), and the tenancy was for a term of years certain not exceeding 12 months, the landlord having given written notice to the tenant that possession might be recovered under Case 14. 'Term of years certain' has the same definition as for Case 13. The court has no dispensation power in the event of a failure to give the requisite notice before the relevant date.

6.2.6 Case 15: residence of minister of religion

Case 15 applies where the dwelling-house is held for the purpose of being available for occupation by a minister of religion as a residence from which to perform the duties of his office. The court must be satisfied, as at the date of the hearing, that the dwelling is required for occupation by a minister of religion as such a residence, and written notice that Case 15 is applicable to the tenancy must have been given before the relevant date, there being no dispensation power vested in the court.

6.2.7 Case 16: persons employed in agriculture

Case 16 relates to persons employed in agriculture. If the dwelling was at any time occupied by a person under the terms of his employment as a person employed in agriculture, then a letting to a person who has not at any time been so employed (and is not the widow of a person so employed) by the landlord, then Case 16 will apply if not later than the relevant date the tenant was given written notice to that effect. The landlord would then be able to recover possession under Case 16 if the court was satisfied that the dwelling-house was required for occupation by a person employed, or to be employed, by the landlord in agriculture. The requirement of a written notice is mandatory (see *Fowler* v *Minchin* and *Springfield Investments Ltd* v *Bell* at 6.2.1 above as examples of the application of this Case).

6.2.8 Cases 17 and 18

These Cases are similarly limited to agricultural tenancies. Case 17 concerns the aftermath of proposals for amalgamations being carried out. Case 18 deals with the occupation of a dwelling-house which is part of an 'agricultural unit' (within the Agriculture Act 1947).

6.2.9 Case 19: protected shorthold tenancies

The form of letting known as the protected shorthold tenancy was created by the Housing Act 1980. It was intended to provide landlords with the opportunity to let houses and flats on terms which would enable them to recover possession expeditiously, without conferring a security of tenure on the tenant, but at the same time giving to the tenant the benefit of rent control. Part I, HA 1988 initiated the phasing out of protected shortholds, they being replaced by the assured shorthold, a means of letting which is more attractive still to the landlord. The effect is that the protected shorthold tenancy is becoming a very rare species.

The only circumstances in which a protected shorthold tenancy may be created on or after 15 January 1989 are where the parties made a contract to create such a tenancy prior to that date, and the tenancy was entered into afterwards. On expiry of the fixed term of a protected shorthold on or after 15 January 1989, the tenant will hold over (as statutory tenant), and be susceptible to a claim under Case 19. Whilst generally the grant of a new tenancy to a regulated tenant on or after 15 January 1989 will confer a protected tenancy on the tenant (see HA 1988, s. 34(1)(b)), this is not the case where the regulated tenancy was a protected shorthold tenancy. If the landlord grants a protected shorthold tenant (or a statutory tenant holding over following expiry of the protected shorthold fixed term) a new tenancy on or after 15 January 1989, that will be an assured shorthold tenancy (see chapter 2, para. 9.2.5) (HA 1988, ss. 34(2),(3)).

It remains important to be able to identify a protected shorthold tenancy, and to understand the requirements of Case 19.

6.2.9.1 Definition

A protected shorthold tenancy must have been granted on or after 28 November 1980 (the date the Housing Act 1980 came into force) for a term certain of not less than one year yet not more than five years. As explained above, in almost all cases, the protected shorthold must have been created before 15 January 1989. The term must not be terminable by the landlord except by re-entry or forfeiture for breach of obligation (interpreted widely in *Paterson* v *Aggio* (1987) 19 HLR 551 to include re-entry on the tenant's bankruptcy). The tenant must not have been, immediately before the grant, a protected or statutory tenant of the dwelling concerned. Before the grant, the landlord must have served notice on the tenant, in prescribed form (SI

1987 No 267), stating that the tenancy was to be a protected shorthold. The tenant has by statute the right to terminate the protected shorthold during the fixed term by giving notice: one month if the term is for two years or less; otherwise, three months.

The court may dispense with the requirement that the tenant be given the prescribed form of notice if it is of the opinion that it is just and equitable to make an order for possession of the dwelling-house (Housing Act 1980, s. 55(2)). In *R. J. Dunnell Property Investments Ltd* v *Thorpe* (1989) 21 HLR 559, the Court of Appeal emphasised the wide meaning of these words, and considered that they vested a similarly wide discretion in the county court judge, whose decision they accordingly refused to reverse.

6.2.9.2 Recovery of possession

The landlord must serve notice on the tenant stating that proceedings for possession under Case 19 may be brought after its expiry. The notice must expire not earlier than two months after it is served, nor (if the tenancy is a periodic tenancy) before the periodic tenancy could be brought to an end by a notice to quit served by the landlord on the same day. The timing of the notice is critical. It must be served in the period of three months immediately preceding the date on which the protected shorthold tenancy comes to an end (i.e., the initial fixed term expires), or, if that date has passed, in the period of three months immediately preceding any anniversary of that date. If the landlord has served a previous 'appopriate' notice, three months must elapse before another notice can be served.

Proceedings must be commenced within three months of the service of an 'appropriate notice'. In *Ridehalgh* v *Horsefield & Isherwood* (1992) 24 HLR 238, the landlord let on protected shorthold in 1985 for a 12-month fixed term. Subsequent fixed terms were granted, the final one expiring in October 1989. A valid Case 19 notice was then served, but the landlord failed to bring possession proceedings within three months of its expiry. This was fatal to the landlord's claim; the court had no power to waive non-compliance with this requirement, and the landlord would have to start again.

Although the tenant who holds over is not a protected shorthold tenant as such, as he will no longer satisfy s. 52(5) of the Housing Act 1980, Case 19 remains open to the landlord. In *Gent* v *de la Mare* (1988) 20 HLR 199, the Court of Appeal accepted that on expiry of the initial one-year fixed term the tenant ceased to be a protected shorthold tenant, but held that Case 19 applied nevertheless whether or not a new tenancy had been granted as the same tenant remained in possession of the dwelling-house.

6.2.10 Case 20

Case 20 provides a mandatory ground for possession for members of the armed forces who might wish to purchase a residential property with a view to occupying it in the future, perhaps (although this is not a requirement) when they return to civilian life. Case 20 is closely related to Cases 11 and 12.

6.2.10.1 Pre-conditions

At the time the landlord ('the owner') acquired the dwelling-house, and at the 'relevant date', he must have been a member of the regular armed forces of the Crown, as defined by s. 1 of the House of Commons Disqualification Act 1975. The letting in question must have been made on or after 28 November 1980. Subject to the power of the court to dispense with these requirements where it considers it just and equitable to order possession, (a) no later than the relevant date, the owner must have given written notice to the tenant that possession might be recovered pursuant to Case 20, and (b) no letting of the dwelling-house since 28 November 1980 may have been on a protected tenancy where such a notice was not served.

6.2.10.2 Conditions at date of hearing

The court must be satisfied that one of conditions (c) to (f) set out at para. 6.2.2.1 above is met, or that the dwelling-house is required as a residence for the owner. As with Case 11, there is no need for the owner to show that his requiring the house is reasonable.

6.3 Suitable alternative accommodation

Although not a separate Case, the court has jurisdiction to make an order for possession where it is satisfied that suitable alternative accommodation is available for the tenant or will be available for him when the order takes effect (RA 1977, s. 98(1)(a)). The court must consider that it is reasonable to make such an order, an issue which is independent of the suitability of the accommodation offered (*Battlespring Ltd* v *Gates* (1983) 11 HLR 6). RA 1977, sch. 15, Part IV goes on to define which accommodation will be considered suitable. The provisions are very similar to those contained in HA 1988, sch. 2, Part III, and the case law which has arisen from the Rent Act provisions is summarised at chapter 2, para. 6.2.2, to which reference should be made. However, the assumption underlying the Rent Act provisions is that the new accommodation will be on protected tenancy rather than assured tenancy. To effect this object, the court has a unique power to create a protected tenancy where it considers that the grant of an assured tenancy would not afford 'the required security' (HA 1988, s. 34(1)(c)) (i.e., security of tenure reasonably equivalent to the security enjoyed by a protected tenant: RA 1977, sch. 15, para. 4(1)).

7 ASSIGNMENT AND SUB-LETTING

7.1 Introduction

The Rent Act 1977, like the Housing Act 1988, confers a status of privilege on a tenancy, not on a particular property. The landlord may not himself have the freehold interest in the property occupied by the tenant, but the Rent Act 1977 is nevertheless capable of application. However, the interests of those superior to the landlord may need to be considered, and the position of the occupying tenant may in consequence be more precarious.

7.2 Assignment

It is essential to distinguish the grant of a sub-tenancy from the assignment of the leasehold interest. The substance of the arrangement, not its terminology, is determinative. If the leaseholder alienates his entire interest, then he will have effected an assignment even though the disposition is described as a sub-tenancy (see *Milmo* v *Carreras* [1946] KB 306; *Grosvenor Estates Belgravia* v *Cochran* (1991) 24 HLR 98). In other words, the tenant who retains a reversion will have granted a sub-tenancy; but if the land will never revert to him he will have assigned his interest. Thus, where A lets a dwelling-house to B for three years, and two years into the term B purports to sub-let to C for a term of five years, C will take by way of assignment rather than as a sub-tenant.

7.2.1 Protected tenancies

Assignment does not cause particular difficulties with regard to protected tenancies. The assignee steps into the shoes of the outgoing tenant, and holds directly from the landlord who granted the lease to the assignor. Although there are grounds for possession available where certain types of assignment have taken place, the landlord must first terminate the protected (contractual) tenancy. That protected tenancy is likely to be for a fixed term, and ready termination by notice may not be possible. If the assignment was in breach of a covenant in the lease, the landlord may be able to forfeit the lease (if he has reserved the right to do so), and claim possession under Case 1. If the assignment was not in breach of covenant, the landlord may be able to claim possession under Case 6 if the assignment occurred without his consent. However, this is a situation where he may not be able to terminate the existing protected tenancy expeditiously, as if the assignment was not in breach of covenant, it is unlikely that it will have activated a right of re-entry reserved in the lease.

Even if the assignment is in breach of covenant (and Case 1 is therefore available), the landlord will be unable to forfeit the lease if he has waived the breach of covenant. The landlord may waive by expressly consenting to the assignee's continued possession (see further, para. 7.3.6 below). Waiver may also be implied, where the landlord performs an unequivocal act indicating an intention that the lease should continue, e.g., by accepting (or even demanding) rent with respect to a time after the assignment (cf. rent arrears outstanding at the date of assignment) (*Matthews* v *Smallwood* [1910] Ch 786). Although the covenant in the lease may provide for assignment only with the landlord's consent, the Landlord and Tenant Act 1927, s. 19 implies a further term into such leases that the landlord shall not unreasonably withhold consent. An assignment which occurs in apparent breach of such a covenant, no consent being given, may accordingly prove to be lawful. Where the covenant is 'absolute', dictating that no assignment shall take place, the 1927 Act does not apparently apply (*Property & Bloodstock Ltd* v *Emerton* [1967] 3 All ER 321, 330, *per* Danckwerts LJ).

7.2.2 Statutory tenancies

Where the tenancy is statutory, the notion of assignment carries substantial difficulties. As the statutory tenancy only continues if and so long as the former protected tenant occupies the dwelling-house as his residence, a purported assignment which involves the parting with possession of the whole dwelling would appear to be invalid. In *Keeves* v *Dean* [1924] 1 KB 685, a statutory tenant purported to assign, and the landlord brought proceedings against the purported assignee on the grounds that he was a mere trespasser. The Court of Appeal upheld the possession order in favour of the landlord. Although the contractual tenant may have had a right to assign pursuant to the original lease, this was not a term or condition of 'the original contract of lease' such as to fall within s. 3(1) of the 1977 Act, but was a right incident to the tenant's estate. That estate was not enjoyed by the statutory tenant.

7.3 Sub-letting

If the tenancy enjoyed by the sub-tenant's immediate landlord is regulated under the Rent Act 1977 (i.e., protected or statutory), the position of the sub-tenant as against the head landlord will depend on the following factors.

7.3.1 Obligation to notify landlord

Where a protected or statutory tenant sub-lets any part of the dwelling-house on a protected tenancy, he must, within 14 days of the sub-letting, supply the landlord with a statement in writing of the sub-letting giving particulars of the occupancy including the rent charged, unless the sub-tenancy in essence replicates an earlier one. A failure to do so without reasonable excuse, or supplying a statement which is false in a material particular, is an offence (RA 1977, s. 139). Where the sub-tenancy is an assured tenancy (now much the more likely situation), s. 139 does not apply.

7.3.2 Sub-letting by protected tenant

The Rent Act regulated tenant has no statutory authority to grant a sub-lease. However, at common law, the leasehold interest, which the protected tenant by definition enjoys, can be disposed of and dealt with in so far as the lease does not provide otherwise. Although Case 6 of the 1977 Act gives a (discretionary) ground for possession where the tenant sub-lets the whole of the dwelling-house or sub-lets part, the remainder already being sub-let (see para. 7.3.8 below), this does not mean that such a sub-letting is unlawful in the absence of an covenant against sub-letting (*Leith Properties Ltd* v *Byrne* [1983] QB 433). Accordingly, if the lease does not expressly prohibit sub-letting, the protected tenant will be free to sub-let. If there is a prohibition, which may be absolute or qualified (no sub-letting 'without the landlord's consent'), a sub-letting may still be lawful if the landlord has consented to it, or waived the breach of covenant in question.

Where a protected tenant sub-lets on or after 15 January 1989, the sub-tenancy will (subject to the usual transitional savings: see chapter 2, para. 3.1) be an assured tenancy under the Housing Act 1988. It is quite possible, therefore, for a dwelling-house to have been let on a protected tenancy, and then sub-let on an assured tenancy.

7.3.3 Sub-letting by statutory tenant

By s. 3(1), RA 1977, the statutory tenant 'shall observe and be entitled to the benefit of all the terms and conditions of the original contract of tenancy, so far as they are consistent with the provisions of this Act.' Thus his power to sub-let will depend on the original lease, subject only to one important proviso, to which the final clause of the above provision alludes. As the statutory tenant retains his status only 'if and so long as he occupies the dwelling-house as his residence', a purported sub-letting of the *whole* property would appear to cause the statutory tenancy to determine. If this is correct, then a statutory tenant cannot ever grant an effective sub-tenancy of the whole of the demised premises. A sub-letting of the whole of the premises demised appears to be equated to an assignment. There is no authority directly on point, but statements to this effect in *Megarry on the Rent Acts* (10th ed., p. 455; see now 11th ed., p. 319) and *Woodfall* (28th ed., vol.3, para.3-0207) were cited with some approval in *Trustees of Henry Smith's Charity* v *Willson* [1983] QB 316, 325.

Even a sub-letting of part of the premises occupied by a statutory tenant carries with it certain intellectual difficulties, as the statutory tenant does not have anything other than a right to occupy to alienate: he has no estate, and it could be argued, on the basis of *Keeves* v *Dean* above, that the right to sub-let is no more a term or condition of 'the original contract of tenancy' than is the right to assign. However, in *Roe* v *Russell* [1928] 2 KB 117, the Court of Appeal decided otherwise. A statutory tenant of a house had purported to sub-let some rooms in the house, and the question arose as to whether the sub-letting (which was not prohibited in the terms of the contractual tenancy) was valid as against the landlord. The Court of Appeal, distinguishing *Keeves* v *Dean*, held that it was. Thus where the statutory tenant purports to sub-let part of the demised premises, the lawfulness will depend on the original contract of tenancy.

An interesting (and undecided) question is whether a statutory tenant who sub-lets on or after 15 January 1989 thereby creates an assured tenancy. There is no prohibition on new statutory tenancies (cf. protected tenancies) arising after the coming into force of the Housing Act 1988. On the other hand, this would appear to be a 'tenancy' capable of falling within Part I of the Housing Act 1988, and would on that analysis be assured.

7.3.4 Statutory intervention

The Rent Act provisions which protect sub-tenants are not noted for their clarity of expression. Central is s. 137(2):

> Where a statutorily protected tenancy of a dwelling-house is determined, either as a result of an order for possession or for any other reason, any sub-tenant to whom the dwelling-house or any part of it has been lawfully sub-let shall, subject to this Act, be deemed to become the tenant of the landlord on the same terms as if the tenant's statutorily protected tenancy has continued.

'Statutorily protected tenancy' means *inter alia* a protected or statutory tenancy (s. 137(4)). In essence, where the head lease terminates and the immediate landlord drops out of the picture, this provision puts the head landlord and the sub-tenant into a relationship of landlord and tenant. As we shall see, an order for possession against the immediate landlord will not be effective without more against the sub-tenant, and in those circumstances, the sub-tenant will step into the immediate landlord's shoes. Likewise if the tenancy terminates 'for any other reason', interpreted as including the death of the existing statutory tenant (*Lewis* v *Reeves* [1952] 1 KB 19), or the statutory tenant's cessation of occupation (*Standingford* v *Bruce* [1926] 1 KB 466). The sub-tenant will hold on whatever terms the immediate landlord did: he may thus become a protected or statutory tenant.

By s. 137(1):

> If a court makes an order for possession of a dwelling-house from—

(a) a protected or statutory tenant . . . and the order is made by virtue of section 98(1) . . . of this Act . . ., nothing in the order shall affect the right of any sub-tenant to whom the dwelling-house or any part of it has been lawfully sub-let before the commencement of the proceedings to retain possession by virtue of this Act, nor shall the order operate to give a right to possession against any such sub-tenant.

It is open to the landlord to bring possession proceedings against both immediate landlord and sub-tenant, or against the sub-tenant alone. As will be seen, grounds for possession which are based on actions of the immediate landlord may be used against the sub-tenant too, though he be innocent of any complicity as such (para. 7.3.8 below). If a possession order is made against both the landlord and the sub-tenant, then it will of course be effective to recover possession. Section 137(1) merely asserts that a possession order against the immediate landlord will not automatically confer the right to recover possession against the sub-tenant where the sub-lease in question was lawful.

7.3.5 Lawfully sub-let

The rights of the protected or statutory tenant to grant a sub-lease are considered fully above. In so far as the tenant had the right to sub-let, and the sub-tenancy is within the scope of that right, the sub-letting will be lawful. If the sub-letting is *prima facie* in breach of a covenant in the tenancy, there may however be the possibility of the landlord having subsequently waived the breach. If the sub-letting is unlawful, then the sub-tenant will be no more than a trespasser vis-à-vis the head landlord, and on the latter terminating the head lease, and recovering possession from the immediate landlord, he will be able to obtain vacant possession.

7.3.6 Waiver

As the lawfulness of the sub-letting is at the very core of protection for the sub-tenant against the head landlord, the question whether a breach of covenant against sub-letting has been waived by that landlord, and the sub-tenancy thereby rendered lawful, has been much litigated. The leading authority is *Oak Property Co. Ltd* v *Chapman* [1947] 1 KB 886. In 1942, a flat was let to a tenant who in due course became statutory tenant. The original lease contained a covenant against sub-letting the flat or any part of it without the landlord's consent, and a right of re-entry was reserved for the landlord in the event of breach. In 1945, the statutory tenant sub-let part of the flat to sub-tenant A; in 1946, the remainder to sub-tenant B. Sub-tenant A subsequently vacated, and the statutory tenant went back into occupation. The head landlords brought possession proceedings against the statutory tenant (who did not contest them) and sub-tenant B. Sub-tenant B argued that her sub-tenancy was rendered lawful by the landlords' waiver in accepting two payments of rent by the statutory tenant after the sub-lease to B had come to their knowledge.

The Court of Appeal circumvented the problem of the statutory tenant having sub-let the whole of the premises by determining that the date for deciding whether the sub-tenancy was lawful was the date of commencement of proceedings, by which time the statutory tenant was occupying once more. On the question of waiver, the Court held (at 899) that although the doctrine did not have the same application to statutory tenancies as to protected (contractual) ones:

> ... a landlord who has acquired full knowledge of a non-continuing breach of covenant by a statutory tenant entitling him to invoke the court's jurisdiction should be entitled thereafter to receive rent and should not, by reason of such receipt, be held to have waived the breach, provided that he makes clear to the tenant at the time of, or before, the receipt that his receipt is without prejudice to his right to go to the court, and provided that he issues his summons for possession within such time as, having regard to all the circumstances of the case, the court hearing the summons regards as reasonable.

In *Oak Property Co. Ltd* v *Chapman*, the landlords had not satisfied this proviso in accepting the rent payments, and as a result they had waived the breach. The sub-letting to B was lawful, and she could continue in possession against the head landlords.

In *Metropolitan Properties Co. Ltd* v *Cordery* (1979) 39 P & CR 10, the Court of Appeal considered the degree of knowledge of the breach which was required to effect a waiver. The sub-tenant had lived in the flat for three years without challenge, entering and leaving the building in the full view of the landlord's porters and dealing with them personally for 18 months concerning a persistent leak in her bathroom. When she notified the landlords formally of her occupancy, they immediately brought possession proceedings. The Court of Appeal held that the sub-letting, initially unlawful as being in breach of covenant, had been waived. The knowledge of the porters was to be treated, on ordinary principles of the law of agency, as that of their employers, the landlords.

7.3.7 Head lease not protected or statutory

By s. 137(3) of the 1977 Act:

> Where a dwelling-house—
>
> (a) forms part of premises which have been let as a whole on a superior tenancy but do not constitute a dwelling-house let on a statutorily protected tenancy; and

(b) is itself subject to a protected or statutory tenancy

then, from the coming to an end of the superior tenancy, this Act shall apply in relation to the dwelling-house as if, in lieu of the superior tenancy, there had been separate tenancies of the dwelling-house and of the remainder of the premises, for the like purposes as under the superior tenancy, and at rents equal to the just proportion of the rent under the superior tenancy.

In *Maunsell* v *Olins* [1975] AC 373, a 106 acre farm was let by the plaintiff to the immediate landlord, who in turn sub-let a cottage on the farm to the defendants. The tenancy of the farm came to an end following service of notice on the immediate landlord. The defendants claimed, however, that they were entitled to stay, and that by virtue of s. 137(3) they now held a tenancy of their cottage directly from the plaintiff. The House of Lords, by a 3:2 majority, confirmed the possession order which had been made, and in doing so interpreted s. 137(3), criticised as 'ambiguous' (Lord Reid at 382), restrictively.

In short, the majority decided that the farm which was the subject-matter of the head lease could not be described as 'premises' within the section, and accordingly the provision did not apply. Unfortunately, the majority of their Lordships did not make very clear what 'premises' did mean. They were relatively sure that Parliament wished to keep sacrosanct the distinction between residential tenancies and other kinds of tenancies, such as business and agricultural tenancies, to which other legislation was intended to apply. In this light, Lord Wilberforce opined (at 388):

So what should 'premises' be taken to mean? One view, the narrowest view, would be that it simply means 'dwelling-houses'. I find this, linguistically, a perfectly possible construction: the phrase, 'premises, not being such a dwelling-house' meaning premises being a dwelling-house but not a protected dwelling-house: the exclusion qualifies and colours the preceding generality. A less narrow view would be to say that 'premises' includes not only dwelling-houses in the normal popular sense, but premises which, for the purposes of the Rent Act, are treated as dwelling-houses. Everybody knows, and the draftsman must be taken to have known, that protection under the Rent Acts is given not merely to single, identifiable, pure dwelling-houses or dwelling units, but also to units of a mixed character — houses let with a garden or yard or a garage or a paddock, houses part (even a substantial part) of which is used for business purposes. This is, of course, an untidy situation and it means that no clear definition of a dwelling-house entitled to protection can be given... But it reflects the reality of life, and the county courts are used,

> and skilful, at solving what are inevitably questions of degree. We should recognise this and, as between the narrow and the less narrow meaning, I would apply to premises the latter which would include any premises which, as a matter of fact, applying accepted principles, would be held to be a dwelling-house for the purposes of the Act.

On its facts, *Maunsell* v *Olins* has been reversed by statute. Section 137(3) now contains a rider, inserted by the Agricultural Holdings Act 1986, s. 100, sch. 14, para. 60, that "premises' includes, if the sub-tenancy in question is a protected or statutory tenancy to which section 99 of this Act applies, an agricultural holding within the meaning of the Agricultural Holdings Act 1986.'

However, the reasoning of *Maunsell* v *Olins* still holds good in other situations. In *Pittalis* v *Grant* [1989] QB 605, the head lease was of a shop with a flat above. The flat was sub-let to the defendants who, following expiry of their term certain, held over as statutory tenants as against their immediate landlord. The head lease was surrendered in 1987, and the head landlords sought possession from the defendants. The Court of Appeal held, following *Maunsell* v *Olins*, that s. 137(3) could only apply if the property that was the subject matter of the head lease was a dwelling-house for the purposes of the 1977 Act. In this case, it clearly was not: indeed the lease of the shop and flat was a business tenancy within Part II of the Landlord and Tenant Act 1954. The Court of Appeal has subsequently followed *Pittalis* v *Grant* in *Bromley Park Garden Estates Ltd* v *George* (1991) 23 HLR 441.

Where the head lease is of a block of flats, or a building containing multiple units of occupation, that lease will not itself be subject to the Rent Act; but the sub-leases to the individual occupiers may be. One would have thought that this was precisely the situation where s. 137(3) would apply, so that on termination of the head lease the individual occupiers would hold directly from the head landlord. However, as a result of the narrow interpretation given to 'premises' in *Maunsell* v *Olins*, this can by no means be assumed, as the block of flats, or other building, is not as such 'a dwelling-house for the purposes of the 1977 Act.'

7.3.8 Recovery of possession from protected or statutory sub-tenant: Case 6

Where, as a result of the operation of s. 137, RA 1977, the head landlord is encumbered with the interest of a protected sub-tenant or the occupation of a statutory sub-tenant, the question of how possession can be recovered arises. Essentially, the position is no different from any other landlord/tenant relationship. However, there is one ground of possession which may be of particular assistance to the landlord: Case 6.

Case 6 applies where without the landlord's consent the tenant has (at any time after certain specified dates) assigned or sub-let the whole of the dwelling-house or sub-let part of the dwelling-house the remainder being already sub-let. There is no requirement that the assignment or sub-letting be in breach of an obligation of the tenancy (*Regional Properties Co. Ltd* v *Frankenschwerth* [1951] 1 KB 631), although a breach of s. 139 of the 1977 Act (para. 7.3.1 above) will usually have occurred. In *Leith Properties Ltd* v *Byrne* [1983] QB 433, a most important decision, the Court of Appeal held that this Case could be used not only against the tenant who assigned or sub-let, but also against the assignee or sub-tenant in question. In 1975, a flat was let to the tenant on a quarterly tenancy, which contained no covenant against sub-letting. This protected tenant then sub-let the flat to a sub-tenant without obtaining the landlord's consent. This was a 'lawful' sub-letting, s. 137 accordingly applied, and on termination of the head lease, the sub-tenant became tenant of the head landlord (s. 137(2)). However, as the sub-lease had been granted without the landlord's consent, possession could be sought under Case 6. Slade LJ stated (at 443):

> Subject to the court considering it reasonable, a landlord may, in our judgment, obtain an order for possession against a lawful sub-tenant or assignee in reliance on Case 6, even though *ex hypothesi* the sub-tenant or assignee will not himself have effected the relevant sub-letting or assignment. Any other construction of Case 6 would in our judgment render it more or less useless to any landlord.

It must be emphasised that Case 6 is a discretionary ground only, and that the court must consider the reasonableness issue in relation to tenant and sub-tenant separately. In *Leith Properties Ltd* v *Byrne*, the Court of Appeal remitted the case to the county court so that the individual circumstances of the sub-tenant could be fully appraised.

8 STATUTORY SUCCESSION TO REGULATED TENANCIES

8.1 Succession by statute

Since 1920, a feature of the Rent Acts has been the transmission of a protected or statutory tenancy on the death of an existing tenant. The circumstances when transmission could occur were initially very limited, but they have gradually expanded, and succession provisions now exist in relation to both assured tenancies (under the Housing Act 1988; chapter 2, para. 8) and secure tenancies (under the Housing Act 1985; chapter 6, para. 7) as well. A particular difficulty with which the courts have had to deal is the relationship between the statutory provisions and the general law of succession, whereby the tenant may have attempted to dispose of his tenancy by his will, or the rules of intestacy would otherwise dictate its destination. This will be discussed first.

A statutory tenancy, being nothing more than a 'status of irremovability', cannot be disposed of by will, and it will not fall into the estate of a deceased tenant (*Lovibond & Sons Ltd* v *Vincent* [1929] 1 KB 687). A protected tenancy, being an estate in land, can be disposed of by will (see Administration of Estates Act 1925, ss. 1(1), 3(1)).

The situation may arise where on death of the tenant, one person is bequeathed the tenancy under the tenant's will (or, in the event of the tenant's intestacy, by operation of the intestacy rules), whilst another person is *prima facie* entitled to succeed under the provisions contained in the Rent Act. In *Moodie* v *Hosegood* [1952] AC 61, the House of Lords considered this issue in relation to a tenant's widow who was in occupation. The tenant having died intestate, the landlord served notice on the Probate judge terminating the contractual tenancy, and argued that this entitled him to an order for possession from the court. The House of Lords, however, decided that the widow held as statutory tenant pursuant to the Rent Act, Lord Morton of Henryton stating:

> ... the widow of the tenant, whether contractual or 'statutory', who was residing with her husband at the date of his death is entitled to the protection given by the Acts. If a contractual tenancy is still subsisting at her husband's death, and devolves upon someone other than the widow, it is not destroyed, but the rights and obligations which would ordinarily devolve upon the successor in title of the contractual tenant are suspended, so long as the widow retains possession of the dwelling-house.

The termination of the contractual tenancy meant only that the landlord would, on the widow's statutory tenancy coming to an end, be entitled to recover possession. If the landlord did not (or could not) terminate the contractual tenancy, and it was still in being when the statutory tenancy came to an end, the contractual tenant would then be entitled to recover possession. According to Lord Morton of Henryton:

> If the contractual tenancy is a lease for years, it will remain in being, but so long as the widow remains in possession she, and not the contractual tenant, is bound to observe the terms and conditions of the lease and has the benefit thereof.

The wait of the contractual tenant may be a long one, longer indeed than was contemplated in *Moodie* v *Hosegood*, as there can now be two statutory successions. The contractual tenancy may itself devolve under the tenant's will or intestacy, and on the death of the (final) statutory successor, the person so entitled will at last gain possession.

Yet whilst *Moodie* v *Hosegood* appears to assert the pre-eminence of the statutory successor over the contractual tenant, a person who qualifies under both heads somewhat strangely takes under the contract rather than the statute. In *Whitmore* v *Lambert* [1955] 1 WLR 495 (in which *Moodie* v *Hosegood* was not cited) a contractual tenant died in 1922, by his will bequeathing his tenancy to his widow. She never took out a grant of probate, but continued to occupy the dwelling as before, paying the rent, for 30 years until her own death in 1953. The Court of Appeal had to decide whether she had in 1922 succeeded her husband and become a statutory tenant under the relevant Rent Act, in which case her daughter would not be able to succeed her in 1953, only one succession being then permitted by statute. After a lengthy review of the facts, the Court determined that she had taken as contractual tenant. It should not be thought that this will necessarily be the situation in all such cases, or that *Whitmore* v *Lambert* is authority for a principle that, where a person who occupies following the tenant's death is both the statutory successor and entitled to the contractual tenancy under the tenant's will or intestacy, they will be occupying pursuant to the contractual tenancy.

8.2 The statutory rules

The complexity of the statutory rules is considerable. They have been frequently amended, most recently by Part I of the Housing Act 1988, and it is essential to determine from the outset the date of death of the original tenant (or the first successor as the case may be), as the rules will differ significantly according to whether the death was before or after the coming into force of the 1988 Act. It should also be noted (although space does not permit further explanation in the text) that where the original tenant died before 28 November 1980, the rules are different still (e.g., a widow but not a widower had priority to succeed).

Although for convenience of exposition the original tenant has been taken to be male and the surviving spouse accordingly female, the provisions applying to deaths on or after 28 November 1980 (which are the ones we shall deal with here) are gender-neutral. The terminology of sch. 1, RA 1977 has given rise to a large body of case law, which will be considered following a statement of the basic statutory rules. Where a word or phrase is italicised in the following text, it will be further explained below.

8.2.1 The first succession

(a) Where the *original tenant* dies before 15 January 1989, he will be succeeded as statutory tenant by:

(i) his *surviving spouse*, if she was *residing in the dwelling-house* immediately before his death (para. 2), or, if this is not applicable,

(ii) a person who was a *member of the tenant's family* who was *residing with the tenant* at the time of and for the period of six months before the tenant's death (para. 3).

(b) Where the *original tenant* dies on or after 15 January 1989 he will be succeeded:

(i) as statutory tenant by his *surviving spouse*, if she was *residing in the dwelling-house* immediately before his death (para. 2, as amended by HA 1988, sch. 4, para. 2) or, if this is not applicable,

(ii) as *assured tenant by succession* by a person who was a *member of the tenant's family* who was *residing with him in the dwelling-house* at the time of and for a period of two years before the tenant's death (para. 3, as amended by HA 1988, sch. 4, para. 3).

8.2.2 The second succession

(c) Where the *first successor* dies before 15 January 1989, and was at the time of his death still a statutory tenant, he will be succeeded as statutory tenant by

(i) his *surviving spouse*, if she was *residing in the dwelling-house* immediately before the death of the first successor (para. 6); or, if this is not applicable, by

(ii) a person who was a *member of the first successor's family* who was *residing with him* at the time of and for a period of six months before his death (para. 7).

(d) Where the first successor dies on or after 15 January 1989, the original tenant having died before 15 January 1989, and the first successor remains statutory tenant at the time of his death, he will be succeeded *as assured tenant by succession* by any person who was *both*

(i) a *member of the original tenant's family* immediately before that tenant's death; and

(ii) a *member of the first successor's family* immediately before the first successor's death and was *residing in the dwelling-house* with the first successor at the time of, and for a period of two years immediately before, the first successor's death.

(e) Where the first successor dies on or after 15 January 1989, the original tenant having died on or after this date as well, then rule (d) will apply provided that the first successor was a *surviving spouse*. If this proviso is not satisfied, there will be no further succession.

8.3 Interpretation of terms

8.3.1 Original tenant

The 'original tenant' is the person who, immediately before his death, was a protected tenant of the dwelling-house or the statutory tenant of it by virtue of his previous protected tenancy (RA 1977, sch. 1, para. 1). If, however, following a statutory succession, the landlord makes a grant of a new tenancy to the successor, the successor will not become the 'original tenant' for the purposes of sch. 1 (RA 1977, sch. 1, para. 10).

8.3.2 First successor

The 'first successor' is the person who becomes statutory tenant under rules (a)(i), (a)(ii) or (b)(i) above. There can be no further succession from a person who takes as assured tenant by succession (under, for example, rule (b)(ii): see further, HA 1988, s. 17(1)(c), (2)(c)), and by denying him the title of 'first successor' there is no possibility of a second succession taking place.

8.3.3 Surviving spouse

The ordinary meaning of 'surviving spouse', which is to be applied in relation to rule (a)(i), is a person who was lawfully married to the original tenant at the time of his death. It is in fact the same phrase as is used in the context of the intestacy rules, and will include a spouse where a decree nisi of divorce, but not a decree absolute, has been pronounced. The ordinary meaning of 'surviving spouse' (excluding those have never been lawfully married but who live together as husband and wife) is also to be applied in relation to rule (c)(i).

The Housing Act 1988 gives an extended definition of 'surviving spouse', which applies to deaths on or after 15 January 1989. Thus, in the case of rule (b)(i), 'a person who was living with the original tenant as his or her wife or husband shall be treated as the spouse of the original tenant' (HA 1988, sch. 4, para. 2). The same extended definition is to be used when deciding, for the purposes of rule (e), whether the person who succeeded the original tenant under rule (b)(i) was a 'surviving spouse': in this case, the death of the original tenant was on or after 15 January 1989.

In determining whether a person qualifies by virtue of this extended definition, the court will look at whether they have been living together in the same household, whether their relationship was relatively settled, and whether they intended it to be permanent. These criteria were not fulfilled in *City of Westminster* v *Peart* (1991) 24 HLR 389, a decision on s. 113 HA 1985, during a short period of reconciliation between two persons who had been previously married to each other.

The parties to the relationship must be respectively male and female. In *Harrogate Borough Council* v *Simpson* (1984) 17 HLR 205, also concerning s. 113, the Court of Appeal refused to allow a woman to succeed to the secure tenancy of her lesbian lover with whom she had lived for some two and a half years. In the words of Watkins LJ (at 210), 'If Parliament had wished homosexual relationships to be brought into the realm of the lawfully recognised state of a living together of man and wife for the purpose of the relevant legislation, it would plainly have so stated in that legislation.' The same must be so for the purposes of the Rent Act 1977 as amended.

In the unlikely event of two persons qualifying as surviving spouse by virtue of this extended definition, only one may succeed as statutory tenant. The spouses may agree this themselves, and in the event of a failure to agree the county court will decide (HA 1988, sch. 4, para. 2(2)). For criteria, see para. 8.4 below.

8.3.4 Residence by successor

There are obvious differences in the periods of residence required of potential successors. The spouse has never had to show more than residence at the time of the tenant's death (although in the case of deaths prior to 28 November 1980, residence had to be 'with' the original tenant). Other family members have had to show six months, and the Housing Act 1988 increases this to two years, with certain transitional savings (see HA 1988, sch. 4, paras. 3(d) and 6). Other differences, the significance of which will be explained below, are as follows:

(a) Rule (a)(ii) does not expressly require residence to have been 'in the dwelling-house', whereas all other rules do.

(b) Save where the tenant died before 28 November 1980, the surviving spouse does not need to show residence 'with' the tenant or the successor as the case may be (rules (a)(i), (b)(i), (c)(i)), whereas other family members do (rules (a)(ii), (b)(ii), (c)(ii), (d), (e)).

8.3.5 Residence in the dwelling-house

It can now be stated with some degree of certainty that where the statute does not expressly require the potential successor to have resided with the tenant *in the dwelling-house*, no such implication will be made. In *Waltham Forest LBC* v *Thomas* [1992] 2 AC 198, the House of Lords held (in relation to succession to secure tenancies) that in the absence of clear words to such effect, s. 87 of the Housing Act 1985 could not be construed as requiring the successor to have resided with the tenant in the dwelling-house to which succession was claimed for the requisite statutory period. The successor had lived with the tenant (his brother) for two and a half years prior to the latter's death, but the local authority landlord claimed that no succession could occur in relation to the dwelling finally occupied by them, as they had only moved there 10 days before the secure tenant died. The House of Lords rejected this argument, overruling the earlier contrary authority of *South Northamptonshire District Council* v *Power* [1987] 1 WLR 1433.

There can be little doubt that *Waltham Forest LBC* v *Thomas* is applicable to the succession rules for Rent Act regulated tenants. Thus, where no express reference is made to residence in the dwelling-house in the above Rules (i.e., rules (a)(ii) and (c)(ii)) it will suffice for the successor to prove residence with the tenant or other predecessor in any property or properties for the requisite period. In all other cases, the requisite residence must have taken place in the dwelling-house to which succession is claimed.

8.3.6 Residing with

According to Sir Raymond Evershed MR in *Edmunds* v *Jones* (1952) [1957] 1 WLR 1118, 1120, these words must be given 'their ordinary popular significance':

> ... the person claiming to succeed to the tenancy of the particular premises must fairly and truly be said to have been residing with the predecessor in those premises in the sense that the successor lived and shared for living purposes the whole of the premises to which he or she claims to have succeeded.

8.3.6.1 Extent of the premises to be shared

The words of Sir Raymond Evershed should not be interpreted as requiring the whole premises to be used by the successor during the predecessor's lifetime. In *Collier* v *Stoneman* [1957] 1 WLR 1108, the Court of Appeal accepted that this would be impossible to satisfy in most cases, although Jenkins LJ's informed social comment that 'In almost every case (other than those concerning husband and wife) it would be found that the tenant and the claimant respectively occupied separate bedrooms' has not perhaps stood the test of time. Thus where a claimant exclusively occupied one room (with her husband and young child), and shared the kitchen of a three roomed flat with the statutory tenant, who was her grandmother, she could be said to be residing with her. *Edmunds* v *Jones* was distinguishable, as there the claimant had been sub-let part of the dwelling by her mother (albeit with the right to use the kitchen in common with her): she could say no more than that she shared the kitchen with her mother, as (*per* Evershed MR at 1120) 'She had no right to go in any other part of the house beyond the confines of her own tenancy.'

8.3.6.2 Intention of claimant

The claimant has to prove that he was residing with the predecessor for the requisite period. 'Residing with' the predecessor is not the same thing as 'living at' the predecessor's house. It connotes a common 'household', or a 'sharing', or a joint 'domestic establishment'. In *Morgan* v *Murch* [1970] 1 WLR 778, the claimant deserted his wife in November 1967, and went to live with his mother in her Rent Act-regulated house. She died in June 1968, and the claimant continued to live there. The Court of Appeal reversed the decision of the county court judge that he had not resided with her for the six months' period immediately before her death. It was not necessary for the claimant to prove an intention to reside permanently, nor that he had given up his previous home.

As with statutory tenants themselves, it is possible for a claimant to have more than one home, and successfully claim to be residing with the predecessor whilst living somewhere else as well, for 'a man may, in law, have more than one place in which he resides as well as more than one place in which he lives' (*per* Winn LJ in *Morgan* v *Murch*, not itself a 'two homes' case, at 782).

In *Hildebrand* v *Moon* (1989) 22 HLR 1, the claimant, who had a flat of her own, moved in with her mother over six months before the latter's death in 1986 in order to nurse her. She had contemplated selling her flat, but did not do so, and intended to remain in her mother's house for the foreseeable future. The Court of Appeal held that she was residing with her mother for the requisite time:

> There is ... no reason why the fact that the daughter returns to her mother's house to help nurse her should lead to the conclusion that the daughter does not from the moment of moving back thereafter reside with her mother. It would, of course, be entirely different if she came back, rather like a professional nurse, to do a job but with the intention of leaving as soon as the job was done.' (per Bingham LJ).

A similar case, which arrived at the opposite conclusion, is *Swanbrae Ltd* v *Elliott* (1986) 19 HLR 86. The claimant was tenant of her own home, where she lived with her 18-year-old son, two miles distant from the house of which her mother was statutory tenant. From September 1984, her mother having become ill with cancer, the claimant slept at the latter house three or four nights a week. Although she regarded this house as her home (it had been the family home, and she had lived there from the age of three until she moved away on her marriage), the Court of Appeal upheld the decision of the county court judge that she was not 'residing with' her mother, as she did not become a 'part of the household' there. It is a case where the existence of another home indicated that the claimant did not possess a genuine intention to reside with the predecessor.

8.3.6.3 Absent predecessor

In *Foreman* v *Beagley* [1969] 1 WLR 1387, the statutory tenant was in hospital for the last three years of her life. The claimant, her son, lived in the flat from October 1967 until his mother's death in June 1968. The Court of

Appeal rejected his claim to succeed to the statutory tenancy, as he had never been a member of his mother's household for the requisite period. However, it is not impossible for one person to 'reside with' another where they have never been in the dwelling at the same time. In *Hedgedale Ltd* v *Hards* (1990) 23 HLR 118, a young man (aged only 19) went to live in his grandmother's flat as his relationship with his mother and stepfather had broken down. The precise order of events was not clearly established by the judge at first instance, but the Court of Appeal proceeded on the basis that the claimant moved in whilst the grandmother was living at his mother's home, recuperating from the effects of an accident. Although she subsequently returned to the flat four months or so later, at Christmas 1987, and lived there until her death in May 1988, it was necessary for the claimant to show that he had been residing with her from an earlier date if the six months' qualifying period was to be met. This he satisfied, in being physically present in the premises during the earlier four-month period and intending to remain there as a member of the household when his grandmother returned. *Foreman* v *Beagley* was distinguishable on two grounds. First, in that case there was clear evidence that when the tenant returned the claimant was going to leave. Secondly, there was no intention that the claimant was to become part of the predecessor's household.

8.3.7 Member of the family

This term is not defined in the Rent Act (as it is in relation to succession to secure tenancies under the Housing Act 1985: see chapter 6, para. 7.1.1), and reference to a substantial body of case law is necessary. Much of the case law concerns the status of the person who was living with the tenant (or successor) as his wife or her husband at the time of the death, and perhaps for many years before: the so-called 'common law spouse'. Where the original tenant died on or after 15 January 1989, such person will now qualify to succeed, and indeed have priority, as a 'surviving spouse' (under rule (b)(i)), but otherwise will have to argue, on the basis of the case law, that they were a member of the tenant's family at the time of the death, and that they succeed by operation of rule (a)(ii). A similar claim will have to be made where a first successor died before 15 January 1989, as rule (c)(i) only applies to the lawfully married spouse; thus the 'common law' spouse will have to prove, in order to satisfy rule (c)(ii), that they were a member of the first successor's family at the time of the successor's death.

The authorities are at one in requiring the courts to interpret the statute in its ordinary, everyday, 'popular' meaning. 'Family' does not mean the same as 'household', and the claimant is required to *be* a member of the predecessor's family, not merely reside with the predecessor as a member of their family. Relationships of blood or marriage have therefore caused little difficulty. Numerous decisions can be found where spouses, siblings, children and grandchildren have successfully brought claims (see, respectively for example, *Salter* v *Lask* [1925] 1 KB 584, *Price* v *Gould* [1930] 46 TLR 411, *Morgan* v *Murch* [1970] 1 WLR 778, *Collier* v *Stoneman* [1957] 1 WLR 1108). There can be little doubt that adopted children, who are by s. 39 of the Adoption Act 1976 to be treated for all purposes as the children of their adoptive parents, will inevitably be members of the family of their adoptive parents. Beyond this, the authorities are less consistent, and less rational.

8.3.7.1 De facto familial relationships

In *Brock* v *Wollams* [1949] 2 KB 388, the claimant lived with the predecessor tenant from 1912 (when she was five or six) until his death in 1948, with the exception of three years at the beginning of the 1940s. She was the subject of a *de facto* adoption, being treated by the tenant as his daughter. (Legal adoption only became possible in 1926, by which time the claimant was nearly of majority.) The Court of Appeal had little difficulty holding that she was a member of the tenant's family.

The courts have, however, been reluctant to treat *de facto* relationships as giving rise to the necessary familial status where the parties to them are adult. In *Ross* v *Collins* [1964] 1 WLR 425, the claimant, who had been the predecessor's sub-tenant, on the death of his wife performed all the necessary household duties and nursed him in his old age. The relationship was platonic, and the parties did not hold themselves out as husband and wife. Russell LJ stated, at 432:

> Granted that 'family' is not limited to cases of a strict legal familial nexus, I cannot agree that it extends to a case such as this. It still requires, it seems to me, at least a broadly recognisable *de facto* familial nexus. This may be capable of being found and recognised as such by the ordinary man — where the link would be strictly familial had there been a marriage, or where the link is through adoption of a minor, *de iure* or *de facto*, or where the link is 'step-', or where the link is 'in-law' or by marriage. But two strangers cannot, it seems to me, ever establish artificially for the purposes of this section a familial nexus by acting as brothers or as sisters, even if they call each other such and consider their relationship to be tantamount to that.

This passage was endorsed by the House of Lords in *Carega Properties S.A. (formerly Joram Developments Ltd)* v *Sharratt* [1979] 1 WLR 928. The claimant lived with the predecessor (the widow of a High Court judge) from 1957 until her death, at the age of 94, in 1976. He was 51 years her junior. Their relationship was, in the words of Lord Diplock, 'platonic and filial', the claimant caring for the predecessor as a devoted child, although he referred to her as his 'aunt'. It was not enough for him to become a member of her family.

A similar conclusion was reached by the Court of Appeal in *Sefton Holdings Ltd* v *Cairns* (1987) 20 HLR 124. Although the claimant had lived in the house of which possession was sought since 1941, being treated by the predecessor's parents as their child (and therefore as the sister of the predecessor), she was not a member of the predecessor's family. In 1941, the claimant was 23, an adult, and the relationship with the predecessor's parents could not be characterised as a *de facto* adoption such as might have entitled her to claim (cf. *Brock* v *Wollams* [1949] 2 KB 388).

8.3.7.2 'Common law' spouses

In *Ross* v *Collins,* Russell LJ emphasised the platonic nature of the relationship between the claimant and the predecessor. It is now clear that in certain circumstances the courts will find that persons of the opposite sex who have been living together and involved in a sexual relationship have established the necessary familial nexus for succession to occur. The early cases made a distinction between 'common law' spouses whose union produced children (and thereby an easily identifiable family unit) and those who were childless. Thus in *Hawes* v *Evenden* [1953] 1 WLR 1169, the tenant's mistress, who had lived with him for some 12 years and given birth to two children by him, was held to be a member of his family, whereas in *Gammans* v *Ekins* [1950] 2 KB 328 a man who had lived for 20 years with the female tenant could not become a member of hers, as they did not have any children. This distinction is, however, no longer valid.

In *Dyson Holdings Ltd* v *Fox* [1976] 1 QB 503, the Court of Appeal, controversially taking the view that they could redefine 'family' in the light of changed social attitudes since 1949, rejected the reasoning of *Gammans* v *Ekins*, and allowed a claimant who had lived with the tenant of a house for 21 years as his wife, albeit not legally married to him, to succeed even though there were no children of their relationship. In deciding whether unmarried cohabitation gives rise to the familial nexus, the court is answering a question of fact, but useful assistance will be gleaned from, *inter alia*:

(a) the presence of children: children are no longer necessary, but they are still very useful, as they strongly suggest the existence of a family unit of which each parent will be presumed to be part.

(b) the length of the relationship: the longer the relationship, the better the chances for the claimant. Length will usually suggest permanence and stability, themselves strong indicators of the presence of a family.

(c) pretence of married status: it is not necessary, but again indicative of the parties' intentions, that they hold themselves out as being a married couple.

In *Helby* v *Rafferty* [1979] 1 WLR 13, the claimant lived with the (female) statutory tenant of a flat for five years prior to her death. They had no children. They shared expenses, and when the tenant fell ill, the claimant nursed her. The tenant did not use the claimant's name, and they did not hold themselves out as a married couple. The claimant was not a member of the tenant's family, and could not succeed.

In *Watson* v *Lucas* [1980] 1 WLR 1493, the claimant and the statutory tenant lived together for nearly 20 years. They had no children, and they did not use the same surname. Although the claimant remained married to another woman throughout this time, he was not thereby prevented from claiming to be a member of the statutory tenant's family, and the Court of Appeal upheld his claim to succeed.

In *Chios Property Investment Co. Ltd* v *Lopez* (1987) 20 HLR 120, the claimant moved into the tenant's flat in 1983, the parties intending to get married as soon as they could afford to. The tenant died in 1985, the cohabitation having lasted no more than two years. There were no children. The claimant was nevertheless held to be a member of the tenant's family.

8.4 Choosing between competing claimants

In certain circumstances, there may be more than one person within the same class who qualifies to succeed the given tenant. Only one may succeed: the tenancy is not transmissible to two or more successors jointly (*Dealex Properties Ltd* v *Brooks* [1966] 1 QB 542). The Rent Act 1977 invites the claimants to agree between themselves who is to succeed: in the event of their failing to agree, the county court is to decide. The Act itself gives no guidance on the principles on which the court is to act.

Somewhat surprisingly, there is only one reported decision of the Court of Appeal. In *Williams* v *Williams* [1970] 1 WLR 1531, the tenant died in 1969, leaving a widower and a son, aged 28, both of whom qualified under the then legislation as members of her family. (Under the 1977 Act as since amended, the surviving spouse would have the priority claim.) The Court of Appeal refused to overturn the county court's decision in favour of the widower, as it was the duty of the judge to balance the competing factors of merit and need. According to Lord Denning MR at 1533, 'From the point of view of *conduct*, the son was the more meritorious; but, from the point of view of *necessity*, the father was the more in need: and the need of the father outweighed the merits of the son.'

9 RESTRICTED CONTRACTS

9.1 Introduction

The restricted contract is a seriously endangered species, and no longer justifies extensive treatment. It formerly provided rent control and a diluted form of security of tenure for many who did not qualify as Rent Act protected tenants. The Housing Act 1980 (HA 1980) effectively removed the statutory system of security, and Part I of the Housing Act 1988 signalled the beginning of the end for the restricted contract. Those agreements which were restricted contracts as at 15 January 1989 continued to be restricted contracts for the time being, and contracts made before that date to enter into contracts on or after it (of which there cannot be many!) will have also given rise to restricted contracts. But as few of these contracts have any statutory security, the number of restricted contracts remaining must be small, and getting smaller. The regulated tenancy will inevitably outlast the restricted contract.

9.2 Definition

There are two kinds of restricted contract:

(a) A contract whereby one person grants to another, in consideration of a rent which includes payment for the use of furniture or for services, the right to occupy a dwelling as a residence, is potentially a restricted contract (RA 1977, s. 19(2)). As the contract must not create a regulated tenancy, the largest category of tenants who qualify are those excluded from protected status by virtue of making payments in respect of board or attendance (RA 1977, s. 7; para. 3.6 above). The occupier may be a licensee, provided that he is allowed to occupy at least one room as a residence to the exclusion of anyone else (*Luganda* v *Service Hotels Ltd* [1969] 2 Ch 209, 219).

(b) A tenancy which cannot be a protected tenancy owing to the application of the resident landlord exception (RA 1977, s. 20) and a tenancy which confers exclusive occupation of one room on a tenant, other accommodation being shared with the landlord (RA 1977, s. 21) (in either case notwithstanding that the rent does not include payments for the use of furniture or for services).

9.3 Exceptions

The 1977 Act makes various exceptions (such as higher value properties; regulated tenancies; agreements with public sector landlords or the Crown; shared ownership leases; and holiday lets). But the most important by far is contained in HA 1988, s. 36(1), which provides that a tenancy or other contract entered into on or after 15 January 1989 cannot be a restricted contract unless it is entered into in pursuance of a contract made before that date. Moreover, a restricted contract may cease to be a restricted contract if on or after that date the amount of the rent is varied (other than pursuant to RA 1977, ss. 78, 79) or the terms of the agreement are so substantially varied as to give rise to a new agreement altogether (HA 1988, s. 36(2), (3)).

9.4 Rent

The rent provisions concerning restricted contracts operate rather differently from those concerning regulated tenancies. Either party to the agreement may refer the contract to a rent assessment committee (termed a 'rent tribunal' in this context: HA 1980, s. 72(2)). The tribunal approves, increases, or reduces the rent to the amount it considers reasonable, and that amount is then registered (RA 1977, ss. 77, 78). A rent tribunal cannot be required to hear a reference within two years of a previous determination unless the parties make joint application, or there has been such change in circumstances as to make the rent registered no longer reasonable (RA 1977, s. 80). The owner can apply for cancellation of the registration once two years have elapsed provided that no restricted contract is in existence (RA 1977, s. 81A, added by HA 1980, s. 71). It is an offence to require, or receive, more than the registered rent, or to charge any premium (RA 1977, ss. 79, 81, 122).

9.5 Security of tenure

All depends on whether the restricted contract was made before or after the commencement of the Housing Act 1980, which removed security of tenure for agreements entered into thereafter (HA 1980, s. 69).

9.5.1 Restricted contracts made before 28 November 1980

A lessee is granted security on referring his restricted contract to the rent tribunal. If the lessor subsequently serves notice to quit on him, it will not take effect until six months after the decision of the tribunal (or such shorter period as it may substitute) (RA 1977, s. 103). The rent tribunal also has jurisdiction to extend the operation of a notice to quit served by a lessor for a period of up to six months on application by the lessee, and it is possible for the lessee to make successive applications frustrating the lessor's attempts to recover possession (RA 1977, s. 104). However, misconduct by the lessee empowers the tribunal to reduce the period of postponement (RA 1977, s. 106), and there is specific provision made for recovery of possession by owner-occupiers (RA 1977, s. 105).

9.5.2 Restricted contract made on or after 28 November 1980

The provisions of RA 1977, ss. 102 to 106, do not apply where the restricted contract was made on or after 28 November 1980 (RA 1977, s. 102A, added by HA 1980, s. 69(3)). The court, on making a possession order in relation to a dwelling-house which is the subject of a restricted contract, may stay or suspend execution, or postpone the date of possession, for such period(s) as it thinks fit, although the delivery up of possession must not be postponed for more than three months from the date of the order, and conditions must be imposed on the tenant unless the court considers that to do so would cause exceptional hardship or be otherwise unreasonable (see generally RA 1977, s. 106A, added by HA 1980, s. 69(2)).

10 HOUSING ASSOCIATION TENANCIES

10.1 Introduction

As we have seen, tenancies granted on or after 15 January 1989 by housing associations (other than fully mutual housing associations) will be capable of being assured tenancies (and normally will be). Part VI of the Rent Act 1977, which provided rent control for certain tenants of housing associations, continues to have some residuary effect, such as to justify an outline here.

10.2 Definition

A tenancy entered into before 15 January 1989 will be a 'housing association tenancy' if the landlord's interest belongs to a housing association, a housing trust, or the Housing Corporation, and the tenancy would be a protected tenancy but for ss. 15 and 16, RA 1977 (which excludes tenancies from protection where the landlord is a registered housing association, a co-operative housing association, the Housing Corporation, Housing for Wales, a charitable housing trust or a housing co-operative) (RA 1977, s. 86). Business tenancies cannot be 'housing association tenancies', nor can 'co-ownership tenancies' (see further, RA 1977, s. 86(2),(3A)).

A tenancy entered into on or after 15 January 1989 may be a housing association tenancy if (HA 1988, s. 35(2)):

(a) it is entered into pursuant to a contract made before that date;

(b) it is granted to a person (alone or jointly with others) who, immediately before the tenancy was granted, was a tenant under a housing association tenancy, the landlord being the same;

(c) prior to the tenancy being granted, the court had made an order for possession against a secure tenant based on the availability of suitable alternative accommodation (i.e., HA 1985, Grounds 9 to 16; see chapter 6, paras. 6.2 and 6.3), the tenancy is of the accommodation in question, and the court declared that the tenancy was to be a housing association tenancy;

(d) the tenancy was granted by a new town corporation, which subsequently (but before 15 November 1990) disposed of its interest (pursuant to New Towns Act 1981, s. 37) to the housing association.

On transfer of the reversion to a body which is not a housing association, a housing trust or the Housing Corporation, the tenancy will no longer be a 'housing association tenancy'. By HA 1988, s. 38, a 'housing association tenancy' entered into before 15 January 1989 which ceases to be so on the transfer of the landlord's reversion subsequent to that date cannot thereby become a protected tenancy. It may become an assured tenancy, as the exclusion of tenancies pre-dating the coming into force of the 1988 Act is here disapplied (see chapter 2, para. 3.1.1).

10.3 Effect

Where a tenancy is a housing association tenancy, the rent may be registered (in a separate part of the register) (RA 1977, s. 87). In such a case, the registered rent is the 'rent limit' (RA 1977, s. 88(2)). Where no registration of the rent has occurred, the 'rent limit' is calculated with reference to the rent agreed between the parties to the tenancy (see, for further details, RA 1977, s. 88(4)). If the rent payable under the tenancy exceeds the rent limit as so determined, the amount of the excess will be irrecoverable from the tenant (RA 1977, s. 88(1)). For means whereby the tenant may recover sums paid in excess of the rent limit, see RA 1977, s. 94.

11 RENT CONTROL

11.1 Introduction

The emphasis of this book is on the various systems of security of tenure prevailing in relation to residential leases. However, as the Rent Acts were introduced in order to impose rent control, security of tenure merely being a necessary corollary, and as the main advantage to tenants of regulated tenancies over assured tenancies is thought to be the applicability of the fair rent provisions, an outline of their effect is offered by way of explanation.

11.2 Registration of rent

Where a tenancy is regulated under the Rent Acts, either party (or both, making joint application) may apply to a rent officer for registration of the rent (RA 1977, s. 67). The rent officer registers the 'fair rent', which, subject to the following text and the possibility of further reference to a rent assessment committee, binds not only the parties but also future tenancies of the dwelling-house in question (RA 1977, ss. 45, 46). The rent officer keeps a register of rents for his registration area, which forms itself an invaluable source of comparable fair rents for future use (RA 1977, s. 66). We will consider the meaning of 'fair rent' shortly. First, the way in which the rent registered affects the regulated tenancy will be dealt with.

If the rent officer registers a rent which is *lower* than the rent currently paid under a protected or statutory tenancy (the 'contractual' or 'existing' rent, as the case may be), then from the date of entry of the rent upon the register the amount by which the current rent exceeds the registered rent is 'irrecoverable' from the tenant (RA 1977, ss. 44(2), 45(2)(a)). It is not a criminal offence for the landlord to obtain more from the tenant. But the landlord cannot sue for the excess, and the tenant may take proceedings (in the county court) for its return from the landlord, or may set off the amount overpaid from future payments of rent (RA 1977, s. 57).

If the rent officer registers a rent which is *higher* than the rent currently paid, the landlord may increase the rent to the amount registered provided that he is contractually entitled to do so, and that he follows the procedure laid down in the 1977 Act. Thus, whilst the tenancy remains protected, the landlord may serve a notice of increase (in prescribed form) on the tenant, giving him such notice as is required under the lease (the statutory minimum being four weeks': RA 1977, s. 45(3)). The effect of serving a valid notice of increase is that the protected tenancy is terminated and a statutory tenancy takes its place (RA 1977, s. 49(4)). Where the tenancy is statutory already, the landlord's task is much more straightforward: he simply serves notice of increase of the appropriate length on the tenant (RA 1977, s. 45(2)(b)).

Once a rent has been registered in relation to a dwelling, no further application may be made to a rent officer for registering a new rent unless both parties join in making it, or there has been a change in the condition of the house, the terms of the tenancy, the furniture provided or any other circumstances taken into consideration at the previous registration so that the rent registered is no longer a fair rent (RA 1977, s. 67(3)).

There is no appeal as such from the decision of the rent officer, but either party may make written objection within 28 days of receiving notice of the rent which has been registered, and the matter is then referred to a rent assessment committee. The rent assessment committee must then inquire into the circumstances of the case, and either confirm the rent registered by the rent officer, or (if they do not consider the rent registered is a fair rent) themselves determine the fair rent for the dwelling-house (see generally RA 1977, sch. 11).

11.3 Fair rent

The Rent Act 1977 does not define 'fair rent' as such. The closest it comes is in s. 70, which instructs rent officers and rent assessment committees that in determining the fair rent regard must be had to all the circumstances *other than personal circumstances*, and in particular to the age, character, locality and state of repair of the dwelling-house; the quantity, quality and condition of any furniture provided; and any premium which has been or may be lawfully required or received. Various matters are to be disregarded, such as disrepair attributable to breaches of obligation of the tenant or his predecessors in title, certain tenants' improvements, and any improvements to or deterioration in furniture provided under the tenancy. Most significantly, 'scarcity value' is to be disregarded, as it must be assumed 'that the number of persons seeking to become tenants of similar dwelling-houses in the locality on the terms (other than those relating to rent) of the regulated tenancy is not substantially greater than the number of such dwelling-houses in the locality which are available for letting on such terms' (RA 1977, s. 70(2)). Thus demand is deemed to be not substantially greater than supply.

The courts have had plenty of opportunity to explain the statutory definition, but have not done so with great activism or enthusiasm. In *Mason* v *Skilling* [1974] 1 WLR 1437, Lord Reid opined, 'A fair rent should be fair to the landlord as well as fair to the tenant', and continued, 'It can be regarded as fair to the landlord that he should receive a fair return on his capital.' In general, the courts have been happy to leave the question of valuation to the rent officers and the rent assessment committees. It is important though to note that the effect of disregarding scarcity was both to introduce artificiality into the exercise, and to hold rents of regulated tenancies, assuming there is a vibrant market, at a level below that of a commercially agreed rent. The imposition of rent control which was involved was of course the very reason for the assault on the Rent Acts mounted in Part I of the Housing Act 1988.

Disregard of the scarcity element has proved central to the exercise of determining a fair rent. Its purport was well expressed by Lord Widgery CJ in *Metropolitan Property Holdings Ltd* v *Finegold* [1975] 1 WLR 349, at 352:

> If the house has inherent amenities and advantages, by all means let them be reflected in the rent under [s. 70(1)]; but if the market rent would be influenced simply by the fact that in the locality there is a shortage, and in the locality rents are being forced up beyond the market figure, then that element of market rent must not be included when the fair rent is being considered. Parliament, I am sure, is not seeking to deprive the landlord of a proper return on the inherent value and quality of this investment in the house, but Parliament is undoubtedly seeking to deprive a landlord of a wholly unmeritorious increase in rent which has come about simply because there is a scarcity of houses in the district and thus an excess of demand over supply.

The effect of the enactment of Part I of the Housing Act 1988, with its encouragement of private sector letting consequential upon the adoption of freely negotiated 'commercial' rents, was at some time sure to be felt in relation to fair rents. The argument which came to be heard with increasing regularity before rent assessment committees was that as supply of properties (on assured tenancy) now frequently exceeded demand, no deduction should be made from the *prima facie* market rent for the house in question, and that it was not the committee's task to set a reasonable rent where the market rent might appear to be excessive. The argument was tested on appeal to the High Court in *B.T.E. Ltd* v *Merseyside & Cheshire Rent Assessment Committee* (1991) 24 HLR 514. The judgment of Hutchison J is of considerable importance.

The facts were mundane. The landlord sought a rent of £30 per week of a three bedroomed terraced house in Liverpool before the rent officer, who fixed a rent of £13. The rent assessment committee apparently accepted the evidence of the landlord that there was an abundance of comparable properties for letting (i.e., that supply exceeded demand), but refused to consider recent lettings to be appropriate comparables as they were at 'market rent'. They determined the fair rent at £16.50, and the landlord appealed under the provisions of the Tribunals and Inquiries Act 1971 to the High Court.

In allowing the landlord's appeal, and setting aside the decision of the rent assessment committee, Hutchison J considered the committee's approach, of having regard essentially only to comparable lettings on regulated tenancy, as being contrary to s. 70(1) of the 1977 Act. The court considered it wrong of the committee to select a range of 'reasonable' rents arbitrarily and set the fair rent of the dwelling in question by comparison with them. In setting a fair rent, appropriate consideration should be given to both regulated tenancy and assured tenancy comparables.

In *Spath Holme Ltd* v *Greater Manchester & Lancashire Rent Assessment Committee, The Times,* 13 July 1994, Harrison J supported the reasoning of Hutchison J in the *BTE* case. His Lordship emphasised that assured tenancy comparables were to be considered by rent assessment committees even where a scarcity of properties for letting is established, provided that the market rent is adjusted to eliminate that element.

The combined effect of these two decisions is highly significant. They can be said to sound the death knell for 'below market' fair rents. As the provision of lettings on assured tenancies increases, in time the rents of regulated tenancies will not differ significantly from those of assured tenancies. Regulated tenancies will remain the more valuable asset, as their security of tenure is greater, and the provisions for succession on death are more generous. But the importance of the distinction will gradually diminish.

11.4 Rent agreements

Agreements between landlords and regulated tenants increasing the rent payable under the tenancy must satisfy detailed statutory requirements (RA

1977, s. 51), failing which the excess of the rent payable as a result of the agreement will be 'irrecoverable' from the tenant (RA 1977, s. 54).

11.5 Premiums

It would be relatively easy to evade the fair rent provisions of the Rent Acts by charging the tenant a large premium on grant of the tenancy. This abuse has long been outlawed, indeed criminalised, but the provisions are becoming increasingly anachronistic. They do not affect assured tenancies (where, consistent with the underpinning philosophy of the free market, the landlord may charge whatever the tenant will pay), and they have never affected long residential tenancies (i.e., tenancies for over 21 years), which tenancies most frequently attract payments of large capital sums. For detail of the law relating to premiums and regulated tenancies, reference should be made to RA 1977, Part IX (ss. 120–128).

FOUR

LONG TENANCIES AT A LOW RENT

Landlord and Tenant Act 1954, Part I
Local Government and Housing Act 1989, sch. 10

1 INTRODUCTION

Many dwellings in England and Wales are held by the occupiers on long leases, for which a substantial premium has been paid. To the uninformed layperson, the arrangements whereby these persons have purchased their houses appear little different from the traditional purchase of a freehold. The 'premium' paid on 'assignment' or 'grant' of a long lease may be similar in amount to prices paid for freeholds in the same vicinity, and the purchasers will probably be taking a term which will not be likely to expire during their lifetime, and may last for hundreds of years. The long leaseholder has become a familiar figure in our conveyancing processes. He is in part the product of the 19th and 20th century building lease (whereby building companies and entrepreneurs encouraged investment in their enterprises by offering generous leasehold terms), and in part the result of the long established, and recently reaffirmed (see *Rhone* v *Stephens* [1994] 2 WLR 429) rule of English law that positive covenants extracted on a conveyance of freehold land cannot be enforced against successors in title.

The long leaseholder is both an embittered and an endangered species: embittered because the long lease, as its term comes to its close, is a depreciating asset; endangered because the latter half of this century has seen legislative intervention entitling many long leaseholders to purchase their landlords' interests ('to enfranchise') and become freeholders. The process is continuing, and in the very near future an entirely new method of holding land, 'commonhold', will be introduced which will *inter alia* provide means of enforcing covenants between those who have similar interests in the same building or development and thereby remove one of the major attractions of granting long leaseholds. This chapter will consider the security of tenure currently provided for long leaseholders, and chapter 5 the rights to enfranchise available to such tenants.

2 THE REGIMES OF SECURITY

2.1 Introduction

Long leases have generally been outside the scope of the Rent Acts. Although in recent years length of term has not been an excluding factor, most long leases, being granted for a premium, are at a low rent, and excluded for that reason (Rent Act 1977 (RA 1977), s. 5; see chapter 3, para. 3.3). Part I of the Housing Act 1988 (HA 1988) adopts a similar policy (HA 1988, sch. 1, para. 3). In the public sector, a tenancy cannot be secure if it is a long tenancy, as defined in s. 115 of the Housing Act 1985 (HA 1985) (HA 1985, sch. 1, para. 1).

Part I of the Landlord and Tenant Act 1954 granted security to tenants on the termination of a 'long tenancy at a low rent', where the 'qualifying condition' was fulfilled for the time being, namely that 'the circumstances (as respects the property comprised in the tenancy, the use of that property, and all other relevant matters) are such that on the coming to an end of the tenancy at that time the tenant would, if the tenancy had not been one at a low rent, be entitled by virtue of the Rent Act to retain possession of the whole or part of the property comprised in the tenancy' (Landlord and Tenant Act 1954 (LTA 1954), s. 2(1)). In other words, the tenancy was to be analysed on the assumption that the tenancy was not at a low rent (within s. 3 of the 1977 Act). If on that assumption, it would qualify for Rent Act protection, and it comprised 'a long tenancy at a low rent', the tenant would then be entitled to the protection of the Rent Act subject to and in accordance with the provisions of Part I of the 1954 Act (LTA 1954, s. 1).

The enactment of the Housing Act 1988 had an impact on the protection of long leaseholders which was not immediately appreciated. Where a long tenancy at a low rent was entered into on or after 15 January 1989, merely assuming that the level of the rent did not exclude it from the Rent Acts was not sufficient for that tenancy to qualify for Rent Act protection. By s. 34(1) of the Housing Act 1988, a tenancy entered into on or after that date cannot, subject to exceptions, be a protected tenancy. It was necessary, therefore, to enact further legislation to protect those long leaseholders whose leases were granted subsequently to the 1988 Act coming into force, and the relevant provisions are to be found in the Local Government and Housing Act 1989, s. 186, and sch. 10.

The provisions of the 1989 Act equate long leaseholders to assured tenants under the Housing Act 1988 rather than Rent Act regulated tenants, and ultimately phase out the 1954 Act with regard to existing long leaseholders as well as those who are granted such leases after the 1989 Act came into force. Whereas the 1954 Act confers on long tenants a Rent Act statutory tenancy on termination of the long lease, the 1989 Act protects them by means of an assured periodic tenancy. As the latter security is not thought to be as good or as effective, it is important from the outset to establish whether a given tenancy is subject to the provisions of the 1954 Act or those of the 1989 Act. Some difficulty has been caused by the rather piecemeal nature of the reforms, and it is possible that certain long tenancies have fallen through the net of protection as a result.

2.2 Tenancies entered into prior to 15 January 1989

A long tenancy at a low rent entered into prior to this date will, if it fulfils the 'qualifying condition' referred to above, be protected by the code contained in Part I of the 1954 Act.

2.3 Tenancies entered into on or after 15 January 1989

2.3.1 1954 Act tenancies?

The legal position of long tenancies at a low rent entered into after the coming into force of the Housing Act 1988 is complex. Certain of these tenancies will remain subject to Part I, LTA 1954. If they are entered into subject to a contract made before 15 January 1989, or they comprise in effect a grant of a new tenancy to an existing tenant, then they could be protected tenancies under the Rent Act were they not at a low rent (see HA 1988, s. 34(1)(a),(b)), and Part I of the 1954 Act can therefore apply to them. There are further, rarer, exceptions in s. 34(1)(c) and (d) (see chapter 3, para. 3.1). But generally, Part I of the 1954 Act will be inapplicable to long tenancies at a low rent entered into on or after 15 January 1989, as the qualifying condition contained in s. 2(1) of the 1954 Act will not be satisfied.

2.3.2 1989 Act tenancies?

As already stated, long tenancies at a low rent entered into on or after 15 January 1989 cannot be assured tenancies if the rent is below the level laid down in sch. 1, para. 3, to that Act. However, by s. 186(2) of the Local Government and Housing Act 1989:

> Schedule 10 to this Act applies, and section 1 of the Landlord and Tenant Act 1954 does not apply, to a tenancy of a dwelling-house—

(a) which is a long tenancy at a low rent, as defined in sch. 10 to this Act; and

(b) which is entered into on or after the day appointed for the coming into force of this section, otherwise than in pursuance of a contract made before that day.

The 'day appointed for the coming into force' of s. 186 of the 1989 Act is 1 April 1990. Thus, tenancies entered into on or after 1 April 1990 are capable of protection under the code of the 1989 Act provided that they were not entered into pursuant to a contract made prior to that date. If the contract was prior to 15 January 1989, however, the tenancy could be subject to Part I of the 1954 Act: see para. 2.3.1 above.

2.4 Tenancies entered into between 15 January 1989 and 30 March 1990 inclusive

Part I of the 1954 Act cannot apply to tenancies entered into on or after 15 January 1989 (save in the exceptional circumstances outlined above) as a tenant holding such a tenancy (assuming it were not at a low rent) would not be entitled on termination at that time to retain possession by virtue of the Rent Act (thus he would not satisfy the 'qualifying condition': LTA 1954, s. 2(1)). And it appears from s. 186(2) of the 1989 Act that the code contained in sch. 10 to that Act cannot apply to tenancies entered into before 1 April 1990. It is thus possible that long leaseholders whose tenancy was granted on or after 15 January 1989, but before 1 April 1990 are outside both protective codes.

It has been argued (by Arden and Hunter, *Current Law Statutes Annotated, 1989*, 42-276) that long tenancies entered into on or after 15 January 1989 can, by an imaginative interpretation of s. 186(3) (see para. 7 below), still come within sch. 10 to the 1989 Act. Condition (a) of that section will be met: the term date for such tenancies will be inevitably after 15 January 1999 (indeed the earliest possible date will be 15 January 2010), and so in any case where security of tenure is being sought the tenancy will have been in existence on 15 January 1999. So will condition (b): this restates the problem which requires solution. However, condition (c), the apparent stumbling block, presupposes that the tenancy being considered was protected by the 1954 Act. If it was entered into on or after 15 January 1989, this will not be the case, and much clearer words were surely necessary if the statute were to have retrospective effect.

Whilst the issue can not by any means be considered as decided, in this author's view there is a lacuna, no doubt unintended, as a result of which most long tenancies at a low rent granted between 15 January 1989 and 30 March 1990 inclusive are not protected by either the 1954 or the 1989 Act.

The practical difficulty facing those who deal with leases granted in this period is that there may be no decision of the courts on this issue until after 2010, when landlords seek to recover possession following expiry of the term certain. It can only be hoped that a landlord or tenant may in an appropriate case seek declaratory relief from the High Court, and thereby provide an earlier indication whether either of these codes apply to such tenants.

3 1954 ACT: DEFINITIONS

Part I of the 1954 Act applies to any 'long tenancy at a low rent', where the 'qualifying condition' is fulfilled. On termination of such a tenancy (on or before 15 January 1999), the tenant shall be entitled to the protection of the Rent Act subject to and in accordance with the provisions of Part I (LTA 1954, s. 1). Those provisions have effect notwithstanding any agreement to the contrary (LTA 1954, s. 17), although an actual surrender of the lease by the tenant (as distinguished from an agreement to surrender) is not struck down. In *Re Hennessey's Agreement* [1975] Ch 252, a 99-year lease provided that if the tenant wished to vacate the premises an option to purchase the residue of the term would arise in favour of the landlord. The option was declared void by Plowman V-C pursuant to s. 17 of the 1954 Act.

3.1 'Long tenancy'

A long tenancy is 'a tenancy granted for a term of years certain exceeding 21 years, whether or not subsequently extended by act of the parties or by any enactment ' (LTA 1954, s. 2(4)). It does not, however, include a tenancy which is, or may become, terminable before the end of the term by the tenant (LTA 1954, s. 2(7)). Nor will this definition allow for 'backdating' of the lease so as to make up the necessary length. In *Roberts* v *Church Commissioners* [1972] 1 QB 278 (a decision on the Leasehold Reform Act 1967), the landlords granted a lease for 10 and a quarter years in 1950. In 1952, the parties agreed to an extension of the term, the landlords then granting a lease for 21 and a quarter years from March 1950 (when the tenants had first gone into possession). This was not a grant for a term certain exceeding 21 years within the statutory definition. Russell LJ said (at 284):

> . . . a tenant must at some point in time be, or have been, in a position to say that, subject to options to determine, rights of re-entry and so forth, he is entitled to remain tenant for the next 21 years, whether at law or in equity.

Where, on the coming to an end of a long tenancy at a low rent within the above definition, the tenant is granted a new tenancy (or becomes by implication of law a new tenant) of the whole or any part of the property comprised therein, that tenancy being at a low rent, the second tenancy will be deemed to be a long tenancy within Part I of the 1954 Act irrespective of its terms (LTA 1954, s. 19(1)). In relation to tenancies from year to year (or other tenancies not granted for a year certain) which are deemed to be long tenancies by virtue of s. 19(1), the provisions of the 1954 Act are to be read as modified by sch. 4 to the Act.

3.2 'At a low rent'

The definition of 'low rent' depends, as do so many definitions in the housing statutes, on the date the tenancy was entered into.

3.2.1 Tenancy entered into before 1 April 1990

If the tenancy was entered into before 1 April 1990, or on or after that date in pursuance of a contract made before that date (in the latter case provided that the property had a rateable value on 31 March 1990), the rent must be less than two thirds of the rateable value of the property (on 'the appropriate day': RA 1977, s. 5(1); see chapter 3, para. 3.2.1).

3.2.2 Tenancy entered into on or after 1 April 1990

If the tenancy was entered into on or after 1 April 1990, the property not having a rateable value on 30 March 1990, the rent must be payable at a rate of £1,000 or less a year if the property is in Greater London, and £250 or less a year if it is elsewhere. Furthermore, the formula contained in s. 2(1A) (inserted by the Reference to Rating (Housing) Regulations 1990, SI 1990 No. 434) must also be applied to the tenancy. These tests, complex though they are, will rarely be used in this context, as almost all long tenancies entered into on or after 1 April 1990 will fall within sch. 10 to the 1989 Act rather than Part I of the 1954 Act. In determining whether the tenancy is at a long rent within these provisions, the court must disregard sums expressed to be payable by the tenant in respect of rates, services, repairs, maintenance or insurance, unless (despite the wording of the lease) they could not have been so regarded by the parties (LTA 1954, s. 2(7)).

3.3 'Qualifying condition'

Not every long tenancy at a low rent as above defined will fall within Part I of the 1954 Act. As we have already seen, the 1954 Act is being phased out, and the date the tenancy is entered into is of vital importance. The tenancy must also fulfil 'for the time being' 'the qualifying condition', that is:

> the circumstances (as respects the property comprised in the tenancy, the use of that property, and all other relevant matters) are such that on the coming to an end of the tenancy at that time the tenant would, if the tenancy had not been one at a low rent, be entitled by virtue of the Rent Act to retain possession of the whole or part of the property comprised in the tenancy (LTA 1954, s. 2(1)).

This requires the court to assume that the rent is sufficiently high that the tenancy could be protected, and then ask itself whether the requirements of the Rent Act 1977 are in all other respects met. The question is to be asked at the time the question arises ('for the time being').

The requirement in RA 1977, s. 1, that the property be 'let as a separate dwelling' would without more cause difficulty in this context, as it has come to be accepted that this phrase relates back to the date of the initial letting, although later consensual changes of use may vary that purpose (see chapter 2, para. 2.3). Where long tenancies are concerned, the date of the initial letting would frequently be in the mid-19th century, and it would be difficult and expensive to adduce convincing or even adequate evidence. Accordingly, by s. 22(3), further assumptions are to be made when determining whether the property or any part of it is 'let as a separate dwelling':

> [T]he nature of the property or part at the time of the creation of the tenancy shall be deemed to have been the same as its nature at the time in relation to which the question arises, and the purpose for which it was let under the tenancy shall be deemed to have been the same as the purpose for which it is or was used at the last-mentioned time.

This has led the courts to concentrate, in the several decisions on s. 2(1), on the purpose to which the property was being put when the long lease expired. Thus, in *Haines* v *Herbert* [1963] 1 WLR 1401, the tenant acquired by assignment the 'butt-end' (the final six weeks) of a 99-year lease of a house which was sub-divided into two large living units, each consisting of two floors. The tenant immediately installed herself in the upper two floors, sleeping there four or five nights a week and cooking some meals there. She slept in the lower two floors for some six nights in total over the six-week period, but that was all. However, she gave evidence (which was believed) that she intended to reconvert the property and occupy it as her dwelling. The Court of Appeal, looking at the state of affairs at the end of the fixed term, held that she occupied the house as her residence, and that it was then let to her as a separate dwelling.

A similar result occurred in *Herbert* v *Byrne* [1964] 1 WLR 519. It was again a 'butt-end' purchase, the final five months of a 99-year term. When the term expired, the tenant was occupying two of the four floors, the other two being sub-let to protected tenants. These sub-lettings did not deter the Court of Appeal from deciding that the house was let as a separate dwelling at the end of the term, and that the tenancy fell within Part I of the 1954 Act.

The tenants in both the above cases were opportunists, seizing the chance of obtaining a statutory tenancy by purchasing what on its face was a fast-depreciating asset. Such factor should not influence the court, as the tenant's knowledge of the Landlord and Tenant Act 1954, and hope of taking advantage of the rights it confers on him, cannot affect the true nature of his occupation (see *per* Salmon LJ in *Herbert* v *Byrne* [1964] 1 WLR 519, 529).

In *Crown Lodge (Surbiton) Investments Ltd* v *Nalecz* [1967] 1 WLR 647, the tenant's house was sufficiently commodious to be outside the Rent Act rateable value limits. The tenant sub-let such parts of the house which he did not occupy personally, and then argued that as the apportioned rateable value of the parts he retained as his dwelling-house was within the Rent Act limits, he was entitled to the protection of the 1954 Act. The Court of Appeal rejected his claim. In considering whether the qualifying condition applied, the whole property let to the tenant must be examined, and as the extent of the property let took it outside the rateable value limits, it could not be brought back in by deeming the part occupied by the tenant to be let to him as a separate dwelling. See, further, *Grosvenor Estates Belgravia* v *Cochran* (1991) 24 HLR 98.

In *Regalian Securities Ltd* v *Ramsden* [1981] 1 WLR 611, the House of Lords re-emphasised the importance of looking at the position between landlord and tenant (as opposed to sub-tenants) in the house as a whole. A penthouse which comprised a maisonette and adjoining flat was let for a term of 42 years in 1936. The term was assigned to the defendant in 1973, following which he occupied the flat and sub-let the maisonette for the reminder of the head lease less one day. The sub-tenant did not vacate as required to do, and remained in *de facto* occupation of the flat until after the term date. Despite this, the House of Lords held that on the term date the penthouse was let to the tenant as a separate dwelling, as there had initially been a single letting for residential purposes, and the intention of the tenant to occupy the penthouse as a single home as soon as he could, together with his right to possession of the penthouse as a whole, indicated that this was also the position at the expiry of the lease.

3.4 Exclusions

There is no list of exclusions from long tenancies at a low rent under the 1954 Act. However, with the obvious exception of tenancies at a low rent, any tenant whose tenancy would be otherwise excluded from Rent Act protection by the 1977 Act will be unable to claim the security of Part I (see

LTA 1954, s. 2(1)). The various exceptions to Rent Act protected status must in each case be examined; and the 1954 Act will not apply where the dwelling is let by a public sector landlord (RA 1977, s. 14). There is also an important provision in s. 2(2) of the 1954 Act, which allows an application to be made to the court within the last 12 months of the fixed term for a declaration that the tenancy is not to be treated as a long tenancy at a low rent to which Part I applies. If the qualifying condition is not fulfilled *at the time of the application*, the court must go on to consider whether the tenancy is likely to be a tenancy to which Part I applies at the term date. If it is not likely, then the court must make the declaration sought, the effect of which is that the tenancy shall not thereafter be treated as a Part I tenancy, even though the usual criteria are satisfied by the expiry of the term. In determining an application by the landlord under s. 2(2), the burden will be on the tenant to prove that circumstances are likely to change between the date of application and the term date (see LTA 1954, s. 20.)

4 1954 ACT: SECURITY OF TENURE

Part I of the 1954 Act operates by continuing automatically the long tenancy at the end of the term. The landlord may seek to better his position in two ways, each requiring service of notices and strict compliance with the provisions of the Act:

(a) The landlord may aim to convert the long tenancy into a statutory tenancy. If he does this, the tenant will continue to occupy the property, on terms determined by an application of the provisions of the 1954 Act, and may seek to have a rent registered. Once the tenant has become a statutory tenant, his security is dependent on the Rent Act 1977, and the landlord may obtain a possession order against him only by satisfying s. 98 thereof (see chapter 3, para. 5.4).

(b) The landlord may seek to recover possession whilst the tenancy is still continuing under the 1954 Act by proving prescribed statutory grounds to do so. The grounds which can be utilised are considerably more limited than those which will be available to the landlord should the tenancy become a statutory tenancy under the Rent Act 1977 as in (1) above, but the advantage of this route to recovery of possession is speed.

4.1 Continuation of long tenancy

By s. 3(1) of the 1954 Act, a tenancy which is current immediately before 'the term date' (i.e., the date of expiry of the term: s. 2(6)), and which is then a long tenancy at a low rent which fulfils the qualifying condition, will not come to an end unless terminated in accordance with the provisions of Part

I of the 1954 Act. While continuing, it will be a tenancy within the Act, and will remain so even though circumstances subsequently change and the qualifying condition ceases to be fulfilled (LTA 1954, s. 3(1)).

4.2 Terms of continuation tenancy

Whilst a tenancy continues after the term date, the rent and other terms remain the same as before. The premises to which the tenant will be entitled following expiry of the fixed term ('the premises qualifying for protection') are to be ascertained by applying the high rent assumption, i.e., the aggregate of the premises to which the tenant would be entitled to retain possession by virtue of the Rent Act were the tenancy not at a low rent (LTA 1954, s. 3(3)). If the continuation tenancy relates to part only of the property comprised in the term certain, the rent payable will be apportioned, the other terms remaining 'subject to any necessary modifications' the same as before (LTA 1954, s. 3(2)).

4.3 Termination of tenancy by tenant

The tenant may bring a long tenancy to an end under the 1954 Act by giving one month's notice in writing (LTA 1954, s. 5). As the tenant is contractually bound under the lease until the fixed term expires, he cannot unilaterally terminate by giving notice to take effect before the term date.

4.4 Termination of tenancy by landlord

The landlord is similarly bound by the terms of his contract with the tenant to grant him exclusive possession until the fixed term expires: thus, he may not terminate by giving notice at any earlier date. Subject to this, the landlord may terminate the long tenancy by giving notice in the prescribed form (SI 1967 No 1831, Forms 1 and 2) to the tenant specifying the date at which the tenancy is to come to an end (LTA 1954, s. 4(1)). The notice must be given 'not more than 12 nor less than six months before the date of termination specified therein, and the date of termination must be no earlier than 'the term date' (s. 4(1),(2)). The notice must specify the premises which the landlord believes to be, or to be likely to be, the premises qualifying for protection (s. 4(3)). It must be in one of two forms:

4.4.1 Notice proposing a statutory tenancy

The landlord's notice may contain proposals for a statutory tenancy, i.e., as to rent and repairs (LTA 1954, s. 7(3)). The notice must ask the tenant whether he is willing to give up possession (s. 4(4)). The tenant has two months from the date of service in which to reply. The Rent Acts will then normally apply to the tenancy (s. 6(1)). However, if the 'qualifying condition' is no longer fulfilled at the end of the two-month period for service, then unless the tenant has by notifying the landlord elected to retain possession, the Rent Acts will no longer apply, and the landlord will be able to recover possession (s. 6(2)).

There are lengthy provisions dealing with the terms on which the former long tenant will hold as statutory tenant under the Rent Act 1977 (see generally LTA 1954, ss. 6 to 10). In essence, the terms on which the statutory tenant is to hold, save as to rent, are as agreed by the parties, failing which agreement the county court makes a determination (s. 7(1); s. 69(1)). These matters must have been agreed, or referred to the court, earlier than two months before the date of termination stated in the landlord's notice, otherwise the landlord's notice shall cease to have effect (s. 7(2)).

The statute does not provide a list of 'considerations' to which the court must have regard in settling the terms of the statutory tenancy. Its duty is to do what is fair between the parties in the light of the state of affairs existing at the date of the hearing:

> One of the obviously material factors in that state of affairs is the bundle of rights and obligations enjoyed or imposed by landlord and tenant by the terms of the current lease. But Parliament has deliberately decided, as may be concluded from the contrast between the terms of s. 35 [dealing with business tenancies] and section 7(1), not to give the terms of the existing lease any priority in the list of considerations which the court should, as a matter of common fairness, take into account in order to determine how to exercise its discretion. (*per* Cumming-Bruce LJ in *Etablissement Commercial Kamira* v *Schiazzano* [1985] QB 93, 102.)

4.4.2 Notice to resume possession

This is a notice by the landlord that, if the tenant is not willing to give up possession at the date of termination of the tenancy of all the property then comprised in the tenancy, the landlord proposes to apply to the court for possession of the property on one or more of the grounds which are available to him under Part I of the 1954 Act, stating the ground(s) on which he proposes to apply (s. 4(3)(b)). The notice must invite the tenant to notify the landlord within two months of the notice being given whether he is willing to give up possession (s. 4(4)). If the tenant notifies the landlord that he is not willing to give up possession ('elects to retain possession': s. 4(6)), or, although no such election has been made, the qualifying condition remains fulfilled two months after service of the landlord's notice, the landlord may then apply to court for a possession order (s. 13(1)). He must make his application not later than two months after the tenant elects to remain in possession, or if no election is made, not later than four months after service of the notice (s. 13(1)). If he fails to make an application within these time limits, the landlord's notice shall cease to have effect (s. 14(2)).

5 GROUNDS FOR POSSESSION

The grounds on which the landlord may apply to the court for possession are set out in s. 12.

5.1 Mandatory ground: redevelopment

The landlord must prove 'that for purposes of redevelopment after the termination of the tenancy the landlord proposes to demolish or reconstruct the whole or a substantial part of the relevant premises' (as defined in LTA 1954, s. 12(2)) (LTA 1954, s. 12).

In *Magdalen and Lasher Charity, Hastings (Trustees)* v *Shelower* (1968) 19 P & CR 389, the landlords served notice to resume possession following expiry of a term certain of 99 years, relying on s. 12(1)(a) as their ground. The Court of Appeal held that they had sufficiently proved the ground. Lord Denning MR, at 392, refused to equate 'proposes' in this section with 'intends' in the reconstruction ground for business tenancies (LTA 1954, s. 30(1)):

> The word 'proposes' is different from the word 'intends'. A man may propose to do a thing without having formed a fixed and settled intention to do it.

This ground is in effect 'mandatory'. If the court is satisfied that possession will be required by the landlord on that ground on the termination of the tenancy, and that the landlord has made such preparations for proceeding with the redevelopment as are reasonable in the circumstances, the court must order the tenant to give up possession on termination of the tenancy (s. 13(2)). The landlord may require the court to make an order for possession effective from a postponed date no later than one year from the date of termination stated in the landlord's notice if the court is satisfied that the requirements of the ground will be met by that postponed date (s. 13(3)).

5.2 Discretionary grounds

The other grounds (set out in LTA 1954, sch. 3) correspond to the 'suitable alternative accommodation' ground, and Cases 1, 2, and 9 of the Rent Act 1977 (see further chapter 3, para. 6). They are 'discretionary':

if on an application made in accordance with section 13(1) the court is satisfied that the landlord has established that ground and that it is reasonable that the landlord should be granted possession, the court shall order that the tenant shall, on the termination of the tenancy, give up possession of all the property then comprised in the tenancy (s. 13(4)).

5.3 Failure to obtain possession

The landlord's notice to resume possession will 'cease to have effect' if he fails to apply to the court within the prescribed time limit, or if the court refuses to make an order for possession, or if he withdraws his application by serving notice in writing to that effect on the tenant. In the latter two of these cases, provision is made for the landlord to serve a notice proposing a statutory tenancy within one month of the proceedings for possession being disposed of, or the withdrawal of the notice to resume possession, as the case may be (see generally, LTA 1954, s. 14).

6 FORFEITURE AND 1954 ACT TENANCIES

The 1954 Act operates largely to provide security for those holding long tenancies at a low rent when the term certain expires. In the absence of a statutory provision dealing with forfeiture, landlords would have a considerable incentive to attempt to forfeit long tenancies for breach of covenant prior to the expiry of the term certain. Similarly, they could bring claims for substantial damages in the hope that tenants would be discouraged from continuing in possession.

Section 16 of the 1954 Act provides some protection for long leaseholders in such circumstances. Where the landlord brings proceedings to enforce a right of re-entry, or forfeiture, or a right to damages in respect of a failure to comply with the terms of the tenancy, the tenant may make application to the court for relief under s. 16. If the court then goes on to make an order for recovery of possession of the premises from the tenant, or for the payment of damages, which orders it may only make if more than seven months of the term certain are unexpired (s. 16(3)), the order will automatically be suspended for a period of 14 days, during which time the tenant may give a further notice to the landlord invoking s. 16. Service of such notice will prevent the order for possession from taking effect. Instead, the tenant will be deemed to be for a term of seven months from the date of the order, at the end of which term the 1954 Act will apply (s. 16(2)). The procedure is not entirely tenant-biased. There may have been a substantial part of the term unexpired, which is translated into a seven-month term with the prospect of continuation under the 1954 Act.

Where less than seven months of the term certain remain unexpired, or the term has expired, the court may not make an order for possession in respect to forfeiture proceedings. Where, however, the term has expired, the court may make damages awards against the tenant in respect of breach of covenant (s. 16(3)). Section 16 does not apply in relation to the following kinds of covenant: to pay rent or rates; to insure or keep insured any premises; not to use any premises for immoral or illegal purposes (s. 16(4)).

7 PHASING OUT OF PART I OF 1954 ACT

By s. 186(3) of the 1989 Act, those long tenancies which remain subject to Part I of the 1954 Act as at 15 January 1999 will be transformed into 1989 Act long tenancies, subject only to a limited exception. The provision reads:

> If a tenancy—
>
> (a) is in existence on 15 January 1999, and
> (b) does not fall within subsection (2) above [for which see para. 2.3.2 above], and
> (c) immediately before that date was, or was deemed to be, a long tenancy at a low rent for the purposes of Part I of the Landlord and Tenant Act 1954,
>
> then, on and after that date (and so far as concerns any notice specifying a date of termination on or after that date and any steps taken in consequence thereof), section 1 of that Act shall cease to apply to it and sch. 10 to this Act shall apply to it unless, before that date, the landlord has served a notice under s. 4 of that Act specifying a date of termination which is earlier than that date.

The only 1954 Act tenancies which will remain subject to those provisions subsequent to 15 January 1999 are those where the landlord has by then initiated the procedure for termination. It would obviously be undesirable for such tenancies to change their status at that stage. If, however, the landlord's notice under s. 4 ceases to have effect (e.g., the landlord fails to apply to the court within the time limit: see LTA 1954, s. 14(2)), then the long tenancy would thereupon become subject to the 1989 Act.

8 1989 ACT: INTRODUCTION

The provisions of sch. 10 to the 1989 Act differ significantly from those of Part I of the 1954 Act in two main respects: they are otherwise substantially similar. Whereas the landlord may, by giving notice to his 1954 Act tenant whose fixed term has expired, convert him into a statutory tenant under the Rent Act 1977, the landlord of a 1989 Act tenant whose term has similarly expired can by notice render him an assured tenant under Part I of the Housing Act 1988. As we have seen, an assured tenant is in a weaker position than a statutory tenant both as regards rent and security of tenure. In addition, the 1989 Act contains provisions for the imposition of an interim rent on the tenant once the landlord has proposed an assured periodic tenancy following expiry of the fixed term. It must be remembered, however, that these provisions will not be operative until 15 January 1999, following which date they will begin to effect long tenancies which were formerly governed by Part I of the 1954 Act (see para. 7 above).

9 1989 ACT: DEFINITIONS

For the most part, sch. 10 to the 1989 Act adopts the same principal definitions used in Part I of the 1954 Act (and, where relevant, Part I, HA 1988) (see 1989 Act, sch. 10, para. 2(2)).

9.1 'Long tenancy'

A long tenancy is (as in the 1954 Act) 'a tenancy granted for a term of years certain exceeding 21 years, whether or not subsequently extended by act of the parties or any enactment, but excluding any tenancy which is, or may become, terminable before the end of the term by notice given to the tenant' (sch. 10, para. 2(3)). Where, on the coming to the end of a long tenancy at a low rent (or a tenancy deemed to be such), the tenant is granted a new tenancy (or becomes by implication of law a new tenant) of the whole or part of the property let under the previous tenancy, then the subsequent tenancy will be deemed to be a long tenancy for the purposes of sch. 10, irrespective of its terms (sch. 10, para. 16(1)). Where the subsequent tenancy is a tenancy from year to year (or any tenancy other than a term of years certain), then sch. 10 will take effect subject to certain modifications (sch. 10, para. 16(2)).

9.2 'At a low rent'

The definition of 'low rent' is the same as that used in relation to Part I of the 1954 Act (see para. 3.2 above) (sch. 10, para. 2(4)).

9.3 'Qualifying condition'

The long tenancy at a low rent must satisfy the 'qualifying condition', in this case 'that the circumstances (as respects the property let under the tenancy, the use of that property and all other relevant matters are such that, if the tenancy were not at a low rent, it would be at that time be an assured tenancy within the meaning of Part I of the Housing Act 1988' (sch. 10, para. 1(1)). For this purpose only, sch. 1 to the 1988 Act must be read with the omission of para. 1 (the exclusion of tenancies entered into before, or pursuant to contracts made before, 15 January 1989) (sch. 10, para. 1(2)). Paragraph 2 of that schedule (excluding high value dwellings) is also read subject to modifications: for the purposes of determining whether the qualifying condition is fulfilled a complex formula is applied (sch. 10, para. 1(2A), added by SI 1990, No 434). In determining the 'nature' and 'purposes' of the letting, the same assumptions are made as in relation to Part I of the 1954 Act (sch. 10, para. 1(7): see further, para. 3.3 above).

9.4 Exclusions

There is no list of exclusions as such, but where a tenancy would be excluded from being an assured tenancy under the 1988 Act it will, subject to what is said above, be outside the protection of the 1989 Act as well. Application may be made for a declaration that the tenancy is not to be treated as within the schedule within the final 12 months of the term, on the same basis as applications under s. 2(2) of the 1954 Act (sch. 10, para. 1(3),(4)).

10 1989 ACT: SECURITY OF TENURE

As with Part I of the 1954 Act, sch. 10 to the 1989 Act operates by continuing automatically the long tenancy at the end of the term. The landlord may seek to improve his position by one of two means:

(a) He may seek to convert the long tenancy into an assured tenancy under Part I of the Housing Act 1988, following which the tenant will occupy as any other assured periodic tenant. The landlord may then seek to recover possession by invoking the possession procedure appopriate to such a tenant, proving where necessary a ground for possession under sch. 2 to that Act.

(b) He may seek to recover possession at an earlier stage: while the tenancy is continuing pursuant to the provisions of sch. 10 to the 1989 Act. In this case, however, the grounds for possession are restricted in number.

10.1 Continuation of long tenancy

A long residential tenancy shall not come to an end by expiry of the fixed term. It will only terminate by compliance with the provisions of sch. 10 (sch. 10, para. 3(1)). The terms of the tenancy after the term date will be the same as those before (sch. 10, para. 3(3)).

10.2 Termination of tenancy by tenant

The tenant may bring a long residential tenancy to an end on or after the term date by giving not less than one month's notice in writing (sch. 10, para. 8).

10.3 Termination of tenancy by landlord

The landlord may terminate the long residential tenancy on or after the term date by giving notice in the prescribed form to the tenant specifying the date at which the tenancy is to come to an end. It must be served not more than 12 nor less than six months before the date specified (sch. 10, para. 4). No form has yet been prescribed: as this procedure will not become operative until 1999, there are no doubt more urgent calls on the time of the Department of the Environment. The notice must be either:

10.3.1 Notice proposing an assured periodic tenancy

The tenancy must be an assured monthly periodic tenancy, at a rent which is such that the tenancy will not be a tenancy at a low rent (sch. 10, para. 9). There are provisions enabling the tenant to challenge the rent or other terms proposed, and jurisdiction is conferred on rent assessment committees to determine disputes on these matters (sch. 10, paras. 10 to 12). Whilst the terms of the assured tenancy are being established, the landlord may apply to a rent assessment committee for an interim rent to be assessed (sch. 10, paras. 6 to 7). Once the assured tenancy has taken effect, the landlord will be able to recover possession only by satisfying the provisions of Part I of the Housing Act 1988.

10.3.2 Notice to resume possession

The landlord may propose to apply to the court for an order for possession on the following grounds:

(a) Ground 6 of the Housing Act 1988 (sch. 2: see chapter 2, para. 6.1.9), unless the tenancy is a former 1954 Act tenancy (sch. 10, para. 5(2)). Ground 6 may be used here although the assured tenant became so by virtue of the succession provisions of the 1977 or 1988 Acts.

(b) Grounds 9 to 15 inclusive of the Housing Act 1988 (sch. 2: see chapter 2, para. 6.2).

(c) The landlord (which must be a body to which s. 28 of the Leasehold Reform Act 1967 applies: sch. 10, para. 5(4); see chapter 5, para. 3.7.5) proposes to demolish or reconstruct the whole or a substantial part of the premises for the purposes of redevelopment after termination of the tenancy.

(d) The premises or part of them are reasonably required by the landlord for occupation as a residence for himself or any son or daughter of his over 18 years of age or his spouse's father or mother and, if the landlord is not the immediate landlord, he will be at the specified date of termination. This ground may not be used where the landlord's interest was created after 18 February 1966 (see further, sch. 10, para. 5(5)).

10.4 Failure to obtain possession

There are similar provisions to those in the 1954 Act (s. 14) concerning the effect of failure by the landlord to obtain possession pursuant to the statutory code (sch. 10, para. 15).

11 SUMMARY

Were it not for the metamorphosis of 1954 Act tenancies into 1989 Act tenancies which will occur on 15 January 1999, the 1989 Act would not come into play on termination of any lease until 2010, and the 1954 Act would remain operative with respect to certain tenancies for decades, and, possibly, centuries. As it is, the 1954 Act will remain dominant as far as proceedings to recover possession at the end of the term are concerned until 1999.

FIVE

ENFRANCHISEMENT AND ASSOCIATED RIGHTS

Leasehold Reform Act 1967

Leasehold Reform, Housing and Urban Development Act 1993

Parts I and II

Landlord and Tenant Act 1987, Part I

1 THE STATUTES

It may be of assistance to list the various statutes conferring a right on the residential tenant to force his landlord's hand, and compel a sale of the reversion, or a grant of a new (and better) lease to him. All are complex, and subject to innumerable exceptions and qualifications. The best known is the so-called tenant's right to buy, now contained in Part V of the Housing Act 1985 (and dealt with in chapter 7). This gives to tenants of public sector landlords, on discounted terms, the right to purchase the freehold reversion of their house, or the right to obtain a long lease of their flat. The longest established analogous right enjoyed by private sector tenants (as well as some in the public sector) is that of enfranchisement, or lease extension, pursuant to the Leasehold Reform Act 1967. This confers the right to purchase the freehold reversion, or the right to a further 50-year lease, on favourable terms to those who hold a long lease of a house at a low rent. The recent Leasehold Reform, Housing and Urban Development Act 1993 makes significant amendments to the 1967 Act, but even more importantly confers two new rights on tenants of flats: collective enfranchisement, forcing the landlord to sell the reversion to the tenants of a building collectively, and individual lease renewal, which can be initiated by the single tenant, but in either case at full market value. Finally, there is Part I of the Landlord and Tenant Act 1987 conferring a right of first refusal on certain tenants in the private sector. As the tenant will be expected to pay the price negotiated by the landlord with his purchaser, purchase is again at the market value. Part III of the same Act (which is not covered here) provides for compulsory acquisition by the tenants of the landlord's interest where the landlord is in breach of an obligation in the lease relating to repair, maintenance, insurance or management. These various rights are complex both in their definition and in their practical enforcement. It is essential that practitioners deal with the relevant statutes at their finger-tips. This book will describe the statutory codes, and in so doing emphasise points of particular difficulty.

A LEASEHOLD REFORM ACT 1967: HOUSES

2 INTRODUCTION

The Leasehold Reform Act 1967 confers on tenants occupying houses under long leases at a low rent the right to enfranchise (i.e., purchase the freehold) or to extend their lease for 50 years. It does not apply to flats. The singular attractiveness of the 1967 Act to the tenant is the method of valuation used. The price to be paid by the tenant is based on the value of the undeveloped land: the site without the building occupied by the tenant upon it. In 1986, trustees of the will of the second Duke of Westminster claimed before the European Court of Human Rights that the Leasehold Reform Act, as expropriatory legislation (which it certainly is) breached Article 1 of the First Protocol to the European Convention on Human Rights and Fundamental Freedoms ('No-one shall be deprived of his possessions save in the public interest'). They did not succeed, as 'The enhancement of social justice within the community could properly be described as being in the public interest' (*James* v *United Kingdom* (1986) RVR 139). Although the 1967 Act was the invention of the Labour Government of Harold Wilson, it has now been extended in its application by the Conservative Government of John Major to include high value properties which were formerly excluded, and must be considered for the foreseeable future unlikely to be repealed or significantly amended.

3 TENANCIES WITHIN THE 1967 ACT

The 1967 Act confers its rights on a tenant who is occupying a leasehold house as his residence where (a) his tenancy is a long tenancy at a low rent;

and (b) at the time he gives notice of his intention to exercise his statutory rights he has been a tenant of the house under such a tenancy, so occupying it, for the last three years, or for three out of the last 10 years (Leasehold Reform Act 1967 (LRA 1967), s. 1(1)). As might be expected, there are certain exceptions and qualifications to these broad rules, which themselves now require further analysis.

3.1 Long tenancy

A long tenancy is a tenancy granted for a term of years certain exceeding 21 years. The tenancy may be legal or equitable (LRA 1967, s. 37(1)(f)). It is immaterial that the tenancy is, or may become, determinable during that term by re-entry or by exercise of a break clause or otherwise. It includes a perpetually renewable lease, unless it is a sub-lease where the mesne tenant is not holding under a long tenancy.

By s. 149(6) of the Law of Property Act 1925, leases for life or for a term of years determinable on death or marriage take effect as leases for a term of 90 years determinable after the death or marriage of the tenant (or other person in question). These leases are deemed to be long tenancies by LRA 1967, s. 1B (inserted by Leasehold Reform, Housing and Urban Development Act 1993 (LRHUDA 1993), s. 64(1)), subject to two important exceptions. Thus, the tenancy will not be a long tenancy:

(a) where the notice is capable of being given at any time after the tenant's death or marriage, the length of the notice is not more than three months, and the terms of the tenancy preclude assignment (other than an assignment by way of exchange: HA 1985, s. 92) and sub-letting of the whole of the premises, (LRA 1967, s. 3(1), amended by LRHUDA 1993, s. 64(2)).

(b) where the tenancy was granted before 18 April 1980, or pursuant to a contract entered into before that date, the tenancy will carry the right to enfranchise (provided it is otherwise within the Act) but not the right to a lease extension (LRA 1967, s. 1B, inserted by LRHUDA 1993, s. 64(1)).

The length of the tenancy will be calculated from the date of execution and delivery which it bears (see *Roberts* v *Church Commissioners* [1972] 1 QB 278, chapter 4, para. 3.1). If, however, the tenant is granted a term of years for less than 21 years, with an option to renew without payment of a premium, which option he then exercises so as to bring the total of the terms granted to more than 21 years, then the 1967 Act will apply to the term originally granted (LRA 1967, s. 3(4)). In *Eton College* v *Bard* [1983] Ch 321, the Court of Appeal decided that a lease granted by a housing association for 93 years or until it should cease to be vested in a member of that association was a long tenancy within s. 3(1) of the 1967 Act. It was treated as being a term of years terminable 'otherwise', i.e., on the happening of a particular event.

Where a tenant's long tenancy at a low rent expires, and he is granted a new tenancy (or one comes into being by implication of law) of the same property or part of it, then the new tenancy will be deemed to be a long tenancy irrespective of its terms (LRA 1967, s. 3(2)). This will be the case even though the tenant assigns, and the assignee can therefore claim the benefit of the 1967 Act. In *Austin* v *Dick Rickards Properties Ltd* [1975] 1 WLR 1033, the tenant under a long tenancy at a low rent was granted a new lease for a term of 15 years. Eight years later, the tenant assigned, and the assignee, after being in occupation for five years (as was then required) successfully claimed enfranchisement, the Court of Appeal holding that s. 3(2) was not conferring merely personal rights on the tenant who is granted the new lease.

A tenancy will be deemed to be a long tenancy where the tenancy is being continued by virtue of Part I or II of the Landlord and Tenant Act 1954 (LTA 1954), or sch. 10 to the Local Government and Housing Act 1989 (LRA 1967, s. 3(5): see chapter 4 generally). A tenancy of a house granted by virtue of Part V of the Housing Act 1985 will also be deemed to be a long tenancy (Housing Act 1985, s. 174).

Where on the coming to an end of a long tenancy, a tenant becomes tenant of the property or part of it under another long tenancy, then the Act will treat the tenancies as one single tenancy (LRA 1967, s. 3(3)). There is further provision for the treatment as one tenancy of separate tenancies (with the same landlord and tenant) of two or more parts of the same house (LRA 1967, s. 3(6)).

3.2 Low rent

The long tenancy must be at a low rent. It is the rent for 'the house and premises' (see para. 4.1 below) which is to be considered. The test differs according to the date the tenancy was entered into, and the Leasehold Reform, Housing and Urban Development Act 1993 has added a further layer of complexity by providing an alternative 'low rent' test for the purposes of enfranchisement claims only.

3.2.1 Basic test (LRA 1967, s. 2(4))

3.2.1.1 Tenancy entered into on or after 1 April 1990

Where the tenancy was entered into on or after 1 April 1990 (other than pursuant to a contract made before that date, the property having a rateable value on 31 March 1990) the annual rent must not exceed £1,000 if the property is in Greater London, or £250 if the property is elsewhere.

3.2.1.2 Tenancy entered into before 1 April 1990

Where the tenancy was entered into before 1 April 1990 (or subsequently, pursuant to a contract made before that date, provided the property had a rateable value on 31 March 1990) the annual rent must not be equal to or exceed two-thirds of the rateable value of the property on the appropriate day or, if later, the first day of the term. The appropriate day is 23 March 1965, or such later day as would be the appropriate day under s. 25(3) of the Rent Act 1977 'in relation to a dwelling-house consisting of the house in question' (LRA 1967, s. 4(1)(a)). By s. 25(3), the appropriate day is

> (a) in relation to any dwelling-house which, on 23 March 1965, was or formed part of a hereditament for which a rateable value was shown in the valuation list then in force, or consisted or formed part of more than one such hereditament, means that date, and
> (b) in relation to any other dwelling-house, means the date on which such a value is or was first shown in the valuation list.

In *Dixon* v *Allgood* [1987] 1 WLR 1689 the tenant was granted a 51-year lease of two derelict cottages and six acres of land in 1964. He reconstructed the cottages, and on 6 February 1967, a rateable value for each cottage, £42 and £34 respectively, appeared on the valuation list. The tenant then built a garage and store room on the forecourt adjacent to one of the cottages, which building was itself separately rated on 22 December 1971 with a rateable value of £24. As at 1981, when the tenant served the landlord with notice of his claim to enfranchise, he was occupying the two cottages as a single dwelling-house, and was paying a rent of £51.44. The House of Lords held that the long tenancy was not at a low rent. Where the appropriate day falls after 23 March 1965, it is the day when the *house* (here being the two cottages), as opposed to the *house and premises*, was first rated either as a single hereditament or (as was the case here) as two or more hereditaments: on 6 February 1967. The rent of £51.44 was not less than two-thirds of the rateable value of £76, and so the tenancy was outside the 1967 Act. If the garages had been built before 6 February 1967, the formula would have taken account of them, as it is the rateable value of the *house and premises* which is to be utilised (see LRA 1967, s. 4(2)).

3.2.1.3 Tenancy granted between August 1939 and April 1963

Where the tenancy was granted between the end of August 1939 and the beginning of April 1963 (not being a building lease as defined) a further test must be satisfied. If at the commencement date of such a lease the rent payable under the tenancy exceeded two-thirds of the *letting value* of the property, then the tenancy will not be at a low rent. The burden of establishing that the tenancy is outside the 1967 Act by virtue of this particular provision will be on the landlord (s. 4(5)). The definition of 'letting value' has been the subject of several decisions of the courts. In *Gidlow-Jackson* v *Middlegate Properties Ltd* [1974] 1 QB 361, the Court of Appeal held that in ascertaining the letting value at the commencement of the tenancy, the court must take account of the restrictions imposed on such a letting by the Rent Acts. However, as most long leases will be granted for a premium, it has accordingly been held in later cases that the court should in assessing the letting value take account also of the decapitalised amount of any premium which was paid at the time: not to do so 'would have the absurd result of making a property which could be let at £100 a year with a premium of £2,000 of equal letting value to another similar property which could be let at £100 a year with no premium' (*per* Stephenson LJ in *Manson* v *Duke of Westminster* [1981] 1 QB 323, 333). The House of Lords have subsequently defined 'letting value' as 'the best annual rent obtainable in the open market for the grant of a long lease on the same terms whether this is achieved by letting at a rack rent or letting at a lower rent plus the payment of a premium' (*Johnston* v *Duke of Westminster* [1986] AC 839, 845, *per* Lord Griffiths). In most cases, the best evidence of letting value (in view of the historical nature of the enquiry) may well be the terms of the very lease under examination, and it will require the party denying this to rebut the presumption.

In determining the 'rent' for the purposes of this section, there should be disregarded any part of the rent expressed to be payable by way of service charges, or for repairs, maintenance or insurance (LRA 1967, s. 4(1)), and in determining 'rent' and 'rateable value', the court should refer to the house and 'premises', as defined at length in s. 2 of the Act. There is power to apportion rent between property which is the subject of a claim under the 1967 Act and property which is not (s. 4(6)).

3.2.2 Alternative test (enfranchisement only) (LRHUDA 1993, ss. 63, 65)

The alternative rent limit imposed by the 1993 Act allows the tenant to argue that although he cannot satisfy the provisions above, he can nevertheless enfranchise. The alternative does not give rise to a claim to extend the lease. By s. 4A, as inserted by LRHUDA 1993, s. 65, the court is to consider the rent payable during the initial year of the tenancy (i.e., the period of one year beginning with the date of the commencement of the tenancy). If no rent was payable in that year, or the aggregate amount payable did not exceed:

(a) where the tenancy was entered into before 1 April 1963, two-thirds of the letting value (see above) of the property (on the same terms) on the date of the commencement of the tenancy;

(b) where the tenancy was entered into between 1 April 1963 and 31 March 1990 (inclusive), or subsequently, pursuant to a contract made before 1 April 1990, provided the property had a rateable value before 1 April 1990, two-thirds of the rateable value of the property on the 'relevant date' (being the date of the commencement of the tenancy, or, if later, the date on which the property first had a rateable value);

(c) in any other case £1,000 if the property is in Greater London, or £250 if elsewhere:

then the tenancy will be treated as a long tenancy at a low rent, for the purpose of conferring on the tenant the right to acquire the freehold of the house and premises.

3.3 House

A tenant holding under a long tenancy at a low rent can only obtain a right to enfranchise or to extend his lease under the 1967 Act in so far as the property he occupies is a 'house', as defined in s. 2 thereof. 'House' includes any building designed or adapted for living in and 'reasonably so-called'. The building need not be structurally detached, nor need it have been or be solely designed or adapted for living in. It may even be divided horizontally into flats or maisonettes, but in such a case, the individual units (the flats) are not separate houses. Where a building is divided vertically, the individual units may be houses but the building as a whole will not be. In *Lake* v *Bennett* [1970] 1 QB 663, as approved by the House of Lords in *Tandon* v *Trustees of Spurgeons Homes* [1982] AC 755, the following propositions were accepted:

(a) whether a building is a house 'reasonably so-called' is a question of law;

(b) a building may reasonably be called a house even though it may also reasonably be called something else.

Thus, a shop with living accommodation above will generally fall within the 1967 Act (for examples, see *Lake* v *Bennett*; *Peck* v *Anicar Properties Ltd* [1971] 1 All ER 517; *Tandon* v *Trustees of Spurgeons Homes*).

In *Sharpe* v *Duke Street Securities NV* (1987) 19 HLR 506 a building was constructed so as to contain two flats, one on the ground floor and one on the first floor. Access to the first floor flat was gained through a hall and staircase from the ground level, themselves divided from the ground floor flat by a wall. The front doors to each flat were side by side in the front porch. When the tenant served notice under the 1967 Act, he had been occupying both flats as a single dwelling for more than three years, and had put a door in the wall dividing the ground floor flat from the hall. The Court of Appeal held that the building could be reasonably called a house. Although by

s. 2(1)(b) buildings divided vertically could not be houses, the provision did not apply where the division did not create separate units as such: here the division was essentially horizontal, between ground and first floor flats. In *Malpas* v *St Ermins Property Co. Ltd* (1992) 24 HLR 537, a similarly divided building was held to be a house although each floor was occupied by a separate family as their respective residence. Dillon LJ said:

> The concept of a house divided into maisonettes is of course one which the Act recognises and which is familiar to anyone who sees what has happened to Victorian houses in central London built in those spacious days for occupation by a single family but now subdivided horizontally into maisonettes sharing a single entrance.

Section 2(2) contains an important exclusion, intended to obviate the conveyancing problems of so-called 'flying freeholds'. Where a house is (a) not 'structurally detached' and (b) a material part of it lies above or below a part of the structure not comprised in the house, then it will not be a house for the purposes of the Act. In *Parsons* v *Viscount Gage (Trustees of Henry Smith's Charity)* [1974] 1 WLR 435, a sub-tenant of three adjoining leasehold properties had converted them into two dwellings. He sought enfranchisement in relation to the dwelling he occupied (the other was sub-let in turn to his son). Part of this dwelling overhung the son's garage. The House of Lords held that s. 2(2) applied. The sub-tenant's dwelling was not 'structurally detached' in that it was not detached from any other structure, and, it being acknowledged that a part of that dwelling lay above a part of the structure not comprised in the house, it was a question of fact for the judge (which had been answered affirmatively) as to whether that part was 'material'. Enfranchisement was not therefore possible. In *Gaidowski* v *Gonville and Caius College, Cambridge* [1975] 1 WLR 1066, on the other hand, the tenant, who occupied as part of his dwelling a room which lay both above and below parts not comprised in the house, sought enfranchisement in relation only to the remainder of his dwelling excluding that room. He was allowed to do so, as the property in relation to which enfranchisement was claimed might reasonably be called a house.

3.4 Occupation by the tenant

The tenant must, at the time he gives notice in accordance with the 1967 Act of his desire to enfranchise or obtain a lease extension, have been tenant of the house under a long tenancy at a low rent, and occupying it as his residence, for the last three years, or for periods amounting to three years in total out of the last 10 (LRA 1967, s. 1(1)(b)). The occupation of the tenant must be in right of the tenancy, and must be as his only or main residence (whether or not he uses it for other purposes) (LRA 1967, s. 1(2)).

The leading authority is *Poland* v *Earl Cadogan* [1980] 3 All ER 544. The tenant had to establish, as was then the condition, five years' occupation. He had taken an assignment of the lease in December 1973. He was away for two months in 1974, and then in October 1975 he and his wife went on a long voyage, leaving instructions with agents to sub-let the property if possible. They returned in January 1977 to find mortgagees lawfully in possession. They sought to exercise the right to enfranchise in December 1978, although they did not in fact recommence living there until 1979, as the house had been rendered uninhabitable when left vacant owing to storm damage. The Court of Appeal held that the tenant had failed to satisfy the condition of occupation. Whilst it was possible for a tenant to continue to occupy when physically absent from the property, the onus was on him to show that the steps he has taken to maintain occupation are clear. The test is not the same as under the Rent Act 1977 (although see HA 1988, s. 1(1)), and the tenant does not lose the benefit of his periods of genuine occupation because of the provisions allowing aggregation. The tenant in *Poland* v *Earl Cadogan* had ceased to occupy. Instructing his agents to sub-let was conclusive:

> [A] tenant cannot be said to be occupying a house as his residence during a period of time in respect of which he has no intention of occupying it or residing in it because of his belief, or expectation, whether it is accurate or not, that he has given up his legal right to occupy or reside in the house. He has, in respect of that period of time, to use the expression used in the judgment of the court in *Brown* v *Brash* [1948] 2 KB 247, 255, no 'animus possidendi': no intention of asserting or exercising an immediate right of possession. That is an essential element (*per* Megaw LJ at 551).

The repossession by the mortgagees in any event interrupted the tenant's occupation: indeed, until the mortgagees reinstated the mortgage with him in September 1977, he could not be held to be satisfying the condition, as he was not occupying 'in right of the tenancy', but by licence of the mortgagees.

If a tenant sub-lets the entirety of the house, he will inevitably cease to occupy (see, for example, *Poland* v *Earl Cadogan* at 550), but, as is implicit in the decision in *Lake* v *Bennett*, above, the sub-letting of some part of the house in question does not take it outside the 1967 Act. By s. 1(2)(a) 'references to a person occupying a house shall apply where he occupies it in part only'. Thus, in *Harris* v *Swick Securities Ltd* [1969] 1 WLR 1604, the tenant, who let three floors of her house on unfurnished tenancies, whilst she continued to occupy the basement, was entitled to claim enfranchisement.

There is an important exception to the general rule that the tenant must have occupied the house as his residence for three years (or three out of 10 years) at the time he gives notice of desire to exercise his rights under the

1967 Act. By s. 7, where a tenant who has been occupying dies, and on his death a member of his family (as defined: see s. 7(7)) becomes tenant in his place under the same tenancy, the successor can count towards the qualifying period any period during which the house was occupied by both the former tenant and the successor (each occupying it as their only or main residence).

3.5 Sub-tenancies

Where the tenant seeking to exercise his rights under the 1967 Act is himself a sub-tenant, the law has to address not only the interests of the freeholder but also those of any intermediaries. This complex exercise is performed by sch. 1 to the 1967 Act, which also deals with questions such as who has the conduct of proceedings on behalf of the landlords.

3.6 High value properties

The Leasehold Reform Act 1967, by s. 1(1), excluded from its operation tenants who were occupying high value properties under long tenancies at a low rent. The provisions, complex in themselves, have been significantly affected by the Leasehold Reform, Housing and Urban Development Act 1993. By LRA 1967, s. 1A, inserted by LRHUDA 1993, s. 63, the tenant of a property which would formerly have been excluded from the operation of the Act by virtue of its excessive value is now given the right to enfranchise, but not the right to a lease extension. Where a tenant is entitled to claim by virtue of s. 1A, the formula for calculating the price payable on enfranchisement is modified, and compensation may be payable to the landlord (see LRA 1967, ss. 9(1C), 9A, as inserted by LRHUDA 1993, s. 66). It remains important to apply LRA 1967, s. 1(1)(a) where the tenant seeks a lease extension (as s. 1A will not apply), and in all cases to discover whether the tenant seeking enfranchisement could have done so without resort to s. 1A, as then the price payable will be calculated on a basis more favourable to him, and the additional statutory compensation will not be payable. The high value limits are as follows. If the limit is exceeded, any enfranchisement will be within s. 1A.

3.6.1 Tenancy entered into before 1 April 1990

Where the tenancy was entered into before 1 April 1990 or subsequently, pursuant to a contract made before that date, the rateable value of the house and premises on the appropriate day (i.e., 23 March 1965, or such later day as would be deemed 'appropriate' by s. 25(3) of the Rent Act 1977: s. 1(4)) must not exceed certain limits set by ss. 1(1), 1(5) and 1(6) of the 1967 Act, as amended by the References to Rating (Housing) Regulations 1990. In assessing rateable value for these purposes, a reduction may need to be made of tenant's improvements (LRA 1967, s. 1(4A), inserted by Housing Act 1980: see also Housing Act 1974, sch. 8).

3.6.2 Tenancy entered into on or after 1 April 1990

Where the tenancy was entered into on or after 1 April 1990 (save where it was entered into pursuant to a contract made before that date and the house and premises had a rateable value on 31 March 1990), a statutory formula must be applied at the date of the contract for the grant of the tenancy, or, if there was no such contract, the date the tenancy was entered into: see further s. 1(1)(a), as amended by the References to Rating (Housing) Regulations 1990.

3.7 Other exclusions

Where the tenant comes within the above conditions, there are relatively few circumstances where his entitlement to claim will be excluded:

3.7.1 Shared ownership leases

The Housing and Planning Act 1986, s. 18 and sch. 4, excludes from the 1967 Act certain shared ownership leases granted by public bodies and housing associations: see further LRA 1967, s. 33A and sch. 4A, added by this later statute. However, other long leases granted by public bodies may qualify for enfranchisement or lease extension under the 1967 Act. As a long lease cannot be a secure tenancy (HA 1985, s. 115), the tenant's right to buy (HA 1985, Part V) cannot apply to such leases.

3.7.2 Leases terminable on death or marriage

Despite amendment by the 1993 Act, there remain certain leases terminable on death or marriage which will remain outside the provisions of the 1967 Act: see para. 3.1 above.

3.7.3 Tenancies of agricultural holdings and other land

LRA 1967, s. 1(3) effectively excludes any house which either is let with other land or premises to which it is ancillary, or is comprised in an agricultural holding within the meaning of the Agricultural Holdings Act 1986. The former of these may require the court to ask what is the 'prime purpose' of the letting (as it does under HA 1988, s. 2 and RA 1977, ss. 6 and 26: see chapter 2, para. 4.1). The latter was considered by the Court of Appeal in *Lester* v *Ridd* [1990] 2 QB 430. In 1982, the plaintiffs purchased the leasehold interest in a house with two acres of land, which land was never used by them as agricultural land. Having occupied for three years, they sought to enfranchise. Their claim was rejected by the Court of Appeal. The

99-year lease under which they held had comprised some 23 acres, all of which had been used for agriculture: it was an agricultural holding. There had been a partition of the land in 1963, without the landlord's consent. The court held that in such circumstances, the house now occupied by the plaintiffs was still comprised in the agricultural holding, being 'the aggregate of the land (whether agricultural or not) comprised in a contract of tenancy which was a contract for an agricultural tenancy' (Agricultural Holdings Act 1986, s. 1(1)).

3.7.4 Houses let by charitable housing trusts

The 1993 Act, s. 67, excludes from the right to enfranchise (but not lease extension) a tenant whose immediate landlord is a charitable housing trust, and the house forms part of the housing accommodation provided by the trust in pursuit of its charitable objects. However, this amendment is not retrospective, in that it does not take away acquired rights. It applies only to (a) tenancies entered into on or after 1 November 1993 (see also LRHUDA 1993, sch. 1, for transitional provisions); and (b) tenancies entered into before then which would only have come within the 1967 Act by virtue of amendments effected by the 1993 Act.

3.7.5 Retention or resumption of land held for public purposes

By s. 28 of the 1967 Act, a Minister of the Crown may certify that certain property (which must be owned by one of the public bodies listed in s. 28(5)) will in the next 10 years be required for 'relevant development' (meaning generally development for the purposes of the public body in question). The effect of such certificate is that tenants of such property will be unable to serve an effective notice of desire to enfranchise or extend the lease. However, if the tenant serves such notice before, or no more than two months after, the certificate is served on him, the tenancy will be treated as having been extended, and if the landlord then wishes to obtain possession, it must apply to the court under s. 17 (see para. 4.8 below). On such application, the Minister's certificate is conclusive as to the required purposes.

3.7.6 Tenancies held of the National Trust

A tenant is not entitled to enfranchise (although he can obtain a lease extension) where an interest in the property is vested inalienably in the National Trust (LRA 1967, s. 32).

3.7.7 Tenancies held of the Crown

The Crown is not bound by the 1967 Act as such. However, a tenant holding from the Crown who would otherwise be able to enfranchise or extend his lease may find that the Crown will voluntarily agree to confer the freehold, or grant another lease, on like terms to those in the Act. Section 33 proceeds on the basis that the Crown will voluntarily participate in the process.

3.7.8 Property transferred for public benefit

The 1993 Act, s. 68 (adding LRA 1967, s. 32A) excludes from the right to enfranchise (but not lease extension) 'qualifying property', being property which is exempted from inheritance tax (or designated as conditionally exempt) as being for the public benefit. This exclusion is not retrospective, and only applies to tenancies created after 1 November 1993 or tenancies which were only brought within the 1967 Act by the 1993 Act.

3.7.9 Compulsory purchase

Exercise of rights under the 1967 Act is not possible where compulsory purchase is taking place (see further, LRA 1967, s. 5(6)).

3.8 No contracting out of the Act

Any agreement relating to a tenancy purporting to exclude or modify the tenant's rights under the 1967 Act or providing for the termination or surrender of the tenancy in the event of a tenant acquiring or claiming such rights or for the imposition of a penalty or disability in that event is likely to be struck down (LRA 1967, s. 23). The agreement may involve third parties: indeed it is not a requirement that the agreement involves both landlord and tenant. In *Rennie & Rennie* v *Proma & Byng* (1989) 22 HLR 129, a transfer of the freehold to a company which could only sell with the consent of a third party fell foul of s. 23, as it purported to exclude or modify (i.e., had the effect of excluding or modifying) any right to acquire the freehold. The provision requiring third party consent to a sale was accordingly void. The House of Lords in *Jones* v *Wrotham Park Settled Estates* [1980] AC 74 held that s. 23 did not invalidate agreements which merely made the terms of enfranchisement more onerous to the tenant (the actual decision in the case has since been reversed by statute: see Leasehold Reform Act 1979). Section 23 does not apply to an actual surrender, as opposed to an agreement to surrender: see *Woodruff* v *Hambro* (1990) 23 HLR 295.

4 THE NATURE OF THE RIGHT

The right conferred on the tenant who satisfies the above provisions is the right to acquire 'on fair terms' the freehold or an extended lease of the house and premises (LRA 1967, s. 1(1)). The right is exercised by service of notice on the landlord by the tenant (LRA 1967, ss. 8, 14). The price payable by the tenant is calculated in accordance with a statutory formula (LRA 1967, s. 9).

4.1 The house and premises

The property to which the tenant is entitled is 'the house and premises', which term is also used in relation to quantifying the rateable value for the purposes of determining whether the tenancy is at a low rent (see para. 3.2 above). The 'premises' mean 'any garage, outhouse, garden, yard and appurtenances which at the relevant time (i.e., the time the tenant serves notice of his desire to enfranchise, etc.) are let to him with the house and are occupied with and used for the purposes of the house or any part of it by him or any other occupant' (LRA 1967, s. 2(3)). Where a landlord let a house to a tenant, and subsequently the tenant took an assignment of a strip of garden, the freehold of which was owned by the same landlord, the garden did not comprise 'premises' within s. 2(3), as it had not been let to the tenant with the house (*Gaidowski* v *Gonville & Caius College, Cambridge* [1975] 1 WLR 1066). There must be a reasonably close connection between the letting of the house and the letting of the garden. In *Methuen-Campbell* v *Walters* [1979] 1 QB 525, the lease comprised a dwelling-house, a garden, and some rough pasture referred to as a 'paddock'. It was argued unsuccessfully that the paddock, which was physically divided off from the garden, was an appurtenance to the house. The Court of Appeal, whilst baulking at the prospect of defining 'appurtenances', stated that the minimum requirement would be that the land in question was within the curtilage of the house (on which see chapter 7, para. 3.1), which this paddock was clearly not.

4.2 Tenant's obligation to take additional property

The landlord can require the tenant to take, as well as any property which falls within this definition, such other premises let with the house but not currently occupied with and used for the purposes of the house (because, for example, the tenant has assigned or sub-let that part of the demised property) where the court is satisfied that it would be unreasonable for the landlord to retain them in the circumstances. The landlord should give notice objecting to their severance from the property the subject of the tenant's claim not later than two months after service of the tenant's notice on him (LRA 1967, s. 2(4)). As additional property which the tenant is obliged to take pursuant to these provisions is thereby defined as 'premises', the price paid by the tenant will take account of this additional property (see LRA 1967, s. 9).

4.3 Landlord's retention of parts of property

The 1967 Act strives to prevent the creation of 'flying freeholds' (see, for example, s. 2(2)). The landlord may object to the acquisition by the tenant of any part of the 'house and premises' which lies above or below other premises (not consisting only of underlying mines or minerals) in which the landlord has an interest, and, failing agreement with the tenant to exclude this part, the court may order that it shall be excluded from the acquisition if it is satisfied that any hardship or inconvenience likely to result to the tenant from its exclusion is outweighed by the difficulties which would be caused to the landlord or other persons interested in the premises (LRA 1967, s. 2(5)). The landlord may also require that underlying minerals be excepted from the acquisition, on the basis that proper provision is made for the support of the house and premises (LRA 1967, s. 2(6)). Where property is excluded from the acquisition by virtue of these provisions, allowance is made in calculation of the purchase price by deeming a surrender of the lease in relation to the parts in question before the tenant exercises his rights by serving notice (LRA 1967, s. 2(7)).

4.4 Effect of enfranchisement

If the tenant succeeds in a claim for enfranchisement under the 1967 Act, he is entitled to a conveyance of the house and premises for an estate in fee simple absolute, subject to the tenancy itself and to tenant's incumbrances (e.g., mortgages over his interest) but otherwise free from incumbrances (e.g., mortgages over the landlord's interest) (LRA 1967, s. 8). From the moment the notice of desire is served on the landlord, it operates as a contract freely entered into for the landlord to make the conveyance of the freehold of 'house and premises' (LRA 1967, s. 5(1)), which contract is registrable by notice or caution in registered land, and as an estate contract in unregistered land. The rights to be conveyed to the tenant on enfranchisement are set out in s. 10 of the 1967 Act.

4.5 Price to be paid

The method of calculation of the price is laid down in the statute. The process of valuation is complex and many factors must be considered. What follows is no more than a thumbnail sketch of the outline principles. Those involved in the process must examine with great care the detailed provisions of the Act itself.

There are essentially two different methods of assessment, and which is used depends upon the value of the house and premises in question! Fortunately, this first step is facilitated by the use of relatively straightforward formulae based upon the rateable value of the house and premises or, where no rateable value exists, the premium and the length of term (see further, LRA 1967, s. 9(1A)). The 1993 Act has made some modification in those cases which have been brought within the 1967 Act by that statute.

If the value of the house and premises does not exceed the limits set out in s. 9(1A), s. 9(1) applies, whereby the price is the value of the freehold of the house and premises on the open market (excluding from that market the tenant and members of his family residing in the house), on the assumption (*inter alia*) that sale is subject to the current tenancy which may be extended under the 1967 Act but which does not carry any right to enfranchise. Thus, it is to be assumed that possession of the house may not be acquired until the existing and extended term have expired, and that in the interim the ground rents are paid to the reversioner. This formula requires capitalisation of the ground rents.

If the value of the house and premises does exceed the limits above, the formula is less favourable to the acquiring tenant. Section 9(1A), as inserted by the Housing Act 1974, s. 118(4) and subsequently amended, dictates that the price is the value of the freehold of the house and premises on the open market (this time including the tenant and his family), the freehold being purchased subject to the tenancy. However, whilst it is to be assumed that the tenant will have the right to remain in possession at the end of the lease pursuant to the LTA 1954, Part I or sch. 10 to the Housing and Local Government Act 1989 (as the case might be), it is also to be assumed that the tenancy carries no rights to enfranchise or extend the lease. A reduction in the price is made where the tenant has improved the property, and it is to be assumed for valuation purposes that the tenant has no liability to carry out repairs, maintenance or redecorations.

If the long tenancy pursuant to which the tenant's right to enfranchise has arisen is only brought within the 1967 Act by ss. 1A or 1B (i.e., by the amendments effected by the 1993 Act), there are three further consequences:

(a) the share of the 'marriage value' to which the tenant is to be regarded as being entitled is not to exceed one half of it;

(b) the assumption that the tenant will be able to remain in possession pursuant to the 1954 or 1989 Act is not to be made;

(c) the landlord may claim compensation for any resulting diminution in the value of any interest he has in other property, and for any other resulting loss or damage referable to his ownership of any interest in other property. Such compensation will then comprise part of the price payable by the tenant.

4.6 Extension of lease

Where the tenant successfully seeks a lease extension, he is entitled to the grant of a tenancy of the house and premises for 50 years commencing at the date of expiry of his existing lease. The terms of the tenancy other than rent are the same as the existing lease, save as to take account of property which has been excluded from the new tenancy (e.g., pursuant to s. 2(4) to (7)), alterations made since the grant of the existing lease, or (where the existing lease derives from more than one separate leases) the combined effect of the different leases (LRA 1967, s. 15(1)). The rent payable under the new tenancy will be a ground rent representing the letting value of the site, without including anything for the value of the buildings, as at the date of its commencement. After a further 25 years, however, the landlord may elect to substitute as the rent the then current letting value of the site by giving written notice to that effect in the 25th year of the tenancy. The reasonable costs of valuation for these purposes are to be met by the tenant (LRA 1967, s. 15(2)). Where a lease is extended pursuant to the 1967 Act, the new tenancy will not carry with it rights to enfranchise or to extend further, nor will the tenant be protected on its expiry by the operation of Part I of the Landlord and Tenant Act 1954 or sch. 10 to the Local Government and Housing Act 1989. Further statutory rights are expressly excluded (LRA 1967, s. 16).

4.7 Procedure

The procedure whereby the rights conferred by the Leasehold Reform Act 1967 are exercised is contained in sch. 3 thereof, and in statutory regulations (see Leasehold Reform (Enfranchisement and Extension) Regulations 1967, SI 1967 No 1879). The tenant activates the statutory machinery by serving notice of his desire to have the freehold or an extended lease, as the case may be, on the landlord. He must use the prescribed form for this purpose (see Leasehold Reform (Notices) Regulations 1967, SI 1967 No 1768: for the effect of inaccuracies or fraud in such notices, see *Cresswell* v *Duke of Westminster* [1985] 2 EGLR 151; *Dymond* v *Arundel-Timms* (1990) 23 HLR 397). Where the tenant's term certain has expired, but he is holding over pursuant to Part I, LTA 1954, he may still exercise his rights under the 1967 Act, but in a case where the landlord has served the tenant with notice seeking to terminate the tenancy, the 1967 Act claim must be made within two months thereof (sch. 3, para. 2). There is a procedure whereby a tenant can claim enfranchisement (only) where the landlord cannot be found (LRA 1967, s. 27).

4.8 Opposition by the landlord

The landlord must give notice in reply to the tenant within two months of the tenant's notice of desire (sch. 3, para. 7; for prescribed form, see SI 1967 No 1768). The landlord has very limited grounds for opposing the tenant's claim under the 1967 Act once it is established that the claim can be properly brought, but if he does wish to oppose the claim (e.g., on the basis that the tenant is not entitled to enfranchise or extend his lease, or that the provisions outlined below apply), he must state the grounds in his notice. Where a claim has been made, the tenancy may not terminate by effluxion of time, or by a landlord's notice to quit, or by termination of a superior tenancy, or by exercise of a right of re-entry without leave of the court (sch. 3, paras. 3, 4).

4.8.1 Reasonably required for residence

Section 18 of the 1967 Act provides that a claim to enfranchise or extend the lease will fail if the landlord obtains an order from the court that he may resume possession on the ground that the house and premises (or part thereof) is reasonably required for the occupation of the landlord or an adult member of the landlord's family (as defined in s. 18(3)). The landlord must apply to the court for such an order between the tenant serving his notice of desire and effect being given to it. However, the landlord will not be able to apply for an order of this kind if his interest was purchased or created after 18 February 1966, and in any event no order will be made if to make an order would cause greater hardship than to make none. If an order is made, the tenant will then be entitled to compensation, calculated in accordance with sch. 2 to the 1967 Act.

4.8.2 Redevelopment rights

Where the tenant applies to extend his lease (but not where he applies to enfranchise), or where a lease extension has been granted, the landlord may apply to the court for an order that he may resume possession of the property on the ground that for purposes of redevelopment he proposes to demolish or reconstruct the whole or a substantial part of the house and premises (LRA 1967, s. 17). If an order is granted to such effect, then possession can be resumed by the landlord, the tenant being in turn entitled to compensation (on which see sch. 2).

4.9 Establishing the terms of the acquisition

Leasehold valuation tribunals have jurisdiction to determine the price payable on enfranchisement, the rent payable following a lease extension, and the compensation payable to a tenant in the event of the landlord asserting that the property is reasonably required for a residence or that redevelopment rights are to be exercised (LRA 1967, s. 21(1)). If application is made to a tribunal for determination of these matters or any of them, or the parties agree, the tribunal may also determine what provisions should be contained in any conveyance or new lease, apportion between the house and premises the rent to be payable, and determine the amount of a sub-tenant's share in relation to compensation payable to a tenant (LRA

1967, s. 21(2)). Otherwise, these matters fall within the jurisdiction of the county court. The county court has exclusive jurisdiction to determine whether a person is entitled to enfranchise or acquire an extended lease, and to what property his rights extend (LRA 1967, s. 20(1)).

5 ESTATE MANAGEMENT SCHEMES

In the first two years after the coming into force of the Leasehold Reform Act 1967, the appropriate Minister could certify that a particular landlord should retain powers of management and control over the development and use of houses in the area (LRA 1967, s. 19). This power, used principally, although not exclusively, to reassure the large inherited urban estates that despite the loss of some freeholds as a result of the new legislation they could still influence the quality of the local environment, required the submission of a scheme to the High Court for its approval. The schemes thus evolved did not prohibit or restrict the enfranchisement of leasehold property; they merely regulated the use of the property in the hands of the tenant who had enfranchised. There was a common interest in landlords and tenants propounding a scheme, and joint application to the court became a possibility (see, for example, *Re Abbots Park Estate* [1972] 1 WLR 598; *Re Abbots Park Estate* (No. 2) [1972] 1 WLR 1597). The opportunity of obtaining a Ministerial certificate arose again in relation to those properties brought within the 1967 Act by the Housing Act 1974 (see the 1974 Act, s. 118).

The Leasehold Reform, Housing and Urban Development Act 1993 contains important provisions concerning estate management schemes. Leasehold valuation tribunals are now given much wider powers. They can terminate or vary existing estate management schemes (a power which has previously been vested in the High Court) (LRHUDA 1993, s. 75). But more significantly, they can also approve new schemes, without the need for a Ministerial certificate or High Court approval (see generally LRHUDA 1993, s. 69) in relation to those houses which have been brought into the 1967 Act by the removal of the high value limits. Applications can be made in the period of two years commencing on 1 November 1993, although if the Secretary of State consents, on being satisfied of particular onerous conditions, late applications may be made (LRHUDA 1993, ss. 70-72). Although the existence of an estate management scheme does not prevent enfranchisement any more than previously, the terms of the purchase of the freehold will of course be subject to the scheme, and there are provisions dealing with contemporaneous applications for approval of a scheme and tenants' notices of desire to enfranchise (LRHUDA 1993, s. 75).

The approval of a scheme under s. 70 of the 1993 Act requires the tribunal to be satisfied that, in order to maintain adequate standards of appearance and amenity and regulate development within the area in the event of tenants' exercising their rights, it is in the general interest that the landlord should retain powers of management (LRHUDA 1993, s. 70(2)). They must have regard primarily to the benefit likely to result from the scheme to the area as a whole, and the extent to which it is reasonable to impose, for the benefit of the area, obligations on tenants acquiring the interest of their landlord. They shall have regard also to the past development and present character of the area and to architectural or historical considerations, to neighbouring areas, and 'to the circumstances generally.' For examples of the operation of similar principles in relation to the LRA 1967, s. 19, see *Re Dulwich College Estate's Application* (1974) 231 EG 845; *Eton College* v *Nassar* [1991] 2 EGLR 271.

B LEASEHOLD REFORM, HOUSING AND URBAN DEVELOPMENT ACT 1993: FLATS

6 COMPARISON OF LRA 1967 AND LRHUDA 1993

As we have seen, the Leasehold Reform Act 1967 has no application to flats. Indeed, the abhorrence of creating 'flying freeholds' by the exercise of enfranchisement was such that provision is made to exempt from the process of acquisition any part of the house and premises lying above or below other property of the landlord (see LRA 1967, s. 2(5) and para. 4.3 above). The difficulties inherent in flying freeholds concern primarily the non-enforceability of positive covenants, such as to repair, between successors in title of adjacent properties. Ultimately this problem is to be addressed by the introduction of commonhold as an alternative method of land-holding. However, whilst the commonhold proposals have reached an advanced stage, and the government has undertaken to legislate, no Bill has yet been put before Parliament.

The Leasehold Reform, Housing and Urban Development Act 1993 does not (contrary to certain popular misconception at the time) introduce a commonhold scheme. It does, however, seek to redress the injustice long leaseholders of flats may have felt in comparing the extent of their rights as against the rights of those holding long leases of houses. The 1993 Act thus confers two alternative rights on these persons: a right of *collective enfranchisement* (which will require the active participation of other tenants in order to be exercised successfully), and a right of *individual lease renewal* (which will not). The legislation is dauntingly complex. It should be emphasised at the outset, however, that the rights conferred by the 1993 Act differ most significantly from those conferred by the 1967 Act in one respect. Whereas the 1967 Act affords the opportunity to long leaseholders of houses to enfranchise at a discount, the 1993 Act is painstaking to ensure that those tenants of flats who enfranchise or obtain lease renewals will pay full compensation to the landlord. Although the proposals in the 1992 Conservative manifesto which spawned this legislation were undoubtedly motivated by a desire to appease the vocal and electorally significant tenant flat lobby, the legislation as drawn pays considerable attention to the need to maintain support for the government amongst the landed classes.

Although there is no overlap between the 1967 Act and the 1993 Act (the former applies to houses, the latter to flats), it should not be thought that the two statutory codes now comprehensively cover all residential property held on long lease. As will be seen, the criteria to be satisfied to be able to claim under the 1993 Act are closely defined without reference to the 1967 Act. There will be many cases of long leaseholders who are unable to bring a claim under either of the statutes.

It remains to be seen how widely tenants seek to exercise these new rights. Collective enfranchisement is an exercise which will require huge effort on the part of those initiating the process, and many may be discouraged by the awesome complexity, inevitable expense and numerous pitfalls. Moreover, until commonhold is introduced, there is no very obvious machinery which tenants who have enfranchised can use to hold the freehold and manage the property other than a corporate landlord, albeit one controlled by themselves. Their status as tenants will be unlikely to change in consequence of exercising their rights under this legislation, although the terms of their leases will presumably be much improved. In the circumstances, individual lease renewal (whereby the long leaseholder will at the end of the present lease be entitled, at a premium, to acquire a new term of 90 years) may prove much the more attractive of these new rights (see also comments on the Act by Bright (1994) Conv. 211; Clarke (1994) Conv. 223; and Davey (1994) 57 MLR 773).

It is generally not possible to contract out of, or modify the rights of a tenant in relation to, collective enfranchisement or individual lease renewal (see further, LRHUDA 1993, s. 93). Application of the Act in relation to Crown land is dealt with by s. 94. Property vested inalienably in the National Trust and property within the precinct of a cathedral church is exempt from the operation of the Act (LRHUDA 1993, ss. 95, 96).

7 COLLECTIVE ENFRANCHISEMENT: SUMMARY

Section 1(1) of the 1993 Act summarises the right of collective enfranchisement as follows:

> This Chapter has effect for the purpose of conferring on qualifying tenants of flats contained in premises to which this Chapter applies on the relevant date [i.e., the date on which the initial notice of the claim is given: s. 1(8)]

the right, exercisable subject to and in accordance with this Chapter, to have the freehold of those premises acquired on their behalf—

(a) by a person or persons appointed by them for the purpose, and
(b) at a price determined in accordance with this Chapter; . . .

The Act broadly contemplates a group of tenants in a building co-operating in the acquisition of the freehold interest in that building. It does not dictate what vehicle the tenants are to use to acquire the freehold, other than to state that there must be a 'nominee purchaser' appointed by them at the outset of the process. It is anticipated that in most cases the tenants will form a company, which company will then acquire the freehold at a price calculated in accordance with the provisions of the Act, and presumably let the flats to the tenants on more favourable terms. Various questions arise in connection with the process. Those who are considering whether to seek collective enfranchisement will need to know in particular:

(a) whether the building on which they have designs is within the 1993 Act;
(b) how many tenants will be required to participate for the acquisition to succeed;
(c) what the price of the acquisition is likely to be, and what other costs are involved.

8 COLLECTIVE ENFRANCHISEMENT: THE QUALIFYING CONDITIONS

8.1 The premises

The premises must consist of a self-contained building or part of a building (see further, LRHUDA 1993, s. 3(2)), the freehold of which building or part is owned by the same person. The premises must contain two or more flats held by 'qualifying tenants' (a term central to the workings of the Act and which will next be considered), and the total number of flats held by such tenants must be not less than two-thirds of the total number of flats contained in the premises (LRHUDA 1993, s. 3(1)).

A 'flat' is defined as 'a separate set of premises (whether or not on the same floor):

(a) which forms part of a building, and
(b) which is constructed or adapted for use for the purposes of a dwelling, and
(c) either the whole or a material part of which lies above or below some other part of the building' (LRHUDA 1993, s. 101(1)).

8.1.1 Excluded premises

Certain premises are excluded from the right to collective enfranchisement (though in such circumstances the individual tenants may still be able to seek lease renewal under Chapter II):

(a) If a part (or parts) of the premises are neither occupied (or intended to be occupied) for residential purposes nor comprised in the common parts, and the internal floor area of that part exceeds 10% of the internal floor area of the premises (see LRHUDA 1993, s. 4(3)), taken as a whole (LRHUDA 1993, s. 4(1)). Where a part is not used as such for residential purposes, but is used in conjunction with a particular dwelling (as, for example, a garage, parking space, or storage area), it shall be taken to be occupied for residential purposes (LRHUDA 1993, s. 4(2)).

(b) If the premises have a resident landlord (see further LRHUDA 1993, s. 10, and case law under the Rent Act 1977, s. 12: chapter 2, para. 3.10; chapter 3, para. 3.11), and do not contain more than four units (LRHUDA 1993, s. 4(4)). 'Unit' is defined as meaning a flat, or any other separate set of premises constructed or adapted for use for the purposes of a dwelling, or a separate set of premises let, or intended for letting, on a business lease (LRHUDA 1993, s. 38(1)).

8.2 Qualifying tenants

It is essential for the claimants to calculate the number of qualifying tenants in relation to the premises of which enfranchisement is to be sought, as the claim will not be tenable if the total number of flats held by such tenants is less than two-thirds of the total number of flats contained in the premises. A tenant may 'qualify' although he does not occupy the flat in question as his only or principal home (indeed he may have sub-let), and in carrying out this calculation, it is therefore unnecessary to go on to consider whether the qualifying tenant is in occupation. However, it should be appreciated that when the claim is initiated, not less than half of the qualifying tenants who give the notice must satisfy a statutory residence condition (LRHUDA 1993, ss. 13(2), 6: see para. 9.5.3 below).

A qualifying tenant of a flat is a tenant of the flat under a long lease at a low rent (LRHUDA 1993, s. 5(1)), both of which terms are defined elsewhere in the Act (see paras. 8.3 and 8.4 below). As no flat shall have more than one qualifying tenant at any one time (LRHUDA 1993, s. 5(3)), it is necessary to provide for the situation where as a result of sub-lettings (on long lease), or the grant of a joint tenancy, there are two (or more) persons who *prima facie* 'qualify' in relation to a single flat. In the former case, the tenant in possession will generally qualify: in the latter, the joint tenants are generally regarded as jointly constituting the qualifying tenant of the flat (LRHUDA 1993, s. 5(4)).

There are important exclusions as follows ((a) to (c) are contained in the 1993 Act, s. 5(2)):

(a) The lease is a business lease (i.e., a tenancy to which Part II, LTA 1954 applies: see LRHUDA 1993, s. 101(1)).

(b) The immediate landlord under the lease is a charitable housing trust (i.e., a housing trust within the Housing Act 1985, s. 6, which is a charity within the Charities Act 1993, s. 96(1)), and the flat forms part of the housing accommodation provided by it in pursuit of its charitable purposes.

(c) The lease was granted as a sub-lease in breach of the terms of the head-lease (such breach not having been waived), and the head-lease was not itself a long lease at a low rent.

(d) The person who would on an application of the above principles be qualifying tenant is the tenant of three flats contained in the premises. In these circumstances, it shall be taken that there is no qualifying tenant of any of those flats (LRHUDA 1993, s. 5(5)). This provision applies to associated companies as well (LRHUDA 1993, s. 5(6)).

8.3 Long leases

Section 7(1) of the 1993 Act defines 'long lease'. The definition is essentially that of the 1967 Act, namely a lease granted for a term of years certain exceeding 21 years, whether or not it is (or may become) terminable before the end of that term by notice, re-entry, forfeiture or otherwise. Case law on the 1967 Act provisions will therefore be applicable (see para. 3.1 above), but care should be taken to apply the statutory provisions of the 1993 Act, as there are some small differences. Perpetually renewable leases, leases granted in pursuance of the secure tenant's right to buy (chapter 7), shared ownership leases (chapter 3, para. 3.4), and most leases terminable after death or marriage qualify (LRHUDA 1993, s. 7(2)). Where a long lease at a low rent has expired, and the tenant is granted a new lease of the same property or part of it, that lease will qualify within the 1993 Act (LRHUDA 1993, s. 7(3)). So, too, where the effect of a renewal of a tenant's lease (pursuant to a covenant to renew without payment of a premium) is to bring the total of the terms granted to more than 21 years (LRHUDA 1993, s. 7(4)). A tenant will qualify whilst his lease is continued by virtue of Part I of the Landlord and Tenant Act 1954 or sch. 10 to the Local Government and Housing Act 1989 (LRHUDA 1993, s. 7(5): see further, chapter 4).

8.4 Low rent

Section 8 of the 1993 Act sets out the test for 'low rent'. It is significantly different from that used for the 1967 Act, in that it is exclusively based upon the 'initial year' of the letting, i.e., the period of one year beginning with the date of the commencement of the term of the lease (LRHUDA 1993, ss. 8(2)(a), 101(5)). Where the lease which has been renewed is treated as a long lease although it is not itself a term exceeding 21 years (LRHUDA 1993, s. 7(4)), then the initial year will be the year following the commencement of the renewed term (LRHUDA 1993, s. 8(5)). 'Rent' is defined for the purposes of this provision as rent reserved as such, disregarding sums expressed to be payable for services, repairs, insurance, costs and so forth (see LRHUDA 1993, s. 8(2)(d)).

8.4.1 Lease entered into on or after 1 April 1990

Where the lease was entered into on or after 1 April 1990 (other than pursuant to a contract made before that date), the aggregate amount of rent payable during the initial year must not have exceeded £1,000 if the flat is in Greater London, or £250 if it is elsewhere.

8.4.2 Lease entered into before 1 April 1990 and on or after 1 April 1963

Where the lease was entered into before 1 April 1990 (or subsequently, pursuant to a contract made after that date, the flat having a rateable value at some time before 1 April 1990) and on or after 1 April 1963, the aggregate amount of the rent payable during the initial year must not have exceeded two-thirds of the rateable value of the flat on the appropriate date (i.e., the date of the commencement of the lease, or, if later, the first date the flat had a rateable value: see also Rent Act 1977, s. 25: LRHUDA 1993, s. 8(2)(b),(c)).

8.4.3 Lease entered into before 1 April 1963

Where the lease was entered into before 1 April 1963, the aggregate amount of rent payable during the initial year must not have exceeded two-thirds of the letting value of the flat on the date of the commencement of the lease. For this purpose 'letting value' is given the same meaning as in s. 4(1), LRA 1967 (LRHUDA 1993, s. 8(3),(4), and see para. 3.2.1.3 above).

9 COLLECTIVE ENFRANCHISEMENT: THE NATURE OF THE RIGHT

9.1 Property to be acquired

The right to acquire the freehold is conferred on those qualifying tenants who satisfy the above conditions. They are also entitled to acquire the freehold of any property which is not comprised in 'the premises' (see para. 8.1 above) but which is owned by the freehold owner of the premises and is at the date on which notice of the claim is given ('the relevant date': LRHUDA 1993, s. 1(8)) *either*:

(a) 'appurtenant property' (i.e., any garage, outhouse, garden, yard or appurtenances belonging to or usually enjoyed with the flat: LRHUDA 1993, s. 1(7)) which is demised by the lease held by a qualifying tenant of one of the flats in the premises (LRHUDA 1993, s. 1(3)(a)); or

(b) property which a qualifying tenant of any flat in the premises is entitled under the terms of his lease to use in common with the occupiers of other premises (LRHUDA 1993, s. 1(3)(b)). It does not matter that the 'other premises' are not contained in the premises of which acquisition is sought. The freeholder may, however, by granting 'permanent rights' over this property (or other property, or by transferring other property outright) prevent the claimants enfranchising in respect of it. The rights granted must ensure that thereafter the occupier of the flat has 'as nearly as may be' the same rights over that property as those enjoyed on the relevant date by the qualifying tenant in question (see generally LRHUDA 1993, s. 1(4)).

It should be mentioned here that those acquiring the freehold may be compelled to take other property pursuant to s. 21(4) of the 1993 Act (see para. 9.5.9 below).

9.2 Leaseback of flats and other units

The freeholder is entitled to claim a leaseback to him on a purchase of the freehold under Chapter I of certain flats or other units in the premises, and in certain circumstances, leaseback is mandatory (LRHUDA 1993, s. 36, sch. 9). The freeholder may elect to take a leaseback in respect of any unit in the premises which is not immediately before the time of acquisition of the freehold ('the appropriate time') a flat let to a person who is a qualifying tenant of it (LRHUDA 1993, sch. 9, para. 4). Where, immediately before the appropriate time, a flat is let under a secure tenancy, the freeholder being the tenant's immediate landlord or (where there have been sub-demises) all intermediate landlords are public sector landlords, then the purchaser must grant a leaseback to the freeholder: so, too, if, the tenancy not being secure, the freeholder is a housing association, and the tenant is not a qualifying tenant of the flat (LRHUDA 1993, sch. 9, paras. 2, 3).

The leaseback, where it operates, and subject to the contrary agreement of the parties or a direction of a leasehold valuation tribunal, is to be a lease granted for a term of 999 years at a peppercorn rent (LRHUDA 1993, sch. 9, Part IV, to which see generally for other terms).

9.3 Effect of enfranchisement

If the claim to collective enfranchisement succeeds, the 'nominee purchaser' is entitled to a conveyance of the freehold of the premises and any other property being acquired, subject to such incumbrances as may have been agreed or determined (LRHUDA 1993, s. 34(1): see further for rights conveyed LRHUDA 1993, sch. 7). Enfranchisement will also effect a transfer to the nominee purchaser of any leasehold interests which are interposed between the freeholder and a qualifying tenant ('intermediate leasehold interests': see generally LRHUDA 1993, s. 2). The purchaser takes free of mortgages (LRHUDA 1993, s. 35, but see sch. 8 for detailed procedures). As with a tenant's notice of desire under the 1967 Act, the service of an initial notice under the 1993 Act is registrable as an estate contract. It is expressly provided that tenants' rights under the 1993 Act shall not take effect as overriding interests (LRHUDA 1993, s. 97(1)).

9.4 Price to be paid

The statute sets out in great detail the method by which the price is to be calculated (LRHUDA 1993, s. 32, sch. 6). The purchaser pays not only for the freehold, but also for any intermediate leasehold interests, or other interests, which are being acquired. In cases where agreement is not reached, the price will be determined by a leasehold valuation tribunal.

9.4.1 Price payable for freehold interest

The price payable for the acquisition of the freehold of the premises is to be determined by aggregation of three elements:

9.4.1.1 The value of the freeholder's interest in the premises

This is the amount which at the valuation date (i.e., the date the value is determined, whether by agreement or by a leasehold valuation tribunal: LRHUDA 1993, sch. 6, para. 1(1)) the freeholder's interest might be expected to realise if sold on the open market (with neither the nominee purchaser nor any participating tenant buying or seeking to buy). This element is based on the capitalised value of the ground rents during the existing (and any extended) term, and the value of the reversion at the expiry of the term. Various assumptions are made. In particular, it is assumed that the purchase is subject to any intermediate or other leasehold interests in the premises which are themselves to be acquired by the nominee purchaser.

9.4.1.2 The freeholder's share of the 'marriage value'

This takes account of the gain to the acquiring tenants of being able to grant themselves new tenancies, subsequent to acquisition, without payment of premium and without restriction as to the length of the term. Thus the 'marriage value' is the difference between (a) the aggregate value of the freehold and intermediate leasehold interests in the premises prior to the acquisition, and (b) the aggregate value of those interests after acquisition. The 'freeholder's share' is no less than 50% of this difference, and may be more if on a sale on the open market a greater proportion would have been determined by agreement between the parties. In most cases, this element will be the largest part of the purchase price to be paid on acquisition. The provisions have been criticised (see in particular Daiches (1993) 43 EG 104) as being poorly drafted, and clarity may require litigation.

9.4.1.3 Compensation for loss resulting from enfranchisement

In addition to the above, the freeholder is entitled to reasonable compensation for loss or damage which he will suffer by virtue of diminution in the value of any interest he has in other property resulting from the enfranchisement, and any other resulting loss or damage referable to his ownership of any interest in other property, such loss to include loss of development value (as defined: see LRHUDA 1993, sch. 6, para. 5(4)).

9.4.2 Price payable for intermediate leasehold interests

Where the nominee purchaser is also acquiring intermediate leasehold interests, a separate price will be payable for each of these interests. This will be the aggregate of the value of the interest concerned, and any amount of compensation payable to the owner of the interest (as determined in accordance with Part III of sch. 6 to the 1993 Act). The holder of an intermediate leasehold interest which is acquired by the nominee purchaser will also be entitled to part of the freeholder's share of the marriage value (see further, LRHUDA 1993, sch. 6, para. 9).

9.4.3 Price payable for other interests

Part IV of sch. 6 makes provision for the calculation of the price payable for the acquisition of freehold interests in appurtenant property or common parts (see above) or interests in property which the freeholder has required the nominee purchaser to take pursuant to s. 21(4) (see para. 9.5.9 below).

9.5 Procedure

9.5.1 The 'reversioner'

A claim is initiated by giving a notice to the 'reversioner' in respect of the premises. As it is this person who conducts proceedings on behalf of the landlords, it is important to both sides to identify him correctly. If the freeholder owns all the reversionary interests which are to be acquired then he will be the reversioner (LRHUDA 1993, s. 9(1)). If there are intermediate leasehold interests, then recourse must be had to sch. 1 to the Act (see s. 9(2)). Normally, the freeholder will act, but the 'relevant landlords', as they are known, may agree otherwise, or the court may on the application of one such landlord appoint some other person (who must himself be a relevant landlord) to act if the respective interests of the relevant landlords in the premises, the freeholder's absence, incapacity, or unwillingness to act, or other special circumstances so require. The court has power to remove the reversioner and appoint another relevant landlord to act in cases of actual or apprehended delay, and may do so not only on application by the landlords themselves, but also on application by the nominee purchaser (LRHUDA 1993, sch. 1, Part I).

9.5.2 The nominee purchaser

The 'initial notice' of the claim must designate the nominee purchaser, and the address at which notices may be given to that person (LRHUDA 1993, s. 13(3)(f)). Although the nominee purchaser does not give the initial notice, it is his or (more accurately in most cases, as the vehicle of a limited company will be used) its duty to conduct the proceedings on behalf of the participating tenants, and ultimately to acquire the freehold and any other interests on their behalf (LRHUDA 1993, s. 15(1)). The participating tenants have power to terminate the appointment of a nominee purchaser by giving notice to that effect, such notice to be given to both the nominee purchaser and to the reversioner, and to state the replacement nominee (LRHUDA 1993, s. 15(3), *et seq*). There is provision too for replacement of the nominee purchaser on retirement or death (LRHUDA 1993, s. 16). The statutory provisions are, however, in the nature of a shell. It is very much up to the participating tenants to decide, inevitably on legal advice, how they wish to proceed, how the nominee purchaser is to be structured, and the rights of individual participating tenants vis-à-vis that 'person'.

9.5.3 The initial notice

The initial notice must give extensive particulars of the enfranchisement claim. Although there is no prescribed form, the details which it must follow are set out verbatim in the statute (s. 13), and it is not proposed to repeat them here. The notice must be given by a certain proportion of the qualifying tenants (as defined at para. 8.2 above) of flats contained in the premises in respect of which the claim is made. These 'participating tenants' (a term used throughout the Act: see further, s. 14) must comprise, at the date of the notice, not less than two-thirds of the total number of qualifying tenants, and their number must be not less than one-half of the total number of flats contained in the premises. This rather strange formula is taking account of the fact that some flats may not have qualifying tenants.

In addition, not less than one-half of the qualifying tenants by whom the notice is given must satisfy 'the residence condition'. The residence condition is that the tenant in question has occupied the flat (or part of it: s. 6(3)) as his only or principal home (on which see chapter 2, para. 2.5) either for the last 12 months or for periods amounting to three years in the last 10 years. It does not matter that he has used it for other purposes (LRHUDA 1993, s. 6(2)). The occupation need not have been in right of the lease, but the condition cannot be satisfied by a company or artificial person (LRHUDA 1993, s. 6(3)). Occupation by one of joint tenants which satisfies the residence condition will suffice (LRHUDA 1993, s. 6(4)).

9.5.4 Reversioner's counter-notice

The reversioner has two months (at least: the initial notice may give him longer: see LRHUDA 1993, s. 13(3)(g)) in which to give a counter-notice to the nominee purchaser admitting or denying the participating tenants' entitlement to exercise the right to collective enfranchisement. If no counter-notice is given within the requisite period, the court has power to proceed to determine the terms of the acquisition (LRHUDA 1993, s. 25). In the case of a denial of the claim, the counter-notice must specify reasons. If the nominee purchaser nevertheless wishes to proceed, he should apply to the court within two months of the giving of the counter-notice, and seek a declaration of entitlement (LRHUDA 1993, s. 22).

9.5.5 Establishing the terms of acquisition

Once entitlement to enfranchise has been established or agreed, the parties should seek to agree the terms of the acquisition. If this does not prove possible, application should be made to a leasehold valuation tribunal, which has jurisdiction to determine matters in dispute, including the price payable on acquisition (LRHUDA 1993, s. 24). Application to the tribunal cannot be made until two months have elapsed from the date of the relevant counter-notice, but must be made before the end of a period of six months commencing with that date (LRHUDA 1993, s. 24(1), (2)).

9.5.6 Vesting orders

The 1993 Act makes provision for vesting orders where the freeholder or other relevant landlords cannot be found (ss. 26, 27).

9.5.7 Costs

The costs of collective enfranchisement will generally be borne by the nominee purchaser (see further, LRHUDA 1993, s. 33). It will therefore be important that, prior to initiating the process of acquisition, the participating tenants agree on their respective contributions to the expenses of the claim. The nominee purchaser will be liable for the costs of the reversioner or other relevant landlords in investigating the claim, valuing interests, deducing title, making copies, and conveying the interests in question. However, the nominee purchaser will not be liable if the initial notice is withdrawn in consequence of the landlord's proof of an intention to redevelop or the inception of compulsory purchase proceedings (see para. 10 below). Nor will he be liable for the costs of a reference to a leasehold valuation tribunal, where it will be expected that each party will bear its own costs.

9.5.8 Conveyance of the property

The acquisition will be completed by conveyance of the freehold of the premises and any other property to the nominee purchaser. For details of the conveyancing effects of this procedure, see LRHUDA 1993, ss. 34 to 36. The reversioner is not obliged to complete until the price, together with the costs for which the nominee purchaser is liable, is paid.

9.5.9 Property of no practical use to the landlord

The reversioner may require the nominee purchaser to acquire interests in other property (LRHUDA 1993, s. 21(4)). The interests in question must be those of the freeholder of the premises being acquired or of any other relevant landlord. The property must either for all practical purposes cease to be of use or benefit to the owner, or cease to be capable of being reasonably managed or maintained by him following the acquisition of his interest in the premises or any other property (such as, for example, property appurtenant to the premises). The reversioner must specify in his counter-notice any such interest it is proposed that the nominee purchaser should take, and if the acquisition does include such interest, the price payable on enfranchisement will include an element in respect of it.

10 COLLECTIVE ENFRANCHISEMENT: GROUNDS OF OPPOSITION

10.1 Intended redevelopment

The reversioner may resist the claim by contending that an 'appropriate landlord' (i.e., the reversioner and/or other relevant landlords, possibly acting together) intends to redevelop the whole or a substantial part of the specified premises (LRHUDA 1993, s. 23). In such a case, the reversioner's counter-notice must state that an appropriate landlord is to apply for an order from the county court declaring that the right to collective enfranchisement shall not be exercisable (LRHUDA 1993, s. 21(2)(c)). The application to the court must then be made within two months of the giving of the counter-notice. Three conditions must be satisfied before the court has jurisdiction to make an order on this basis (LRHUDA 1993, s. 23(2)):

(a) Not less than two-thirds of all the long leases on which flats contained in the premises are held are due to terminate within the period of five years beginning with the date notice was given under s. 13. This requires the court to look at all the long leases, not just those held by the participating or qualifying tenants (and apparently not just long leases at a low rent). It will be difficult for many landlords to overcome this hurdle.

(b) For the purposes of redevelopment the applicant intends, once the leases have so terminated, to demolish or reconstruct, or to carry out substantial works of construction on the whole or a substantial part of the premises.

(c) The applicant could not reasonably do the above without obtaining possession of the flats demised by those leases.

The latter three elements are very similar to the provision contained in LTA 1954, s. 30(1)(f), on which a large body of case law has built up, to which reference should be made, and HA 1988, sch. 2, Ground 6 (see chapter 2, para. 6.1.9). There is one important difference in that here the intention, whilst it must be present at the date of the application of the order, may relate to a time nearly five years into the future.

If the landlord establishes these three elements, the court *may* make an order pursuant to s. 23(1). This provision appears to confer a discretion on the court, but there is no indication in the statute as to how the discretion is to be applied. If an order is made, the initial notice will cease to have effect (LRHUDA 1993, s. 23(4)). If the court dismisses the application, on the other hand, the reversioner's counter-notice will be declared to be of no effect, and the reversioner will be required to give a further counter-notice by a date specified by the court (LRHUDA 1993, s. 23(5)). Whilst this would normally admit the claim, there seems no reason why it should not deny it, on the basis that it does not fall within the statutory provisions, or even intimate another application to the court for an order under s. 23. The latter would only be worth pursuing in the event of new evidence (e.g., of intention) being adduced.

10.2 Compulsory purchase procedures

Compulsory purchase will prevent the successful acquisition of the freehold by virtue of collective enfranchisement (see further, LRHUDA 1993, s. 30).

10.3 Designation of premises etc. for inheritance tax purposes

The designation of the premises, or any other property specified in the initial notice, for inheritance tax purposes, or an application for designation, will prevent collective enfranchisement (see further, LRHUDA 1993, s. 31). In certain circumstances, the person applying for designation will be liable for the costs of the participating tenants and the nominee purchaser (LRHUDA 1993, s. 31(5)).

11 ESTATE MANAGEMENT SCHEMES

The policy of estate management schemes has already been outlined (see para. 5 above). A landlord (or two or more landlords of neighbouring areas acting jointly) may apply to a leasehold valuation tribunal for approval of a scheme within the two-year period commencing on 1 November 1993 (or subsequently with Ministerial consent). In the event of approval being given (on the grounds set out in LRHUDA 1993, s. 70 and outlined at para. 5), the landlord will retain such powers of management over the area as the scheme provides, despite the acquisition of that landlord's interest in properties by virtue of the right of collective enfranchisement (see generally LRHUDA 1993, ss. 69 to 73). If an application for a scheme is made subsequent to the commencement of proceedings to instigate enfranchisement, the nominee purchaser may withdraw the initial notice, without penalty as to costs. If this does not occur, the reversioner should serve the counter-notice, following which there will be a stay of proceedings pending the determination of the application for a scheme (LRHUDA 1993, s. 74).

12 INDIVIDUAL LEASE RENEWAL: SUMMARY

By s. 39(1) of the 1993 Act:

> This Chapter has effect for the purpose of conferring on a tenant of a flat, in the circumstances mentioned in subsection (2), the right, exercisable subject to and in accordance with this Chapter, to acquire a new lease of the flat on payment of a premium determined in accordance with this Chapter.

The claim under Chapter II, whilst based on many of the concepts in Chapter I, is an independent claim. Thus, a tenant may seek renewal of his lease whether or not collective enfranchisement is an available alternative. It is suspected that the practical administrative difficulties of collective enfranchisement will turn many tenants towards lease renewal, and that these provisions will be invoked with much greater regularity than those in Chapter I.

13 INDIVIDUAL LEASE RENEWAL: QUALIFYING CONDITIONS

These are relatively few (see generally LRHUDA 1993, s. 39). The presence of a resident landlord does not prevent tenants who otherwise qualify from making a claim, nor does the use of some part of the building containing the flat for non-residential purposes.

(a) The premises must be a 'flat', as defined in s. 101(1) (see para. 8.1).

(b) The tenant must be a 'qualifying tenant' of the flat, as defined in s. 5 (see para. 8.2), at the date notice to claim is given. For these purposes, he can still be a qualifying tenant although he is a tenant of more than one flat in a particular building. However, as he must satisfy the residence condition below in relation to any flat of which lease renewal is claimed, he is unlikely to be able to establish rights over more than one flat at any one time. If a tenant does not qualify, for example, because the tenancy is a business tenancy within Part II, LTA 1954, he will be unable to claim lease renewal.

(c) At the date the notice of claim is made, the tenant must have occupied the flat (or part of it) as his only or principal home for the last three years, or for periods amounting to three out of the last 10 years (whether or not he has used it for other purposes). Such occupation need not be in right of the lease, and occupation by a company, artificial person or corporation sole will not suffice. Occupation for the relevant period by one of two or more joint tenants will satisfy the condition.

14 INDIVIDUAL LEASE RENEWAL: THE NATURE OF THE RIGHT

14.1 Effect of renewal

The tenant who establishes his claim is entitled to be granted, in substitution for his existing lease, a new lease of the flat at a peppercorn rent for a term expiring 90 years after the term date of the existing lease (LRHUDA 1993, s. 56(1)). The new lease will also be subject to the 1993 Act, and so it will be possible for the tenant to exercise, apparently *ad infinitum* (at least until the legislation is amended) these rights (LRHUDA 1993, s. 59(1)). On grant of the new lease 'none of the statutory provisions relating to security of tenure [presumably the Landlord and Tenant Act 1954, Part I, and the Local Government and Housing Act 1989, sch. 10] shall apply' to it (LRHUDA 1993, s. 59(2)). On expiry of the new lease, the tenant will not be able to exercise rights under those statutes; but as he will continue to have rights under the 1993 Act the inability to use them is not a serious handicap. For the position of sub-tenants following the grant of the new lease, see further LRHUDA 1993, s. 59(2) to (4).

14.2 Price to be paid

14.2.1 Premium payable for leasehold

The premium to be paid by the tenant for the new lease is calculated by aggregating three elements (see generally, LRHUDA 1993, s. 56(1), sch. 13). Valuation is to be made as at the date when all terms of the acquisition (apart from those relating to the premium, etc). have been determined either by agreement or by a leasehold valuation tribunal (LRHUDA 1993, sch. 13, para. 1). The three elements are:

14.2.1.1 *The diminution in value of the landlord's interest in the flat*

This is the difference between (a) the value of the landlord's interest in the tenant's flat prior to the grant of the new lease and (b) the value of that interest once the new lease is granted. The landlord's interest is to be valued on the basis of the amount which at the valuation date it might be expected to realise if sold on the open market by a willing seller, with the tenant not buying or seeking to buy, assuming (*inter alia*) sale subject to the tenant's lease and any other intermediate leasehold interests, and that no right of collective enfranchisement or individual lease renewal should be exercisable by the tenant of the flat. The tenant's improvements should be disregarded in conducting the valuation exercise.

14.2.1.2 *The landlord's share of the marriage value*

As with marriage value under collective enfranchisement, this is the value of the advantage conferred on the tenant of being able to combine his and the landlord's interests. The value of the tenant's interest, landlord's interest, and any intermediate leasehold interests prior to the grant of the new lease (determined as at the valuation date) is to be deducted from the value of the same interests subsequent to the lease being granted. If there are intermediate leasehold interests, their holders will be entitled to be paid a part of this sum (see LRHUDA 1993, sch. 13, para. 10).

14.2.1.3 *Compensation payable to the landlord*

The tenant also has to pay reasonable compensation to the landlord in respect of any loss or damage (including loss of development value) referable to the landlord's ownership of his interest which he will suffer as a result of the new lease being granted.

14.2.2 Sums to be paid to others

The tenant is also liable to pay to holders of intermediate leasehold interests a sum in respect of the diminution in value of that person's interest, together with compensation for any loss suffered by him in consequence of the grant of the new lease.

14.3 Procedure

The qualifying tenant initiates his claim by giving notice both to the landlord and to any third party to the tenant's lease (LRHUDA 1993, s. 42(2)). 'The landlord' is defined in s. 40 as the person most proximate to the tenant who has the power to grant a lease of the relevant length. In most cases, this will be the freeholder. If the landlord on whom the notice is to be served (termed by the Act 'the competent landlord': s. 40(4)) is not the tenant's immediate landlord, sch. 11 has effect with regard to the procedure to be adopted. As with 'the reversioner' in the collective enfranchisement process, 'the competent landlord' conducts the proceedings on behalf of the landlords' side. Any other person who is a party to a lease apart from the tenant and the immediate landlord is a 'third party' to the tenant's lease (LRHUDA 1993, s. 62(1)). The tenant can demand that the immediate landlord (or his agent) supply him with information concerning those with interests in the lease (LRHUDA 1993, s. 41), thereby enabling him to ensure that he gives notice to all appropriate parties.

The tenant's notice must specify the details of the tenant's claim (reference should be made to LRHUDA 1993, s. 42(3) for the detailed requirements to be satisfied), and specify the date by which the landlord must respond by counter-notice. The giving of notice is treated as giving rise to a contract freely entered into between landlord and tenant (LRHUDA 1993, s. 43(4)). On receipt of the tenant's claim, the competent landlord has two months (or longer if the tenant's notice gives him longer) to give a counter-notice. This counter-notice may admit the claim or not, giving reasons in the latter case, and it may also state that the landlord intends to apply for an order under s. 47(1) on the ground of intended redevelopment (see para. 14.7 below). If the landlord refuses to admit the tenant's claim on the basis that he has no right to a lease renewal, he must apply to the county court for an order to that effect within two months of the giving of the counter-notice (LRHUDA 1993, s. 46).

14.4 Establishing the terms of the new lease

Where the terms of the new lease are in dispute at the end of the two-month period beginning with the date the counter-notice was given, a leasehold valuation tribunal has jurisdiction, on application of landlord or tenant, to determine the matters in dispute. Application must be made within six months of the date of the counter-notice (LRHUDA 1993, s. 48). Where no counter-notice is given, the tenant can ask the court to determine the terms of the new lease (LRHUDA 1993, s. 49). The court has power to make vesting orders in favour of tenants in circumstances where the landlord cannot be found, or his identity cannot be ascertained (LRHUDA 1993, s. 50).

14.5 Costs

The costs of the application for a new lease will generally fall on the tenant (see generally LRHUDA 1993, s. 60). These will include the cost of any investigation reasonably undertaken of the tenant's right, any valuation of the tenant's flat, and the legal costs of the grant of a new lease. However, where the tenant's proposed acquisition is curtailed by the landlord's proof of an intention to redevelop (see para. 14.7 below) or the inception of compulsory purchase procedures, no costs liability will be incurred. In the event of the terms of the acquisition being referred to a leasehold valuation tribunal, the parties will be expected to bear their own costs of those proceedings.

14.6 Grant of the new lease

The landlord is not obliged to execute the new lease until the premium, together with any other sums payable, including costs and rent arrears, have been tendered (LRHUDA 1993, s. 56(3)).

14.7 Landlord's intention to redevelop

The landlord may resist the tenant's claim on the ground that he intends to redevelop, on much the same basis as he can resist claims for collective enfranchisement (LRHUDA 1993, s. 47). However, the provision is subtly wider in its impact. Whereas the landlord has the formidable obstacle in connection with a collective enfranchisement claim of establishing that two-thirds of all long leases in the premises are due to terminate within five years of the tenant's initial notice, here he need only establish that the lease of this individual tenant is due to terminate within that time-scale. Thus, there is a large incentive to tenants who wish to claim lease renewal under the 1993 Act to give notice to that effect before the last five years of their lease.

C LANDLORD AND TENANT ACT 1987, PART I: RIGHTS OF FIRST REFUSAL

15 INTRODUCTION

The Landlord and Tenant Act 1987 was enacted following the Report in 1985 of the Committee of Inquiry on the Management of Privately Owned Blocks of Flats, established by the Department of the Environment and chaired by Edward Nugee QC ('the Nugee Report'). The legislation sought to ameliorate the difficulties of management frequently encountered in relation to private sector flats, particularly those held on long lease. New remedies were given to tenants faced with bad management by their landlord, such as obtaining the appointment of a manager, and, ultimately, in the event of further default, applying for an acquisition order vesting the landlord's interest in a purchaser nominated by them (see Parts II and III of the Act respectively). Complaints by tenants of being given insufficient information were addressed by the introduction of a more effective statutory regulation of service charges than previously existed, and rights to information as to the insurance arrangements in place were also conferred. But it is Part I of the 1987 Act which concerns us here, as it gives to certain tenants of flats the right to compel sale of the landlord's interest to them, although the landlord is not in breach of any obligation.

Part I grants a 'right of first refusal' when the landlord intends to make a relevant disposal of an interest in their premises. The right is collectively exercised. A majority of the tenants in the property having decided to exercise this right, they will purchase at the price negotiated by the landlord with the intended purchaser, i.e., in most cases at 'market value'. If the landlord does not inform the tenants of the disposal he intends to make, or otherwise fails to comply with the provisions of the Act, the tenants may prevent him from making the disposal, or, if it has already been made, may enforce their rights against their new landlord. The Act has been quite widely used by tenants to acquire their landlord's interest, and it is not thought that the enactment of the collective enfranchisement provisions in Part I, LRHUDA 1993 will seriously affect its popularity, for the reasons set out at para. 6 above.

Part I of the 1987 Act is operative in the private sector only (nor does it apply to most housing associations). Sadly, as has been judicially remarked, the Act is 'ill-drafted, complicated, and confused' (*per* Sir Nicolas Browne-Wilkinson V-C in *Denetower Ltd* v *Toop* [1991] 3 All ER 661, 668).

16 QUALIFYING CONDITIONS

16.1 The premises

The premises must consist of the whole or part of a building; they must contain two or more flats held by 'qualifying tenants'; and the number of flats held by such tenants must exceed 50% of the total number of flats contained in the premises (LTA 1987, s. 1(2)). For these purposes, 'flat' is defined (by Landlord and Tenant Act 1987 (LTA 1987), s. 60(1)) as:

> a separate set of premises, whether or not on the same floor, which (a) forms part of a building, and (b) is divided horizontally from some other part of that building, and (c) is constructed or adapted for use for the purposes of a dwelling.

16.1.1 Excluded premises

Certain premises are excluded from the operation of Part I of the 1987 Act (LTA 1987, s. 1(3),(4)):

(a) Where a part (or parts) of the premises is or is intended to be occupied otherwise than for residential purposes, and the internal floor area of that part (or parts) exceeds 50% of the internal floor area of the premises taken as a whole (disregarding the internal floor area of any common parts).

(b) Any premises at a time when the landlord's interest is held by an 'exempt landlord'. These are largely public sector landlords (for example, local authorities), but also include the Housing Corporation, Housing for Wales, registered housing associations, and (unregistered) fully mutual housing associations (LTA 1987, s. 58(1)).

(c) Any premises at a time when the landlord's interest is held by a 'resident landlord', as defined (narrowly) in s. 58(2). The landlord must have occupied a flat in the premises (which are not a purpose built block of flats) as his only or principal residence for the previous 12 months to satisfy this condition.

16.2 Qualifying tenants

The 1987 Act adopts a peculiar exclusory definition (LTA 1987, s. 3(1)). Any tenant of a flat qualifies, other than a tenant whose tenancy is:

(a) a protected shorthold tenancy;
(b) a business tenancy (within Part II, LTA 1954);
(c) a tenancy terminable on the cessation of his employment;
(d) an assured tenancy (and therefore also an assured shorthold tenancy) or an assured agricultural occupancy.

Thus which tenants *will* qualify? Protected or statutory tenants under the Rent Act 1977 will, all other things being equal. Most long leaseholders will qualify, provided they are paying a rent which is sufficiently low to prevent them being assured tenants under the Housing Act 1988 (see further, chapter 2, para. 3.3). But secure tenants will not, as their landlords will be exempt (LTA 1987, s. 58(1)). The exclusion of assured tenants means that the Act is mainly operative in relation to those who hold a long lease at a low rent.

There is no requirement that qualifying tenants must reside: thus, absentee tenants who have sub-let can still exercise rights under this statute. In such a situation, the sub-tenant will not himself normally qualify. However, if the tenant is tenant of three or more flats in the same premises, all of which tenancies *prima facie* qualify, he will not be a qualifying tenant of any of them (LTA 1987, s. 3(2), as amended by Housing Act 1988, s. 119, sch. 13, para. 2), and then any sub-tenants may be able to claim (see LTA 1987, s. 3(4)). A corporate tenant cannot by assigning or sub-letting two (or more) flats to associated companies retain qualifying status, as it will be deemed to be tenant of all those flats let to any associated companies (LTA 1987, s. 3(3)).

17 NATURE OF THE RIGHT

The Act operates by requiring the landlord who is proposing to alienate his interest in the premises to give notice to the qualifying tenants of flats contained in them of any 'relevant disposal'. The notice is to be treated by the tenants as an offer to them, which they may or may not accept. If they accept it, in accordance with conventional contract law, a binding contract will arise. It is important for both landlord and tenant to be able to identify a relevant disposal, and to recognise the legal consequences of the provisions of Part I, and, in particular, failure to comply with them.

17.1 Relevant disposal

A 'disposal' for these purposes may take effect by the creation or transfer of an estate or interest, and it includes the surrender of a tenancy and the grant of an option or right of pre-emption. It excludes a disposal under the terms of a will or under the law relating to intestacy (LTA 1987, s. 4(3)). A disposal is 'relevant' if it is a disposal by the landlord (including certain disposals by a mortgagee in exercise of its power of sale: s. 4(1A)) of any estate or interest, legal or equitable, in premises to which the Act applies, including the disposal of any such estate or interest in any common parts (as defined in s. 60(1)) of any such premises (LTA 1987, s. 4(1)).

17.1.1 Excluded disposals

Although many disposals are excluded by the Act, and can therefore take place without an offer notice being served on the qualifying tenants, most 'commercial' disposals will be caught. The disposals excluded tend not to be at arm's length, and are listed in s. 4:

(a) the grant of a tenancy of a single flat (possibly with appurtenant premises, as defined: s. 4(4));

(b) a disposal of any interest of a beneficiary in settled land, or of any interest under a mortgage, or any incorporeal hereditament;

(c) a disposal consisting of the creation of an estate or interest by way of security for a loan;

(d) a disposal to a trustee in bankruptcy or to the liquidator of a company;

(e) a disposal pursuant to certain orders under the Matrimonial Causes Act 1973 (ancillary relief on divorce, etc.) or the Inheritance (Provision for Family and Dependants) Act 1975 (making reasonable financial provision for the family and dependants of a deceased person out of his estate);

(f) certain disposals in pursuance of compulsory purchase procedures;
(g) a disposal by way of gift, if to members of the landlord's family (as defined: s. 4(5),(6)) or a charity;
(h) certain disposals between charities of their functional land;
(i) a disposal of land held on trust where a trustee has been appointed or discharged;
(j) a disposal by two or more members of the same family either to fewer of their number, or to a different combination of members of the family (one of which must be a transferor);
(k) a disposal pursuant to an option or right of pre-emption binding on the landlord, or pursuant to any other obligation binding him, created in the latter case before the commencement of the 1987 Act (i.e., 1 February 1988);
(l) a disposal consisting of the surrender of a tenancy in pursuance of a covenant, condition, or agreement contained in it;
(m) a disposal to the Crown;
(n) a disposal by a corporate landlord to an associated company.

17.1.2 Options

It can be seen that where an option or right of pre-emption is concerned, it is the grant of the right, not its exercise, which triggers the tenants' statutory right of first refusal. The grant of an option is a 'disposal' by virtue of s. 4(3). A transfer pursuant to the exercise of an option, whilst also a disposal, is not a 'relevant disposal': see (k) above.

17.2 Obligation on landlord

The landlord is obliged, when he proposes to make a 'relevant disposal' affecting premises to which Part I applies, to serve a notice on the qualifying tenants (LTA 1987, s. 5(1)). No form is prescribed for the notice, but it must, *inter alia*, give particulars of the principal terms of the disposal, notably the estate or interest being disposed of, and the consideration required by the landlord, and state that the notice constitutes an offer to the tenants to dispose of the property on those terms. The notice must also specify the period in which the tenants may accept, which period must not be less than two months after the date of service of the notice (LTA 1987, s. 5(2)). The landlord will be deemed to have complied with his obligation to serve the qualifying tenants if he has served 90% of them, or, where there are less than 10 such tenants, all but one of them (LTA 1987, s. 5(4)). Where a landlord fails to serve an offer notice on qualifying tenants, and yet appears to be proceeding to dispose in contravention of the 1987 Act, it is open to the tenants concerned to apply for an injunction restraining the disposal in question (see LTA 1987, s. 19).

17.3 Acceptance by the qualifying tenants

Exercise of the statutory right of first refusal is a collective venture. The tenants have a period of at least two months beginning with the date of the offer notice to accept the landlord's offer (LTA 1987, s. 5(2)(c)). Acceptance must be by 'the requisite majority' of qualifying tenants of the constituent flats, being more than 50% of the qualifying tenants of those flats (not restricted to those who were served by the landlord) at the date of the expiry of the period for acceptance of the landlord's offer (LTA 1987, s. 6(1)(b); s. 5(6)). They accept by serving notice (an 'acceptance notice') on the landlord, and they should then nominate a 'person' (which is likely to be a limited company formed for the purpose) to act on their behalf in connection with the acquisition.

The acceptance of the landlord's offer operates to freeze further dealing with 'the protected interest' (i.e., the estate and interest in the property as specified in the offer notice: s. 6(9)). The landlord cannot dispose of it to anyone other than a person (or persons) nominated for the purposes of the acquisition by the requisite majority of the qualifying tenants for the duration of 'the relevant period'. This is a period consisting of (a) the period during which acceptance had to be made, and (b) if a person is nominated within that period by the qualifying tenants, a further period of three months. At the end of this 'relevant period', the nominated person should be in place to conduct any further negotiations on behalf of the qualifying tenants. Although the landlord is not specifically prohibited from disposing at that stage, the Act achieves its objective by enabling tenants to claim an injunction preventing sale of the landlord's interest, or to enforce their rights of first refusal against a purchaser of the landlord's interest (LTA 1987, s. 11; see para. 17.5 below). Any purchase of the landlord's interest in the premises will be subject to the tenants' leases.

As an alternative to unqualified acceptance of the offer notice, the tenants may make a counter-offer to the landlord, proposing different terms. The landlord may accept this counter-offer, in which case a similar process to that above is initiated, subject to necessary modifications. But (consistent with the general principles of contract law) there is no obligation on the landlord to accept a counter-offer, and the landlord has in these circumstances the right to dispose of his interest to any other person on the terms of the offer notice for a period of 12 months (see para. 17.4 below).

17.4 Rejection or default by the tenants

The broad tenor of the Act is that if the landlord complies with its procedures, but for whatever reason the tenants fail to exercise their statutory right of first refusal, the landlord then has 12 months in which to dispose of the property in question to any person he chooses, on the terms of the offer notice, or on the terms agreed with the tenants before the default took place. The 12-month period runs from different dates, according to which of the following provisions are invoked, and they should be specifically referred to. The situation will arise:

(a) if no person is nominated by the tenants during the period specified in the offer notice (LTA 1987, s. 6(3));

(b) if the offer contained in the notice is not accepted by notice served by a requisite majority of qualifying tenants during the specified period, no counter-offer being made (LTA 1987, s. 7(1));

(c) if the landlord rejects a counter-offer by notice (and does not make a fresh offer: see s. 8) (LTA 1987, s. 7(5));

(d) if the nominated person withdraws from the transaction (LTA 1987, s. 9(1));

(e) if the landlord has served notice on the qualifying tenants stating that the premises have ceased to be premises within the Act and that the offer notice should therefore be treated as not having been served (LTA 1987, s. 10(1);

(f) if the landlord has, despite using his best endeavours, including the institution of proceedings where appropriate, failed to obtain the consent of a person whose consent is required (e.g., the landlord's interest is itself leasehold, and the lease contains a covenant against assignment) (LTA 1987, s. 10(4); see also s. 6(7));.

(g) if three months have elapsed since the end of the period in which the tenants could have accepted the offer notice, and no binding contract has been entered into by the landlord and the nominated person (LTA 1987, s. 10(4)).

In cases (d) to (g) above, any disposal by the landlord must be for a consideration no less than, and on other terms corresponding to, the terms agreed between the landlord and the qualifying tenants. In all other cases, no such terms having been agreed, any disposal must be for a consideration no less than, and on other terms corresponding to, the terms contained in the landlord's offer notice. In only one case may the landlord dispose of the protected interest for a price less than that agreed with the tenants or contained in the offer notice (and on any other terms he thinks fit): where the landlord has lawfully rescinded the contract between himself and the nominated person (e.g., for misrepresentation) (LTA 1987, s. 10(6)).

17.5 Purchase notice procedure

We turn next to the remedies provided by the 1987 Act for non-compliance with the rights which it confers. The main remedy is to be invoked not against the landlord himself (although in circumstances where a disposal is anticipated, injunctive action may be possible: see LTA 1987, s. 19), but against a purchaser of his interest. Thus, where a relevant disposal is made in contravention of Part I of the 1987 Act (e.g., the landlord fails to serve an offer notice at all; or some other provision is not properly complied with), the qualifying tenants (acting by a requisite majority) of the constituent flats may invoke the purchase notice procedure against their new landlord (see further, LTA 1987, ss. 11, 12).

The premises in which the flats are contained must remain premises to which the 1987 Act applies. The tenants may seek information first, by serving notice on the transferee under the original disposal requiring him to furnish particulars of the terms of the disposal (LTA 1987, s. 11). The request for particulars must be served within two months of the requisite majority being served with notice of the change of landlord (under Landlord and Tenant Act 1985, s. 3) or with any other documents indicating that the transfer has taken place, and must be complied with by the landlord within one month (LTA 1987, s. 11(2)).

The tenants' next step is to serve a 'purchase notice' on the new landlord (LTA 1987, s. 12). This must be done within three months of any request for particulars being answered by the landlord, or, where no request has been served, within three months of the date on which the change of landlord came to the notice of the tenants. In essence, the purchase notice requires the new landlord to dispose of the estate or interest the subject matter of the original disposal to the person(s) nominated by the qualifying tenants. The terms of the purchase, including the consideration, are the terms of the original disposal. The court has power to compel a purchaser to comply with the requirements of a purchase notice (LTA 1987, s. 19). The coercive power of the court is the ultimate, and most effective, sanction. Moreover, reversioners who engage in several consecutive disposals of the reversion (or a severance of the landlord's interest) will find that the court has ample powers to enforce the tenants' rights (LTA 1987, ss. 16, 19).

17.6 Protection of the purchaser

There is no requirement that the rights of first refusal contained in the Landlord and Tenant Act 1987 be registered, and there is thus a substantial risk that a purchaser may unknowingly find himself the subject of an application by tenants compelling him to sell his interest to them. The new landlord may seek some assurance by himself serving notices on the tenants of flats contained in premises which he is proposing to purchase, and he may by appropriate compliance with statutory procedures safeguard his position (see further, LTA 1987, s. 18).

17.7 Jurisdiction of leasehold valuation tribunal

The rent assessment committee, here known as a leasehold valuation tribunal, is given jurisdiction to hear and determine any question arising in relation to matters specified in a purchase notice (LTA 1987, s. 13). However, whilst a tribunal may consider matters such as the property to be transferred, it may not review the consideration payable *de novo* (e.g., *Cousins* v *Metropolitan Guarantee Ltd* [1989] 2 EGLR 223; *Gregory* v *Saddiq* [1991] 1 EGLR 237). Nor may it consider whether a purchase notice is valid (see *Denetower Ltd* v *Toop* [1991] 3 All ER 661, 669). This latter issue would be a matter for the county court (LTA 1987, s. 52).

17.8 Costs

Generally, the procedures of the 1987 Act envisage the parties paying their own costs: no doubt a considerable disincentive to tenants who are contemplating exercising their rights. However, the Act provides for costs to be paid:

(a) by a landlord who decides no longer to dispose of his interest, or a nominated person who decides no longer to proceed with the acquisition, if the withdrawal from the transaction occurs more than four weeks after the period for acceptance of the offer notice has expired (LTA 1987, s. 9(6));

(b) by the nominated person, where no binding contract has been entered into within three months of the expiry of the period in which the landlord's offer notice could have been accepted, and the landlord has accordingly given notice enabling him to dispose on the terms of the offer notice to any other person (see further, LTA 1987, s. 10(5));

(c) by the nominated person, where having served a purchase notice, he subsequently decides not to proceed (or he becomes aware that the number of qualifying tenants desiring to proceed has fallen below the requisite majority, in which case he must serve notice to withdraw) (LTA 1987, s. 14).

SIX

SECURE TENANCIES

Housing Act 1985, Part IV

1 GENERAL INTRODUCTION

The Housing Act 1980 introduced the so-called council tenants' charter, the most celebrated element being the right to buy. Prior to 1980, public sector tenants had no statutory security of tenure, and whilst they could negotiate a purchase of their dwellings from their local authority landlord, councils had no incentive to reduce their housing stock by way of sale. The 1980 Act, and subsequent legislation (see chapter 1, para. 4), has transformed the land-holdings of local authorities, to such an extent that some have no, or no significant, housing remaining in their control. There remain, however, many tenants within this housing sector. Their statutory rights are largely dependant on their being 'secure tenants'.

The status of secure tenancy confers on the occupier (a) a security of tenure pursuant to Part IV of the Housing Act 1985 (HA 1985), whereby the landlord will be unable to obtain possession without obtaining an order of the court on proof of prescribed grounds; and (b) subject to various important qualifications, exclusions and exceptions, the right to buy the freehold of a house or take a long lease (usually of 125 years) of a flat. A secure tenant also may have the right (again subject to qualifications) to exchange his property with another secure tenant ('assignment by way of exchange').

2 DEFINITION

The principal definition of 'secure tenancy' is contained in s. 79(1), HA 1985:

> A tenancy under which a dwelling-house is let as a separate dwelling is a secure tenancy at any time when the conditions described in sections 80 and 81 as the landlord condition and the tenant condition are satisfied.

The landlord condition (further considered below) broadly requires the landlord to be within the public sector. The tenant condition (see also below) imposes a requirement of residential occupation upon the person in question. Many of the terms here used are similar or identical to terms in the private sector legislation, and cross reference will therefore be necessary for further explanation. It should, however, be noted that a secure tenant cannot also be a protected tenant, statutory tenant, or assured tenant: the codes are mutually exclusive.

2.1 'Tenancy'

A secure tenancy may be a tenancy (on which see the case law digested at chapter 2, para. 2.1). However, it may also be a licence. By s. 79(3) of the 1985 Act, 'The provisions of this Part apply in relation to a licence to occupy a dwelling-house (whether or not granted for a consideration) as they apply in relation to a tenancy.' This provision, by confining the extended definition to Part IV of the Act, is understood to preclude secure tenants who are only licensees from claiming the right to buy (see *per* Balcombe LJ in *Westminster City Council* v *Clarke* (1991) 23 HLR 506, 516). Licensees who entered the dwelling-house (or any other land) as a trespasser and were granted the licence as a temporary expedient cannot be secure tenants under s. 79(3) (HA 1985, s. 79(4)).

The scope of s. 79(3) has been significantly narrowed by the decision of the House of Lords in *Westminster City Council* v *Clarke* [1992] 2 AC 288, where Lord Templeman, giving the single speech, held that a licensee could only claim to be a secure tenant if he had been granted exclusive possession of a separate dwelling-house. The council owned and managed a hostel for homeless single men, including those with personality disorders and physical disabilities. Mr Clarke was offered accommodation in this hostel, being granted a licence to occupy which provided that he did not obtain a right to exclusive occupation of any room, and did not become a tenant of the council. He paid a weekly charge for his accommodation. The House of Lords held that he did not obtain exclusive possession, and could not therefore be a secure tenant. The grant of exclusive possession would be inconsistent with the purposes for which the hostel had been provided, as it was in the interests of both the occupiers and the council that persons could be moved from room to room, and asked to share where necessary. Lord Templeman stressed that this was a very special case which depended on 'the peculiar nature of the hostel maintained by the council, the use of the hostel by the council, the totality, immediacy and objectives of the powers exercisable by the council and the restrictions imposed on Mr Clarke.'

The insistence on exclusive possession as a requirement for a licence to qualify as a secure tenancy appears to deprive s. 79(3) of much of its impact. Since *Street* v *Mountford*, the presence of exclusive possession has led in most cases to the finding of a tenancy. A rent is not necessary for s. 79(3), but neither is it necessary for a tenancy (see *Ashburn Anstalt* v *Arnold* [1989] Ch 1, at chapter 2, para. 2.1.7). There are several acknowledged situations where despite a grant of exclusive possession a licence rather than a tenancy will be created (see chapter 2, para. 2.1), but it is difficult to envisage these falling within the scope of Part IV of the 1985 Act. A licence will be created where the parties did not intend to create legal relations, perhaps in the context of a family arrangement: but this is unlikely to occur where a public sector landlord is concerned. A licence will be the norm where the occupier holds a 'service occupancy' (the accommodation being provided by his employer who requires him to occupy for the better performance of his duties of employment); but such agreements will be likely to be excluded anyway from secure tenancy status (see HA 1985, sch. 1, para. 2, at para. 3.2 below).

Although the grant of a licence to a person entering as a trespasser will not confer a secure tenancy (see s. 79(4) above), the grant of a tenancy to such a person may do. However, such a grant will not readily be implied. In *Westminster City Council* v *Basson* (1990) 23 HLR 225, the defendant to possession proceedings had not entered as a trespasser: she had been invited by the secure tenant to cohabit with him. When he left, she stayed. The council made it clear that her occupation was unlawful, and demanded charges for her 'use and occupation' of the property. Although the defendant had successfully applied to another department of the council for a 'rent rebate', and remained in occupation for over 12 months before the council commenced possession proceedings, the Court of Appeal refused to infer a tenancy from this course of conduct.

2.2 'Dwelling-house'

A dwelling-house may be a house or a part of a house (such as a flat) (HA 1985, s. 112(1)). The security of the secure tenant is the same whether the dwelling is a house or a flat, but the distinction is significant to the exercise of the right to buy (chapter 7, para. 1). A secure tenancy will be operative in relation both to the house or flat itself and land let together with it (unless the land is agricultural land exceeding two acres) (HA 1985, s. 112(2); see further, chapter 2, para. 4.1).

2.3 'Let as a separate dwelling'

The requirement that the dwelling-house be let as a separate dwelling is common to Part I of the Housing Act 1988 and the Rent Act 1977, as well as this statute (see chapter 2, para. 2.3, and chapter 3, para 2.3). It involves, without more, the tenant having the exclusive use of the essential living rooms of a separate dwelling-house (*Cole* v *Harris* [1945] KB 474). The Housing Act 1988 (ss. 3, 10) and the Rent Act 1977 (s. 22) mitigate this requirement by providing special forms of protection for tenants who share essential common parts, such as kitchens and bathrooms, with persons other than the landlord. No such leniency is shown to those who claim to be secure tenants. Thus, in *Central YMCA Housing Association Ltd* v *Saunders* (1990) 23 HLR 212, the Court of Appeal rejected the claim of an occupier of a room in a Y.M.C.A. hostel to be a secure tenant where his kitchen facilities were shared, and cooking in the room itself was prohibited: there was no letting of a dwelling-house as a separate dwelling (see also *Central YMCA Housing Association Ltd* v *Goodman* (1991) 24 HLR 109).

The letting must be 'as a dwelling'. A letting as a business is therefore outside the scope of the 1985 Act. Business tenancies within Part II of the Landlord and Tenant Act 1954 cannot in any case be secure tenancies (see HA 1985, sch. 1, para. 11; para. 3.11 below).

2.4 'At any time when'

This phrase allows tenancies or licences to move in and out of Part IV of the 1985 Act where particular elements of the agreement change. 'It would therefore appear that a tenancy can at one time be a secure tenancy, cease to be a secure tenancy and become a secure tenancy again if in the interim period it has not been determined' (*per* Parker LJ in *Crawley Borough Council* v *Sawyer* (1987) 20 HLR 98).

2.5 The landlord condition

The landlord condition is described in HA 1985, s. 80. The interest of the landlord must belong to one of: a local authority; a new town corporation; a housing action trust; an urban development corporation; the Development Board for Rural Wales; and certain housing co-operatives. If the landlord's interest belongs to more than one body, only one of which satisfies the landlord condition, the tenancy cannot be secure (*R* v *Plymouth City Council, ex parte Freeman* (1987) 19 HLR 328).

2.5.1 Housing associations

Prior to the coming into force of the Housing Act 1988, many tenancies and licences granted in the housing association sector were secure tenancies, as the Housing Corporation, charitable housing trusts and many housing associations (i.e., registered housing associations which were not co-operative housing associations, and unregistered housing associations which were co-operative housing associations) satisfied the landlord condition. The 1988 Act initiated the shift of housing associations from the public to the private sector, and as part of this policy the definition of 'landlord condition' was amended to exclude these bodies. However, there are important exceptions and savings, as a result of which there are still a significant number of lettings by housing associations (as defined), the Housing Corporation and charitable housing trusts which may be secure tenancies:

(a) A tenancy or licence entered into before 15 January 1989, where the landlord, immediately before that date, was one of these bodies (Housing Act 1988 (HA 1988), sch. 18, saving 4).

(b) A tenancy or licence entered into in pursuance of a contract made before 15 January 1989 (HA 1988, s. 35(4)(c)).

(c) A tenancy or licence granted on or after 15 January 1989 to a person who, immediately before it was entered into, was a secure tenant, it being granted by the secure tenant's landlord (HA 1988, s. 35(4)(d)).

(d) A tenancy or licence granted to a person as suitable alternative accommodation in consequence of an order of the court, the court considering that an assured tenancy would not afford the required security, and directing that the dwelling should be held on secure tenancy (HA 1988, s. 35(4)(e)).

(e) A tenancy or licence granted pursuant to an obligation under s. 554(2A) of the 1985 Act (a new tenancy to an owner occupier of a defective dwelling: see generally HA 1985, Part XVI) (HA 1988, s. 35(4)(f)).

(f) Where, on or after 15 January 1989, the landlord's interest in a dwelling held on regulated (i.e., Rent Act protected or statutory) tenancy becomes vested in a housing association or similar body (HA 1988, s. 35(5)).

2.6 The tenant condition

The tenant condition requires the tenant to be an individual (see chapter 2, para. 2.4), who occupies the dwelling-house as his only or principal home (HA 1985, s. 81). The tenant condition is identical to that required for qualification as an assured tenant in the private sector (see chapter 2, para. 2.5), and similar to that required for occupation for the purposes of the Leasehold Reform Act 1967. Case law under the Rent Acts (chapter 3, para. 4.1), where the residential qualification is subtly different, must be treated with care. In *Crawley Borough Council* v *Sawyer* (1987) 20 HLR 98, a tenant of a council flat went to live with his girlfriend (also in local authority accommodation), and was away for over a year, during which time the electricity and gas were disconnected as a result of the tenant's non-payment of bills. Shortly after service of the notice to quit, the tenant returned to the flat. The Court of Appeal upheld the tenant's contention that he had remained a secure tenant, on the basis that he had intended to return to the flat and had left furniture there. Whilst he may have had a home with his girlfriend during the period of absence, his principal home throughout remained the flat.

It is accordingly not necessary for the tenant to be physically in occupation. Where the tenant is physically absent, the tenant condition will continue to be satisfied if the tenant has left some physical evidence on the premises (such as furniture), and intends to return, provided that the place in which he is presently living has not displaced the premises as his principal home. Where there are joint tenants, it is sufficient for one of them to occupy the dwelling-house as his only or principal home (HA 1985, s. 81). If at any time the tenant condition ceases to be satisfied, the contractual tenancy will nevertheless subsist until it is lawfully terminated (see, e.g., *Croydon LBC* v *Buston* (1991) 24 HLR 36.

2.6.1 Husband and wife

The Matrimonial Homes Act 1983 (MHA 1983) makes similar qualifications in relation to the tenant condition for secure tenancies as are made in relation to the occupation requirements for assured and protected tenancies (MHA 1983, s. 1; see further, chapter 2, para. 2.5.2). Thus, if a husband is the secure tenant of the matrimonial home, and leaves his wife, her occupation of the home will suffice to satisfy the tenant condition. She will be entitled to make rent payments to the landlord. In due course, she may (and should) seek to have the tenancy transferred to her in any divorce proceedings.

3 EXCLUSIONS

A tenancy is not a secure tenancy if it falls within any of the exceptions contained in sch. 1 to the 1985 Act. There is a further list of exclusions from the right to buy (HA 1985, sch. 5), which is outlined below in chapter 7, para. 3).

3.1 Long leases: para. 1

A 'long tenancy' for these purposes is defined in s. 115 to which reference should be made. Essentially, the definition is the same as for the the Landlord and Tenant Act 1954, Part I, the Leasehold Reform Act 1967, sch. 10 to the Local Government and Housing Act 1989 and similar legislation (on which see chapters 4 and 5 above). A tenancy for a term certain exceeding 21 years is thus excluded from protection, as too is a tenancy granted pursuant to the right to buy. Whilst such tenancies cannot be secure, and will also be excluded from security of tenure under the 1954 and 1989 Acts, a public sector tenant of a house holding under a long lease at a low rent may be able to claim enfranchisement or a lease extension under the 1967 Act. Likewise, a public sector tenant of a flat may be able to exercise collective enfranchisement, or claim renewal of his lease under the Leasehold Reform, Housing and Urban Development Act 1993, Part I.

3.2 Premises occupied in connection with employment: para. 2

A 'service occupancy' is a licence rather than a tenancy (see *Street* v *Mountford* [1985] AC 809, 818; chapter 2, para. 2.1). Whilst it may confer exclusive possession on the occupier, as required by *Westminster City Council* v *Clarke*, and would therefore appear to qualify as a secure tenancy pursuant to s. 79(3) of the 1985 Act, provision is made by this paragraph to exclude it from secure tenancy status. A tenancy is excluded if the tenant is an employee of the landlord, or of any other public sector body listed in para. 2, and his contract of employment (or apprenticeship, express, implied, oral, or in writing) requires him to occupy the dwelling-house for the better performance of his duties. Specific provision is made for employees of a police force or fire authority (para. 2(2),(3)). Where the premises have been subject to a service occupancy within a period of three years before the grant of a tenancy, the landlord may by written notice to the tenant continue to exclude the premises for a further period (para. 2(4)).

Normally, the contract of employment will have to specify clearly the requirement that the employee reside in the property. In *Hughes* v *Greenwich LBC* [1994] 1 AC 170, a headmaster of a boarding school lived in a house in the school grounds (but not within its curtilage) built for his occupation by the education authority. His contract of employment did not contain an express term requiring him to live in this house, and the House of Lords refused to imply one. Implication of such a term would only be made where the landlord could show it was essential that the employee should live in the house in order to do his job. Mere provision of a facility for an employee was not enough. It was necessary that the employer imposed an obligation on the employee to use that facility. A term requiring a school caretaker to live in a house adjacent to the school was implied in *South Glamorgan County Council* v *Griffiths* (1992) 24 HLR 334. Although this decision was not cited in *Hughes* v *Greenwich LBC*, it is felt that it can stand as a construction of the particular circumstances surrounding the caretaker's employment.

The Court of Appeal in *Griffiths* rejected an argument by the occupier, based on a literal interpretation of the statute, that on his retirement para. 2 would no longer apply (as he would thereupon cease to be an employee) and he would become a secure tenant. Acceptance of such an argument would have produced a most unsatisfactory situation, as on any termination of employment (including summary dismissal for good cause), the very time when the landlord wished to recover possession, the occupier would become secure. However, Ralph Gibson LJ gave an important warning (at 340):

> Local authorities, or other landlords affected by these provisions, will be well advised to act promptly because the court may well infer a change in the nature of the occupation after any significant delay; but the local authority will retain the ability to act fairly and with consideration without immediate loss of the right to recover possession.

A variation in the terms of a tenant's employment may lead to the tenancy becoming, or ceasing to be, secure. In *Elvidge* v *Coventry City Council* [1993] 3 WLR 976, the tenant was employed as a water bailiff at a countryside park managed by the council. On his subsequent promotion to an assistant ranger, the council altered his conditions of employment so that his occupation of a cottage in the park became a term of his contract of employment. Although he had been a secure tenant initially, the Court of Appeal confirmed that this change to his contractual terms, whereby he was now required to occupy the cottage for the better performance of his duties, deprived him of secure status due to the application of sch. 1, para. 2(1).

3.3 Land acquired for development: para. 3

A tenancy will not be secure if the dwelling-house is on land which has been acquired for development and the dwelling-house is used by the landlord, pending development of the land, as temporary housing accommodation. 'Development' means the carrying out of building, engineering, mining or other operations in, on and over or under land, or the making of any material change in the use of any buildings or other land (see generally Town and Country Planning Act 1990, s. 55). It has been established that the land may have been acquired for development by a predecessor of the landlord, and that the nature of the development plans may change or be modified (*Attley* v *Cherwell District Council* (1989) 21 HLR 613; *Hyde Housing Association* v *Harrison* [1991] 1 EGLR 51). It is implicit in the provision that a development must be pending, and thus if there are no relevant plans at any given time the exception will cease to apply (*Lillieshall Road Housing Co-operative Ltd* v *Brennan* (1991) 24 HLR 195). However, it has been suggested *obiter* that intended development of any part of the land which was acquired with the dwelling-house in question will suffice, even though the development will not affect the site on which the dwelling-house itself stands (*per* Lloyd LJ in *Lillieshall Road Housing Cooperative Ltd* v *Brennan*).

A landlord will use a dwelling-house as temporary housing accommodation wherever he lets it for use as a residence: it is immaterial that prior to the letting the landlord may have contemplated using it for other purposes (*Attley* v *Cherwell District Council*, at 617). The length of the letting is not decisive: in *Attley* v *Cherwell District Council*, the grant of a 10-year lease was held to be within the exclusion, as the landlord intended in the long term to use the land for industrial development.

3.4 Accommodation for homeless persons: para. 4

Where accommodation is provided for homeless persons in pursuance of certain provisions of Part III of the 1985 Act, a period of grace of 12 months will arise during which any tenancy granted by the landlord will not be secure. The landlord need not itself be under the statutory duty to house: thus, the exclusion can apply where some other public sector body is requested by the local housing authority to assist in the provision of homes (*Family Housing Association* v *Miah* (1982) 5 HLR 94). Accommodation of this kind will also be excluded from assured tenancy protection (where the landlord is in the private sector, for example, a housing association) by virtue of HA 1988, s. 1(6),(7), on which see chapter 2, para. 3.14).

The homelessness provisions which activate the exclusion are:

(a) Section 63 (duty to house pending inquiries in case of apparent priority need).

(b) Section 65(3) (duty to house temporarily a person found to have priority need but to have become homeless intentionally).

(c) Section 68(1) (duty to house pending determination whether conditions for referral of application are satisfied).

The 12-month period runs not from the date of the tenancy (or licence) but from the date the tenant receives notification pursuant to the provisions of Part III. The landlord may give notice to the tenant during the 12-month period that the tenancy is secure, in which case the exclusion will no longer apply. On expiry of the 12-month period, the occupier will usually obtain a secure tenancy. In *Eastleigh Borough Council* v *Walsh* [1985] 1 WLR 525, the House of Lords held that where a homeless person had been granted exclusive possession of the dwelling-house (possibly just a bed-sitting room), the normal *indicia* of tenancy being present (see *Street* v *Mountford*, above at chapter 2, para. 2.1), the occupier would be a tenant despite the initially temporary nature of the arrangement. However, exclusive possession is essential. Its absence will prevent the court from holding that the occupier has a licence to occupy within s. 79(3), and the licence route to protection as a secure tenant will thereby also be barred (see *Westminster City Council* v *Clarke*, at para. 2.1 above).

3.5 Temporary accommodation for persons taking up employment: para. 5

A landlord which lets to persons who are moving into the area for the purposes of employment may, by serving notice on them prior to the tenancy, prevent it from being secure for a period of 12 months from the date of its grant. The tenant must not have been resident in the district (of the local housing authority) in which the dwelling-house is situated immediately before the grant. He must have obtained employment in that district or its surrounding area (i.e., the area consisting of each district which adjoins it) before the grant, and the tenancy must have been granted for the purpose of meeting his need for temporary accommodation in order to work, and to find permanent accommodation there.

3.6 Short-term arrangements: para. 6

Prior to the enactment in 1980 of a code for security of public sector tenants, a device came into common usage whereby a private sector landlord would let through the medium of a local authority to a residential tenant in order to prevent the tenant claiming the privileges of the Rent Acts. The local authority was the tenant's immediate landlord, and accordingly the Acts did not apply (Rent Act 1977 (RA 1977), s. 14, nor would Part I, HA 1988: see sch. 1, para. 12 thereof). This provision excludes such arrangements from secure tenancy status as well, the intention being to encourage private sector landlords to assist in the provision of housing for public sector tenants. It is apparently much used: in *Tower Hamlets LBC* v *Abdi* (1992) 25 HLR 80, 83, the Court of Appeal was informed by counsel that so-called:

> private leased accommodation ... has to a great extent supplanted bed and breakfast accommodation as temporary accommodation for the homeless. It is a means by which local housing authorities can obtain the temporary use of private sector accommodation for the homeless.

The dwelling-house must have been leased to the landlord for temporary housing accommodation on terms which include provision for the lessor to obtain vacant possession from the landlord on the expiry of a specified period or when required by the lessor. Despite the use of the word 'leased' in the statute, the Court of Appeal has given effect to the exclusion where the arrangement between the lessor and the landlord was by way of licence only (*Tower Hamlets LBC* v *Miah* (1991) 24 HLR 199).

Two provisions attempt to prevent abuse of the exclusion. The lessor must not be a body which can itself grant secure tenancies (i.e., can satisfy the landlord condition). The landlord must not have an interest in the dwelling-house other than under the lease or as mortgagee: thus leasebacks with private sector bodies will not avoid the grant of secure tenancies to the occupiers.

3.7 Temporary accommodation during works: para. 7

If a tenant who is not a secure tenant of the dwelling-house he occupies as his home ceases to occupy it whilst works are being carried out, he will not be secure tenant of any dwelling-house made available for him in the meantime.

3.8 Agricultural holdings: para. 8

A tenancy of a dwelling-house comprised in an agricultural holding, which is occupied by the person responsible for the control of the farming of the holding will not be secure (see also text on HA 1988, sch. 1, para. 7 at chapter 2, para. 3.7; RA 1977, s. 10).

3.9 Licensed premises: para. 9

If the dwelling-house consists of or includes premises licensed for the sale of intoxicating liquor for consumption on the premises, the tenancy will not be secure (see text on HA 1988, sch. 1, para. 5 at chapter 2, para. 3.5; RA 1977, s. 11).

3.10 Student lettings: para. 10

The exclusion of student lettings, whilst similar in effect to exclusions contained in HA 1988, sch. 1, para. 8 and RA 1977, s. 8, is very different in its operation. Before the grant of the tenancy, the landlord must inform the tenant by written notice that in his opinion this exception applies. The tenancy must be granted for the purpose of enabling the tenant to attend a 'designated course' at an educational establishment (i.e., a university or establishment of further education), which establishment the notice must specify. Courses are designated by statutory instrument (see the Secure Tenancies (Designated Courses) Regulations 1980, SI 1980 No 1407). The exception will continue to apply for a period of six months beyond the date the tenant ceases to attend the course. If, despite the letting being made on this basis, the tenant does not last six months on the course, the exception will apply for the first six months of the tenancy.

3.11 1954 Act tenancies: para. 11

A tenancy cannot be secure if it is within Part II of the Landlord and Tenant Act 1954 (i.e., it is a business tenancy). The discussion at chapter 2, para.

3.4 is relevant. Occupation of the dwelling for the purposes of a business will take the tenancy out of Part IV of the 1985 Act, provided that the use made is not insignificant. However, a change of use from business to dwelling will not bring a public sector tenancy into the protection of the 1985 Act unless a new agreement between the landlord and the tenant can be inferred. In *Webb* v *Barnet LBC* (1988) 21 HLR 228, a tenant ran a garage business from the dwelling-house and garage let to him on a 21-year lease. He ceased trading, and subsequently contended that he had become a secure tenant. The Court of Appeal, following *Pulleng* v *Curran* (1980) 44 P & CR 58 and *Russell* v *Booker* (1982) 5 HLR 10, rejected his claim. A unilateral change of use, although it would have the effect of taking the tenancy outside the Act of 1954, did not automatically bring it within the Act of 1985.

3.12 Almshouses: para. 12

A licence to occupy a dwelling-house which is an almshouse is not a secure tenancy if various conditions are satisfied (see further, HA 1985, sch. 1, para. 12).

4 THE TERMS OF THE SECURE TENANCY

Whilst many of the terms on which a secure tenant holds from his landlord will be determined by the agreement of the parties, certain important areas of obligation, notably the rent payable, the alienation of the tenant's interest, and tenants' improvements, are significantly affected by statute. Variation of the terms of a secure tenancy is governed by a statutory procedure.

4.1 Rent

There is no statutory system of rent control applicable to secure tenants. A secure tenant who is aggrieved by the level of rent demanded by his public sector landlord must seek recourse through the difficult channels of judicial review. The statutory power of the local housing authority to fix rents is to be found in HA 1985, s. 24. This enables an authority to make 'such reasonable charges as they may determine for the tenancy or occupation of their houses' (s. 24(1)), and they are further obliged from time to time to review rents and to make such changes, either of rents generally or of particular rents, as circumstances may require (s. 24(2)). Since 1990, a local authority must have had particular regard to the principle of 'proportionality', namely that 'the rents of houses of any class or description should bear broadly the same proportion to private sector rents [i.e., rents recoverable where property is let on assured tenancy] as the rents of houses of any other class or description' (HA 1985, s. 24(3),(4), as inserted by Local Government and Housing Act 1989, s. 162). This does not require local authorities to equate its rents to those in the private sector, but simply to have regard to the need to maintain a differential between various types of property (e.g., three bedroomed houses as against bedsitting flats) similar to that existing in the private sector.

The burden of proving that a local authority has set a rent which is unreasonable falls squarely on the tenant or other occupier, and it is a heavy one (*Smith* v *Cardiff Corporation* [1955] Ch 159). Very few applications for judicial review have been successful, as courts have shown themselves unwilling to intervene in an area which is largely seen as one of discretion for the landlord authority. A review of the case-law is beyond the scope of this book, but the reader is referred to the leading decisions of *Belcher* v *Reading Corporation* [1950] 1 Ch 380, *Luby* v *Newcastle under Lyme Corporation* [1964] 2 QB 64, and *Wandsworth LBC* v *Winder (No 2)* (1987) 19 HLR 204, as well as the full discussion in *Sweet & Maxwell's Encyclopaedia of Housing Law* 1-0048, *et seq.*

4.2 Alienation

A secure tenant may not assign save in certain exceptional circumstances. He may permit lodgers to occupy, but may not (save with the landlord's written consent) sub-let or part with the possession of part of the dwelling-house.

4.2.1 Assignment

Assignment of secure tenancies is generally prohibited: indeed they are 'not capable' of being assigned (HA 1985, s. 91(1)). However, there are significant exceptions as follows (HA 1985, s. 91(3)):

(a) an 'assignment by way of exchange' (HA 1985, s. 92).

(b) an assignment in pursuance of an order under the Matrimonial Causes Act 1973, s. 24 on divorce, nullity or judicial separation.

(c) an assignment to a statutory successor (i.e., the person who would be entitled to succeed to the tenancy were the tenant to die immediately before the assignment).

(d) an assignment which does not fall within the above exceptions of a term certain granted before 5 November 1982: in which case the tenancy, although assignable, will on assignment cease to be secure (HA 1985, s. 91(2)).

4.2.2 Assignment by way of exchange

The Housing Act 1985, s. 92, allows a secure tenant to exchange his tenancy with that of another secure tenant or of an assured tenant whose landlord is a registered housing association or similar body. Any secure tenant who is a party to the exchange must obtain the written consent of his landlord, but such consent is not to be withheld save on a ground or grounds specified in sch. 3 to the 1985 Act (HA 1985, s. 92(3)). The landlord must particularise his ground(s) of opposition to the exchange within 42 days of the tenant's application for consent, or be disentitled from relying on them (HA 1985, s. 92(4)). The landlord's consent may be conditional on the assignor paying any outstanding rent, and/or remedying any breach of obligation, but not otherwise (HA 1985, s. 92(5),(6)). In the event of the landlord withholding consent otherwise than on a specified ground, the tenant can treat the consent as given, and proceed to assign (HA 1985, s. 92(3)).

4.2.3 Assignment in ancillary relief on divorce, etc.

The court has power under the Matrimonial Causes Act 1973, s. 24, to make property adjustment orders between the divorcing spouses, and it may order the transfer of a tenancy from one to the other in the exercise of this jurisdiction: the tenancy is treated as 'property' within the provision. The court also has power under MHA 1983 (s. 7; sch. 1) to order the transfer of a secure tenancy from one spouse to another, or from two spouses (holding jointly) to one. In either case, the significance of decree absolute must be appreciated. If a husband is sole secure tenant of the matrimonial home, and deserts his wife with no intention to return, the tenant condition will continue to be satisfied whilst they remain married (see MHA 1983, s. 1(6)). Thus the tenancy will remain secure. Following decree absolute, the tenant condition will only continue to be satisfied if the tenancy is transferred to the former wife, as her occupation cannot any longer be deemed to be that of her husband.

4.2.4 Assignment to successor

This enables the secure tenant to assign *nter vivos* and thereby elect which of two or more qualifying successors shall take his tenancy. An assignment in breach of the terms of the lease to a successor will nevertheless take effect. In *Peabody Donation Fund* v *Higgins* [1983] 1 WLR 1091, a father who was a secure tenant assigned his tenancy to his daughter without seeking the landlord's consent, as under the lease he was obliged to do. The Court of Appeal held that the assignment was effective, although it might give rise to an action for possession against the daughter based upon the breach of obligation (HA 1985, sch. 2, Ground 1: see below).

4.2.5 Lodgers and sub-letting

A secure tenant is expressly given the right to allow any persons to reside as lodgers in the dwelling-house (HA 1985, s. 93(1)) (although in doing so, he should take care that he does not grant a lease, or contravene the law against overcrowding). A person will be a lodger if the landlord (i.e., the secure tenant) provides such extensive services, requiring unrestricted access to the room in question, that exclusive possession has not been granted (see *Street* v *Mountford* [1985] AC 809).

A secure tenant may not sub-let or part with possession of *part* of the dwelling-house without the written consent of the landlord. Such consent cannot be unreasonably withheld, and if it is, it may be treated as given: in which case, the tenant may lawfully sub-let or part with possession as the case may be (HA 1985, s. 94). Alternatively, the tenant may ask the county court for a declaration that the landlord's consent is being unreasonably withheld (HA 1985, s. 110(2)(b)). In such proceedings, the landlord must prove that withholding or refusal of consent is not unreasonable (HA 1985, s. 94(2)). The provisions of the Landlord and Tenant Act 1988 (imposing *inter alia* a qualified duty on the landlord to consent to assignment within a reasonable time) do not apply to secure tenancies (see Landlord and Tenant Act 1988, s. 5(3)).

Whilst there is no statutory prohibition on sub-letting or parting with possession of the *whole* of the dwelling-house (although the landlord may, and probably will, impose such a term), such action will result in the tenancy ceasing to be secure, even if the landlord's consent was obtained, and it will not subsequently be able to become a secure tenancy (HA 1985, s. 93(2)).

4.2.6 Tenant ceasing to be secure

If a tenant goes out of occupation (or for some other reason the tenant condition is not satisfied), the restrictions on assignment and sub-letting will continue to apply, with necessary modifications (see generally, HA 1985, s. 95). This useful provision ensures that a non-occupying tenant, by losing the status of being a secure tenant, does not thereby improve his position in this respect.

4.3 Other terms

4.3.1 Repairs and improvements

The Housing Act 1985 does not impose repairing obligations on the landlord of a secure tenant (see the more general provisions of Landlord and Tenant Act 1985, s. 11 *et seq.*), but the Secretary of State is empowered to make regulations for the promulgation of schemes whereby secure tenants can themselves carry out repairs which their landlord is obliged to perform, and then recover the cost (or some part of it) from the landlord (HA 1985, s. 96). The first (and, so far, only) 'right to repair' scheme of this kind was introduced by SI 1985 No 1493.

Sections 97 to 101 of the 1985 Act make specific provision for secure tenants' improvements (and have effect in place of the more general provision in the Landlord and Tenant Act 1927, s. 19(2)). Every secure tenancy will contain a term that the tenant will not make any improvement (i.e., any alteration in, or addition to, a dwelling-house, as explained in s. 97(2)) without the landlord's consent (HA 1985, s. 97(1)). The landlord must not withhold consent unreasonably, or impose conditions on the giving of consent which are unreasonable (HA 1985, ss. 97(3), 99(3)). The burden of proof of reasonableness in these matters rests on the landlord (see further, HA 1985, ss. 98, 99). Where an improvement is lawfully made by the secure tenant, an increase in the rent whilst the improver remains tenant may not be made solely on the basis of that improvement (HA 1985, s. 101).

4.4 Variation of terms

The terms of a secure periodic tenancy may be varied in accordance with HA 1985, s. 103. This provision is necessary, as otherwise the tenant would have no incentive in agreeing a variation against his interests with the landlord, who cannot terminate the tenancy without recourse to the court on prescribed grounds. Variation is therefore effected by the landlord serving notice of variation on the tenant no less than four weeks (or the length of the rental period, if longer) before the varied terms are intended to come into effect. Save where the variation concerns rent (or other payments in respect of services or facilities provided by the landlord or rates), the landlord must serve a notice preliminary to the notice of variation inviting the tenant to comment on the proposals. However, whilst the landlord is obliged to consider these comments, he is not obliged to act upon them. The sole statutory right of the tenant in relation to a notice of variation is to give notice to quit before the notice takes effect (HA 1985, s. 103(6)). Short of seeking judicial review of the landlord's actions, on the grounds that the landlord is acting as no reasonable landlord would act, the tenant is powerless to resist the variation proposed. For an example of an unsuccessful application for judicial review of a variation, see *R* v *Brent LBC, ex parte Blatt* (1991) 24 HLR 319.

The landlord may vary the terms of any secure tenancy by agreement with the tenant, or by activating some provision in the lease providing for variation (such as a rent review clause) (HA 1985, s. 102(1)). These will be the only possibilities available to a landlord where the tenancy is a term certain, as the variation notice procedure described above only applies to periodic tenancies. For an example of an unsuccessful attempt by a tenant to prove a contractual variation, see *Palmer* v *Metropolitan Borough of Sandwell* (1987) 20 HLR 74.

5 SECURITY OF TENURE

The landlord will only be able to take the initiative and recover possession of a dwelling-house let on secure tenancy by obtaining a possession order from the court. However, if the occupier ceases to be a secure tenant, Part IV of the 1985 Act will no longer apply, and recovery of possession will be much facilitated.

5.1 Loss of secure status

The secure tenant may himself terminate the tenancy or licence pursuant to which he occupies the dwelling-house, as a result of which Part IV of the 1985 Act will no longer be applicable. In *Greenwich LBC* v *McGrady* (1982) 6 HLR 36, Sir John Donaldson MR succinctly stated that 'the Act of 1980 [as it then was] operates to give security where landlords give notice to quit; it does not give security where tenants give notice to quit.' Thus, although Part IV of the 1985 Act restricts the right of the landlord to terminate a secure tenancy, no such restriction operates in relation to a tenant. Where a tenant has terminated the tenancy, the landlord may then be able to recover possession on the basis that he no longer has any legal right to possession: in short, that he is a trespasser. However, the landlord should realise that he must still obtain a possession order from the court where despite termination of the tenancy the former secure tenant continues to reside in the dwelling-house (Protection from Eviction Act 1977, s. 3(1): see chapter 8, para. 2.2).

Where the secure tenancy is *periodic*, the principal means of termination by the tenant will be service of a notice to quit on the landlord. Its length will depend on the terms of the tenancy. However, a notice will be ineffective unless it is in writing and is given not less than four weeks before the date on which it is to take effect (Protection from Eviction Act 1977, s. 5(1)). This provision applies equally to 'periodic licences', which may include some secure tenancies (by virtue of the HA 1985, s. 79(3): see para. 2.1 above).

Where the secure tenancy is a *term certain*, the tenant may exercise a right conferred in the lease to terminate by notice (i.e., under a 'break clause'). Alternatively, he may surrender his interest to the landlord, either by deed, or 'by operation of law'. This latter possibility will require more than the tenant simply going out of occupation (see, for example, *Preston Borough Council* v *Fairclough* (1982) 8 HLR 70). Although in such circumstances the tenancy will cease to be secure (the 'tenant condition' no longer being satisfied), the tenancy itself will not necessarily terminate unless it can be established (by the landlord) that in leaving the tenant was intending to give up his interest in the property (*R* v *Croydon L.B C., ex parte Toth* (1986) 20 HLR 576; *City of Westminster* v *Peart* (1991) 24 HLR 389, 400). If the tenant's action does not terminate the tenancy, the landlord must give the notice required under the lease (paying due heed to the Protection from Eviction Act 1977, s. 5(1)) prior to commencing possession proceedings.

Where a secure periodic tenancy is held by more than one person, as joint tenants, it may be terminated by notice to quit given by one only of the joint tenants (*Hammersmith & Fulham LBC* v *Monk* [1992] 1 AC 478). A surrender of a secure tenancy held by more than one will however require the participation of both or all joint tenants (*Leek & Moorlands Building Society* v *Clark* [1952] 2 QB 788), as will the exercise of a break clause to terminate a secure term certain (*Hounslow LBC* v *Pilling* [1993] 1 WLR 1242).

5.2 Landlord-initiated recovery of possession

A landlord cannot bring a secure tenancy to an end except by obtaining an order of the court (HA 1985, s. 82(1)).

5.2.1 Periodic tenancies

Where the secure tenancy is a periodic tenancy, the landlord can make application pursuant to any of the grounds set out in sch. 2. This application will be for an order terminating the tenancy and granting possession to the landlord. The procedure which the landlord must follow is set out in s. 83, and described below. The jurisdiction of the court to make a possession order is derived from s. 84.

5.2.2 Terms certain

The landlord cannot forfeit a secure tenancy as such. Where the secure tenancy is a term certain, he must first apply to the court for an order terminating the tenancy. He must be able to show that the lease contains a provision for re-entry or forfeiture, and that had the tenancy not been secure the court would have made an order forfeiting the lease. An order terminating the term certain will not of itself entitle the landlord to recover possession, as on termination of a term certain, whether by effluxion of time, or on the court making an order terminating it prior to its expiry, a periodic tenancy will arise by operation of law (HA 1985, s. 86). Whilst the landlord may apply to the court for an order terminating both the term certain and the s. 86 periodic tenancy, thereby granting possession to the landlord, the court is unlikely, save in cases of serious tenant default, to make an immediate order for possession. It is more likely that the court will make an order under s. 82(3) terminating the term certain. In the event of further default, the landlord should then make application for a possession order.

5.2.3 Possession orders

The jurisdiction of the court to grant possession of a dwelling-house let on secure tenancy is governed by s. 84, which provides that the court shall not make an order except on one or more of the grounds set out in sch. 2. None of these are 'mandatory', in the sense that on proof the court is required to order possession. Grounds 1 to 8 (Part I of sch. 2) are 'discretionary': the court must consider it reasonable to make the order. Grounds 9 to 11 require the court to be satisfied that suitable accommodation will be available for the tenant when the order takes effect. Grounds 12 to 16 require the court to be satisfied *both* that it is reasonable to make the order *and* that suitable accommodation will be available when the order takes effect.

5.2.4 Consent orders

As the jurisdiction of the court is restricted by s. 84 of the 1985 Act, an order 'by consent' will only be effective if the court is satisfied that a ground for possession is established, and that the other requirements (i.e., reasonableness, and/or suitable alternative accommodation are met). The case-law discussed in relation to the Rent Act 1977 at chapter 3, para. 5.5 is pertinent here. In *Wandsworth LBC* v *Fadayomi* [1987] 1 WLR 1473, a possession order made 'by consent' against a secure tenant was successfully challenged by his wife, as the court had failed to investigate the suitability of the alternative accommodation being provided in relation to her, and no express admission of the existence of grounds for possession had been made. However, the decision was distinguished in *Bruce* v *Worthing Borough Council* (1993) 26 HLR 223, where the very status of the tenant was an issue before the court. The judge was held to have made sufficient investigation to enable him to make an order on the basis that the tenant was not a secure tenant at all. In those circumstances, it was not material that he had not specifically investigated the existence of grounds for possession under the 1985 Act.

5.3 Procedure

The landlord must, prior to commencing proceedings, serve on the tenant a 'notice seeking possession' (HA 1985, s. 83), which must state, *inter alia*, the ground(s) on which possession is to be sought. 'This is a warning shot across the bows of the tenant and the object of it is to warn him that unless he repairs what is stated as the ground upon which possession is going to be sought, he is going to be liable to court proceedings' (*per* Oliver LJ in *Torridge District Council* v *Jones* (1985) 18 HLR 107). Thus, any ground on which the court makes an order must have been specified in the notice seeking possession (HA 1985, s. 84(3)). The court may grant leave to alter or add to such a notice (HA 1985, s. 84(3)), but it would normally be proper to adjourn the proceedings to allow the tenant to adduce further evidence in the event of an application for leave at trial of the action. Thus, it is very much in the landlord's interests to serve a full and proper notice at the outset.

The form of the notice seeking possession is prescribed in the Secure Tenancies (Notices) Regulations 1987 (SI 1987 No 755). If the tenancy is a periodic tenancy, the notice must specify a date (not earlier than the date on which the tenancy could be terminated by notice to quit) after which possession proceedings may be begun, and those proceedings must be commenced no later than 12 months after that specified date. The court shall not entertain proceedings begun before or after the dates in question (HA 1985, s. 83(1)).

The notice must state 'the particulars' of the ground(s) relied on. In *Torridge District Council* v *Jones* (1985) 18 HLR 107, the landlord wished to rely on Ground 1 (see below), and gave as particulars the statement 'The reasons for taking this action are non-payment of rent.' This re-statement of part of the ground itself was not enough. The specification must be sufficient 'to tell the tenant what it is he has to do to put matters right before the proceedings are commenced'. In *Dudley Metropolitan Borough Council* v *Bailey* (1990) 22 HLR 424, the landlord's notice departed from the form prescribed in that it referred to the 'reasons for taking proceedings' rather than the 'particulars of each ground'. The Court of Appeal held that this was a notice 'substantially to the same effect' as that specified in the regulations, and such a notice was sanctioned by the regulations themselves (SI 1987 No 755, para. 2(1)). Error in the particulars, in overstating the rent liability of the tenant, did not invalidate the notice, as long as at the time of the notice the landlord genuinely intended to prove those matters.

5.4 Suitable alternative accommodation

Suitable alternative accommodation is defined in Part IV of sch. 2. The certificate of a local housing authority that they will provide suitable accommodation by a specified date is conclusive evidence of those facts (para. 4). In the absence of such a certificate, the landlord must satisfy the court that the premises are sufficiently secure, and that the accommodation is reasonably suitable for the needs of the tenant and his family. The premises will satisfy the security test if they are to be let on secure tenancy, protected tenancy, or assured tenancy, provided that it is neither an assured shorthold tenancy nor a tenancy under which the landlord might recover possession pursuant to Grounds 1 to 5 of the HA 1988 (sch. 2: see chapter 2, para. 6.1 above) The case law on the analogous provisions in the Rent Act 1977 is relevant on the needs of the tenant and his family, and is summarised at chapter 2, para. 6.2.2 above. Where the tenant's family does not wish to continue to live under the same roof, the court may require separate accommodation to be provided for (say) the tenant and his wife (see *Wandsworth LBC* v *Fadayomi* [1987] 1 WLR 1473, where it was also held that such a wife was entitled to be joined as a party to the possession proceedings).

6 GROUNDS FOR POSSESSION

The grounds for possession will now be outlined. Certain of these are very similar to grounds appropriate to assured or regulated tenancies, and cross reference to case law under the Housing Act 1988 and, more particularly, the Rent Act 1977, is frequently necessary.

6.1 Grounds 1 to 8: court may order possession if it considers it reasonable

Where the landlord sets out to recover possession on any of Grounds 1 to 8 inclusive, it must satisfy the court that it is reasonable to make the order sought. The question of reasonableness has been thoroughly examined by the case law on similar provisions in the Rent Act 1977, to which reference should be made (see chapter 2, para. 6.2.1). Where possession proceedings are based on grounds 1 to 8 (or Grounds 12 to 16), the court has power to adjourn for such period or periods as it thinks fit, and on making an order for possession on those grounds, it has wide powers to stay or suspend the execution of the order, or postpone the date of possession, although it must in doing so impose conditions with respect to the payment of rent arrears or mesne profits unless it considers that to do so would cause exceptional hardship to the tenant or would otherwise be unreasonable (HA 1985, s. 85(2), (3)). In the event of conditions being complied with, the court may discharge or rescind the possession order. The extended discretion of the court is only available prior to execution of the order in question. Once a warrant for possession has been executed, the tenant who wishes to set it aside must either have the possession order on which it was issued set aside, or prove that the warrant was obtained by fraud or that there had been an abuse of the process or oppression in its execution (see *Leicester City Council* v *Aldwinckle* (1991) 24 HLR 40, *Hammersmith & Fulham LBC* v *Hill* [1994] Times Law Reports 219).

6.1.1 Ground 1: Rent arrears or breach of obligation

'Rent lawfully due from the tenant has not been paid.' The rent must be 'lawfully due': thus the tenant can advance any defence to Ground 1 which would have been available to him had the action been one for the rent itself. The provision does not state when the rent has to have been unpaid, and the *quantum* is unspecified: *any* failure to pay rent at the due date would appear in most cases to activate the ground. The fact that the tenant has by trial paid (or at least tendered) all arrears will not take him outside Ground 1, although it will be extremely unlikely in those circumstances that the court will consider it reasonable to make a possession order. In *Woodspring District Council* v *Taylor* (1982) 4 HLR 95, the Court of Appeal reviewed the exercise of discretion in relation to Ground 1. They considered that an immediate possession order against tenants who had lived in the house for 24 years and had only fallen into rent arrears on the husband's unemployment was an order which no reasonable judge could have made, even though the arrears were substantial (£557) at the date of trial.

The second limb of Ground 1 is the breach or non-performance of an obligation of the tenancy. Factors such as the remediability and seriousness of the breach will no doubt weigh with the judge when he determines whether it is reasonable to grant the order sought. A recent example is *Sheffield City Council* v *Jepson* (1993) 25 HLR 299. In breach of a covenant in the lease, the tenant kept a dog. Although there was no evidence of misbehaviour by this particular dog, the Court of Appeal overturned the decision of the county court judge that it could not be reasonable to order possession in such circumstances. The covenant was reasonable, the breach was deliberate and persistent. The action was remitted to the county court for further consideration of the question of reasonableness. See also *Green* v *Sheffield City Council* (1993) 26 HLR 349.

6.1.2 Ground 2: tenant misconduct or conviction

The tenant or any person residing in the dwelling-house has been guilty of conduct which is a nuisance or annoyance to neighbours (*sic*: cf. 'adjoining occupiers' in the equivalent provision under RA 1977 (Case 1) and HA 1988 (sch. 2, Ground 14)), or has been convicted of using the dwelling-house or causing it to be used for illegal or immoral purposes (see further, chapter 2, para. 6.2.7 above).

6.1.3 Ground 3: deterioration in condition of dwelling-house

This provision is similar to Ground 13 in relation to assured tenancies (on which see chapter 2, para. 6.2.6).

6.1.4 Ground 4: deterioration in condition of furniture in dwelling-house

This provision is similar to Ground 15 in relation to assured tenancies (on which see chapter 2, para. 6.2.8).

6.1.5 Ground 5: false statement by tenant

The tenant from whom possession is sought is the person to whom the tenancy was granted (i.e., the original tenant, there not having been any assignments), and the landlord was induced to grant the tenancy by a false statement made knowingly or recklessly by the tenant. A good example of the operation of this Ground can be found in *Rushcliffe Borough Council* v *Watson* (1991) 24 HLR 124. A secure tenant of a housing association property made an application for housing to the landlords indicating that she was currently 'sharing with family or friends', a statement found by the judge to be knowingly false. The Court of Appeal upheld the possession order he made. In doing so, they accepted the need for the court in cases based on this ground to balance the interests of the tenant in being housed with the public interest of discouraging deceitful applications which result in the unjust relegation on the housing list of honest applicants.

6.1.6 Ground 6: premium paid on assignment by way of exchange

The tenancy was assigned to the tenant, or to a predecessor who is a member of his family who is residing in his dwelling-house, by an assignment by way of exchange (see para. 4.2.2 above), and a premium was paid either in connection with that assignment or the assignment which the tenant or predecessor himself made by way of exchange. For this purpose, 'premium' means any fine or other like sum and any other pecuniary consideration in addition to rent.

6.1.7 Ground 7: misconduct by employee tenant in relation to certain accommodation

This is a complex, and probably little used, ground. Many tenants employed by their landlord will not qualify as secure tenants as a result of sch. 1, para. 2 (see para. 3.2 above). Where they do qualify, Ground 7 will be available to the landlord seeking possession on proof of three elements:

(a) the dwelling-house forms part of, or is within the curtilage (see chapter 7, para. 3.1) of a building which is held mainly for purposes other than housing purposes, and consists mainly of accommodation other than housing accommodation, and

(b) the dwelling-house was let to the tenant or predecessor in title in consequence of his being in the landlord's employment, and

(c) the tenant or other person residing in the dwelling-house has been guilty of conduct such that, having regard to the purpose for which the building is used, it would not be right for him to continue in occupation.

6.1.8 Ground 8: temporary accommodation whilst works carried out

Where a secure tenant accepts alternative accommodation whilst works are being carried out on the dwelling-house which he occupies as his only or principal home, doing so on the understanding that on completion of the works he will give up occupation, the landlord may, when the works are completed and the dwelling-house available for occupation again, seek possession pursuant to Ground 8.

6.2 Grounds 9 to 11: the court may order possession if suitable accommodation is available

The issue of reasonableness does not here arise. If the landlord establishes that suitable alternative accommodation is available, and proves one of Grounds 9 to 11, the court must order possession. The possession order must take effect within 14 days, or a maximum of six weeks in cases of exceptional hardship (Housing Act 1980, s. 89). The definition of suitable alternative accommodation is to be found in Part IV of sch. 2. See further para. 5.4 above.

6.2.1 Ground 9: overcrowding

The dwelling-house is overcrowded within Part X of the 1985 Act, in such circumstances as to render the occupier guilty of an offence. The formula for overcrowding is contained in Part X.

6.2.2 Ground 10: demolition or reconstruction

The landlord intends, within a reasonable time of obtaining possession of the dwelling-house, to demolish or reconstruct the building or that part of it comprising the dwelling-house, or to carry out work on that building or on land let together with (and therefore treated as part of) the dwelling-house. Provided he cannot reasonably do this without obtaining possession of the dwelling-house, he can re-possess on proof that suitable alternative accommodation will be available to the tenant when the order takes effect.

This provision is based upon the Landlord and Tenant Act 1954, s. 30(1)(f), and HA 1988, sch. 2, Ground 6, has since adopted similar principles (albeit in the context of a mandatory ground). The question of intention has been much discussed in the case law on the 1954 Act, and is summarised at chapter 2, para. 6.1.9 above. In *Wansbeck District Council* v *Marley* (1987) 20 HLR 247, the Court of Appeal gave lengthy consideration to Ground 10. The tenant occupied a cottage adjacent to a swimming pool, her late husband having formerly been superintendent of the pool. The council had plans to incorporate the cottage and the pool into a country park, and wished to recover possession of the cottage in order to accommodate a warden. The works proposed to the cottage involved no more than constructing a doorway connecting it to another building. The council failed on two grounds. First, although it was not necessary to establish the intention to carry out the works by resolution of the local authority (following *Poppet's (Caterers) Ltd* v *Maidenhead Borough Council* [1971] 1 WLR 69, 72), such intention as was shown by other evidence was not sufficiently 'clearly defined and settled' (*Cunliffe* v *Goodman* [1950] 2 KB 237). Secondly, the council had not established that such works as were proposed could not reasonably be done without obtaining possession of the cottage.

6.2.3 Ground 10A: redevelopment schemes

The dwelling-house is in an area which is the subject of a redevelopment scheme approved by the Secretary of State or the Housing Corporation (see Part V of sch. 2), and the landlord intends within a reasonable time of obtaining possession to dispose of the dwelling-house in accordance with the scheme; *or* part of the dwelling-house is in such an area, the landlord intends within a reasonable time of obtaining possession to dispose of that part, and for that purpose reasonably requires possession of the dwelling-house.

Redevelopment schemes were introduced by the Housing and Planning Act 1986. They involve the disposal and redevelopment (or *vice versa*) of dwelling-houses held on secure tenancies after consultation with the tenants concerned.

6.2.4 Ground 11: charitable landlord

The landlord is a charity, and the tenant's continued occupation of the dwelling-house would conflict with the objects of the charity.

6.3 Grounds 12 to 16: court may order possession if it considers it reasonable and suitable alternative accommodation is available

The court has a discretion to order possession if the landlord establishes both one of Grounds 12 to 16 and the availability of suitable alternative accommodation. On reasonableness and suitable alternative accommodation, see paras. 5.4 and 6.1 above. The court has the same jurisdiction to adjourn, stay, suspend and postpone as for Grounds 1 to 8.

6.3.1 Ground 12: dwelling-house part of building held for non-housing purposes; now required for landlord's employee

The dwelling-house forms part of (or is 'within the curtilage of') a building which is held mainly for purposes other than housing purposes, and consists mainly of accommodation other than housing accommodation, or is situated in a cemetery. It must have been let to the tenant or a predecessor in title of his in consequence of the tenant or predecessor being in the landlord's employment (or in the employment of another public sector body as listed). The employment has ceased, and the landlord now reasonably requires the dwelling-house for the residential occupation of another employee. This ground imposes quite different requirements from Ground 7, which is also applicable to tied occupiers.

6.3.2 Ground 13: accommodation for the physically disabled; Ground 14: accommodation for persons in especially difficult circumstances; Ground 15: 'sheltered' accommodation for persons with special needs

These three similar grounds focus on particular types of accommodation. They enable landlords to regain possession where there is no longer any person at whom the accommodation is aimed residing in the dwelling-house, and the landlord now requires it for occupation by such a person. Ground 14 is specifically limited to housing associations and housing trusts (which will only rarely be letting on secure tenancy: see para. 2.5.1 above).

6.3.3 Ground 16: accommodation too extensive for statutory successor

As with the other grounds in Part III of the Schedule, Ground 16 facilitates housing management by the landlord. A secure tenant has died, and a successor (see para. 7 below) is now residing in the dwelling-house. The accommodation afforded by the dwelling-house is, however, more extensive than is reasonably required by the successor. The landlord may in these circumstances offer alternative accommodation to the successor: in the event of the offer being rejected, the landlord may invoke this ground. Any notice seeking possession based on this ground must be served between six and 12 months after the former tenant's death: there is no discretion to waive this time limit. Ground 16 may not be used against the tenant's spouse.

7 STATUTORY SUCCESSION

On the death of a secure tenant, the devolution of the tenancy will depend on whether, at the time of death, it is a periodic tenancy or a term certain.

7.1 Periodic tenancy

A secure periodic tenancy will vest in a statutory successor in accordance with the following rules, which take precedence over any contrary devolution directed in the will of the deceased tenant or the operation of the intestacy rules. The successor must, at the time of the tenant's death, occupy the dwelling-house as his only or principal home (see chapter 2, para. 2.5). He or she must be either (a) the tenant's spouse (i.e., lawfully married spouse), in which case no further occupation requirement is to be fulfilled; or (b) another member of the tenant's family, who has resided with the tenant throughout the 12-month period ending with the tenant's death (HA 1985, s. 87). If more than one person is qualified to succeed, a spouse, if there is one, has priority; otherwise, the landlord determines which of the claimants should succeed to the tenancy (HA 1985, s. 89(2)).

If no person qualifies pursuant to these provisions, the will or the intestacy rules dictate the destiny of the tenancy. On such devolution the tenancy will cease to be secure (and will not subsequently become secure) unless in pursuance of an order under the Matrimonial Causes Act 1973, s. 24 (i.e., where on divorce the court orders the transfer of the tenancy from one spouse to the other) (HA 1985, s. 89(3),(4)).

7.1.1 Member of the family

A person is a member of a tenant's family if he falls within the statutory definition of this term (HA 1985, s. 113), which includes, as well as spouses, persons who 'live together as husband and wife' (see *City of Westminster* v *Peart* (1991) 24 HLR 389). It has been held that this cannot include two persons of the same sex (*Harrogate Borough Council* v *Simpson* (1984) 17 HLR 205). A person is a member of the tenant's family if he is their parent, grandparent, child, grandchild, brother, sister, uncle, aunt, nephew or niece (relationships by marriage, of the half-blood, and step-relationships being included, and an illegitimate child being treated as the legitimate child of his mother and reputed father) (HA 1985, s. 113(2)). The 12-month period of occupation with the tenant which the successor must establish need not have been in the house or flat of which a secure tenancy is now claimed, as held by the House of Lords in *Waltham Forest LBC* v *Thomas* [1992] 2 AC 198:

> It does not matter whether the successor and the tenant resided together in one or more houses or whether the residences were all council houses provided they resided together in a council house at the moment of death and provided that the successor and the tenant resided together during the period of 12 months prior to the death of the tenant.
>
> (*per* Lord Templeman at 204).

7.1.2 Exclusions

The general principle is to allow for one succession under the statute, but no more. This policy is effected by s. 88. Where the tenant was at the date of his death himself a successor, no person will qualify to succeed him. The tenant will be a successor if:

(a) the tenancy he held vested in him by virtue of s. 89;

(b) he was a joint tenant, and became sole tenant (presumably by survivorship, or possibly release: see *Bassetlaw District Council* v *Renshaw* [1992] 1 All ER 925);

(c) the tenancy arose as a periodic tenancy on termination of a fixed term, that tenancy having been granted to some other person (or jointly to him and some other person);

(d) he became tenant by reason of assignment;

(e) he became tenant on the tenancy being vested in him on the death of the previous tenant.

If a new tenancy intervenes, however, succession will become possible once more: the slate will be wiped clean. In *Bassetlaw District Council* v *Renshaw*, the claimant's parents had occupied the property for some seven years. His father served notice terminating the tenancy, following which his mother entered into a new agreement with the council whereby she became sole tenant. On her death, some two months later, the claimant was entitled to succeed as secure tenant. His mother was not a successor within the meaning of the Act.

7.2 Term certain

If the tenancy is for a fixed term, it will devolve according to the will of the tenant, or the operation of the intestacy rules. The tenancy will remain secure until the act of vesting, or disposal, has been carried out, but on that occurrence, it will cease to be secure unless the person on whom it devolves would be qualified to succeed by virtue of the above principles, or the transfer is in pursuance of an order under s. 24 of the Matrimonial Causes Act 1973 (HA 1985, s. 90).

SEVEN

THE RIGHT TO BUY

Housing Act 1985, Part V

1 INTRODUCTION

Part V of the Housing Act 1985 (HA 1985) is the current source of the right to buy provisions, although, as will be seen, there have been important amendments affecting them, most recently in Part II of the Leasehold Reform, Housing and Urban Development Act 1993 (LRHUDA 1993). 'The right to buy' is the statutory shorthand for two rights: (a) the right to acquire the freehold of a dwelling-house which is a 'house' (as opposed to a flat) and of which the landlord owns the freehold; (b) the right to be granted a lease (normally for 125 years at a rent not exceeding £10 per annum) of a dwelling-house which is either a flat, or a house of which the landlord does not own the freehold.

These rights are subject to many conditions, exceptions, and qualifications. They have proved to be very attractive to tenants, not least because the price of acquisition is below the market value of the property: the tenant obtains a discount based on the length of time he has been a public sector tenant. Ancillary rights conferred by the 1980 Housing Act, and preserved in the 1985 consolidation, such as the right to a mortgage and the right to deferred completion, have not proved as popular, and are in the process of repeal. Shared ownership leases are being replaced by sale on 'rent to mortgage terms'.

Part V of the 1985 Act confers a statutory right on secure tenants, which the parties to the agreement cannot contract out of. Nor can a person letting to a public sector body which fulfils the 'landlord condition' so tailor his leases as to prohibit or restrict the exercise of the right to buy by those holding as sub-tenants (see HA 1985, s. 179).

2 QUALIFYING CONDITIONS

2.1 Secure tenants

The right to buy is conferred on secure tenants only (HA 1985, s. 118(1); see chapter 6 for definition). It seems that those few licensees who are secure tenants by virtue of s. 79(3) of the 1985 Act (see chapter 6, para. 2.1) do not have the right to buy, as they are only secure tenants for the purposes of that Part of the Act (i.e., Part IV), and the right to buy provisions are contained in Part V. This anomaly, which arose on consolidation in 1985, was identified by Balcombe LJ in *Westminster City Council* v *Clarke* (1991) 23 HLR 506. Its practical effect is, however, small, as the House of Lords in *Clarke* have severely limited the circumstances in which a licensee will enjoy a secure tenancy (see Housing Act 1985, Part V).

Where a secure tenancy is a joint tenancy, the right belongs jointly to all the joint tenants, or to such one or more as may be agreed between them. One at least of the joint tenants to whom the right is to belong (by agreement) must occupy the dwelling-house as his only or principal home (see generally, HA 1985, s. 118(2)). There is also the possibility of a 'deemed' joint tenancy arising (see para. 2.1.1 below).

The tenant must remain secure until completion of the acquisition or grant of the lease. In *Sutton LBC* v *Swann* (1985) 18 HLR 140, the tenant ceased to occupy the dwelling-house as his only or principal home after he had served a notice claiming to exercise the right to buy, and the landlords had admitted his claim, but before grant of the long lease. He could not then compel the landlords to grant the lease. See also *Muir Group Housing Association Ltd* v *Thornley* (1992) 25 HLR 89; *Jennings* v *Epping Forest District Council* (1993) 25 HLR 241.

2.1.1 Sharing the right to buy

A secure tenant may require that not more than three members of his family, who are not joint tenants but who occupy the dwelling-house as their only or principal home, should share the right to buy with him. If he does this, he and the other(s) concerned will be treated as joint secure tenants for the purposes of Part V (HA 1985, s. 123). The tenant can select for these purposes:

(a) his spouse (i.e., the person to whom he is lawfully married);

(b) any other member of his family (as defined in HA 1985, s. 186: includes a person with whom the tenant is living as husband and wife) who has been residing with him for the 12-month period prior to the notice exercising the right to buy (see chapter 6, para. 7.1.1);

(c) any member of the tenant's family (who does not satisfy the residence condition in (b) above) where the landlord consents.

In each case, the person selected must at the time of service of the notice exercising the right to buy be occupying the dwelling-house as his only or principal home.

The person who by these means shares the right to buy is then treated for the purposes of the application as a joint tenant (HA 1985, s. 123(3)), and, indeed, a secure tenant. In *Harrow LBC* v *Tonge* (1992) 25 HLR 99, a secure tenant required that her daughter share in the exercise of the right to buy pursuant to s. 123. The secure tenant died before the acquisition was completed. The daughter could not succeed to her mother's secure tenancy as her mother had herself been a successor (see HA 1985, s. 87; chapter 6, para. 7.1.2). The Court of Appeal held that she could nevertheless compel the landlord to convey the property to her (by means of injunction: HA 1985, s. 138(3)), as for the purposes of the right to buy application she was treated as a joint secure tenant with her mother, and she continued to occupy the house as her only or principal home after her mother's death.

In *City of Bradford MBC* v *McMahon* [1994] 1 WLR 52, a superficially similar case, a secure tenant served a notice claiming to exercise her right to buy. Shortly afterwards, her daughter and son-in-law came to live with her, but the tenant died before the conveyance of the freehold was completed. The daughter and son-in-law could not compel the landlord to complete. They did not share in the purchase (the secure tenant had not invoked s. 123), and as they had not lived in the property for a 12-month period, they were not themselves entitled to succeed to her secure tenancy (in which case they may have been able to invoke s. 136: see para. 5.9 below).

It is essential that the person claiming to exercise the right to buy continues to occupy the dwelling as his only or principal home up to the date of completion or grant (HA 1985, s. 123(1); *Harrow LBC* v *Tonge* (1992) 25 HLR 99, 103, *per* Nourse LJ).

2.2 Qualifying period

The right to buy does not arise until the 'qualifying period', as defined in sch. 4 to the Act, is at least two years. Where the secure tenancy is a joint tenancy, it is sufficient for one of the joint tenants to qualify in this sense (HA 1985, s. 119).

Schedule 4 to the 1985 Act serves a dual purpose, as the qualifying period is also applied in calculating the discount to which the tenant is entitled. In effect, it is time as a public sector tenant which matters, whether or not the tenancy or tenancies have been held of this landlord, of these premises, or even whether they have been secure. 'Public sector tenancy' is defined as a tenancy, other than a long tenancy, under which a dwelling-house was let as a separate dwelling, at any time when the 'landlord condition' and 'tenant condition' are satisfied. These 'conditions' are defined in sch.4, paras. 7 to 9.

Although in almost all cases they will be to the same effect as ss. 80 and 81 in the body of the 1985 Act (see chapter 6, paras. 2.5 and 2.6), there are certain differences (e.g., the inclusion of time spent as a tenant of certain Scottish and Northern Irish public bodies), and the provisions themselves should be checked.

A period will qualify (see generally for detail sch. 4, paras. 2 to 5A):

(a) where the secure tenant (now claiming to exercise the right to buy), or his spouse (if living together at the date the claim is made), or a deceased spouse of his (if living together at the time of death) *either* was a public sector tenant *or* was the spouse of a public sector tenant and occupied as his or her only or principal home the dwelling-house of which his or her spouse was tenant;

(b) where the public sector tenant became such on the death of his parent or his parent otherwise ceasing to be public sector tenant, a period during which the new tenant has (since reaching the age of 16) occupied as his only or principal home a dwelling-house of which his parent was public sector tenant, as long as two years did not elapse between the date the child ceased so occupying and the date the parent died or otherwise ceased to be public sector tenant;

(c) certain periods spent occupying accommodation provided as a member of the armed forces may count;

(d) periods during which the secure tenant, his spouse or deceased spouse was a qualifying person for the purposes of the preserved right to buy may count. Time before the 1985 (or even 1980) Act can count: see HA 1985, s. 185.

3 EXCLUSIONS

3.1 Right to buy does not arise

Schedule 5 specifies 10 situations in which the right to buy will not arise. The numbering which follows replicates that of the relevant paragraphs in the schedule (paragraphs 6 and 8 have been repealed):

(1) The landlord is a housing trust or a housing association and is a charity (see *Hounslow LBC* v *Hare* (1990) 24 HLR 9).

(2) The landlord is a co-operative housing association.

(3) The landlord is a housing association which has not at any time received grant aid (under various listed statutory provisions).

(4) The landlord does not own the freehold or an interest sufficient to grant a lease (i) in relation to a house, as defined (see para. 4.1 below), for a term exceeding 21 years; (ii) in relation to a flat, for a term of not less than

50 years. The commencement date of the lease is deemed for these purposes to be the date the tenant's notice claiming exercise of the right to buy is served on the landlord.

(5) The dwelling-house forms part of, or is within the curtilage of, a building which is held mainly for purposes other than housing purposes, and consists mainly of accommodation other than housing accommodation, or is situated in a cemetery, *and* it was let in consequence of the tenant (or a predecessor in title of his) being in the employment of the landlord or some other listed public body. A dwelling-house will only fall 'within the curtilage' of another building if, looking at the physical situation of the land and all the circumstances, it is 'so intimately associated with' the building as 'to form part and parcel' of it (*Methuen-Campbell* v *Walters* [1979] 1 QB 525, 543, *per* Buckley LJ). Thus, a house built on the edge of the grounds of a college, at some distance from any of the college buildings, did not come within the curtilage of any relevant building, and the lecturer who occupied the house could exercise the right to buy (*Dyer* v *Dorset County Council* [1989] QB 346, as followed in *Barwick* v *Kent County Council* (1992) 24 HLR 341).

(7) The dwelling-house has features which are substantially different from those of ordinary dwelling-houses and are designed to make it suitable for occupation by physically disabled persons; it is one of a group of dwelling-houses which it is in the practice of the landlord to let for occupation by physically disabled persons; and a social service or special facilities are provided wholly or partly for the purpose of assisting those persons. (In other words, sheltered accommodation for the physically disabled.)

(9) The dwelling-house is one of a group of dwelling-houses which it is the practice of the landlord to let for occupation by persons suffering from a mental disorder, a social service or special facilities being provided (i.e., sheltered accommodation for the mentally disordered).

(10) The dwelling-house is one of a group which are particularly suitable (having regard to location, size, design, heating systems and other features) for occupation by *elderly persons*; which it is the practice of the landlord to let for occupation by *persons aged 60 or more* (or by them and physically disabled persons); and special facilities (which here must include the services of a warden) are provided for their assistance. Where the tenant's notice was served prior to 11 October 1993, the italicised words above should be read in both cases as 'persons of pensionable age': the provision has been amended to eliminate discrimination between the sexes (LRHUDA 1993, s. 106(1), (3); SI 1993, No 2134, sch. 1, para. 4).

(11) Individual dwelling-houses which are particularly suitable (having regard to location, size, design, heating system and other features) for occupation by elderly persons, and were let to the tenant (or a predecessor in title of his) for occupation by a person, not necessarily the tenant, who was

aged 60 or more. The dwelling-house must first have been let before 1 January 1990. The tenant must challenge the landlord's contention (in his notice denying the right to buy) by application to the Secretary of State rather than the county court. This provision, and its procedure, has been significantly amended by the 1993 Act: the amended version outlined above will apply where the tenant's notice exercising the right to buy is served on or after 11 October 1993 (see further LRHUDA 1993, s. 106(2), (3); SI 1993 No 2134, r. 4(b), sch. 1, para. 4).

(12) The dwelling-house is held by the landlord on tenancy from the Crown, i.e., there is an interest in the land (e.g., the freehold) superior to that of the landlord, and that interest belongs to the Crown. However, the right to buy is not excluded if the landlord is entitled under the terms of its lease to grant a lease without the consent of the appropriate authority, or if the authority gives its consent to the lease in question. The 'appropriate authority', defined in para. 12(2) is the particular arm of the Crown responsible for the land involved.

3.2 Right to buy cannot be exercised

In two circumstances, the right to buy, although it has *arisen*, cannot be *exercised*:

(a) Where the person (or one of the persons) to whom the right to buy belongs has a bankruptcy petition pending against him; is an undischarged bankrupt; or has made a composition or arrangement with his creditors the terms of which have yet to be fulfilled (HA 1985, s. 121(2)). This provision protects the landlord who would be reluctant to proceed with a sale in what appear to be unpropitious financial circumstances.

(b) If the tenant is obliged to give up possession of the dwelling-house in pursuance of an order of the court or will be so obliged at a date specified in the order (HA 1985, s. 121(1)). This provision, which dictates the relationship between the security of tenure and the right to buy of secure tenants, has proved peculiarly difficult to operate. The issue is whether, and if so, when and how, a landlord can take the initiative where the tenant has sought to exercise his right to buy by seeking possession of the dwelling-house on one or other of the grounds in sch. 2 to the 1985 Act (see chapter 6, para. 6).

In *Enfield LBC* v *McKeon* [1986] 1 WLR 1007, a secure tenant (who had succeeded to the tenancy on the death of her father) served notice exercising her right to buy. The landlord by notice admitted the tenant's right, but then two weeks later served a notice seeking possession (pursuant to HA 1985, s. 83) citing Ground 13 (i.e., the accommodation occupied by the tenant was more extensive than she reasonably required). In reply, the tenant sought a declaration from the court of her entitlement to completion of the acquisition of the freehold under Part V of the 1985 Act. The Court of Appeal held that s. 121(1) applied to prevent her from exercising the right to buy. The right to buy was 'exercised' 'each and every time when the tenant takes a step towards the implementation of his right to purchase .... 'If, therefore any of the circumstances set out in [s. 121] subsist at any time between the time when he serves his [s. 122] notice and completion, his right to buy ceases to be exercisable (*per* Slade LJ at 1015).

It should be noted that in *McKeon*, the landlord served notice under s. 83 prior to any agreement (or even negotiation) on the terms of the acquisition. The above statements of Slade LJ are therefore *dicta* only, and in *Dance* v *Welwyn Hatfield District Council* [1990] 1 WLR 1097, where the Court of Appeal distinguished *McKeon*, they were not followed.

In *Dance* v *Welwyn Hatfield District Council* the tenants served notice exercising the right to buy, which the landlord by notice admitted. The terms of the acquisition having been agreed, the tenants elected to defer completion. Finally, they served notice requesting completion within three weeks. The landlord did not comply with this notice, four days after its expiry serving a notice seeking possession on the tenants based on Ground 10 of sch. 2 to the 1985 Act (landlord intending to demolish, etc). The tenants sought an injunction directing the landlord to convey the dwelling-house to them, and the landlords counter-claimed for possession. The Court of Appeal held in favour of the tenants, and granted the injunction sought. The case was clearly distinguishable from *Enfield LBC* v *McKeon*, as the landlord had served its s. 83 notice subsequent to the date on which it should have complied with the requirements of the tenants' completion notice. By that time, the tenants had exercised their right to buy, and it was too late for the landlords to invoke s. 121.

Yet on a strict application of Slade LJ's *dicta* in *McKeon*, s. 121 was still applicable, as the right to buy was being 'exercised' up until the date of completion itself.

It is tentatively submitted that the two decisions are to be reconciled by allowing the landlord to invoke s. 121 at any time prior to the tenant's lawful service of a notice to complete. This will itself require all matters relating to the grant to have been agreed or determined (see HA 1985, s. 138(1)). It remains unclear what the landlord must have done before this stage is reached. A strictly literal interpretation of s. 121 would seem to indicate that the existence of a court order is necessary, but this seems unduly onerous, and in *Dance* v *Welwyn Hatfield District Council*, Nourse LJ appears to indicate (at 1105) that the service of a notice seeking possession may prevent the tenant from exercising the right to buy. The landlord's application for a possession order would then have to be dealt with before the success or otherwise of the tenant's attempt to exercise the right to buy would be known.

4 THE TERMS OF THE ACQUISITION OR GRANT

4.1 The property

The secure tenant is entitled to a conveyance or lease of the dwelling-house. This will include land let together with the dwelling-house (unless it is agricultural land exceeding two acres), and also land which has not been let with it, but which is or has been used for the purpose of the dwelling-house, provided that the tenant by written notice requires the land to be included in the purchase, and it is reasonable for the land to be so included (HA 1985, s. 184). The tenant may make this request for the inclusion of additional land at any time prior to completion of the right to buy.

Whether the tenant is entitled to a conveyance of the freehold or a lease will depend in part on whether the dwelling-house is a 'house' or a 'flat'. A dwelling-house is a house if, and only if, it is 'a structure reasonably so-called, so that (a) where the building is divided horizontally, the flats or other units into which it is divided are not houses; (b) where a building is divided vertically, the units into which it is divided may be houses; (c) where a building is not structurally detached, it is not a house if a material part of it lies above or below the remainder of the structure' (HA 1985, s. 183(2)). A dwelling-house which is not a 'house' as so defined is a 'flat' (HA 1985, s. 183(3)). The terminology is taken with slight modifications from the Leasehold Reform Act 1967, s. 2, and reference should be made to the case law on that provision for further particulars (see chapter 5, para. 3.3).

4.2 Conveyance of freehold

The secure tenant is entitled to a conveyance of the freehold where the dwelling-house is a 'house' of which the landlord is the freeholder. On completion, the secure tenancy will come to an end, and the purchaser will obtain a largely unencumbered freehold (HA 1985, s. 139). The detailed provisions of the conveyance are set out in sch. 6 (Parts I and III) to the 1985 Act. Charges over the landlord's interest are dealt with in accordance with Part IV of that schedule: in general, charges (other than tenant's incumbrances) over the freehold are extinguished, although the landlord's personal liability (e.g., in respect of any debt secured by a charge) will persist.

Where the dwelling-house is a house of which the landlord does not own the freehold, a secure tenant who gives notice claiming the right to buy on or after 11 October 1993 is entitled to a conveyance of the freehold provided that all interests superior to that of the landlord are held by a body satisfying the landlord condition (see chapter 6, para. 2.5) or a registered housing association which is not excepted from the right to buy by sch. 5 to the 1985 Act (paras 1 to 3; chapter 6, para. 2.5.1). This extension to the tenant's right to buy was made by the Secretary of State exercising his powers pursuant to s. 171 of the 1985 Act, and the detailed provisions are to be found in the Housing (Extension of Right to Buy) Order 1993 SI 1993 No 2240.

4.3 Grant of lease

The secure tenant is entitled to a new lease where the dwelling-house is a 'flat', or where it is a house of which the landlord does not own the freehold, and which does not fall within the provisions of the Housing (Extension of Right to Buy) Order 1993 referred to above (HA 1985, s. 118(1)(b)). The length of the lease will depend upon the interest of the landlord in the dwelling-house. If its interest is 'not less than' a lease for a term of which more than 125 years and five days are unexpired (thus a freehold would clearly suffice), the term of the right to buy lease will be not less than 125 years (HA 1985, sch. 6, para. 12(1)). If the landlord's interest is less than this, the term to which the tenant will be entitled is a term expiring five days before the first day on which the term of any lease under which the landlord holds any part of the dwelling-house is to expire (HA 1985, sch. 6, para. 12(2)). It should be remembered that if the landlord's interest in the dwelling-house is for 21 years or less (in the case of a 'house') or for less than 50 years (in the case of a 'flat'), the right to buy does not arise (HA 1985, sch. 5, para. 4: see para. 3.1 above).

Where the landlord has previously granted one or more leases since 8 August 1980 in relation to another or other flats in the same building for the term to which the tenant(s) were entitled under Part V of the 1985 Act, the lease of the flat in respect of which the right to buy is now being exercised may be granted so as to expire at the end of the term for which the other lease or leases have been granted (HA 1985, sch. 6, para. 12(3)). Thus, the landlord may so manage his long leases of flats in a particular building that they will expire contemporaneously.

The other terms of the lease are to be found by reference to Parts I and III of sch. 2. For the effect of the grant of the new lease on charges over the leasehold interest, see Part IV thereof.

The lease of a *house* (as opposed to a flat) granted by virtue of Part V of the 1985 Act is to be treated as a long tenancy for the purposes of the Leasehold Reform Act 1967 notwithstanding that it is granted for a term of 21 years or less (HA 1985, s. 174). Thus, the tenant will *prima facie* have the right to enfranchise or extend the lease (see further, chapter 5, para. 2 *et seq.*). The price payable on enfranchisement shall be determined in accordance with s. 9(1A) of the 1967 Act (chapter 5, para. 4.5) where the long tenancy is a lease granted in pursuance of the right to buy (HA 1985, s. 175). The lease of a flat granted by virtue of Part V of the 1985 Act is similarly to be treated as a long lease for the purposes of the collective enfranchisement and individual lease extension provisions of Part I of the Leasehold Reform, Housing and Urban Development Act 1993 (see LRHUDA 1993, s. 7(1)(c); chapter 5, para. 6 *et seq.*).

4.4 The price to be paid

The amount to be paid for a dwelling-house on conveyance or grant is the 'value', as defined by s. 127, less the 'discount' to which the purchaser is entitled (HA 1985, s. 126(1)). The calculation is made on the 'value' at the 'relevant time', i.e., the date on which the notice claiming to exercise the right to buy is served (HA 1985, s. 122).

4.4.1 The value

The value is the price which the dwelling-house would obtain if sold on the open market by a willing vendor. Improvements by tenants (and certain others) are to be disregarded, and it is to be assumed that any service charges or improvement contributions payable will be not less than the figures given in the landlord's s. 125 notice (HA 1985, s. 127(1)). *Where the freehold is being conveyed*, it is assumed that the vendor is selling for an estate in fee simple with vacant possession; that neither the tenant nor a member of his family residing with him wanted to buy; and that the dwelling-house is to be conveyed with the same rights and subject to the same burdens as it would be in pursuance of Part V (HA 1985, s. 127(2)). *Where a lease is being granted*, it is assumed that the vendor is granting a lease with vacant possession for the term to be granted; that neither the tenant nor a member of his family residing with him wanted to take the lease; that the ground rent would not exceed £10 per annum; and that the grant was to be made with the same rights and subject to the same burdens as it would be in pursuance of Part V (HA 1985, s. 127(3)). In most cases, valuation will be agreed between the parties. In the event of dispute, the matter should be referred to the district valuer, who has exclusive jurisdiction to determine it (HA 1985, s. 128).

4.4.2 The discount

The discount is a percentage calculated by reference to the 'qualifying period' (see para. 2.2 above). *Where the dwelling-house is a 'house'*, the discount is 32% plus 1% for each complete year by which the qualifying period exceeds two years: the maximum total discount is 60%. *Where the dwelling-house is a 'flat'*, the discount is 44% plus 2% for each complete year by which the qualifying period exceeds two years: the maximum total is 70%. These formulae may be amended (by increasing the discount only) by ministerial order (HA 1985, s. 129(2A),(2B), as amended by the Housing and Planning Act 1986, s. 2). Where joint tenants are exercising the right to buy, the discount is taken to be the highest discount of those participating (HA 1985, s. 129(3)). Where, after a notice claiming the right to buy has been served, another person becomes secure tenant (e.g., by succession on death), that person will be entitled to the same discount as the person who served the notice (HA 1985, s. 136(1); *McIntyre* v *Merthyr Tydfil District Council* (1989) 21 HLR 320).

The discount will be reduced in the case of a purchaser who has previously exercised the right to buy in relation to another dwelling-house (see further, HA 1985, s. 130). In all cases, the discount must not reduce the price payable below the 'cost-floor', being the amount of costs incurred in respect of the dwelling-house in the eight-year period prior to the service of the tenant's notice claiming to exercise the right to buy (HA 1985, s. 131, as amended by HA 1988, s. 122). For how the expenditure is to be calculated, see Housing (Right to Buy) (Cost Floor) Determinations 1984 and 1992; Housing (Right to Buy) (Cost Floor) (Amendment) Determination 1989. The maximum discount in any one case has been set at £50,000 (Housing (Right to Buy) (Maximum Discount) Order, SI 1989 No 513).

4.5 Mortgage

The secure tenant had until recently 'the right to a mortgage', i.e.,the right to leave the whole or part of the purchase price and costs payable outstanding on mortgage (HA 1985, ss. 132 to 135). Such a right is not available where the tenant's notice claiming to exercise the right to buy is served on or after 11 October 1993, and these provisions have been repealed with appropriate savings (LRHUDA 1993, s. 107; SI 1993 No 2134, r. 4(b), sch. 1, para. 4(1)).

4.6 Future disposals

Where the right to buy has been exercised, and the freehold conveyed or the lease granted as the case may be, the vendor will have no right of pre-emption in the event of a re-sale by the purchaser (save in very limited circumstances). However, the purchaser who has benefited from a discount (as most will have) must covenant to pay to the landlord on demand, in the event of a 'relevant disposal' within three years of the conveyance or grant, the discount to which the secure tenant was entitled, reduced by one third for each complete year which has elapsed since the date of the conveyance or grant (HA 1985, s. 155(1),(2)). The covenant is expressed to be binding on successors in title of the secure tenant, and liability under the covenant takes effect as a charge on the dwelling-house (see further, HA 1985, s. 156).

A disposal is a 'relevant disposal' for these purposes if it is a further conveyance of the freehold or an assignment of the lease; or the grant of a lease for a term of more than 21 years other than at a rack rent (thus a letting of the dwelling-house at market value will not activate the covenant) (HA 1985, s. 159). A disposal of part of the dwelling-house will be caught. Exempted are disposals to 'qualifying persons' (i.e., members of the tenant's family: s. 160(2)); a vesting of the whole of the dwelling-house under a will or on intestacy; and a disposal of the whole of the dwelling-house pursuant to a property adjustment order on divorce, etc. (Matrimonial Causes Act 1973, s. 24) or pursuant to an order for family provision from the estate of a deceased person (Inheritance (Provision for Family and Dependants) Act 1975, s. 2) (HA 1985, s. 160(1)). Compulsory disposals (defined in HA 1985, s. 161) are also exempted, as are disposals of land included in the purchase by virtue of its being let with or used for the purposes of the dwelling-house (i.e., pursuant to HA 1985, s. 184) (HA 1985, s. 160(1)).

A local authority, the Development Board for Rural Wales, or a housing association may, on executing a conveyance or grant of a dwelling-house situated in a National Park, or an area of outstanding natural beauty, or a designated rural area, require that the tenant covenant that he will not make a 'relevant disposal' which is not an 'exempted disposal' (see above) without the landlord's written consent, and that he will not dispose of the dwelling-house by way of tenancy or licence without such consent. Provision is made to allow for disposal to persons who have had their place of work, or their only or principal home, in the area or region in question for the previous three years (see generally, HA 1985, s. 157). The covenant may, with the consent of the Secretary of State or the Housing Corporation, take the form of a right of pre-emption activated by a disposal within the period of 10 years from the date of the conveyance or grant (HA 1985, s. 157(4); see further s. 158). A general consent has been given by the Secretary of State to the insertion of such covenants (Ministerial Letter, 22 September 1980, para. 28).

5 PROCEDURE

5.1 Tenant's notice claiming to exercise the right to buy

The tenant initiates the right to buy procedure by serving written notice on the landlord (HA 1985, s. 122). The form of notice has been prescribed (as enabled by HA 1985, s. 176), and is contained, as 'RTB 1', in the Housing (Right to Buy) (Prescribed Forms) Regulations 1986, SI 1986 No 2194 (as amended by SI 1993 No 2246, with respect to notices served on or after 11 October 1993). Service of this notice on the landlord will bind any persons purchasing the landlord's interest in the dwelling-house (HA 1985, s. 137). The tenant may withdraw the notice at any time (HA 1985, s. 122(3)). If the tenant wishes any members of his family to join in the right to buy (see para. 2.1.1 above), he should state this in the notice.

5.2 Landlord's notice admitting or denying the right to buy

The landlord normally has four weeks in which to serve its notice in reply (eight weeks where there has been a change of landlord during the previous two years: HA 1985, s. 124(2)). The notice, which must be in writing, must either admit or deny the claim, in the latter case giving reasons (HA 1985, s. 124(1)). In the event of the tenant wishing to challenge the landlord's denial of the claim, application should then be made to the county court for a ruling (HA 1985, s. 181).

5.3 Landlord's notice of purchase price

Where the tenant's right to buy has been established, following the landlord's admission or the determination of the county court, the landlord must serve a notice pursuant to s. 125, stating the terms of the acquisition. In particular, it must state the price at which (in the landlord's opinion) the tenant is entitled to have the freehold conveyed or the lease granted, and it must state how the figure has been arrived at by giving details of the value, improvements disregarded, and the discount (HA 1985, s. 125(2)). In addition, it should state the provisions which the landlord contends should be included in the conveyance or grant, any service charges or improvement contributions claimed to be recoverable, any relevant structural defects, and give notice of other statutory rights to which the tenant may be entitled (HA 1985, ss. 125(3) to (5), 125A, 125B). Where the tenant's s. 122 notice was served on or after 11 October 1993, the landlord should comply with the amended version of s. 125(5) (contained in LRHUDA 1993, s. 104), which takes account of the amendments to secure tenants' statutory rights made by that Act. The s. 125 notice must be served within eight weeks of the right to buy being established where the freehold is to be conveyed, and 12 weeks where a leasehold interest is to be granted (HA 1985, s. 125(1)).

If the tenant wishes to challenge the price claimed by the landlord in its s. 125 notice, he should refer the question to the district valuer for a determination (HA 1985, s. 128): on questions of value, he has exclusive jurisdiction. If the tenant wishes to contest other terms of the acquisition, application should be made to the county court (HA 1985, s. 185).

5.4 Tenant's notice of intention

Where the right to buy procedure is invoked by a s. 122 notice served on or after 11 October 1993, a further stage is added to the process. Following service of the landlord's notice of purchase price (under s. 125), the tenant must serve a written notice on the landlord (stating either that he intends to pursue his claim to exercise the right to buy, or that he withdraws the claim) or serve a notice under s. 144 (as amended) claiming to exercise the right to acquire on rent to mortgage terms (see further, para. 7 below) (HA 1985, s. 125D(1), added by LRHUDA 1993, s. 105(1)). This allows the landlord to discover whether the tenant does wish to proceed with the acquisition once he is able to make an informed decision. The tenant has 12 weeks in which to serve notice under s. 125D, the time running from the landlord's s. 125 notice, or, where the value of the dwelling-house has been determined by the district valuer, the date of service of the notice of the determination (HA 1985, s. 125D(2), added as above).

5.5 Landlord's notice in default

The landlord's remedy for the tenant's failure to serve a notice under s. 125D above is to invoke the default procedure laid down by s. 125E (also added by LRHUDA 1993, s. 105(1)), the ultimate sanction being the deemed withdrawal of the tenant's s. 122 notice (and thereby the termination of the procedure).

5.6 Duty to convey

Once the right to buy has been established, and 'all matters relating to the grant and to the amount to be left outstanding or advanced on the security of the dwelling-house have been agreed or determined', the landlord is under a legal duty to convey the freehold or grant the lease as appropriate (HA 1985, s. 138(1)). The landlord may only resist the tenant's claim at this stage by showing that the tenant is no longer a secure tenant, that the right to buy has not been established, that all other matters have not been agreed or determined, or, finally, that the tenant has failed to pay the rent or any other payment due from him as a tenant (e.g., a service charge) for a period of four weeks after it has been lawfully demanded (HA 1985, s. 138(2)). It is too late for the landlord to initiate proceedings for the recovery of possession (pursuant to Part IV of the 1985 Act) in an attempt to prevent exercise of the right to buy (HA 1985, s. 121(1); *Dance* v *Welwyn Hatfield District Council*; see para. 3.2 above).

The duty to complete is enforceable by injunction (HA 1985, s. 138(3)). There is no stage in the process of 'exchange of contracts'. Instead, the court is asked to accept that agreement (or determination) has taken place, and that the duty to complete has therefore arisen. The court has no discretion to refuse an injunction on the basis of considerations of hardship. Only where there is a proven ground enabling a court properly to resist an order of specific performance (e.g., mistake, misrepresentation, or fraud), which would itself negate the fulfilment of the conditions in s. 138(1), may the court refuse the tenant the injunction sought (see *Taylor* v *Newham LBC* [1993] 1 WLR 444).

5.7 Other remedies of the tenant

5.7.1 Delay procedure

The Housing Act 1988 introduced a delay procedure whereby in certain circumstances the tenant seeking to exercise the right to buy is entitled to have his payments of rent deducted from the purchase price of the house or flat. The provisions are to be found in ss. 153A and 153B of the 1985 Act, added by the 1988 Act, s. 124. The tenant instigates the procedure by serving an 'initial notice of delay' on the landlord. He may do this where the landlord has failed to serve a notice admitting or denying the claim (s. 124) or a notice of purchase price (s. 125) within the respective time limits or (more widely) 'where the tenant considers that delays on the part of the landlord are preventing him from exercising expeditiously his right to buy' (HA 1985, s. 153A(1)). The notice must give the landlord a minimum period of one month in which to respond by serving a counter-notice together with any notice required. If the landlord fails to serve within the time limit, the tenant may then serve an 'operative notice of delay', as a result of which any payment of rent (but not a sum on account of rates, or a service charge as defined in HA 1985, s. 621) made by the tenant is to be 'taken into account', i.e., the rent payments made are to be set off against the purchase price of the dwelling-house. If the rent payments are referable to a period of over 12 months, the tenant is credited with an additional (punitive) sum of 50% of the total payments made (HA 1985, s. 153B). Moreover, any period during which rent payments are applied towards the purchase price is subtracted from the period during which the purchasing tenant has to repay his discount in the event of a subsequent disposal (HA 1985, s. 155(3A), added by HA 1988, sch. 17, para. 41).

The landlord can prevent further application of these provisions by serving a valid counter-notice. In any event, the delay procedure will be obviated on completion of the acquisition, or by withdrawal of the tenant's application to exercise the right to buy. For prescribed forms, see Housing (Right to Buy Delay Procedure) (Prescribed Forms) Regulations 1989, SI 1989 No 240, as amended (where notice claiming exercise of the right to buy is served on or after 11 October 1993) by SI 1993 No. 2245.

5.7.2 Ministerial intervention

An alternative line of attack for a tenant who perceives dilatory tactics being employed by the landlord is to seek the assistance of the Secretary of State, who has wide powers to intervene where it appears to him 'that tenants generally, a tenant or tenants of a particular landlord, or tenants of a description of landlords, have or may have difficulty in exercising effectively or expeditiously the right to buy' (HA 1985, s. 164(1)). The powers are exercised by serving notice to such effect on the landlord, and enable the Minister to do 'all such things as appear to him necessary or expedient' to enable secure tenants of the landlord to exercise their right to buy (HA 1985, s. 164(5)). In particular, he may execute orders vesting property in tenants, and thereby taking the matter entirely out of the hands of the local authority. The power has been described by Lord Denning MR in the leading case (*Norwich City Council* v *Secretary of State for the Environment* [1982] QB 808, 827) as 'a very great power to be used only after careful consideration'. Ancillary ministerial powers are to be found in the 1985 Act, ss. 166 to 171.

5.8 Landlord's remedies

There is no obligation on the tenant to complete once matters have been agreed or determined as aforesaid. Indeed, the tenant has the express right to withdraw from the acquisition at any time (HA 1985, s. 122(3)). The landlord who wishes to know one way or the other may serve on the tenant a notice to complete. In the event of the tenant failing to comply with two consecutive notices to complete, the s. 122 notice will be deemed to be withdrawn, and the right to buy procedure thereby terminated. For details of this procedure, see HA 1985, ss. 140, 141.

5.9 Change of tenant after notice claiming right to buy

Where, following inception of the right to buy process, a new tenant becomes secure tenant, either under the same tenancy, or under a periodic tenancy arising on termination of the secure term certain (under s. 86), the new tenant can adopt the application: he is deemed to be in the same position as the former tenant (HA 1985, s. 136). Thus, on the death of a secure periodic tenant, the successor who takes the tenancy by virtue of s. 89 will be able to continue with the application: likewise where a term certain is transmitted to a person qualified to succeed (see HA 1985, s. 90). *Inter vivos* assignments of secure tenancies are rare (see chapter 6, para. 4.2.1), but where they are effective, the assignee will be able to proceed with a pending acquisition. Assignments by way of exchange (HA 1985, s. 92) are, however, excluded from the operation of this provision.

The new tenant is treated as if he were the former tenant. Thus, he is entitled to the discount to which the former tenant was entitled (see *McIntyre* v *Merthyr Tydfil Borough Council* (1989) 21 HLR 320). If the s. 122 notice was served on or after 11 October 1993, and the landlord has subsequently served a notice of purchase price on the former tenant, the new tenant must serve a notice of intention (see para. 5.4 above) on the landlord within 12 weeks of his becoming a secure tenant, or, if later, the date of service of the district valuer's determination of the value of the dwelling-house (HA 1985, s. 136(2), as amended by LRHUDA 1993, s. 105(2)). However, the transfer of the secure tenancy will normally abrogate the rights of those members of the former tenant's family sharing in the purchase by virtue of s. 123 (see HA 1985, s. 136(6)).

5.10 Change of landlord after notice claiming right to buy

Where the landlord's interest changes following service of a s. 122 notice, the tenant's application will generally be unaffected, unless the new landlord is exempt from the right to buy (HA 1985, s. 137). For the position where the landlord's interest changes prior to the secure tenant exercising the right to buy, see para. 6 below.

5.11 Costs

The tenant is not liable for the landlord's costs in relation to the right to buy procedure, and any agreement which purports to impose such a liability on the tenant is rendered void (HA 1985, s. 178(1)).

6 THE PRESERVED RIGHT TO BUY

The situations where the public sector landlord may alienate the reversion of dwelling-houses let on secure tenancy have multiplied in recent years (see chapter 1, paras. 3 and 4). The loss of the property to the private sector (which now includes housing associations) has a potentially dramatic effect on the availability of the right to buy, as with the disposal of the reversion, the 'landlord condition' will cease to be satisfied, and the necessary pre-condition to the right to buy, namely secure tenant status, will be lost. The Housing and Planning Act 1986, by adding provisions (ss. 171A to 171H) to the Housing Act 1985, introduced the 'preserved right to buy' to deal with this problem.

The right to buy will be preserved where a person ceases to be a secure tenant of a dwelling-house by reason of a disposal by the landlord of an interest in it to a person who does not satisfy the landlord condition (a 'qualifying disposal') (HA 1985, s. 171A(1),(2), subject to minor exceptions in s. 171A(3)). The right will continue to be preserved so long as the dwelling-house is occupied by a 'qualifying person' (i.e., the former secure tenant, or each of joint secure tenants, and certain successors: see further, s. 171B(3),(4)) as his only or principal home (s. 171B(1)). A change of dwelling-house will not affect the preserved right to buy, provided the landlord is the same person (or a connected company) (s. 171B(6)).

Where the right to buy is preserved by these provisions, Part V of the 1985 Act applies subject to such modifications and exceptions as are effected by regulation (HA 1985, s. 171C(1)). Reference should be made to the Housing (Preservation of Right to Buy) Regulations 1993 (SI 1993 No 2241). The schedules to these regulations conveniently set out Part V of the 1985 Act as it applies to the preserved right to buy.

The preserved right to buy is registrable by notice in the Land Registry. A duty is imposed on a person selling subject to the preserved right to buy to state this in the instrument effecting the disposal, and to list the dwelling-houses being occupied by secure tenants (HA 1985, sch. 9A, para. 1). The Chief Land Registrar shall, in such a case, enter a notice in the register protecting the rights of the qualifying persons (HA 1985, sch. 9A, para. 4). This notice is essential, as these rights will not effect a purchaser of the landlord's interest unless they are registered: they cannot take effect as overriding interests (HA 1985, sch. 9A, para. 6). The duty cast on the vendor and the Chief Registrar is in mandatory terms, and it is assumed that qualifying persons who lose their rights, and thereby suffer loss, as a result of a breach of such duty, would be able to sue in tort.

The preserved right to buy will continue to bind successors of the landlord, provided it is registered in accordance with sch. 9A, and provided a new landlord does not satisfy the landlord condition, in which case the qualifying person will be able to rely on the 'standard' right to buy once again (HA 1985, s. 171D). Any disposal of less than the landlord's whole interest, or of part of the dwelling-house, save to the qualifying person(s), requires the consent of the Secretary of State, as separation of interests will clearly render exercise of the preserved right to buy more difficult (HA 1985, s. 171D(2) to (4)). However, on a termination of the landlord's interest in the dwelling-house (e.g., by exercise of a right of entry, but not generally by merger), the right to buy will cease to be preserved, although if such termination is caused by the landlord's act or omission, compensation may be payable (HA 1985, s. 171E).

7 THE RIGHT TO ACQUIRE ON RENT TO MORTGAGE TERMS

The Housing Act 1980 responded to the secure tenant who for one reason or another found the exercise of the right to buy as such difficult or onerous by creating the option of taking a 'shared ownership lease' over the dwelling-house (see generally HA 1985, ss. 143 to 151). By this device, the secure tenant purchases a proportion of the beneficial interest of the property (usually 50%: the 'initial share') on long lease, yet remains periodic tenant, paying a rent, in respect of the remainder. The tenant can subsequently purchase the remainder incrementally, normally in so-called 'additional shares' of 12.5%, until the whole beneficial interest in the dwelling-house has been acquired, at which stage the tenant is entitled to have the legal estate conveyed to him.

LRHUDA 1993, Part II, replaces shared ownership leases with the concept of acquisition 'on rent to mortgage terms'. However, where the secure tenant served his notice claiming to exercise the right to buy prior to 11 October 1993, a shared ownership lease remains a possibility. Acquisition on rent to mortgage terms is only applicable where the notice is served on or after that date (see SI 1993 No 2134, r. 4(b), sch. 1, para. 4(1)).

The provisions concerning acquisition on rent to mortgage terms are to be found in the 1993 Act, ss. 108 to 120. They replace existing provisions in the 1985 Act (ss. 143 to 151). In summary, the secure tenant who has claimed to exercise the right to buy, and whose right has been established, may elect to acquire on this basis instead. He will not be permitted to do so if he is entitled to housing benefit, or if exercise of the right to buy is precluded by s. 121 (see para. 3.2 above). On proof of entitlement, and satisfaction of a procedure involving notice and counter-notice, the tenant will be entitled on making an 'initial payment' (probably itself financed by building society funding) to an immediate transfer of the freehold, the landlord retaining a 'share' in the property representing the sum the tenant has left outstanding. As the tenant occupies, and pays the rent, those rental payments will be used to defray the liability to the landlord such that in time the landlord's share will be redeemed by the acquiring tenant. At the same time, the tenant may be paying instalments under the building society mortgage securing their loan which has enabled the tenant to make the initial payment.

EIGHT

PROTECTION FROM EVICTION

1 INTRODUCTION

The policy of the law is to discourage landlords of residential property who wish to recover possession from the use of self-help, and to encourage them to use the legal process. The Protection from Eviction Act 1977 (PEA 1977) accordingly restricts the methods which landlords can use to terminate their leases (or licences), in particular by prohibiting them from forfeiture by peaceable re-entry, and by requiring in most cases a minimum written notice of four weeks to be given, and further prevents recovery of possession other than by resort to the courts even where the lease or licence has been effectively terminated.

Part I of the Housing Act 1988 amended the 1977 Act in several important respects, legitimising the use of peaceful self-help in circumstances where the landlord and tenant are in close physical proximity, where the landlord has public duties to perform, or where the nature of the agreement is precarious or non-commercial. The provisions as amended are complex, the pitfalls for the landlord are many and deep, and the penalties for non-compliance are severe. Eviction of a residential occupier in contravention of the 1977 Act can result in either or both civil and criminal liability. Civil liability results in the award of substantial damages; criminal conviction carries a maximum sentence of two years' imprisonment, and/or an unlimited fine.

2 TERMINATION OF THE LEASE OR LICENCE

Termination of the lease pursuant to which the tenant is occupying is sometimes subsumed into a particular statutory code. A secure tenancy cannot be terminated by the landlord except by obtaining an order of the court under Part IV of the 1985 Act (see chapter 6, para. 5.2). An assured tenancy is treated similarly, although a fixed term assured tenancy can be terminated by the landlord giving notice as entitled to under the terms of the lease (see chapter 2, para. 5.3). There are no restrictions in the Rent Act 1977 on termination of a protected tenancy, although on such termination a statutory tenancy will arise if the tenant occupies the dwelling-house as his residence (chapter 3, para. 4.1). In any case where the landlord is entitled to terminate a lease (or licence), the landlord must ensure that he terminates it in accordance with its terms. He must also be aware of the further restrictions which are imposed by the Protection from Eviction Act 1977.

2.1 Forfeiture by the landlord

A fixed term tenancy (see chapter 2, para. 4.2.1) will generally terminate by expiry of the term or by either party giving notice as provided in the lease. Alternatively, the landlord may have reserved the right to re-enter in the event of a breach of covenant by the tenant, and seek to end the lease on the occurrence of such a breach. This latter action, also known as forfeiture, is not available where the tenant has an assured tenancy or a secure tenancy (see chapter 2, para. 5.3.1; chapter 6, para. 5.2.2). Forfeiture of a protected tenancy will give rise to a statutory tenancy if the tenant continues to occupy the dwelling-house as his residence, and the landlord will not be able to recover possession from such a tenant by exercising a right of re-entry. However, forfeiture of the protected tenancy will be the necessary first step to recovery of possession in cases where it cannot be terminated by other more convenient means (e.g., by notice to quit).

If the landlord seeks to forfeit a lease, he must satisfy various statutory provisions outside the 1977 Act. Thus if he forfeits for breach of the covenant to pay rent, he must by statute have made a rent demand of the tenant, unless the terms of the tenancy exclude such a requirement, or there is at least six months rent in arrear (see Common Law Procedure Act 1852, s. 210). The tenant then has the right to stay the proceedings by payment of rent arrears at certain times (see County Courts Act 1984, s. 138; Supreme Court Act 1981, s. 38), and may apply for relief from forfeiture. If the landlord forfeits for breach of any other covenant, he must serve a 'section 146 notice' on the tenant, specifying the breach, requiring the tenant to remedy it if it is capable of remedy, and demanding compensation, before he can proceed to forfeit (see Law of Property Act 1925, s. 146). The tenant, and holders of derivative interests such as sub-tenants and mortgagees, will then be able to seek relief from forfeiture from the court.

The landlord's right to 're-enter' and terminate the lease by physically retaking possession, is removed by s. 2, PEA 1977 while 'any person' (not just the tenant) is lawfully residing in the premises or any part of them. Enforcement of such a right, albeit reserved by the lease, by self-help methods, is unlawful, and the landlord who evicts a tenant, or lawful sub-tenant, in purported exercise of his right of re-entry, may incur civil and criminal liability for unlawful eviction. The person must however be 'lawfully residing'. If the tenant has sub-let the whole of the dwelling-house in breach of a covenant in the head-lease, and the landlord has not waived that breach (by, for example, demand or acceptance of the rent subsequent to the date when he ought reasonably to have known of the breach), physical re-entry should not contravene s. 2.

The effect of s. 2 is that a landlord who wishes to forfeit a residential lease which is capable of being forfeited (i.e., it is not an assured or secure tenancy) should do so by issuing court proceedings and serving them on the tenant. Forfeiture will occur on service, and the landlord will then seek an order of the court confirming his right to recover possession.

2.2 Notice to quit

A periodic tenancy is generally terminated by one party giving to the other a notice to quit. The length of the notice is a matter for the agreement of the parties. In the absence of such agreement, the law will infer that notice of the length of the period should be given (quarterly tenancy, three months; monthly tenancy, one month), save that a yearly tenancy will be terminable by six months' notice. Thus, at common law, a weekly tenancy is terminable by giving notice of one week. However, PEA 1977, s. 5(1), provides that (irrespective of the agreement of the parties) no notice to quit any premises let as a dwelling shall be valid unless it is in writing, contains 'prescribed information', and is given not less than four weeks before the date on which it is to take effect. The 'prescribed information', which is contained in the sch. to the Notices to Quit Etc. (Prescribed Information) Regulations 1988 (SI 1988 No 2201) tells the tenant (or licensee: see below) that if he does not leave the dwelling the landlord must get an order for possession from the court before he can be lawfully evicted, and that the landlord cannot apply for such an order until the notice to quit has run out. It further informs the tenant that he can obtain advice from a solicitor (possibly on legal aid), and information from a Citizen's Advice Bureau, a Housing Aid Centre, or a rent officer.

Although the parties cannot 'contract out' of the notice provisions of the Protection from Eviction Act, where the landlord gives a shorter notice to quit than that required by statute, it appears that the invalidity may be cured by the parties treating the notice as valid and acting upon it (*Elsden* v *Pick* [1980] 1 WLR 898). However, an invalid notice given by one only of two joint landlords (or tenants) cannot be validated without the complicity of both (see further *Hounslow LBC* v *Pilling* [1993] 1 WLR 1242).

The statutory requirements for a notice to quit apply to a periodic licence to occupy premises as a dwelling, as well as to a lease (s. 5(1A), PEA 1977). Each licence must be carefully construed to see what notice is contractually required. The statute imposes a minimum length, and if the licensee is entitled to a longer notice under his contract, that must of course be given. However, there is some doubt as to which licences are 'periodic' for these purposes. In *Norris* v *Checksfield* [1991] 1 WLR 1241, an employee's licence to occupy a bungalow pursuant to his contract of employment was held to terminate contemporaneously with his employment. It lasted for the duration of his employment, and was not a 'periodic licence'. There was accordingly no need to give four weeks' notice pursuant to s. 5(1A).

Section 5 does not apply to an 'excluded tenancy' which is entered into on or after 15 January 1989, other than pursuant to a contract made before that date; nor does it apply to any 'excluded licence', whenever made (s. 5(1B)). In such cases, the period of notice to be given will therefore be that contractually agreed, and there will be no requirement that the notice be in writing or contain prescribed information. For what constitutes an 'excluded tenancy' or an 'excluded licence', see para. 4 below.

It should be noted that a tenant, or licensee, is also obliged by s. 5 to give four weeks' written notice to quit any premises let as a dwelling and to give four weeks' written notice to terminate a periodic licence to occupy premises as a dwelling. However, as no information has been prescribed for tenants' or licensees' notices, there is at present no additional requirement.

3 RECOVERY OF POSSESSION

It is a major and costly mistake for the landlord to assume that termination of the tenancy or licence agreement thereby enables him to recover possession, using force if necessary.

3.1 Prohibition of eviction without due process of law

Where any premises have been let as a dwelling under a tenancy (or occupied under a licence) and the tenancy or licence has come to an end, it is unlawful for the owner to enforce against the occupier his right to recover possession other than by proceedings in court where the occupier continues to reside in the premises (or part of them). This important provision, contained in s. 3(1), PEA 1977, does not apply to 'statutorily protected tenancies' or to certain excluded tenancies and licences (see para. 4 below). It protects 'the occupier', being the person lawfully residing in the premises at the termination of the former tenancy or licence (s. 3(2)).

In the event of non-compliance with s. 3 of the 1977 Act, an attempt by the landlord to recover possession may incur civil and/or criminal liability. In *Haniff* v *Robinson* [1993] QB 419, the landlord had obtained a possession order against a Rent Act statutory tenant, and had even applied to the court for a warrant of execution (to be executed by the court bailiff), when he forcibly ejected her. The Court of Appeal held that the effect of s. 3 was to protect the occupier until there had been proper execution of the order by the court. The act of the landlord was unlawful, it constituted an eviction within s. 27(1) of the Housing Act 1988 (HA 1988), and damages of £28,000 were awarded to the tenant.

3.2 Statutorily protected tenancies

As other chapters in this book testify, many tenancies and licences, within and beyond the residential sector, are protected by statutes which confer on the tenant or licensee a security of tenure. It is a common feature of such protective codes that possession can only be recovered with the sanction, and pursuant to an order of, the court. Thus, whilst s. 3, PEA 1977 does not apply to 'statutorily protected tenancies', it should not be thought that recovery of possession is therefore unregulated. Far from it: these codes are sophisticated and complex regulatory instruments. The operation of s. 3 is simply unwarranted.

'Statutorily protected tenancy' is defined by s. 8 of the 1977 Act. It includes, within the residential sector, protected tenancies; assured (and assured shorthold) tenancies; long tenancies (within Part I of the Landlord and Tenant Act 1954 or sch. 10 to the Housing and Local Government Act 1989); Rent (Agriculture) Act 1976 protected occupancies and statutory tenancies; and, beyond, business tenancies under Part II of the 1954 Act. Notable omissions here are a secure tenancy (under Part IV of the Housing Act 1985 (HA 1985)) and a statutory tenancy (under the Rent Act 1977 (RA 1977)), to which s. 3 accordingly applies (see, for an example of the latter, *Haniff* v *Robinson*, above).

4 EXCLUDED TENANCIES AND LICENCES

If a tenancy or licence is 'excluded' by s. 3A of the 1977 Act, then, subject to the transitional provisions outlined below, the landlord does not have to give the statutory minimum four weeks' notice to quit and, once the agreement for occupation has been terminated, can recover possession by exercising peaceable self-help. However, the landlord is subject to the same limitations concerning forfeiture (under s. 2) as for other tenancies. The excluded tenancies and licences are as follows (s. 3A).

4.1 Occupier sharing accommodation

A tenancy or licence where the occupier whose accommodation is shared, under its terms, with the landlord (or licensor) will be excluded if the landlord occupied as his only or principal home, immediately before the tenancy or licence was granted and at the time it came to an end, premises of which the whole or part of the shared accommodation formed part. Sharing accommodation with a member of the landlord's family (as defined in HA 1985, s. 113) will have similar effect, provided that the landlord himself also occupied as his only or principal home premises in the same building as the shared accommodation, that building not being a purpose built block of flats (for which definition see HA 1988, sch. 1, Part III; chapter 2, para. 3.10.1). The accommodation which must be shared is not limited to living accommodation (cf. RA 1977, ss. 21, 22; HA 1988, ss. 3, 10; chapter 2, para. 2.3.7), but it does not include areas used for storage, staircases, passages, corridors, or other means of access. Presumably, a sharing with the landlord of a bathroom, or even a WC, would cause the tenancy or licence to be excluded. Sharing requires the occupier to have the use of the accommodation in common with the other person, whether or not others also share its use, and sharing with one of two or more joint landlords will suffice. It should be emphasised that a tenancy which is excluded from protection under the Rent Act 1977 or Part I, HA 1988 by virtue of the resident landlord exception will not necessarily be an excluded tenancy for these purposes, as the respective provisions are not coterminous: for example, it is not necessary for a 'resident landlord' to share any accommodation with the tenant.

4.2 Temporary expedient to trespasser

A tenancy or licence granted as a temporary expedient to a person who entered the premises (or any other premises) as a trespasser is excluded, whether or not, before the tenancy or licence began, another tenancy or licence had been granted to him (cf. HA 1985, s. 79(4), chapter 6, para. 2.1).

4.3 Holiday let

A tenancy or licence conferring on the occupier the right to occupy for a holiday only is excluded (cf. HA 1988, sch. 1, para. 9; RA 1977, s. 9; chapter 2, para. 3.9).

4.4 Rent-free tenancy or licence

A tenancy or licence granted otherwise than for money or money's worth is excluded.

4.5 Rights of occupation in a hostel

A licence (but not a tenancy) conferring rights of occupation in a hostel provided by one of various public bodies is excluded. 'Hostel' is defined in

s. 622, HA 1985. Although the exclusion only affects licences, it may be difficult for an occupier of hostel accommodation to establish that his public sector landlord intended to grant him exclusive possession in the light of the decision of the House of Lords in *Westminster City Council* v *Clarke* [1992] 2 AC 288 (see further, chapter 6, para. 2.1).

4.6 Transitional provisions

The above exclusions were only introduced, by amendment of the 1977 Act, on the coming into force of the Housing Act 1988 on 15 January 1989. There are important transitional savings.

An excluded *tenancy* which was entered into before 15 January 1989, or subsequently, but pursuant to a contract made before that date, will still be subject to the provisions of ss. 3 and 5 of the 1977 Act. In other words, recovery of possession must be by way of proceedings in court if the occupier continues to reside in the premises after his tenancy comes to an end, and any notice to quit must be in writing, contain the prescribed information, and be of at least four weeks' duration. If, however, the terms of the excluded tenancy are subsequently varied so as to affect the amount of rent payable, other than by operation of provisions in the Rent Act 1977, a new tenancy will be deemed to be then entered into. That new tenancy will not be subject to ss. 3 and 5. If the rent is not varied, but other terms are, it will remain open to the landlord to argue that a new tenancy has arisen (e.g., by surrender and re-grant), with the same consequences in terms of the Protection from Eviction Act.

An excluded *licence* is not subject to the same savings as an excluded tenancy. If, however, the licence in question is a restricted contract (see chapter 3, para. 9), entered into on or after 28 November 1980, it appears that s. 3 will nevertheless apply to it (see s. 3(2A)).

5 CIVIL LIABILITY: INTRODUCTION

An occupier who is evicted or harassed cannot bring a civil claim based on breach of s. 1, PEA 1977 (*McCall* v *Abelesz* [1976] QB 585). However, he will probably be able to sue the landlord (or others involved) for damages or an injunction pursuant to one or other common law causes of action. The choice of cause of action is important, as it may affect the heads of damage, and hence the level of damages, which are available. Matters are further complicated by Part I, HA 1988, which created a new statutory tort of unlawful eviction, giving rise to damages assessed on a statutorily prescribed basis. This latter remedy is the most attractive currently available to an evicted occupier who does not wish to return to the premises. Action may be brought under the statute and in contract and/or tort, although the plaintiff may not be compensated twice for the same loss. However, not all cases will fall within the scope of the statutory tort (see, for example, *Ramdath* v *Daley* (1993) 25 HLR 273, where the evicted occupier was reinstated into the premises). It is essential, therefore, that the occupier who wishes to bring an action against his landlord surveys the entire range of remedies.

6 CAUSES OF ACTION

6.1 Breach of the covenant for quiet enjoyment

A covenant to this effect may be expressed in the document pursuant to which the occupier resides in the property. It will in any event be implied into a lease or agreement for lease (*Budd-Scott* v *Daniel* [1902] 2 KB 351). It does not protect the tenant from eviction or interference by anybody, but it does protect him against interference with his quiet and peaceful possession and enjoyment of the premises by the landlord, or by persons claiming through or under the landlord (*Kenny* v *Preen* [1963] 1 QB 499), in either of which cases the defendant should be the landlord. Examples of a breach of the covenant are the landlord threatening the tenant with physical violence, and the landlord cutting off the tenant's gas and electricity (*Kenny* v *Preen; Perera* v *Vandiyar* [1953] 1 WLR 672).

A claim based on breach of the landlord's covenant for quiet enjoyment is a claim in contract. Neither exemplary nor aggravated damages can be awarded where this is the only cause of action (see paras. 7.3 and 7.4 below). Although a covenant for quiet enjoyment will not be implied into a mere licence to occupy property, the court may imply some term preventing the landlord from unduly interfering with the licensee's occupation and use of the property (see, for example, *Smith* v *Nottinghamshire County Council, The Times*, 13 November 1991).

6.2 Trespass

Three forms of trespass may be relevant in proceedings of this nature: trespass to land; trespass to goods (conversion); and/or trespass to the person (assault).

6.2.1 Trespass to land

A tenant has by definition been granted exclusive possession of the property, as a consequence of which he has the right to exclude all others, including the landlord. The landlord who enters unlawfully, i.e., without the tenant's permission and without any lawful right (reserved by the lease) to do so, commits trespass. Where the landlord's entry was initially lawful, it may nevertheless become trespass if on being asked to leave he does not do so within a reasonable time. A licensee may have exclusive possession of his property as against the landlord (see chapter 2, para. 2.1): if so, he can maintain an action against him in trespass.

6.2.2 Trespass to goods

Where the landlord (or any other person) directly interferes with goods belonging to the occupier, such as clothes or furniture, by damaging them or removing them from the property, he will be guilty of trespass.

6.2.3 Trespass to the person

A battery is committed when the defendant intentionally and directly applies force to the plaintiff (e.g., striking him). An assault is committed when he causes the plaintiff to apprehend the infliction of a battery on him. Both are forms of trespass, giving rise to liability for damages, which, in the event of injury being occasioned, may be substantial.

6.3 Nuisance

A private nuisance is committed when the defendant unlawfully interferes with the plaintiff's use or enjoyment of land. It is well recognised that a landlord can therefore cause a nuisance in law to his tenant. It is more doubtful whether an occupier who has no interest in the land (e.g., a licensee) can bring an action based on nuisance, and in *Malone* v *Laskey* [1907] 2 KB 144, the wife of the occupier was denied the right to sue for this reason. In *Khorasandjian* v *Bush* [1993] QB 727, the majority of the Court of Appeal, in allowing a plaintiff to claim an injunction restraining persistent harassment by unwanted telephone calls, held that she could bring an action based on nuisance although she had no interest in her parents' home where the calls were being received. It is unclear whether this authority will be extended beyond its own special facts, but it does lend some support to an argument that the plaintiff in an action for private nuisance need not necessarily have a proprietary interest in the land he occupies.

7 DAMAGES

The assessment of damages where the plaintiff occupier establishes liability is by no means straightforward. In most cases, some special and general damages are awarded. There may also be the possibility of aggravated or exemplary damages.

7.1 Special damages

The plaintiff may claim for property which has been lost or damaged by the defendant's tortious actions. Where property has been totally lost or destroyed, the defendant will be liable for its value. Where it has been damaged, he will be liable for the resultant diminution in value, which is normally interpreted as meaning the cost of repair. Other items of loss which may be recovered as 'special' (i.e., quantified) damages include the cost of alternative accommodation whilst the plaintiff was out of his property.

7.2 General damages

The plaintiff may obtain 'general' (i.e., unquantified) damages for any personal injury which has been caused by the defendant in carrying out the eviction or harassment in question. These will be assessed with reference to established general principles (see, for example, Kemp & Kemp, *The Quantum of Damages*). The plaintiff may also be able to obtain as general damages compensation for the loss of the right of occupation itself, as well as damages for distress, humiliation, etc., more commonly referred to (and discussed below as) aggravated damages.

7.3 Exemplary damages

In *Rookes* v *Barnard* [1964] AC 1129, where Lord Devlin (with whose speech the other four Law Lords agreed) reviewed in detail the circumstances in which exemplary damages could be awarded, it was held that conduct by the defendant calculated to make a profit for himself which may exceed the compensation payable to the plaintiff would give rise to a claim of this nature. The application of exemplary damages to cases of unlawful eviction was encouraged by Lord Hailsham of St Marylebone LC in *Broome* v *Cassell & Co* [1972] AC 1027, 1079:

> How, it may be asked, about the late Mr Rachman, who is alleged to have used hired bullies to intimidate statutory tenants by threats of violence into giving vacant possession of their residences and so placing a valuable asset in the hands of the landlord? My answer must be that if this is not a cynical calculation of profit and cold-blooded disregard of a plaintiff's rights, I do not know what is.

The object of exemplary damages is punitive rather than compensatory. In this, they provide a major exception to what is a general rule of the common law. They have been criticised as leading to a confusion between the functions of the civil and criminal courts (see, for example, *McGregor on Damages*, 15th ed., pp. 254, 264 *et seq.*), and the Court of Appeal has recently called a halt to any unprecedented application of the concept: 'this is not a developing field of the law' (per Stuart-Smith LJ in *A.B.* v *South West Water Services Ltd* [1993] QB 507, 516). That said, there are many decisions subsequent to *Broome* v *Cassell & Co.* where the lower courts have awarded, or upheld awards of, exemplary damages to evicted plaintiffs, although the awards have not been particularly high. Thus, in *Drane* v *Evangelou* [1978] 1 WLR 455, an award of £1,000 was upheld by the Court of Appeal: the same result occurred in *Guppy's (Bridport) Ltd* v *Brookling* (1983) 14 HLR 1, and *Asghar* v *Ahmed* (1984) 17 HLR 25. In *Millington* v *Duffy* (1984) 17 HLR 232, the court would have awarded considerably more than £500 had exemplary damages been claimed, and in *Branchett* v *Beaney* [1992] 3 All ER 910, the Court of Appeal upheld an award of £3,250.

The principles of assessing exemplary damages are somewhat elusive. In particular, the relationship between aggravated and exemplary damages remains blurred, and several of these decisions are correspondingly difficult to analyse. It has been accepted that the profit obtained by the landlord is not in any sense a ceiling to the damages which may be awarded (*McMillan* v *Singh* (1984) 17 HLR 120). That said, the plaintiff need not prove that the defendant did in fact make a profit in fact. Exemplary damages are available once it is established that the defendant carried out the requisite profit-loss calculation prior to committing the tort.

Exemplary damages can only be claimed where the cause of action is trespass or (probably) private nuisance (on the latter, see *Guppy's (Bridport) Ltd* v *Brookling*, as discussed in *A.B.* v *South West Water Services Ltd* at 522 to 523.) Thus, exemplary damages cannot be awarded where the only claim is for breach of contract (i.e., the covenant for quiet enjoyment) (*Kenny* v *Preen*), unless, possibly, the claim includes an allegation of trespass which is proved (*Drane* v *Evangelou* above). As exemplary damages require the defendant to have made a calculation of profit as against liability for compensation, it will be only rarely that a defendant who is not the landlord (or a person with an interest in the property) obtains exemplary damages. In *Ramdath* v *Daley* (1993) 25 HLR 273, the plaintiff obtained an award of exemplary damages (of £2,000) against the landlord, and a separate one (of £2,500) against the landlord's son. The latter award was set aside on appeal on the basis that he had not concerned himself sufficiently closely with the landlord's interests. However, in *Sampson* v *Wilson* (1994) 26 HLR 486, an award of £2,000 exemplary damages was made against an agent of the landlord whose conduct was 'that of a man who must be reckoning there is money to be made'.

7.4 Aggravated damages

The relationship between aggravated and exemplary damages has not always been clear, and the line between them has proved difficult for the courts to draw. Thus, despite Lord Hailsham's confirmation in *Broome* v *Cassell & Co.* (at 1072C) that aggravated and exemplary (or punitive) damages had acquired 'separate and mutually exclusive meanings as terms of art in English law', there have been cases where the court has awarded a global sum encompassing both aggravated and exemplary damages (with the apparent sanction of Lord Hailsham, at 1072G-H), and the Court of Appeal has approved the practice of not attempting to extricate the punitive from the non-punitive element (see, for example, *Guppy's (Bridport) Ltd* v *Brookling*, at p. 26; *Branchett* v *Beaney* [1992] 3 All ER 910, 914). This is unfortunate, as it leads to unnecessary confusion to run the two heads of damage together. The bases of aggravated and exemplary damages are essentially distinct, as Nourse LJ recently acknowledged in *Ramdath* v *Daley*, where he stated the distinction concisely and compellingly:

> Aggravated damages and exemplary damages are not only different in themselves; they are awarded for two different purposes. Aggravated damages are awarded to compensate the plaintiff for injury to his proper feelings of dignity and pride and for aggravation generally, whereas exemplary damages are awarded to punish the defendant.

It now seems to be accepted that aggravated damages cannot be awarded for breach of the landlord's covenant for quiet enjoyment. In *Branchett* v *Beaney*, the plaintiff claimed *inter alia* damages in respect of her frustration, mental distress, injured feelings and annoyance consequent upon the defendant's unlawful construction of an access road across her garden. Whilst this was sustainable in relation to a cause of action in trespass (which the plaintiff in fact proved), the Court of Appeal held that it was not where the only allegation was breach of contract. In general, a contract breaker is not liable for such matters, save where the very object to the contract is to provide pleasure, relaxation, peace of mind or freedom from molestation (*Addis* v *Gramophone Co. Ltd* [1909] AC 488; *Watts* v *Morrow* [1991] 1 WLR 1421). The Court of Appeal held in *Branchett* v *Beaney* (obiter, at 918) that a covenant for quiet enjoyment in a contract of lease would not normally fall within this exception.

8 STATUTORY TORT OF UNLAWFUL EVICTION

Where the plaintiff occupier can bring his claim within s. 27, HA 1988, he should do so, as the amount of damages obtainable will in almost all cases be substantially higher than a claim at common law. The common law causes of action should not be forgotten, however, as even where a claim is brought under s. 27 damages at common law may also be awarded.

8.1 Elements of tort

The tort can be committed by means of what may be termed 'actual' or 'constructive' eviction. 'Actual' eviction occurs where the landlord (or any person acting on his behalf) unlawfully deprives the residential occupier of any premises of his occupation of the whole or part of the premises (s. 27(1)). 'Constructive' eviction occurs where the landlord (or any person acting on his behalf) *either* attempts unlawfully to deprive the residential occupier of his occupation (i.e., attempts an actual eviction as above), *or* does acts likely to interfere with the peace or comfort of the residential occupier or members of his household, or persistently withdraws or withholds services reasonably required for the occupation of the premises as a residence, in doing so knowing or having reasonable cause to believe that this conduct is likely to cause the residential occupier of the premises to give up occupation or to refrain from exercising any rights or remedies in respect of them (i.e., commits the offence of harassment contrary to s. 1(3A), PEA 1977: see para. 9.7 below) *and* (in either of the above cases) as a result the residential occupier gives up occupation of the premises (s. 27(2)).

Although constructive eviction involves, in one case, proof (on the balance of probabilities) of commission of the offence of harassment, neither harassment nor attempted eviction without more incur liability under s. 27. The residential occupier must have given up residential occupation as a result of the acts in question. If the landlord can establish that prior to the acts taking place, the residential occupier was going to cease to occupy, he may be able to deny that the giving up of occupation was as a result of the landlord's conduct.

As the tort is so closely modelled on the criminal offences of unlawful eviction and harassment contained in the Protection from Eviction Act 1977, it will be necessary to construe the Housing Act provisions in the light of the case law on those offences (see para. 9 below). 'Residential occupier' has the meaning given to it by the 1977 Act (s. 27(9): para. 9.2 below.) Moreover, the landlord has the same defences to a claim. In particular, it is a defence for the defendant to prove that he believed (with reasonable cause) that the residential occupier had ceased to reside in the premises at the time the eviction or attempted eviction took place; or that where liability is based on harassment, he had reasonable grounds for doing the acts or withdrawing or withholding the services in question (s. 27(8)).

8.2 Tort must be committed after 9 June 1988

Although Part I, HA 1988 did not come into force until 15 January 1989, these provisions were given an earlier operative date to frustrate landlords, who knew that the law was being strengthened, from evicting tenants and others before the commencement date. The Report stage of the Housing Bill in the House of Commons saw a significant broadening of the scope of the provisions, and so it was thought to be the appropriate day to choose. In *Jones* v *Miah* (1992) 24 HLR 578, defendants who carried out an eviction on 18 October 1988 argued that this element of retrospectiveness in the provisions was contrary to European Community Law, in particular art. 7 of the European Convention for the Protection of Human Rights and Fundamental Freedoms. Their challenge failed before the Court of Appeal, partly on the ground that this article applies to criminal, not tortious, provisions.

8.3 The appropriate defendant

Although the tort may be committed by persons acting on behalf of the landlord, the statute appears to indicate that liability can only fall on the landlord himself: s. 27(3) stipulates 'where this section applies, the landlord in default shall . . . be liable to pay', and the general purpose of the provisions, namely to deprive those who profit from the eviction of the profit they would otherwise have made, gives further support to this. However, in *Sampson* v *Wilson,* (1994) 26 HLR 486, Judge Roger Cook, sitting as a Judge of the High Court, Chancery Division, gave judgment for damages under the statute against a sub-agent of the landlord as well as the landlord himself, by application of the general rule that where a principal is liable for the torts of his agent, they are to be regarded as joint tortfeasors. It may be doubted whether this rule should hold in the face of the relatively clear statutory wording, and it cannot be said that the issue has been definitively decided.

'Landlord' means the person who, but for the occupier's right to occupy, would be entitled to occupation of the premises; and any superior landlord under whom that person derives title (s. 27(9)). Where the defendant had not yet completed the purchase of the freehold of the relevant premises, but contracts had been exchanged, he was nevertheless held to be the landlord, as he was owner of the freehold interest in equity, and had been licensed by the legal owner (the vendor) to go into occupation (*Jones* v *Miah* (1992) 24 HLR 578).

8.4 Defence of reinstatement

In two circumstances, the reinstatement of the residential occupier will prevent a finding of liability against the landlord (s. 27(6)). If, before the date the proceedings to enforce liability are finally disposed of, the former residential occupier is reinstated in the premises in such circumstances that he becomes again residential occupier of them, no liability will arise. If, (presumably subsequent to this date), at the request of the former residential occupier, the court makes an order as a result of which he is reinstated, no liability will arise. There is no obligation on the evicted occupier to accept, or even consider, an offer of reinstatement by the landlord. Unless the occupier in fact returns to occupy the premises as provided by s. 27(6), neither of these defences will be available to the landlord. It may be that unreasonable refusal of an offer to reinstate may lead to a reduction in the amount of damages payable (see para. 8.8 below), but that is all. Reinstatement requires the occupier to be allowed to return on the same terms as previously, with the premises in a similar state of repair. In *Tagro* v *Cafane* [1991] 1 WLR 378, a tenant obtained an injunction against her landlord who had evicted her, and then returned to her flat to find the locks damaged, property missing, and fixtures and fittings damaged. Lord Donaldson MR stated, 'Reinstatement does not consist in merely handing the tenant a key to a lock which does not work and inviting her to resume occupation of a room which has been totally wrecked.'

8.5 Assessment of damages

The damages payable where liability for unlawful eviction is established are not at large: they are to be calculated in strict accordance with s. 28 (s. 27(3)). The basis of assessment is the difference (as at the time the residential occupier ceased to occupy the premises) between the value of the landlord's interest on the assumption that the occupier continues to have the same right to occupy as before, and the value of the landlord's interest on the assumption that he has ceased to have such a right (s. 28(1)). In short, in most straightforward cases, it is the value to the landlord of vacant possession of the premises.

8.6 Valuation of the landlord's interest

This can be a complex matter, and in the few cases which have so far reached the Court of Appeal, there has been an underlying tension between the lawyers and the surveyors on whose evidence the calculation will normally have to be made. The interest to be valued is his interest in the *building* in which the premises are comprised, together with its curtilage (s. 28(2)). It is to be assumed that the landlord is selling that interest on the open market to a willing buyer; that neither the residential occupier nor any member of his family wishes to buy; and that is unlawful to carry out any substantial development of any of the land in which the interest subsists, or to demolish the whole or part of any building on that land (s. 28(3)). Thus 'there shall be no increase in the damages because the effect of the tenant being dispossessed is that it enables some very valuable development to take place' (*per* Lord Donaldson MR in *Tagro* v *Cafane* above). Development pursuant to a general development order, or a change of use resulting in the building being used as one or more dwelling-houses, is excluded from the general meaning of substantial development (s. 28(6)).

8.7 Effect of occupier's security

The more secure the occupier was in the premises at the time of the eviction, the larger the sum of damages will be. This is entirely consistent with the underlying concept of compensating the plaintiff for 'loss of the right to occupy'. Thus, where the residential occupier had limited security, the landlord's interest will be valued at a level much closer to its value with vacant possession than will be the case if the occupier is, for example, protected by the Rent Act. The damages will be commensurately lower.

In *Nwokorie* v *Mason* (1993) 26 HLR 60, the evicted occupier was entitled to four weeks' notice, but had no further security. Possession could have been obtained against her within six months of notice being given. The plaintiff's expert put the consequent reduction on the freehold value of the property attributable to her occupation at £4,500. As the defendant's surveyor had proceeded on an incorrect basis, the Court of Appeal upheld the award of damages of £4,500 under the Housing Act 1988, although it was inferred that the reduction seemed rather high. The same result is likely to occur if the defendant fails to call valuation evidence (*Tagro* v *Cafane*).

In *Jones* v *Miah* (1992) 24 HLR 578, the three plaintiffs had been protected tenants. The landlord's interest in the building was a leasehold interest, which had been assigned to them together with a subjacent restaurant, and the goodwill, fixtures, and chattels of the business there carried on for a total sum of £85,000. It was necessary to take the apportioned price of the lease, being £50,000, and then deduct the value of the landlord's interest with the protected tenants having ceased to occupy. This left a figure of £25,000 basic damages, which the Court of Appeal divided between the three plaintiffs, rounded down, and awarded £8,000 each.

8.8 Reduction of damages

The court may reduce the damages payable under s. 28 in two circumstances only (s. 27(7)). If, prior to the eviction, the conduct of the plaintiff, or of any other person living with him, was such that it was reasonable to mitigate the damages payable, then a reduction may be made. As the object of the provisions is to prevent landlords resorting to self-help, one would not expect this jurisdiction to be frequently invoked. In *Ekwuru* v *Greycroft Ltd*, unreported, 3 February 1994, the Court of Appeal upheld a substantial reduction in damages where the plaintiff tenant had been arrested and remanded in custody on charges of fraud, as a result of which his housing benefit (the only source of funds for the rent) was stopped.

Reduction may also occur where, before proceedings were begun, the landlord offered to reinstate the occupier in the premises and the occupier either unreasonably refused the offer, or (the occupier having already obtained alternative accommodation) it would have been unreasonable of him to refuse the offer had he not obtained that accommodation. If proceedings were commenced which did not initially include a claim for damages under the Housing Act 1988, an injunction perhaps being claimed instead, the landlord will be able to make a valid offer to reinstate up to the date the proceedings are amended to incorporate the statutory damages claim (*Tagro* v *Cafane* [1991] 1 WLR 378). But an offer to give a key and readmit the occupier, without putting the flat into proper order, would not comprise an offer of reinstatement (*Tagro* v *Cafane*). Once proceedings are in being which include a claim for damages under the Housing Act 1988, any offer of reinstatement by the landlord can be rejected by the evicted occupier without fear of prejudice to his rights to damages. It will also frequently be the case that the circumstances of the eviction are such that it will in no way be unreasonable of the occupier to refuse the landlord's offer.

8.9 Relationship between Housing Act damages and common law

Section 27(5) states that damages shall not be awarded both in respect of common law liability and in respect of liability under the Housing Act on account of the same loss. In *Nwokorie* v *Mason* (1993) 26 HLR 60, the Court of Appeal applied a rigorous set-off between Housing Act damages and damages at common law. The plaintiff obtained in the county court £500 general damages, £1,000 'exemplary damages', and £4,500 Housing Act damages. The Court of Appeal reduced his award by £1,500, the amounts awarded outside the Housing Act. The award of general damages was for nothing more than the loss of the right to occupy, which was precisely the loss for which the statutory award was made: it should therefore be set off. The award of exemplary damages was, in truth, an award of aggravated damages, being based on the manner of the eviction which had been calculated to cause the plaintiff humiliation and shame. This was likewise damages in respect of his loss of the right to occupy, and accordingly stood to be set off as well.

It may be doubted whether the Court of Appeal was justified in setting off the aggravated damages award. In principle, a plaintiff who has suffered substantial trauma as a result of the manner in which the eviction took place should obtain greater damages than one who has not. However, an award of exemplary damages should be set off, although there are several county court decisions and one High Court decision where the court has made such an award as well as damages under the Housing Act (see, for example, *Chniouer* v *Nicholades,* Legal Action, September 1991, p. 18; *Dowkes* v *Athelston,* Legal Action, March 1993, p. 15; *Grocia* v *Flint,* Legal Action, March 1993, p. 15; *Mangan* v *Kincade,* Legal Action, September 1993, p. 17; *Sampson* v *Wilson* (1994) 26 HLR 486). If it is not, the defendant will in effect be punished twice over for the same tort.

8.10 Jurisdiction

The county court has jurisdiction to hear and determine any question arising under ss. 27 and 28, HA 1988, and accordingly it would normally be appropriate to bring proceedings in that court (see s. 40(1)).

9 CRIMINAL LIABILITY

9.1 Unlawful eviction

Section 1(2), PEA 1977 sets out the elements of the offence of unlawful eviction. The defendant must unlawfully deprive a residential occupier of his occupation of the premises or any part thereof, or attempt to do so. He will not be guilty if he proves that he believed, and had reasonable cause to believe, that the residential occupier had ceased to reside in the premises.

9.2 Residential occupier

The 'victim' of the offence must be a residential occupier, who is defined in s. 1(1) of the 1977 Act as 'a person occupying the premises as a residence, whether under a contract or by virtue of any enactment or rule of law giving him the right to remain in occupation or restricting the right of any other person to recover possession of the premises. ' This is a wide definition, covering persons whose tenancy or licence may be excluded from the protection of other provisions in the 1977 Act, as well as those who hold pursuant to statutorily protected tenancies. It is not necessary that the premises are the residential occupier's only or even principal residence. In determining whether the person was occupying the premises as a residence, the case law on s. 2(1), RA 1977 (chapter 3, para. 4.1.2) is to be used: *Schon* v *Camden LBC* (1987) 53 P & CR 361.

9.3 Premises

It has been unhelpfully stated in another context (see chapter 3, para. 7.3.7) that 'premises' 'is an ordinary word of the English language which takes colour and content from the context in which it is used', and that it has 'no recognised and established primary meaning' (*per* Viscount Dilhorne in *Maunsell* v *Olins* [1975] AC 373, 383). It is clearly not necessary for 'premises' to comprise a dwelling-house as such. In *Norton* v *Knowles* [1969] 1 QB 572, 'premises' were defined as being the composite unit of a caravan and the land on which it was standing. In *Thurrock U.D.C.* v *Shina* (1972) 23 P & CR 205, the Divisional Court held, unsurprisingly, that 'premises' could include a single bed-sitting room.

9.4 Deprivation of occupation of the premises

It has been established that this phrase must be read in the light of the heading of Part I of the 1977 Act, i.e., 'Unlawful eviction and harassment'. The acts of the defendant must accordingly have 'the character of an eviction': *R* v *Yuthiwattana* (1984) 80 Crim App Rep 55, 63, *per* Kerr LJ. In that case, the defendant owner had refused to replace a key which the tenant had lost, as a result of which the tenant could not enter his flat for a day and a night. Whilst denying that the eviction must be permanent to constitute an offence, Kerr LJ considered that cases of 'locking out', or not admitting the occupier on one or even more isolated occasions, were more appropriately to be dealt with as unlawful harassment. As occupation is such a flexible concept, tenants who are absent, albeit temporarily, for some time continuing in 'occupation' (see chapter 3, para. 4.1.4), it is difficult in circumstances such as these to find that a deprivation of occupation has occurred: see further, *Schon* v *Camden LBC* above.

9.5 Belief that the residential occupier had ceased to reside

The burden of proof of this defence is placed firmly on the defendant, who must establish reasonable cause for his belief. The belief must exist at the time of the eviction. If the defendant subsequently discovers facts which give him reasonable cause to change his belief, he will not then become guilty of the offence: see, for example, *R* v *Davidson-Acres* (1980) Crim LR 50. A variant of this defence is where the defendant believes, with reasonable cause, that the person in occupation has no right to be there, in other words that he is not a 'residential occupier' within s. 1(1); see *R* v *Phekoo* [1981] 1 WLR 1117, below.

9.6 Unlawfulness

The act of the defendant in evicting the residential occupier must be unlawful, in the sense of a breach of the occupier's rights in the civil law. This should not, however, be a particularly large obstacle to a prosecution, as self-help by the landlord will in most cases contravene s. 2 or 3 of the 1977 Act, or, in the case of a statutorily protected tenancy, the statute which accords it protection.

9.7 Harassment

Since the enactment of the Housing Act 1988, there have been two distinct offences of harassment. Section 1(3) requires proof of intention, but may be committed by 'any person'. Section 1(3A), added by the 1988 Act, s. 29, may only be committed by the landlord or his agent, but proof of intention as such is not required.

By s. 1(3) of the 1977 Act:

> If any person with intent to cause the residential occupier of any premises—

(a) to give up the occupation of the premises or any part thereof, or
(b) to refrain from exercising any right or pursuing any remedy in respect of the premises or any part thereof;

does acts likely to interfere with the peace or comfort of the residential occupier or members of his household, or persistently withdraws or withholds services reasonably required for the occupation of the premises as a residence he shall be guilty of an offence.

The offence under s. 1(3A) does not, as stated above, require the intent stipulated at the outset of s. 1(3). The 'acts' or withdrawal or withholding of services are the same as for the s. 1(3) offence, the prosecution having also to prove that the defendant knows, or has reasonable cause to believe, that the conduct is likely to cause the residential occupier to give up the occupation of the whole or part of the premises or to refrain from exercising any right or pursuing any remedy in respect of the whole or any part of the premises.

9.8 No ingredient of unlawfulness

Unlike s. 1(2), neither of the offences of harassment contain an express ingredient of 'unlawfulness', and in *R* v *Burke* [1991] 1 AC 135, the House of Lords decided that it was not a necessary ingredient of the offence contrary to s. 1(3) that the defendant's actions were in breach of the residential occupier's civil law rights. The defendant prevented his tenants from using lavatories outside their demised property by padlocking or storing furniture in them, and disconnected the front door bell which communicated with the tenants' flats. These actions were not in breach of the tenancy agreements, as the judge found that the tenants had no right that a particular lavatory should be kept available for their use, and no right that a system of front door bells should be maintained by the defendant. The House of Lords nevertheless upheld the defendant's conviction. The object of creating the offence of unlawful harassment in 1965 was, *per* Lord Griffiths at 147, 'to make any action likely to interfere with the peace or comfort of the occupier a criminal offence if it was performed with the evil intention of forcing the occupier to give up occupation of the premises, "intention" in this context meaning with the purpose or motive of causing the occupier to give up occupation of the premises. ' The offence contrary to s. 1(3), which can be committed by any person (not just the landlord) against any residential occupier (not just the tenant) was clearly not confined to a contractual relationship between harasser and victim.

9.9 Acts do not include omissions

In *R* v *Zafar Ahmad* (1986) 18 HLR 416, the defendant landlord commenced carrying out extensive works of construction without the tenant's consent, as a result of which the tenant's flat was rendered temporarily uninhabitable. However, the court found that he believed that the tenant had given her agreement to these works. The prosecution case, based on his failure to reinstate the flat into a habitable condition, succeeded at trial but was rejected by the Court of Appeal, Glidewell LJ holding, at 423, that 'the words of this Act do not impose a responsibility to rectify damage which the defendant has already caused by an act done without either of the intentions necessary to constitute an offence under section 1(3).' An omission to act cannot, therefore, of itself incur liability under s. 1(3).

However, an omission to act may be part of a course of conduct which, viewed as such, comprises harassment under the 1977 Act. This is the explanation for the Court of Appeal upholding the conviction of unlawful harassment in *R* v *Yuthiwattana* (1984) 16 HLR 49. Whilst the refusal of the defendant to replace the occupier's door key could not be said without more to be an 'act' under s. 1(3), no argument to this effect was pursued in the Court of Appeal. The defendant's entry uninvited into the flat, appropriation of his tape recorder and records, and sundry threats of eviction provided ample evidence of acts of harassment.

9.10 Intention that occupier should give up occupation permanently?

In *Schon* v *Camden LBC* (1987) 53 P & CR 361, the defendant sought to argue that he did not intend that the occupier should leave the flat permanently, but only whilst certain works were carried out at the premises. The Court of Appeal held that this was a good defence as in the time involved (two weeks) the occupier would not cease to 'occupy' the premises as her residence. As long as the occupier intended to return into occupation, and had left some physical manifestation of that intention on the premises, she would not in law cease to occupy.

9.11 Section 1(3) creates one offence, not two

In *Schon* v *Camden LBC*, above, Glidewell LJ emphasised that s. 1(3) creates one offence only, that of an act calculated to interfere with the residential occupier's peace and comfort, which may be done with one of two intentions: either the intention to cause the occupier to give up occupation of the premises, or the intention to cause the occupier to refrain from exercising any right (etc.). The significance of this is that the prosecution may charge in the alternative, and ask the jury or justices to reach a verdict on either basis. One presumes that s. 1(3A) is to be similarly interpreted.

9.12 Belief that victim not a residential occupier

In *R* v *Phekoo* [1981] 1 WLR 1117, the defendant was charged with harassment under s. 1(3) of two individuals whom, he contended, he did not know were residential occupiers. He believed they were squatters. The Court of Appeal held that this was a defence to the charge, and should be left to the jury, although it was incumbent on the defendant to show reasonable grounds for his belief.

9.13 Penalties

The maximum penalties for unlawful eviction or harassment (there is no distinction between them for these purposes) are a fine or two years' imprisonment or both on indictment; a fine or six months' imprisonment or both on summary conviction (s. 1(4)).

9.14 Using or threatening violence to secure entry

A further pitfall for landlords is provided by s. 6 of the Criminal Law Act 1977, which imposes criminal liability on a person who without lawful authority uses or threatens violence for the purpose of securing entry into any premises for himself or another. There must be someone present on the premises who is opposed to the entry, and the defendant must know that this is the case. 'Lawful authority' is not constituted by the defendant having an interest in, or a right to possession or occupation of the premises: thus the fact that a landlord is seeking to exercise a right of re-entry which has arisen is no defence. It is however a defence (the burden of proof being on the defendant) that the defendant was himself a displaced residential occupier (see further, ss. 6(3), 12). The maximum penalties on conviction of an offence contrary to Criminal Law Act 1977, s. 6 (summarily triable only), are six months' imprisonment and/or a fine not exceeding level five on the standard scale.

Index